Essentials of WJ V™ Assessment

Essentials of Psychological Assessment Series
Series Editors, Alan S. Kaufman and Nadeen L. Kaufman

Essentials of CAS2 Assessment
by Jack A. Naglieri and Tulio M. Otero

Essentials of Child and Adolescent Psychopathology, Second Edition
by Linda Wilmshurst

Essentials of Cognitive Assessment with KAIT and Other Kaufman Measures
by Elizabeth O. Lichtenberger, Debra Y. Broadbooks, and Alan S. Kaufman

Essentials of Conners Behavior Assessments™
by Elizabeth P. Sparrow

Essentials of Creativity Assessment
by James C. Kaufman, Jonathan A. Plucker, and John Baer

Essentials of Cross-Battery Assessment, Third Edition
by Dawn P. Flanagan, Samuel O. Ortiz, and Vincent C. Alfonso

Essentials of DAS-II® Assessment
by Ron Dumont, John O. Willis, and Colin D. Elliott

Essentials of Dyslexia Assessment and Intervention
by Nancy Mather and Barbara J. Wendling

Essentials of Evidence-Based Academic Interventions
by Barbara J. Wendling and Nancy Mather

Essentials of Executive Functions Assessment
by George McCloskey and Lisa A. Perkins

Essentials of Forensic Psychological Assessment, Second Edition
by Marc J. Ackerman

Essentials of Gifted Assessment
by Steven I. Pfeiffer

Essentials of IDEA for Assessment Professionals
by Guy McBride, Ron Dumont, and John O. Willis

Essentials of Individual Achievement Assessment
by Douglas K. Smith

Essentials of Intellectual Disability Assessment and Identification
by Alan W. Brue and Linda Wilmshurst

Essentials of KABC-II Assessment
by Alan S. Kaufman, Elizabeth O. Lichtenberger, Elaine Fletcher-Janzen, and Nadeen L. Kaufman

Essentials of KTEA™-3 and WIAT®-III Assessment
by Kristina C. Breaux and Elizabeth O. Lichtenberger

Essentials of MCMI®-IV Assessment
by Seth D. Grossman and Blaise Amendolace

Essentials of Millon™ Inventories Assessment, Third Edition
by Stephen Strack

Essentials of MMPI-A™ Assessment
by Robert P. Archer and Radhika Krishnamurthy

Essentials of MMPI-2® Assessment, Second Edition
by David S. Nichols

Essentials of Myers-Briggs Type Indicator® Assessment, Second Edition
by Naomi L. Quenk

Essentials of NEPSY®-II Assessment
by Sally L. Kemp and Marit Korkman

Essentials of Neuropsychological Assessment, Second Edition
by Nancy Hebben and William Milberg

Essentials of Nonverbal Assessment
by Steve McCallum, Bruce Bracken, and John Wasserman

Essentials of PAI® Assessment
by Leslie C. Morey

Essentials of Planning, Selecting, and Tailoring Interventions for Unique Learners
by Jennifer T. Mascolo, Vincent C. Alfonso, and Dawn P. Flanagan

Essentials of Processing Assessment, Second Edition
by Milton J. Dehn

Essentials of Psychological Assessment Supervision
by A. Jordan Wright

Essentials of Psychological Testing, Second Edition
by Susana Urbina

Essentials of Response to Intervention
by Amanda M. VanDerHeyden and Matthew K. Burns

Essentials of Rorschach® Assessment
by Tara Rose, Michael P. Maloney, and Nancy Kaser-Boyd

Essentials of Rorschach Assessment: Comprehensive System and R-PAS
by Jessica R. Gurley

Essentials of School Neuropsychological Assessment, Third Edition
by Daniel C. Miller and Denise E. Maricle

Essentials of Specific Learning Disability Identification, Second Edition
by Vincent C. Alfonso and Dawn P. Flanagan

Essentials of Stanford-Binet Intelligence Scales (SB5) Assessment
by Gale H. Roid and R. Andrew Barram

Essentials of TAT and Other Storytelling Assessments, Second Edition
by Hedwig Teglasi

Essentials of Temperament Assessment
by Diana Joyce

Essentials of Trauma-Informed Assessment and Interventions in School and Community Settings
by Kirby L. Wycoff and Bettina Franzese

Essentials of Treatment Planning, Second Edition
by Mark E. Maruish

Essentials of WAIS®-IV Assessment, Second Edition
by Elizabeth O. Lichtenberger and Alan S. Kaufman

Essentials of WISC®-IV Assessment, Second Edition
by Dawn P. Flanagan and Alan S. Kaufman

Essentials of WISC-V® Assessment
by Dawn P. Flanagan and Vincent C. Alfonso

Essentials of WISC-V Integrated Assessment
by Susan Engi Raiford

Essentials of WJ IV® Cognitive Abilities Assessment
by Fredrick A. Schrank, Scott L. Decker, and John M. Garruto

Essentials of WJ IV® Tests of Achievement
by Nancy Mather and Barbara J. Wendling

Essentials of WMS®-IV Assessment
by Lisa Whipple Drozdick, James A. Holdnack, and Robin C. Hilsabeck

Essentials of WNV™ Assessment
by Kimberly A. Brunnert, Jack A. Naglieri, and Steven T. Hardy-Braz

Essentials of Working Memory Assessment and Intervention
by Milton J. Dehn

Essentials of WPPSI™-IV Assessment
by Susan Engi Raiford and Diane L. Coalson

Essentials of WRAML2 and TOMAL-2 Assessment
by Wayne Adams and Cecil R. Reynolds

Essentials of WRAML3 and EMS Assessment
by Wayne V. Adams, David V. Sheslow, and Trevor A. Hall

Essentials of Evaluating Bias in Intelligence Testing
by Craig L. Frisby

Essentials of WJ V™ Assessment
by Erica M. LaForte Nancy Mather, and W. Joel Schneider

Essentials

of WJ V™ Assessment

Erica M. LaForte, Nancy Mather, and
W. Joel Schneider

WILEY

Published by John Wiley & Sons, Inc., Hoboken, New Jersey.

For general information on our other products and services or for technical support, please contact our Customer Care Department within the United States at (800) 762-2974, outside the United States at (317) 572-3993 or fax (317) 572-4002.

Wiley also publishes its books in a variety of electronic formats. Some content that appears in print may not be available in electronic formats. For more information about Wiley products, visit our web site at www.wiley.com.

Library of Congress Cataloging-in-Publication Data Applied for:

Paperback ISBN: 9781394296552
ePub ISBN: 9781394296569
ePDF ISBN: 9781394296576
oBook ISBN: 9781394296583

Cover Design: Wiley
Cover Image: © Robert/stock.adobe.com

Set in 10.5/13pt AdobeGaramondPro by Straive, Pondicherry, India

CONTENTS

SERIES PREFACE

In the *Essentials of Psychological Assessment Series*, we have provided the reader with books that deliver key *practical* information in the most efficient and accessible manner. Typically, books fall into one of two categories. The first category features specific topics in a variety of domains, such as specific learning disabilities, social-emotional learning, neuropsychological assessment, cross-battery assessment, and adaptive behavior assessment. These books are intended for professionals in psychology and education—and for graduate students in these or related disciplines—who are committed to providing assessment and intervention services.

A second category of books in this series, such as *Essentials of WJ V™ Assessment*, is devoted to a single test. These books offer a concise yet thorough review of an instrument, with special attention to the details of administration, scoring, interpretation, application, and tips for best-practice use of the test. Students can rely on series books in both categories for a clear and concise overview of the important assessment tools and key topics informing skillful practice delivered efficiently, and ethically in their chosen fields. Experienced clinicians will feel equally at home with this series in their efforts to remain on the cutting edge of new research and new instruments as well as new editions of assessments in an array of diverse fields.

Wherever feasible, visual cues highlighting key points are used alongside systematic, step-by-step guidelines. Chapters are focused and succinct. Topics are organized for an easy understanding of the essential material related to a particular test or topic. Theory and research are continually woven into the fabric of each book, always to enhance the practical application of the material. With this series, we aim to challenge and assist readers interested in psychological and educational assessment to aspire to the highest level of competency by arming them with the resources they need for knowledgeable, informed practice. We have long been advocates of "intelligent" testing—the notion that numbers are meaningless unless they are brought to life by the clinical acumen and expertise of examiners. Assessment must be used to make a difference in the child's or the adult's life, or why bother testing? All books in the series—whether devoted to specific tests or general topics—are consistent with this credo. We want this series to help our readers, novice and veteran alike, to benefit from the intelligent assessment approaches of the authors of each book.

In *Essentials of WJ V™ Assessment*, Drs. LaForte, Mather, and Schneider provide important insights into both the administration and interpretation of these tests. The WJ V builds on the strong foundation of the test's four prior versions, continuing to provide a psychometrically sound assessment tool that can be used with both children and adults. Among other enhancements, the fifth edition is now administered on a digital platform using a computer and an iPad with automated scoring. The navigation through each test on the Riverside Score platform is fully automated. The platform manages basal and ceiling rules and includes integrated test timers and audio-recorded stimuli. The digital test design improves the portability of test materials, streamlines and improves the efficiency and accuracy of test administration, and enhances the engagement of examinees. The tests are now organized into two batteries, the Tests of Cognitive Abilities (WJ V COG) and the Tests of Achievement (WJ V ACH), and a library of supplemental tests. The WJ V COG contains 5 new tests and a newly configured 8-test General Intellectual Ability (GIA) cluster aligned to contemporary CHC theory. The WJ V ACH battery includes 8 new tests that provide more in-depth coverage of oral language, reading comprehension, written language, and math problem solving, It includes all of the tests needed to assess the 8 areas of specific learning disability eligibility. In addition, the WJ V includes a Virtual Test Library (VTL) of 15 tests measuring aspects of phonological processing, working memory, and rapid automatized naming that may be used independently or in combination with either the WJ V COG or WJ V ACH. As with prior editions, CHC theory provides the theoretical framework for test interpretation and chapter 2 describes advances in this theory in detail. Both beginning and experienced practitioners familiar with assessment in general, and WJ assessments in particular, will find useful information that goes beyond what is provided in the WJ V Examiner's Manual. While the WJ V is a complex instrument, these chapters provide users with clear explanations of test features, as well as the use and interpretation of the scores. The final chapter of this edition provides illustrative case studies that have been written by several professionals in the field.

Alan S. Kaufman, PhD, and Nadeen L. Kaufman, EdD, Series Editors
Neag School of Education, University of Connecticut

ACKNOWLEDGMENTS

We would like to express our sincere appreciation to the numerous dedicated assessment professionals who help children and adults understand their unique strengths and weaknesses and prescribe targeted interventions and accommodations designed to foster their success.

We would like to acknowledge Dr. Eric Snader and Gabriel Jeantete, who helped develop the WJ V Examiner's Manual, and Dr. Katy Genseke, Cindy Currie, and Hayley Jennings at Riverside Insights for their assistance in providing platform technical specifications and obtaining permissions.

We would also like to thank Barbara J. Wendling for her contributions on past editions of the *Essentials of WJ Achievement*. She was a co-author on both the first edition, *Essentials of WJ III® Tests of Achievement Assessment* and the second edition, *Essentials of WJ IV® Tests of Achievement*, and her past contributions are still apparent in this edition.

We are appreciative of our colleagues who contributed WJ V case studies to Chapter 9: Dr. Lynne Jaffe, Dr. Edward Schultz, Dr. Martha Youman, and Dr. John Garruto. We are thankful to Emily Mather for her feedback and help in editing the first draft of several chapters.

We are grateful to Mr. Nathanael Mcgavin, our managing editor, and his staff at Wiley for their editorial support. We are also appreciative of Drs. Alan and Nadeen Kaufman for their encouragement in writing this book.

Finally, the late Dr. Richard Woodcock has had a profound effect on our professional lives and we are grateful for his influence, inspiration, and mentorship. We acknowledge his many contributions that have led to diagnostic and practical tools for assessment professionals.

One

WJ V OVERVIEW

Although many standardized instruments exist for measuring cognitive and academic performance, the Woodcock-Johnson® (WJ) has been one of the most widely used tests since its original publication in 1977. The latest revision, the *Woodcock-Johnson® V* (WJ V™; McGrew et al., 2025b), provides examiners with an even more comprehensive instrument. The WJ V contains 60 individually administered tests that are designed to measure general intellectual ability, specific cognitive abilities, oral language, and achievement. Depending upon the purpose of the assessment, the WJ V may be used independently or in conjunction with other assessment instruments.

Essentials of WJ V™ Assessment is an easy-to-use guide and reference for professionals and practitioners who wish to learn the key features of this instrument. This guide is appropriate for a wide array of professionals, whether their goal is to learn how to administer the test or simply to increase familiarity with the instrument. The topics covered in this guide include administration, scoring, interpretation, and application of the WJ V. All chapters include "Rapid Reference," "Caution," and "Don't Forget" boxes that highlight or summarize important points. At the end of each chapter, a "Test Yourself" section is provided to help review and reinforce the key information presented. These features make this guide an ideal resource for both in-service and graduate training in WJ V administration and interpretation. Examiners may wish to read the book from cover to cover or turn to individual chapters to find specific information. Rapid Reference 1.1 provides basic information about the WJ V and the publisher.

Essentials of WJ V™ Assessment, First Edition. Erica M. LaForte, Nancy Mather, and W. Joel Schneider.

Rapid Reference 1.1

Basic Information About the WJ V

- **Test name:** Woodcock-Johnson V
- **Authors:** Kevin S. McGrew, Nancy Mather, Erica M. LaForte, and Barbara J. Wendling
- **Publication date:** 2025
- **Age normative range:** 4 to 90+
- **Grade normative range:** K.0 through 12.9
- **Publisher:** Riverside Insights (www.riversideinsights.com)
- **Website:** *Riverside Score*® (www.riversidescore.com)
- **Price:** Contact the publisher for subscription pricing

WJ V HISTORY AND DEVELOPMENT

The original Woodcock-Johnson was published as the *Woodcock-Johnson Psycho-Educational Battery* (WJ; Woodcock & Johnson, 1977). The WJ provided the first comprehensive, co-normed battery of cognitive abilities, achievement, and interests. The tests in the 1977 WJ measured a continuum of human abilities across a wide age range and provided common norms for interpretation.

The *Woodcock-Johnson–Revised* (WJ-R®; Woodcock & Johnson, 1989) was designed to expand the diagnostic capabilities of the WJ. The tests were divided into two main batteries, the WJ-R Tests of Cognitive Ability (WJ-R COG) and the WJ-R Tests of Achievement (WJ-R ACH), with each containing a Standard Battery and the Supplemental Battery that were housed in separate easel test books.

Like its predecessor, the *Woodcock-Johnson III* (Woodcock et al., 2001) had two primary batteries: the WJ III Tests of Cognitive Abilities (WJ III® COG) and the WJ III Tests of Achievement (WJ III ACH). The *WJ III Diagnostic Supplement* (WJ III DS; Woodcock et al., 2003) provided 11 additional cognitive tests that further expanded the range of interpretive options. Together, these batteries comprised a comprehensive system for measuring general intellectual ability (*g*), specific cognitive abilities, oral language, and achievement across a wide age range.

The next edition, the *Woodcock-Johnson IV* (Schrank et al., 2014a), comprised three batteries: the WJ IV Tests of Cognitive Abilities (WJ IV COG; Schrank et al., 2014b), the WJ IV Tests of Achievement (WJ IV ACH; Schrank et al., 2015a), and the WJ IV Tests of Oral Language (WJ IV OL; Schrank et al., 2015b). Together, these three batteries provided a comprehensive set of individually administered, norm-referenced tests for measuring general intellectual abilities, academic achievement, and oral language. As with prior versions, the normative data for the three batteries were based on the same individuals who were administered the cognitive, oral language, and achievement tests. This comprehensive assessment system facilitated exploring and identifying individual strengths and weaknesses across cognitive, oral language, and academic abilities.

The WJ V is an update and revision of the WJ IV and is administered almost exclusively in digital format. The WJ V contains two batteries: the WJ V Tests of Cognitive Abilities (WJ V COG; McGrew et al., 2025a) and the WJ V Tests of Achievement (WJ V ACH; Mather et al., 2025a). Several additional tests are contained in the WJ V Virtual Test Library (WJ V VTL; Mather et al., 2025b). The VTL tests, when administered alone or in conjunction with tests from the WJ V COG and WJ V ACH, provide additional information about an individual's cognitive abilities, oral language, and achievement. The WJ V includes an Examiner's Manual (Mather et al., 2025c) and a Technical Manual (LaForte et al., 2025) that are both available in PDF format on the *Riverside Score*® digital platform.

As with all prior editions of the Woodcock-Johnson, one of the most important features of the WJ V is that the normative data for all 60 tests are based on the same sample of individuals. This *conorming* provides greater accuracy and validity when making comparisons among and between an individual's cognitive, achievement, and oral language scores and provides options for data-based score comparison procedures.

CHANGES FROM THE WJ V

Examiners who are familiar with the WJ IV will find it easy to learn the overall structure and organization of the WJ V. Like prior editions, the WJ V is designed to facilitate *selective testing* by combining tests from the COG, ACH, and VTL to address specific referral questions or test specific hypotheses about an examinee's abilities and achievement. The WJ V maintains the traditional high standards for technical quality and psychometric rigor. All tests were re-normed to reflect the 2020 census for population demographics, based on a sample of 5,837 children and adults from across the United States.

Perhaps the biggest change for WJ IV users is the complete digital transformation of the battery in the WJ V. The WJ V is administered via the *Riverside Score*® digital platform by an examiner working on a laptop computer. The examinee sees visual stimuli on an iPad and, if applicable, hears auditory stimuli from the iPad speaker. For many of the test items, the examinee taps responses on the iPad screen. During testing, all data are captured in real time by the platform, eliminating the risk of data loss in case the Wi-Fi connection is interrupted. Many examiner testing tasks, including score calculations, starting item selections, continuation decisions, and basal and ceiling rules, are automated by *Riverside Score*®, decreasing overall testing time and examiner errors while increasing efficiency and examinee engagement. Chapter 3 provides more information about the *Riverside Score*® platform.

Several new tests have been added to the WJ V COG to reflect the current theoretical broad ability structure under Cattell-Horn-Carroll (CHC) theories. The auditory processing (Ga) tests were moved from the COG battery to the WJ V VTL. The composition of the General Intellectual Ability (GIA) cluster changed significantly from the WJ IV to WJ V.

It is now comprised of eight tests instead of seven, no longer includes a measure of auditory processing (Ga), and contains more robust measures of comprehension-knowledge (Gc) and fluid reasoning (Gf) by including the new Matrices (Gf) and Verbal Analogies (Gc, Gf) tests. The new COG Visual Working Memory (Gwm, Gv) and Symbol Inhibition (Gs) tests tap into working memory and inhibitory control, two aspects of executive functioning.

The WJ V ACH battery has also undergone significant content updates. Two new tests, Paragraph Reading Comprehension and Story Comprehension, provide more ecologically valid measures of reading comprehension and oral comprehension, respectively, than the cloze-procedure tests (such as Passage Comprehension and Oral Comprehension) alone. Oral Language Samples, a new test of oral expression, provides an oral language parallel to the tasks in the WJ V Written Language Samples test (formerly Writing Samples), allowing an examiner to directly compare an examinee's written and oral ideational skills. A new writing test, Sentence Writing Accuracy, assesses mechanics such as spelling, punctuation, and capitalization to better represent the types of writing tasks a student encounters in the classroom. A new test of math problem solving, Math Problem Identification, mimics real-world applications of math concepts that require an individual to assess whether sufficient information exists to solve a problem. Two other new ACH tests, Number Sense and Magnitude Comparison, measure skills that are important for early math learning. Together with the existing WJ IV tests, the new WJ V tests provide more robust and ecologically valid assessment of the eight achievement areas for evaluation of specific learning disabilities (SLD).

In the WJ IV, the tests measuring aspects of oral language were contained in a separate battery (WJ IV OL). In the WJ V, the oral language tests have been redistributed into the COG, ACH, and VTL. Additionally, several new tests were developed for the WJ V VTL to increase the diagnostic utility of the WJ V. Four new tests of rapid automatized naming (RAN)—Rapid Letter Naming, Rapid Number Naming, Rapid Phoneme Naming, and Rapid Quantity Naming—together with the existing Rapid Picture Naming test tap into the cognitive processes underlying reading and math achievement. The new Sound Reversal test and the existing Sound Blending, Segmentation, Sound Substitution, and Sound Deletion tests provide robust measurement of phonological awareness and phonological manipulation.

Rapid Reference 1.2 provides a summary of several differences between the WJ IV and WJ V.

THEORETICAL FOUNDATIONS

Like both the WJ III and WJ IV, the WJ V is based on current theory and research on the structure and function of human cognitive abilities. The theoretical foundation is derived from the Cattell-Horn-Carroll theory of cognitive abilities (CHC; McGrew, 2005; Schneider & McGrew, 2018). Although this theory is most commonly discussed in relation to the WJ V COG, it can also be applied to the WJ V ACH and the WJ V VTL. This overarching theory provides a framework for describing performance, interpreting results, and measuring human performance across the continuum of cognitive abilities, oral language, and achievement.

Rapid Reference 1.2

Examples of Changes from the WJ IV to the WJ V

- The delivery mode changed from paper-and-pencil administration in the WJ IV to primarily digital administration in the WJ V, using a laptop and an iPad.
- The digital platform automates many administration tasks, removing the need for the examiner to monitor basal and ceiling rules and compute scores manually.
- All test data are captured and updated in real time during administration by the *Riverside Score®* platform and stored on a secure server. .
- The norms were updated to reflect the 2020 U.S. census.
- Many new tests and clusters were added.
- Tests from the WJ IV Tests of Oral Language were moved into the WJ V COG, WJ V ACH, and WJ V VTL.
- The WJ V COG battery structure was updated to reflect contemporary CHC theory.
- The WJ V ACH battery was updated to provide more robust clusters measuring the eight SLD identification areas.
- Optional Response Style and Behavior Checklists were added to all tests so examiners can document important qualitative information from the test session.

CHC theory is a combination of two research-based theories: *Gf–Gc* theory, based on the work of Drs. Raymond Cattell and John Horn, and the three-stratum theory, based on the work of Dr. John Carroll. Both theoretical models focus on multiple broad abilities, each of which subsumes several narrow cognitive abilities. For more information about CHC theory, see Schneider and McGrew (2018), the *WJ V Technical Manual* (LaForte et al., 2025), and Chapter 2 of this book. Rapid Reference 1.3 provides a brief description of the broad CHC abilities measured by the WJ V.

Rapid Reference 1.3

Broad CHC Abilities Measured by the WJ V

- **Comprehension-Knowledge (Gc):** the depth and breadth of both general and specific declarative and procedural knowledge that is valued by a culture
- **Fluid Reasoning (Gf):** the ability to solve novel or unfamiliar problems
- **Working Memory Capacity (Gwm):** the ability to maintain information in memory and manipulate the information
- **Learning Efficiency or Long-Term Storage (Gl):** the ability to learn and store new information over time
- **Visual Processing (Gv):** the ability to use mental imagery to solve problems often involving nonlinguistic images, such as shapes and patterns
- **Retrieval Fluency (Gr):** the rate and fluency at which an individual can access known information in memory

- **Cognitive Processing Speed (Gs):** the ability to control attention and quickly perform simple cognitive tasks
- **Auditory Processing (Ga):** the aspect of Ga that is measured is phonological processing (the ability to hear phonemes and to blend sounds into words, segment words into parts, and manipulate sounds within words)
- **Reading and Writing (Grw):** mastery of skills and the depth and breadth of knowledge related to reading and writing
- **Quantitative Knowledge (Gq):** the depth and breadth of declarative and procedural knowledge related to mathematics
- **Domain-Specific Knowledge (Gkn):** the depth and breadth of specialized knowledge in a field

Adapted from Schneider and McGrew (2018) and the *WJ V Technical Manual* (LaForte et al., 2025).

DON'T FORGET

The tests in the WJ V VTL can be used alone or with tests from the WJ V COG or WJ V ACH.

ORGANIZATION OF THE WJ V

The WJ V comprises two batteries: the WJ V Tests of Cognitive Abilities (WJ V COG) and the WJ V Tests of Achievement (WJ V ACH). The WJ V Virtual Test Library (WJ V VTL), which is available to all WJ V users, contains 15 additional tests that can be administered alone, or in combination with tests from the WJ V COG or WJ V ACH to increase the breadth, depth, and diagnostic utility of an assessment.

WJ V TESTS

Rapid References 1.4–1.6 contain the CHC broad ability classification, test description, and task demands for the tests in the WJ V COG, WJ V ACH, and the WJ V VTL, respectively. Several of the tests are mixed measures that include two broad CHC abilities.

WJ V CLUSTERS

The WJ V tests are organized into groups of two or more, called *clusters*, for interpretive purposes. Cluster scores are generally more reliable than individual test scores and are useful for interpreting both within-ability strengths and weaknesses and between-ability comparisons. Some tests contribute to more than one cluster. For example, in the WJ V COG, the Spatial Relations test combines with Block Rotation to form the Visual Processing (Gv) cluster, and it also contributes to the eight-test GIA cluster.

Rapid Reference 1.4

WJ V COG Test Broad CHC Classifications, Descriptions, and Task Demands

Test	Broad CHC Classification	Description and Task Demands
Oral Vocabulary	Gc	Measures oral vocabulary. The test consists of two subtests: Synonyms and Antonyms. Requires providing a synonym or antonym for a word presented orally and on the tablet screen.
Matrices	Gf	Measures inductive reasoning. Requires inducing a rule and deducing which among four options best completes the rule-based pattern in a figural matrix. Early items contain 2×2 matrices; later items contain 3×3 matrices.
Spatial Relations	Gv	Measures visualization and mental rotation processes. Requires determining which two or three 2-dimensional puzzle pieces, from among six options, fit together to form the shape shown in the key.
Story Recall	Gl	Measures meaningful (i.e., narrative) memory and retrieval. Requires listening to short stories from an audio recording and then retelling the stories with as much detail as possible.
Semantic Word Retrieval	Gr	Measures the rate and fluency of accessing information stored in long-term memory (four different trials of 1 minute). Requires saying as many words as possible that fit into the respective category (things to eat or drink, names of people, animals, and things to wear).
Verbal Attention	Gwm	Measures attentional control and auditory working memory. Requires hearing a series of intermingled digits and animals presented from an audio recording and then answering a specific question about the sequence, such as, "Tell me the animal that came before five."
Number-Pattern Matching	Gs	Measures processing speed (timed 3 minutes). Requires tapping pairs of identical 1- to 3-digit numbers among rows of six numbers.
Verbal Analogies	Gc, Gf	Measures oral vocabulary, inductive reasoning, and deductive reasoning. Requires saying a word to complete a verbal analogy (e.g., A is to B as C is to …).

Test	Broad CHC Classification	Description and Task Demands
Analysis-Synthesis	Gf	Measures deductive reasoning. Requires learning to use a key containing colored squares to solve puzzles and then using deductive reasoning to solve each puzzle and name the missing color(s). With the exception of the last several items, immediate feedback is provided for both correct and incorrect answers.
Block Rotation	Gv	Measures visual-mental rotation processes. Requires determining which two, from among five options, 3-dimensional block figures match the figure shown in the key.
*Story Comprehension**	Gl	Measures meaningful (i.e., narrative) memory and retrieval. Requires listening to short stories from an audio recording and then answering story-specific comprehension questions read orally by the examiner.
Phonemic Word Retrieval	Gr	Measures the rate and fluency of accessing information stored in long-term memory (four different trials of 1 minute). Requires saying as many words as possible that begin with a different initial sound.
Numbers Reversed	Gwm	Measures attentional control and auditory working memory. Requires hearing a sequence of numbers from an audio recording and then saying the numbers in reverse order.
Letter-Pattern Matching	Gs	Measures processing speed (timed 3 minutes). Requires tapping pairs of identical letter combinations of one to four letters among rows of letters or letter combinations.
General Information	Gc	Measures general knowledge and vocabulary. This test consists of two subtests: Where and What. Requires answering the questions "Where would you find …?" and "What would you do with …?" that are read orally by the examiner.
Concept Formation	Gf	Measures inductive reasoning. Requires learning rules for solving puzzles that require grouping pictures based on shape, size, color, and/or quantity and then stating the rule that explains how one or more pictures is/are different from the other pictures in each puzzle. With the exception of the last several items, immediate feedback is provided for both correct and incorrect answers.

Test	Broad CHC Classification	Description and Task Demands
Number Series	Gq, Gf	Measures mathematical knowledge and reasoning. Requires seeing a series of numbers with one number missing and determining the underlying rule to provide the missing number.
Visual-Auditory Learning	Gv, Gf	Measures visual memory, associative memory, and fluid reasoning. Requires learning the relationships between words and pictures (rebuses) and then reading "sentences" formed by the rebuses. Sentences increase in difficulty as new rebuses are presented, and oral feedback and error correction are provided. This task mirrors the early process of learning to read.
Symbol Inhibition	Gs	Measures processing speed (timed 3 minutes). Requires tapping successive colored shapes in a row of shapes and not tapping the shape(s) that are identical to the shape(s) shown in the key at the top of the screen. The task becomes more complex as additional shapes are added to the key.
Visual Working Memory	Gwm, Gv	Measures visual-spatial working memory. Requires viewing a pattern of dots on the screen (one to nine dots presented inside randomly displayed patterns of squares), then completing a simple visual distractor task while concurrently retaining the dot patterns in active memory. Immediately upon completing the visual distractor task, the task requires recalling the location of the dots from the first screen (in randomly displayed patterns of 2–23 empty boxes).

Note: New tests are in *italics*.
*Can be used as part of the WJ V COG or WJ V ACH batteries.
Adapted from Table 2.1 in the WJ V Technical Manual (LaForte et al., 2025).

Likewise, in the WJ V ACH, the Word Attack test combines with Letter-Word Identification to form the Basic Reading Skills cluster, and it also combines with Spelling of Sounds to form the Phoneme-Grapheme Knowledge cluster. There are 17 tests on the WJ V that do not contribute to any clusters; these tests may be used to supplement WJ V cluster score interpretation.

Test	Broad CHC Classification	Description and Task Demands
Magnitude Comparison	Gs, Gq	Measures knowledge of numerical concepts and magnitude recognition speed (timed for 2 minutes). Requires choosing the greater value in each pair of numerical values; values are expressed as fractions, numbers, decimals, and groups of shapes.
Number Sense	Gq	Measures mathematical vocabulary, knowledge of number relationships, and the abilities to judge, compare, and estimate size, quantity, position, and volume. Requires providing oral responses to math-related questions that are read orally by the examiner.
Spelling of Sounds	Ga, Grw	Measures aspects of phonological and orthographic coding. Requires spelling nonsense words that conform to conventional English spelling rules.
Oral Reading	Grw	Measures word-reading accuracy and prosody (expression). Requires reading sentences aloud that gradually increase in difficulty.
Reading Recall	Grw, Gl	Measures reading comprehension and meaningful memory. Requires reading a passage silently one time and then retelling the information in the passage with as much detail as possible.
Academic Vocabulary	Gc, Gkn	Measures knowledge of specialized vocabulary in areas such as mathematics, science, and humanities. Requires responding to vocabulary questions that are read orally by the examiner.
Academic Facts	Gc, Gkn	Measures specialized knowledge of areas such as mathematics, science, and humanities. Requires responding to questions that are read orally by the examiner.
Letter-Writing Fluency	Gs	Measures working memory, lexical access, and fine motor efficiency (timed for 30 seconds). Requires writing the letters of the alphabet from memory in any order and then copying a model of the alphabet in order.

Note: New tests are in *italics*.
*Can be used as part of the WJ V COG or WJ V ACH batteries.
Adapted from Table 2.1 in the WJ V Technical Manual (LaForte et al., 2025).

Rapid Reference 1.6

WJ V VTL Test Broad CHC Classifications, Descriptions, and Task Demands

Test	Broad CHC Classification	Description and Task Demands
Nonsense Word Repetition	Ga, Gwm	Measures attentional control, auditory processing, and auditory working memory. Requires listening to a nonsense word presented from an audio recording and then pronouncing the nonsense word exactly as presented.
Rapid Picture Naming	Gs, Gr	Measures processing speed and naming facility (timed for 1 minute). Requires naming pictures of common objects presented in successive rows.
Animal-Number Sequencing	Gwm	Measures attentional control and auditory working memory. Requires listening to an intermingled list of animals and digits presented from an audio recording and then rearranging the presented words, first naming all the animals in order and then naming all the numbers in order.
Sound Reversal	Ga	Measures phonological processing and working memory. Requires listening to a simple word and then saying the sounds in the word backward to form a new word.
Rapid Letter Naming	Gs, Gr	Measures processing speed and speed of letter retrieval, a narrow ability of processing speed. Requires naming single letters presented in successive rows. There is a 1-minute time limit.
Understanding Directions	Gwm, Gf	Measures auditory working memory, fluid reasoning, attentional control, and oral language comprehension. Requires studying a detailed picture scene for 10 seconds and then following prompts from an audio recording to tap specific elements of the picture in a prescribed order.
Sound Blending	Ga	Measures phonological processing. Requires listening to a series of syllables presented from an audio recording and then blending the sounds together to pronounce a whole word.
Rapid Phoneme Naming	Gr, Ga	Measures processing speed, naming facility, and auditory processing (timed for 1 minute). Requires pronouncing phonemes (e.g., /m/) for single letters (graphemes) presented in successive rows.

Test	Broad CHC Classification	Description and Task Demands
Memory for Words	Gwm	Measures attentional control and auditory working memory. Requires listening to a list of unrelated words presented from an audio recording and then repeating them in the same order.
Segmentation	Ga	Measures phonological processing. Requires listening to a word and then breaking the word into parts (compound words, syllables, phonemes).
Rapid Number Naming	Gs, Gr	Measures processing speed and naming facility (timed for 1 minute). Requires naming single-digit numbers presented in successive rows.
Sentence Repetition	Gwm	Measures attentional control, auditory working memory, and oral language comprehension. Requires listening to a list of words, phrases, and sentences presented from an audio recording and then repeating each exactly as presented.
Sound Deletion	Ga	Measures phonological manipulation. Requires deleting a phoneme or word part from a word presented from an audio recording and then saying the new word.
Rapid Quantity Naming	Gs, Gv	Measures processing speed, naming facility, and visualization (timed for 1 minute). Requires saying the number of dots in each pattern of one to nine dots that are presented in successive rows.
Sound Substitution	Ga	Measures phonological manipulation. Requires replacing part of a word with a new word part presented from an audio recording and then saying the new word.

Note: New tests are in *italics*.
Adapted from Table 2.1 in the WJ V Technical Manual (LaForte et al., 2025).

DON'T FORGET

Reminders to Examiners

- The WJ V comprises two batteries, the WJ V COG and the WJ V ACH. Additionally, tests in the WJ V VTL can be used alone or in combination with tests and clusters from these two batteries.
- The WJ IV oral language tests have been redistributed in the WJ V COG, WJ V ACH, and WJ V VTL.

- Important diagnostic information can be obtained by administering tests and clusters from across the WJ V.
- It is not necessary to administer all of the WJ V tests; you may select tests to administer based on the referral question(s).

PSYCHOMETRIC PROPERTIES

Intended to be broadly applicable from the preschool to the geriatric levels for either comprehensive or focused assessments, the WJ V, like its predecessors, was developed with a strong emphasis on technical quality.

NORMS

Normative data were based on a single sample of individuals who were administered tests from the COG, ACH, and VTL. The norming study included 5,837 individuals between the ages of 3 and 90+ years from geographically diverse U.S. communities representing all regions of the country. The sample included 3,599 children ages 3 through 17 and 2,238 adults and was selected to be representative of the United States population for geographic location, sex, race, ethnicity, and education level. The school-age (K–12) sample included 3,106 individuals, and the adult nonschool sample (16–90+ years of age and not enrolled in secondary school or college) included 1,688 individuals. Individuals were randomly selected with a stratified sampling design that controlled for five specific variables: census region, age, sex, race/ethnicity, and parent education (K–12 sample only) or educational attainment (adult sample only).

For the school-age sample, data were gathered throughout the calendar year rather than gathering data at only one or two points in the school year. This produces continuous-year norms without the large breaks, or jumps, that occur in the scores when normative data is collected at only one or two points during the school year. The grade norms are reported for each tenth of the school year from the first month of kindergarten (K.0) through the last month of 12th grade (12.9). The age norms are reported for each month from ages 4 years, 0 months through 99 years, 11 months.

All of the tests except Letter-Writing Fluency[1] were normed across the entire age range from 4 to 90+ years. While it is *possible* to obtain norm-referenced scores for any examinee within this age range, some tests are not appropriate or sufficiently reliable for children younger than 5, 6, or 7 years. For this reason, the publisher has recommended an age range (see Rapid References 1.7 and 1.8) for each WJ V test and cluster. In most cases, the minimum age recommendations were based primarily on the test content

[1] The Letter-Writing Fluency test contains norms for ages 4–9 only. You may administer the test to examinees outside of this age range, but you will only obtain *W* scores and AE/GE scores; you will not obtain scores that require norm tables, such as *W* DIFF scores, *z* scores, or standard scores.

WJ V Test	Recommended Age Range	Reliability for Children	Reliability for Adults
Sound Blending	4 and up	0.86	0.88
Rapid Phoneme Naming	6 and up	0.85	0.90
Memory for Words	4 and up	0.82	0.80
Segmentation	4 and up	0.90	0.90
Rapid Number Naming	4 and up	0.96	0.89
Sentence Repetition	4 and up	0.81	0.79
Sound Deletion	5–11 only	0.82	N/A
Rapid Quantity Naming	4 and up	0.95	0.91
Sound Substitution	6–12 only	0.83	N/A

Rapid Reference 1.8

Recommended Administration Ages and Reliability Coefficients for WJ V Clusters

WJ V Test	Recommended Age Range	Reliability for Children	Reliability for Adults
COG General Intelligence Clusters			
General Intellectual Ability	6 and up	0.97	0.97
Brief Intellectual Ability	6 and up	0.91	0.92
Gf-Gc Composite	6 and up	0.94	0.95
COG CHC Broad Ability Clusters			
Comprehension-Knowledge (Gc)	5 and up	0.91	0.93
Fluid Reasoning (Gf)	6 and up	0.90	0.91
Auditory Working Memory Capacity (Gwm)	5 and up	0.89	0.90
Cognitive Processing Speed (Gs)	4 and up	0.98	0.98
Retrieval Fluency (Gr)	5 and up	0.93	0.95

WJ V Test	Recommended Age Range	Reliability for Children	Reliability for Adults
Long-Term Storage (Gl)	6 and up	0.94	0.94
Visual Processing (Gv)	4 and up	0.90	0.90
Phonological Awareness (Ga)	4 and up	0.92	0.93
CHC Narrow Ability and Clinical Clusters			
Phonological Manipulation (Ga)	6–11 only	0.90	N/A
Auditory Memory Span (Gwm)	4 and up	0.88	0.87
Cognitive Efficiency (CE)	4 and up	0.91	0.92
Phonemic Retrieval Fluency (Gr)	6 and up	0.94	0.96
RAN–Reading (Gs, Gr)	6 and up	0.88	0.84
RAN–Math (Gs, Gr)	4 and up	0.87	0.79
Oral Language Clusters			
Oral Language	6 and up	0.93	0.93
Listening Comprehension	6 and up	0.89	0.87
Oral Expression	4 and up	0.88	0.88
Vocabulary	5 and up	0.91	0.94
Reading Clusters			
Brief Reading	5 and up	0.94	0.93
Basic Reading Skills	5 and up	0.96	0.94
Reading Fluency	6 and up	0.98	0.99
Reading Comprehension	6 and up	0.93	0.92
Math Clusters			
Brief Math	6 and up	0.94	0.94
Math Calculation Skills	6 and up	0.96	0.96
Number Concepts	5 and up	0.94	0.94
Math Problem Solving	5 and up	0.93	0.94
Writing Clusters			
Brief Writing	6 and up	0.96	0.96
Basic Writing Skills	6 and up	0.97	0.96
Spelling Skills	6 and up	0.93	0.92
Written Expression	7 and up	0.94	0.95

WJ V Test	Recommended Age Range	Reliability for Children	Reliability for Adults
Cross-Domain Achievement Clusters			
Broad Achievement	7 and up	0.98	0.98
Academic Skills/Brief Achievement	6 and up	0.97	0.96
Academic Fluency	7 and up	0.98	0.98
Academic Applications	5 and up	0.95	0.95
Academic Knowledge	5 and up	0.92	0.94
Phoneme-Grapheme Knowledge	6 and up	0.92	0.91

and task demands but were also informed by the performance of the children in the WJ V norming study. For example, it is not appropriate to administer a test such as Paragraph Reading Comprehension to a child who cannot read; and indeed, with some rare exceptions, most children younger than age 6 in the norming study were not able to read the passages in the Paragraph Reading Comprehension test well enough to obtain a nonzero score on the test. If you administer Paragraph Reading Comprehension to an examinee who is younger than the minimum recommended age range of 6 and they obtain a raw score of 0, you can still obtain a norm-referenced score for the test; however, the reliability of the score will be low because the student is at the *floor* of the test's range of measurement. For this reason, exercise caution when you interpret test results for an examinee who is younger than the minimum recommended age for the test, especially if the examinee obtains a raw score of 0.

RELIABILITY

Reliability refers to the precision of a test score, or "the degree to which scores are free from random errors of measurement for a given group" (AERA et al., 2014). *Reliability coefficients* are expressed as values from 0 (not reliable, or high measurement error) to 1 (perfectly reliable, or no measurement error). In the context of educational and psychological assessments, reliabilities of 0.80 and above are generally considered strong. In IRT, measurement error is estimated separately for each possible raw-score point value on the test; therefore, it is possible for a test to exhibit differential reliability values across the ability range covered by the test. A *marginal IRT reliability coefficient* is computed as:

$$1-\frac{SEM^2}{SD^2}, \qquad (1.1)$$

where *SEM* is the IRT conditional standard error of measurement and SD^2 is the variance of the IRT ability scores for the sample of examinees. In the WJ V, reliability coefficients for the nontimed tests were computed using Equation 1.1 and are reported in the WJ V Technical Manual (LaForte et al., 2025) for six different age groups.

For most speeded tests (e.g., Letter-Pattern Matching, Math Facts Fluency), *alternate-form reliability coefficients* were computed. An alternate-form reliability coefficient is the correlation between scores from two forms of a test administered to the same sample of examinees. For Letter-Writing Fluency, Semantic Word Retrieval, and Phonemic Word Retrieval—speeded tests for which there is only one form—*test-retest reliability coefficients* were computed. A test-retest reliability coefficient is the correlation between scores from two administrations of the same test to a sample of examinees.

Rapid Reference 1.7 contains the reliability coefficients for the WJ V tests for children (ages 4–17, excluding ages for which the test is not recommended) and adults (ages 18+). Most tests have reliability coefficients of 0.80 or higher.

Rapid Reference 1.8 contains the reliability coefficients for the WJ V clusters for children (ages 4–17, excluding ages for which the cluster is not recommended) and adults (ages 18+). Most clusters have reliability coefficients of 0.90 or higher.

VALIDITY

Validity is a primary consideration when using test scores to make decisions. The WJ V Technical Manual (LaForte et al., 2025) provides extensive evidence to support the validity of the WJ V score interpretations, including expert consensus content evaluation, developmental growth curve analysis, exploratory and confirmatory factor analysis, and concurrent correlations with other cognitive, achievement, and oral language batteries. The performance of subsamples of examinees with attention-deficit/hyperactivity disorder (ADHD), autism spectrum disorder (ASD), specific learning disability in reading, writing, and math, language impairment, and intellectual disability, and a subsample of gifted examinees, is also reported.

Ensuring proper test score use and interpretation is the responsibility of the test user. Administering the tests correctly will minimize threats to validity that could arise due to administration or scoring errors. Before administering the WJ V, you must be familiar with the structure and organization of the battery to ensure that you select the most appropriate tests and clusters to address the referral concern(s). Study the WJ V Examiner's Manual and Chapters 3 through 6 of this book to ensure that you know how to correctly administer the tests according to standardized procedures. Review the test content to become familiar with how to pronounce all the words on the tests and how to correctly assign scores to the examinee's responses. Practice administering the tests with a colleague or family member prior to conducting an evaluation with a client or student. Before using the WJ V as part of a comprehensive evaluation, read the WJ V Technical Manual to ensure that the interpretations you are making from the WJ V scores are valid and defensible.

CAUTION

Possible Kinds of Test Misuse

- Being unfamiliar with the content and organization of the test
- Not completing proper training or study for test use
- Not strictly adhering to standardized administration procedures
- Not understanding both the applications and limitations of test scores

USES OF THE WJ V

Because it is a comprehensive instrument, the WJ V can be used with confidence in a variety of settings and for multiple purposes. The wide age range and breadth of coverage allow the tests to be used for educational, clinical, or research purposes from preschool to the geriatric level. Uses of the WJ V include: (a) establishing an individual's present cognitive and achievement performance levels, (b) determining strengths and weaknesses among abilities, (c) comparing an individual's performance to age or grade peers, (d) exploring eligibility for special programs, (e) monitoring educational progress across the school years, (f) investigating the effectiveness of curricula, and (g) assisting with rationales for recommendations that propose specific curricular adaptations and modifications.

The conorming of the WJ V tests results in a "best-practice" scenario for identifying an individual's unique strengths and weaknesses, as well as for obtaining information for instructional planning and programming. Additionally, the conorming of the WJ V tests provides information and statistical models that are especially useful for documenting the nature of an individual's strengths and weaknesses and for determining ability/achievement comparisons.

Intra-Ability Comparison Procedures (including Intra-Cognitive, Intra-Achievement, and Academic Skills/Academic Fluency/Academic Applications procedures) are useful for understanding an individual's strengths and weaknesses, diagnosing and documenting the existence of specific disabilities, and acquiring the most relevant information for educational and vocational planning. *Ability/Achievement Comparison Procedures* (including General Intellectual Ability/Achievement, Gf-Gc Composite/Other Abilities, and Academic Knowledge/Achievement) are sometimes used as part of the selection criteria for SLD programs. See Chapter 7 for further discussion about the use and interpretation of these comparison scores.

DON'T FORGET

Purposes and Uses of the WJ V

- Describing individual strengths and weaknesses
- Determining present performance levels
- Assisting with the diagnosis of disabilities

- Determining intra-ability strengths and weaknesses and documenting ability/achievement comparisons
- Planning accommodations
- Assessing growth
- Evaluating programs
- Conducting research

POSSIBLE WJ V LIMITATIONS

As with all test revisions, some of the changes in the new edition may not appeal to all examiners. In some cases, a favorite test is no longer available or a scoring procedure has been changed or modified. Rapid Reference 1.9 lists some possible limitations to the use of the WJ V.

WJ V RESOURCES

The *WJ V Examiner's Manual* (Mather et al., 2025c) and the *WJ V Technical Manual* (LaForte et al., 2025) are available on the *Riverside Score®* (www.riversidescore.com) platform and provide detailed information about the WJ V. The examiner's manual presents the basic principles of individual clinical assessment, specific information regarding uses of the tests, and suggested procedures for learning to administer, score, and complete the interpretative portions of the WJ V. The development, norming, and technical characteristics of the tests are described in the separate technical manual.

Rapid Reference 1.9

Possible WJ V Limitations

- The change from paper-and-pencil administration to primarily digital administration may be difficult for some examiners.
- Some digital platform procedures, such as setting up a test session, managing accounts, and running reports, are not always intuitive. There is a learning curve for the examiner.
- Not having a paper test record form makes error analysis more difficult on some tests.
- Some schools or other organizations may not have sufficient internet speed and signal strength for online testing.
- Schools and organizations that do not already own iPads will need to purchase them.
- Some examinees may have limited prior experience with tablet devices.
- The removal of the Spanish tests may be problematic for bilingual examiners.

TEST YOURSELF

1. **Major changes from the WJ IV include:**
   (A) Digital administration
   (B) The elimination of a separate oral language battery
   (C) Updated norms to represent the 2020 U.S. census demographics
   (D) All of the above
2. **The only materials needed to administer the WJ V are a laptop and an iPad. True or False?**
3. **You can obtain age-based scores for a 6-year-old student on any WJ V test. True or False?**
4. **You can obtain grade-based normative scores on the WJ V for an examinee who is in their third year of a 4-year college degree program. True or False?**
5. **The tests in the VTL may be used alone or with either the WJ V COG or the WJ V ACH. True or False?**
6. **Which of the following tests is new in the WJ V ACH?**
   (A) Letter-Word Identification
   (B) Sentence Writing Fluency
   (C) Oral Language Samples
   (D) Applied Problems
7. **The WJ V contains procedures for calculating an ability-achievement comparison. True or False?**
8. **You are testing a 5-year-old student and want to include the Reading Comprehension cluster, which includes the Passage Comprehension and Paragraph Reading Comprehension tests. Which of the following is true?**
   (A) You should administer ***only*** Passage Comprehension because it is recommended for examinees ages 5 and older.
   (B) You should not administer either test because the Reading Comprehension cluster is not recommended for examinees younger than age 6.
   (C) You should not administer either test because the scores will not be reliable at age 5.
   (D) You should use your professional judgment to determine whether to administer both tests.
9. **If you want to interpret a particular cluster score, you must administer all the tests that contribute to the cluster. True or False?**
10. **CHC theory is only relevant to the WJ V COG. True or False?**

ANSWERS

1. **D.**
2. **False.** A Response Booklet is still needed for several tests in the WJ V ACH.
3. **True.** Although some tests are not recommended for children as young as 4, 5, or 6, you can obtain norm-referenced scores for any individual who is 4 through 90+ years of age on any test. The only exception is Letter-Writing Fluency, which provides norms for ages 4 through 9 only.

4. **False.** Grade-based normative scores are available on the WJ V for grades K.0 through 12.9 only.
5. **True.**
6. **C.**
7. **True.**
8. **D.** Although the WJ V provides recommended age ranges for all tests and clusters, use your professional judgment to determine if a test is appropriate for a particular examinee. In this example, if a 5-year-old student can read well enough to receive a nonzero raw score on both tests, then it is appropriate to administer the Reading Comprehension cluster and interpret the examinee's score.
9. **True.**
10. **False.**

REFERENCES

American Educational Research Association [AERA], American Psychological Association [APA], & National Council on Measurement in Education [NCME]. (2014). *Standards for educational and psychological testing.* American Educational Research Association.

LaForte, E. M., Dailey, D., & McGrew, K. S. (2025). *Technical manual.* Woodcock-Johnson V. Riverside Assessments, LLC.

Mather, N., McGrew, K. S., LaForte, E. M., & Wendling, B. J. (2025a). *Woodcock-Johnson V Tests of Achievement.* Riverside Assessments, LLC.

Mather, N., McGrew, K. S., LaForte, E. M., & Wendling, B. J. (2025b). *Woodcock-Johnson Virtual Test Library.* Riverside Assessments, LLC.

Mather, N., Wendling, B. J., Snader, E. H. (Contributor), & Jeantete, G. T. (Contributor). (2025c). *Examiner's manual.* Woodcock-Johnson V. Riverside Assessments, LLC.

McGrew, K. S. (2005). The Cattell–Horn–Carroll theory of cognitive abilities: Past, present, and future. In D. P. Flanagan & P. L. Harrison (Eds.), *Contemporary intellectual assessment: Theories, tests, and issues* (2nd ed., pp. 136–181). Guilford Press.

McGrew, K. S., Mather, N., & LaForte, E. M. (2025a). *Woodcock-Johnson V Tests of Cognitive Abilities.* Riverside Assessments, LLC.

McGrew, K. S., Mather, N., & LaForte, E. M. (2025b). *Woodcock-Johnson V.* Riverside Assessments, LLC.

Schneider, W. J., & McGrew, K. S. (2018). The Cattell–Horn–Carroll theory of cognitive abilities. In D. P. Flanagan & E. M. McDonough (Eds.), *Contemporary intellectual assessment: Theories, tests, and issues* (4th ed., pp. 73–163). Guilford Press.

Schrank, F. A., McGrew, K. S., & Mather, N. (2014a). *Woodcock-Johnson IV.* Riverside Assessments, LLC.

Schrank, F. A., McGrew, K. S., & Mather, N. (2014b). *Woodcock-Johnson IV Tests of Cognitive Abilities.* Riverside Assessments, LLC.

Schrank, F. A., Mather, N., & McGrew, K. S. (2015a). *Woodcock-Johnson IV Tests of Achievement*. Riverside Assessments, LLC.

Schrank, F. A., Mather, N., & McGrew, K. S. (2015b). *Woodcock-Johnson IV Tests of Oral Language*. Riverside Assessments, LLC.

Woodcock, R. W., & Johnson, M. B. (1977). *Woodcock-Johnson Psycho-Educational Battery*. Riverside Assessments, LLC.

Woodcock, R. W., & Johnson, M. B. (1989). *Woodcock-Johnson Psycho-Educational Battery—Revised*. Riverside Assessments, LLC.

Woodcock, R. W., McGrew, K. S., & Mather, N. (2001). *Woodcock-Johnson III*. Riverside Assessments, LLC.

Woodcock, R. W., McGrew, K., Mather, N., & Schrank, F. (2003). *Diagnostic supplement to the WJ III Tests of Cognitive Abilities*. Riverside Assessments, LLC.

Two

THEORETICAL BASIS OF THE WOODCOCK-JOHNSON V

[I]n theory, there is no difference between theory and practice, while in practice, there is.

—Benjamin Brewster (1882, p. 202)

[N]othing is so practical as a good theory.

—G. Stanley Hall (1882, p. 310)

In a comprehensive assessment, it is not long before we are confronted with more data than can be juggled in our heads, and we become lost in the details. A good theory gives us a framework on which we can sort the details into meaningful categories and make sense of the relations among the data. With a large battery of tests like the *Woodcock-Johnson V,* an organizing framework is all the more necessary. The primary theoretical basis of the WJ V is the Cattell-Horn-Carroll Theory of Cognitive Abilities (CHC Theory: McGrew, 1997a, 2005, 2009; Schneider & McGrew, 2012, 2018).

CHC Theory combines an inclusive, ever-expanding taxonomy of cognitive abilities with a set of explanations for how the abilities develop, how they interrelate, and how they influence important life outcomes such as adaptive, educational, and occupational functioning. With a solid understanding of CHC Theory, the complexity of the WJ V's many scores is much reduced, and the results can be interpreted with fluency and confidence.

Essentials of WJ V™ Assessment, First Edition. Erica M. LaForte, Nancy Mather, and W. Joel Schneider.

THE ORIGINS OF CHC THEORY

The roots of CHC theory date back to the start of the previous century, when Charles Spearman generated the first theory of intelligence grounded in empirical observation and formalized by statistical theory. Spearman's successors—students, friends, and arch-rivals—have taken on the work of extending and amending what is known about intelligence.

Spearman's Two Factor Theory

Spearman (1904) proposed that we can learn about psychological phenomena by measuring them in diverse ways and inspecting the patterns of correlations amongst the measurements. He invented what came to be known as *factor analysis*, a statistical tool that helps researchers see subtle patterns in how various psychological measurements correlate. Spearman measured diverse cognitive abilities in several samples of school-age students. In Spearman's data, the overall pattern was not subtle: Almost all of the correlations were positive. This finding has been replicated many thousands of times in diverse samples with diverse tests. Despite an exhaustive search, there is no replicated evidence of any pair of cognitive abilities with nonpositive correlations (Carroll, 1993; Jensen, 1998). What does this mean?

At first, Spearman hypothesized that a single ability (general intelligence, or *g*) could account for all of the positive correlations. That is, cognitive test performance correlates positively because all test performance was hypothesized to be influenced by a single ability. Spearman (1923, 1927) believed that this ability was a general-purpose mental function that perceived relationships, patterns, and rule-like behavior in what one observed and was perhaps rooted in a kind of energy-like phenomenon that could be used interchangeably by many mental functions.

Spearman called his theory the two-factor theory of intelligence, which sounds like he believed there were two intelligence factors. He did not. Rather, he held that all test performance was influenced by two kinds of ability: a general factor and a specific factor that was unique to each test. Although Spearman wrote mostly about the importance of the general factor, he was quite clear that specific factors can matter a great deal in specific tasks and contexts (Hart & Spearman, 1912).

Thurstone's Primary Mental Abilities

Eventually, data from other scholars and from Spearman's own studies compelled him to moderate his claim: The general factor of ability was the *primary* reason abilities are correlated, but a small number of "group factors" were needed to account for some excess correlation among groups of tests that appeared to measure distinct abilities (Spearman, 1927). That is, additional factors were needed because some groups of tests correlated with each other more highly than could be explained by a single general factor. For example, Spearman referred to verbal tests as his "hierarchy breaker" (Cattell, 1987, p. 39) because their correlations with each other were much stronger than their correlations with other tests, and the precise hierarchical structure in the correlations implied by a single general factor was, therefore, not tenable. Not long afterward, other group factors were reliably found, and Spearman devoted a chapter to these factors in his 1927 textbook.

What are these additional factors that are neither general nor specific, but somewhere in between? Since adequate methods for their discovery became available nearly a century ago, the field has generated a consistent set of answers. Thurstone's (1931) advances in multiple factor analysis allowed him to study large batteries of tests ideally suited to understanding the structure of ability. A series of analyses (Thurstone, 1934, 1935, 1938, 1940) revealed a set of what Thurstone called *primary mental abilities* (Reasoning, Verbal Comprehension, Spatial Visualization, Associative Memory, Number Facility, Word Fluency, and Perceptual Speed). Although the names differ slightly, it is easy to map Thurstone's primary mental abilities onto the broad factors of CHC theory presented later in this chapter (i.e., Gf = Reasoning, Gc = Verbal Comprehension, Gv = Spatial Visualization, Gl = Associative Memory, Gs = {Perceptual Speed, Number Speed}).

Later, Thurstone and others found that the list of primary abilities needed some additions and that each of these broad abilities could be divided into smaller, narrow factors of ability (Adcock & Webberley, 1971; Ekstrom et al., 1976; French et al., 1963; Thurstone, 1950). There were different types of spatial visualization, different types of verbal knowledge, different types of memory, and so forth. Over the decades, theorists have used different terms, have elaborated on Thurstone's results, and have organized and emphasized their findings in different ways, but no credible evidence has contradicted Thurstone's initial findings in any fundamental way.

DON'T FORGET

Spearman believed that the general factor of ability was the primary reason abilities are correlated, but a small number of "group factors" were needed to account for some excess correlation among groups of tests that could not be explained by a single general factor. Thurstone later identified a set of seven *primary* mental abilities, each containing multiple *narrow* abilities.

Cattell's Two General Abilities: Gf-Gc Theory 1.0

Although Spearman hypothesized that only one general factor of intelligence was needed in his theory, he allowed for the possibility that the general factor might actually be a group of functions (Spearman, 1904, p. 284). His student, Raymond Cattell (1943), hypothesized that there were at least two general factors of ability, general fluid intelligence (g_f) and general crystallized intelligence (g_c). Cattell did not reject Spearman's idea of general intelligence but rather, elaborated upon it.

Theoretically, Cattell's fluid intelligence was essentially the same as Spearman's *g*, a general relation-perceiving function of the whole brain. It was responsible for generating new knowledge in unfamiliar situations. Crystallized intelligence, however, was the set of learned knowledge structures that contributed to intelligent action. For example, the first time one solves an unfamiliar puzzle, fluid reasoning is required to see its patterns and acquire insights about how the puzzle works. The second time, the puzzle can be solved by recalling the previous solution, and little additional reasoning is required.

Cattell used the fluid/crystallized distinction as a metaphor to characterize how the two abilities differed—no literal fluids or crystals are involved in the theory. Fluid intelligence can be used fluidly to solve almost any kind of problem; it is a truly general-purpose mechanism. Crystallized intelligence is the residue of past applications of fluid intelligence. Once a solution is "crystallized" in memory, it is useful in a narrower range of applications.

Cattell compared fluid reasoning to the thin, fragile outer layer of living coral polyps in a coral reef, and he compared crystallized intelligence to the underlying layers of (dead) coral exoskeletons that make up the robust structure of the reef and create the conditions in which coral colonies thrive. Whereas fluid intelligence is responsible for new insights and knowledge, it is vulnerable to injury, disease, and toxins, and it is easily compromised by fatigue, distraction, and intoxication. By contrast, crystallized intelligence is the repository of past insights and it creates the conditions for additional learning—expertise is difficult to acquire at first, but once established, experts rapidly take in new information that is within the domain of their expertise (Ericsson, 2017; Ericsson & Kintsch, 1995; Horn, 2007; Horn & Blankson, 2005).

Like coral structures under the delicate layer of living coral, crystallized intelligence is relatively robust—once something is learned, it tends to stay learned. Of course, brain diseases, such as Alzheimer's, dementia, and brain injuries can diminish a person's learned capacities, but their effect on fluid reasoning tends to be even greater (Bajpai et al., 2022; Blair, 2006).

Whereas crystallized ability tends to increase into late adulthood, fluid reasoning begins to decline in early adulthood (Horn & Cattell, 1967; Tucker-Drob et al., 2019, 2022). In the WJ V, this pattern is clearly evident when comparing the *W* scores (ability scores not adjusted for age) for crystallized[1] and fluid abilities across ages. In Figure 2.1, both abilities increase rapidly until the end of adolescence. In young adulthood, Gf declines gradually at first and with increasing steepness in late adulthood. By contrast, Gc increases gradually from young adulthood to middle age and decreases gradually in late

DON'T FORGET

Fluid reasoning is responsible for generating new knowledge in unfamiliar, or novel, situations and tends to decline in early adulthood. Crystallized knowledge is acquired through learning and experience and tends to increase into late adulthood. Of the two, fluid reasoning is more vulnerable to injury, disease, and toxins, and is more easily compromised by fatigue, distraction, and intoxication.

[1] Crystallized ability (Gc) is called comprehension-knowledge in the WJ V.

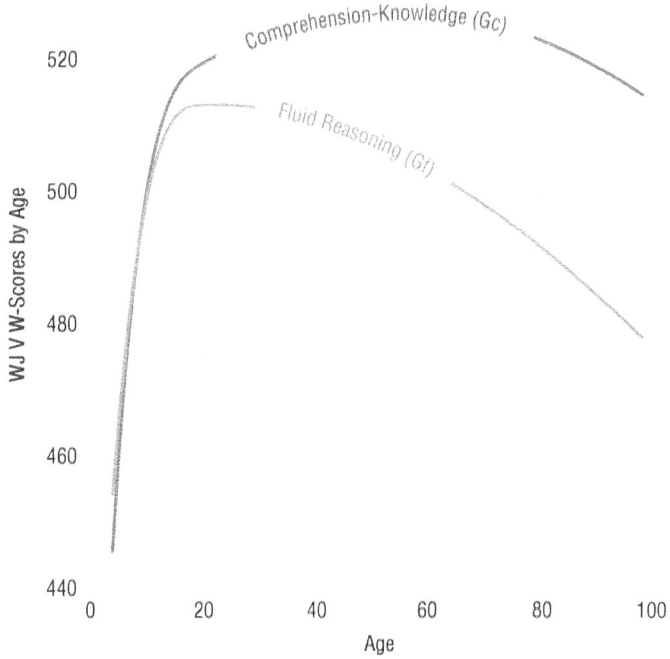

Figure 2.1 WJ V Fluid Reasoning (Gf) and Comprehension-Knowledge (Gc) *W* Scores by Age

adulthood. Of course, these trends are averages and are not necessarily the trajectory of any one individual. For example, people who develop dementia would, by definition, have steeper declines than people who do not.

An Integration of Cattell and Thurstone: The Theory of Fluid and Crystallized Intelligence 2.0

In the same way that Cattell elaborated on his mentor's theory, Cattell's student John Horn elaborated on his own mentor's ideas. Horn titled his dissertation "Fluid and Crystallized Intelligence: A factor-analytic study of the structure among primary mental abilities." His hypothesis was that the correlations among Thurstone's primary abilities would be explained by Cattell's fluid and crystallized factors. The results were largely confirmatory of Cattell's ideas—if one extracts two factors from the ability tests, then the results look a lot like Cattell's original theory; however, a deeper dive into the analyses suggested some refinements were needed. The theory was expanded to incorporate a range of broad abilities resembling Thurstone's primary mental abilities.

Over the next several decades, Horn and Cattell continued to expand and refine Gf-Gc theory to the point that it became a comprehensive summary of what was known about the structure, growth, and action of various cognitive abilities (Cattell, 1987; Horn, 1982, 1985).

At the same time, there were worthy rival theories brewing (e.g., Das et al., 1975; Gardner, 1983; Guilford, 1967; L. Guttman, 1954; Humphreys, 1962; Sternberg, 1985; Vernon, 1950), each of which made important contributions to our understanding of intelligence. How could one decide among the various models? The persuasive credibility of the Gf-Gc theory received a big boost from an unexpected source.

A Re-Analysis of Hundreds of Studies: Carroll's Three-Stratum Theory

John Carroll, a student of Thurstone's, had a sophisticated theory of intelligence of his own and a number of excellent papers on verbal abilities and foreign-language learning abilities (Carroll, 1941, 1978, 1979, 1989). After retirement, Carroll decided to re-analyze every study of the structure of intelligence he could find (461 studies!), apply the same analysis to each study, and write up the results in an 800-page masterpiece (Carroll, 1993).

Although he had no preconceived intention of doing so, Carroll's results largely replicated the findings of Horn and Cattell's Gf-Gc theory. Because Carroll's evidence base was many times larger than Horn and Cattell's, his theory made a number of fine-grained distinctions that Gf-Gc theory did not—he found evidence for 70 narrow abilities, 8 broad abilities, and 1 general ability. Carroll's broad abilities and many of his narrow abilities are nearly identical to the lists of abilities compiled by Cattell (1987) and Horn (1980, 1985), in part because they drew from the same sources and also because Carroll honored the work that came before him.

What made Carroll's work persuasive was his reputation as a dispassionate scholar and the mammoth scope of his work. If one wants to contradict Carroll, one needs to marshal high-quality evidence to contend with his 461 datasets. Most commercially available intelligence tests are broadly consistent with Gf-Gc theory and/or Carroll's work, and the majority of new tests draw on these theories directly.

Much has been made of what, at first glance, appears to be a major difference between Horn and Cattell's Gf-Gc theory and Carroll's Three-Stratum Theory. Carroll's theory has a general factor at the apex of his hierarchy of abilities, and Gf-Gc theory does not. Carroll believed that fluid intelligence and general intelligence were highly correlated but distinguishable abilities operating in the here and now (Carroll, 2003). Horn acknowledged that factor analyses of abilities returned a general factor in every factor analysis ever conducted (Horn & Blankson, 2005; Horn & McArdle, 2007) but believed Cattell's (1971) hypothesis that this statistical finding was a result of fluid intelligence acting over the course of development—fluid intelligence was "invested" in other abilities, causing them to correlate. This idea, known as Cattell's (1971) Investment Theory, has largely been supported (Ackerman, 2018; Bardach et al., 2023; Blanch & Blanco, 2025; Kvist & Gustafsson, 2008; Thorsen et al., 2014; von Stumm & Ackerman, 2013), though the

DON'T FORGET

Cattell's Gf-Gc theory structure does not include a general intelligence (g) factor, whereas Carroll's Three-Stratum theory does.

mechanism may not be as simple, consistent, or one-sided as Cattell thought (Kievit et al., 2017; Scherrer et al., 2024; Watrin et al., 2022).

In discussing the difference between Horn and Carroll, this author sometimes jokes that one of them believed in the central importance of an ability that is so general that it influences every aspect of performance and also every other ability, . . . and the other theorist believed in *g*.

Is this a distinction without a difference? To some degree, yes. Fluid intelligence, starting with Cattell (1943), was explicitly isomorphic to Spearman's *g*. Is there any difference between thinking of *g* as an ability vs. *g* as a statistical finding? This difference is subtle and probably not worth the contention, rancor, and vitriol the debate has generated. In Horn's view, it is important to distinguish between general intelligence in the here-and-now that can be used to solve problems in real time (i.e., fluid intelligence) and the cumulative influence fluid intelligence can have over the course of a lifetime. If a person's fluid intelligence stayed constant, then there would be no reason to distinguish between *g* and Gf; however, with maturation, Gf increases dramatically until young adulthood and then decreases gradually throughout adulthood. Because all intelligence scores are adjusted for age, none of these developmental effects figured into any of Carroll's analyses.

In addition, some people have sometimes small, sometimes large losses of Gf due to disease, injury, and substance abuse. These fluctuations of fluid reasoning, according to Horn, cause different patterns of learning and different patterns of correlations among abilities, which influence the calculations underlying statistical *g*. People who are severely incapacitated by brain injury or brain disease rarely participate in standardization samples of intelligence tests. Thus, we do not usually see in standardization samples the very people for whom the difference between Gf and *g* might matter. Thus, in many normal samples, Gf and *g* have perfect or near-perfect correlations (Reynolds et al., 2013; L. G. Weiss et al., 2013a, 2013b), but, for some populations, the distinction matters (Blair, 2006; Kvist & Gustafsson, 2008).

If *g* is the explanation for the positive correlations among broad abilities, then Carroll's theory would say that 100% of the reason that abilities correlate is due to the general intelligence that one has right now. Horn's theory would say that much of it is due to the general intelligence one has right now (i.e., fluid intelligence), but some of the correlation is also due to past effects of one's general intelligence. That is a clear difference, but this is not the sort of difference of opinion that is worth losing friends over.

For healthy people whose background is similar to that of the test's standardization sample, a general intelligence score based on a diverse set of tests is the best measure of fluid reasoning—one's global capacity to reason, learn, and solve problems in real time. Is there any reason to have tests specifically designed to measure fluid reasoning directly? Yes! If we have reason to believe that a person's capacity to reason, learn, and solve problems has been compromised in the recent past, then a psychometrically pure measure of Gf is a useful tool, even if it is a little less reliable than a general ability measure. In addition, if a person's ability to reason, learn, and solve problems would be underestimated by including measures of language and verbal knowledge (e.g., a person who grew up in a language community different from that of the standardization sample), then a direct measure of fluid reasoning that does not require language or verbal knowledge is likely to be much more informative than a general intelligence measure contaminated by language.

The Cattell-Horn-Carroll Theory of Cognitive Abilities

The original *Woodcock-Johnson Psycho-Educational Battery* (Woodcock & Johnson, 1977) did not have a named theory guiding its development, though Woodcock was clearly paying attention to then-current developments in the field, including measures of reasoning, visual and auditory processing, and structured learning tasks. When revision work began, it was clear that the 1977 WJ was compatible with Gf-Gc Theory. The much-expanded 1989 *Woodcock-Johnson Psychoeducational Battery—Revised* (Woodcock & Johnson, 1989) was intended as a direct operationalization of Gf-Gc theory, and John Horn was a frequent consultant on the project. After Carroll published his analyses in 1993, he and Horn both consulted on the development of the *Woodcock-Johnson III* (Woodcock et al., 2001).

In the 1990s, Richard Woodcock, Kevin McGrew, Dawn Flanagan, and others began publishing clinically oriented articles and books on how to use Gf-Gc theory to interpret any set of cognitive tests (Flanagan et al., 2000; McGrew, 1997b; McGrew & Flanagan, 1998; Woodcock, 1993). They referenced Carroll's model and used his terms for many abilities, but they thought of his work as an extension of Gf-Gc theory, which, indeed, it was; however, because Horn and Carroll had strong differences of opinion about the nature of the *g* factor, there was a need to distinguish between them.

Before the publication of the *Woodcock-Johnson III*, Horn and Carroll agreed that there was utility in referring to the similarities between their theories with an umbrella term, the *Cattell-Horn-Carroll theory of cognitive abilities*, or CHC theory. As it turned out, both Horn and Carroll had reservations about the term (McGrew, 2023), but it has, indeed, been a useful way of talking about a common set of broad and narrow abilities without having to bicker endlessly about the *g* factor (Schneider & McGrew, 2019). CHC theory does not replace either Gf-Gc theory or the Three-Stratum theory. It is instead more like a superordinate category in the same way that *cola* refers to a variety of fizzy drinks with similar ingredients and taste profiles, even though the people who make them and the people who drink them have strong opinions about how they differ. The superordinate category of *cola* does not imply that we must mix various brands of cola into a single glass. CHC theory, likewise, maintains Gf-Gc theory and Three-Stratum theory as distinct but highly similar ideas.

Now that Cattell, Horn, and Carroll have all passed away, Kevin McGrew, later joined by W. Joel Schneider, took on the task of tending and updating CHC theory. They see themselves as stewards of this line of work; they do not see the theory as their property. Rather, CHC theory is collectively owned by all intelligence researchers, and Schneider and McGrew have outlined a set of steps and procedures by which other scholars can contribute to its extension and update (Schneider & McGrew, 2018), and many scholars have done so (e.g., Allen & Mayer, 2022; Biesok et al., 2024; Callis et al., 2023; Chang

Rapid Reference 2.1

CHC Broad Abilities

CHC Broad Abilities Measured in the WJ V:

- Fluid Reasoning (Gf)
- Comprehension-Knowledge (Gc)
- Working Memory Capacity (Gwm)
- Long-Term Storage (Gl)
- Retrieval Fluency (Gr)
- Cognitive Processing Speed (Gs)
- Reading and Writing (Grw)
- Quantitative Knowledge (Gq)
- Visual Processing (Gv)
- Auditory Processing (Ga)

CHC Broad Abilities Not Measured in the WJ V:

- Reaction and Decision Speed (Gt)
- Psychomotor Speed (Gps)
- Domain-Specific Knowledge (Gkn)
- Olfactory Abilities (Go)
- Tactile Abilities (Gh)
- Kinesthetic Abilities (Gk)
- Psychomotor Abilities (Gp)
- Emotional Intelligence (Gei)

et al., 2024; Geiger et al., 2024; Mayer et al., 2024; Schneider et al., 2016; Unsworth, 2024; Walker et al., 2024; S. Weiss & Wilhelm, 2022; Wilhelm & Kyllonen, 2021; Woodcock et al., 2018). Rapid Reference 2.1 lists the broad abilities in the current conception of CHC theory (Schneider & McGrew, 2018).

Although CHC theory began as a two- or three-level hierarchy, it has evolved to recognize intermediate categories. Intermediate abilities are not quite broad and not quite narrow, but somewhere in between. CHC theory has explicitly borrowed from Vernon's (1950) hierarchical theory and its successor theory Verbal-Perceptual-Rotation theory (VPR: Johnson & Bouchard, 2005) the idea that abilities are not arranged in strict strata (i.e., general, broad, narrow, specific) but lie on a smooth continuum of generality ranging from very broad to very specific.

CHC theory will continue to evolve with incoming data. Current efforts have been devoted to understanding how different abilities interact and influence each other. McGrew (2023) suggested that one may soon see CHC theories in the plural, as there are now several more variations in the CHC tradition. That said, there are a few contradictions in the variations, and none of the suggested changes have any bearing on how to resolve the core difference between Gf-Gc theory and Three-Stratum Theory. Should CHC theory's evolution ever lead to any radical changes, a name change might be necessary, but given the stability of findings since Thurstone, that need might never arise.

CHC ABILITIES AND THE WJ V

This section describes the CHC broad and narrow abilities that are measured by the WJ V. Not all tests fit neatly into the CHC taxonomy of narrow abilities; many measure clear blends of two or more known abilities. Some are blended so thoroughly that it is hard to say exactly which abilities are measured to which degree. There is an important distinction between tests that blend abilities because of careless test design and tests that blend abilities by necessity. Dribbling skill in soccer (i.e., what most people in the world refer to as *football*) is necessarily entangled with running and agility. One might measure running and agility separately, but neither of these measurements would do the job of measuring dribbling skill.

General Ability (g)

The WJ V General Intellectual Ability (GIA) cluster score is an equally weighted average of the Oral Vocabulary, Matrices, Spatial Relations, Story Recall, Semantic Word Retrieval, Verbal Attention, Number-Pattern Matching, and Verbal Analogies test scores. The GIA is a strong predictor of most forms of achievement and can be used for identifying the extremes of intelligence (i.e., intellectual disability and giftedness).

Fluid Reasoning (Gf)

Fluid reasoning is the ability to solve unfamiliar problems in real time. Fluid reasoning's narrow abilities can be distinguished by process (inductive vs. deductive reasoning) and by content (verbal, figural, numeric).

Inductive reasoning If fluid reasoning is the core of human intelligence, then inductive reasoning is at the very center of the core. Inductive reasoning is the ability to discover patterns and rule-like behavior that govern how phenomena behave. Consider this series of lines:

| || ||| ||||

It is clear that they are grouped such that the number of lines increases by one in each group. If the series were extended, then what is, likely the next set of lines? If the pattern holds, then it will be five lines like this:

|||||

In everyday experience, there are no guarantees that phenomena will conform to any pattern we have inductively discovered; however, inductive reasoning gives us a sense of what is most likely to happen next. Not only can we make predictions about what will happen next, but we can also make predictions about what will happen next given an action we choose. That is, accurate prediction of outcomes sometimes allows for control of outcomes. Thus, inductive reasoning is a powerful tool for guiding intelligent action.

The act of extending a series like this requires two steps: making an inference about the rule that governs the series using inductive reasoning and predicting the next item in the sequence using deductive reasoning. The complete sequence of induction and deduction is a *predictive inference.*

One of the reasons that inductive reasoning is thought to be at the core of all intelligence is that predictive inference appears to be the central function of the cerebral cortex (Hawkins, 2004, 2021). That is, neurons in the cortex are constantly using information they receive to make predictions about what information they are about to receive next. Specifically, columns of neurons create predictive models of low-level sensations, intermediate-level representations of objects, and high-level abstract ideas. As Hawkins (2021) explains,

> The brain creates a predictive model. This just means that the brain continuously predicts what its inputs will be. Prediction isn't something that the brain does every now and then; it is an intrinsic property that never stops, and it serves an essential role in learning. When the brain's predictions are verified, that means the brain's model of the world is accurate. A mis-prediction causes you to attend to the error and update the model.
>
> We are not aware of the vast majority of these predictions unless the input to the brain does not match. As I casually reach out to grab my coffee cup, I am not aware that my brain is predicting what each finger will feel, how heavy the cup should be, the temperature of the cup, and the sound the cup will make when I place it back on my desk. But if the cup was suddenly heavier, or cold, or squeaked, I would notice the change. We can be certain that these predictions are occurring because even a small change in any of these inputs will be noticed. But when a prediction is correct, as most will be, we won't be aware that it ever occurred. (p. 48)

Most neurons appear to be using the same algorithm throughout the cortex to create predictive models (Hawkins & Ahmad, 2016). Is this the explanation for why all abilities are correlated? Perhaps. Whatever the explanation, the role of predictive inference (inductive reasoning) runs all the way down from high-level reasoning to individual neurons processing sensory information.

Deductive reasoning Whereas inductive reasoning is the discovery of pattern or rule-like behavior that governs a behavior, deductive reasoning is the application of that rule to predict what follows. Inductive reasoning is the process of using known facts to discover new rules and patterns. Deductive reasoning is the process of using known rules and patterns to discover new facts. For example, if we accept the premise that only humans write poetry and also accept the premise that there are no humans living on Europa, one of Jupiter's moons, then we can deduce a new fact that no poems are being written on Europa. Of course, a premise might be wrong, and our reasoning will lead us astray. Perhaps a group of poetry-loving astronauts has been sent secretly to Europa. Perhaps a robotic probe to Europa is currently churning out haikus by the millions in its spare computing time.

Content Facets in Fluid Reasoning

Whereas inductive and deductive reasoning refer to the type of processing, the content that we are reasoning about also matters. We can reason inductively and deductively about verbal concepts, geometric figures, and numerical quantities (Beauducel et al., 2001; R. Guttman & Greenbaum, 1998; Lakin & Gambrell, 2012; Marshalek et al., 1983).

Rapid Reference 2.2 contains the WJ V fluid reasoning (Gf) tests and the narrow CHC ability measured by each. Concept Formation and Matrices are both inductive reasoning tests that use geometric figures. Because the figures in Concept Formation are very simple, the spatial reasoning requirement is minimized. By contrast, many studies of matrix tasks find that performance on them also involves a fair bit of spatial reasoning.

Verbal Analogies is primarily an inductive reasoning task with verbal concepts. Number Series is primarily an inductive reasoning task with quantitative information. Because many math curricula give explicit instruction on how to solve number series tasks, Number Series will not operate as a fluid reasoning test for all people. Indeed, the evidence presented in the WJ V Technical Manual suggests that Number Series sometimes loads on the

Rapid Reference 2.2

WJ V Fluid Reasoning (Gf) Tests

- **Concept Formation (COG):** Inductive reasoning with geometric figures
- **Matrices (COG):** Inductive reasoning with geometric figures; may require spatial reasoning
- **Verbal Analogies (COG):** Primarily inductive reasoning with verbal concepts
- **Number Series (COG):** Inductive reasoning; may require academic (quantitative) knowledge
- **Analysis-Synthesis (COG):** Primarily deductive reasoning with visual figures; may require quantitative reasoning

same factor as reading and writing skills, suggesting that it has become an academic skill for many examinees.

Although each of the inductive reasoning tasks requires at least some deductive reasoning, the primary difficulty in answering the questions correctly is inferring the relationships and rules that govern the stimuli presented. The only test that is primarily a test of deductive reasoning is Analysis-Synthesis. On this test, one is given all of the rules for each item. As the test progresses, the rules increase in complexity, and it becomes progressively harder to apply those rules deductively. Although Analysis-Synthesis uses geometric figures, its structure is decidedly math-like. Thus, it appears to be mostly a measure of quantitative deductive reasoning.

Visual Processing (Gv)

Visual Processing refers to the ability to perceive objects, create mental representations of them, and transform and manipulate them in one's mind. There are many narrow abilities within the Gv domain, but the WJ V focuses only on the narrow ability of visualization (see Rapid Reference 2.3). The tests that most directly measure visualization are Spatial Relations and Block Rotation, both of which require manipulating mental images.

Visualization can play an important role in many people's understanding of quantity and in developing accurate intuitions about geometry (Wang & Carr, 2020). Spatial ability is also known to be important for people entering technical fields like engineering (Buckley et al., 2019; Lubinski, 2010; Uttal et al., 2013).

Carroll and many other scholars found that there is not always a clear distinction between Gv and Gf, especially when the Gf tests have spatial content. The WJ Technical Manual finds evidence for the separation of Gf and Gv, but it is still important to remember that the strong Gv component of Matrices and Concept Formation can lead to interpretive difficulties (e.g., scoring low on Matrices not because of poor general ability but because of visual-spatial processing problems). In such cases, follow-up testing is recommended.

Auditory Processing (Ga)

Auditory processing is frequently misunderstood to have something to do with the understanding of language at the level of conversations. It does not. It instead refers to lower-level perceptions of sound (e.g., pitch discrimination, sound localization, and memory for

Rapid Reference 2.3

WJ V Visual Processing (Gv) Tests

- **Block Rotation (COG):** Primarily visualization
- **Spatial Relations (COG):** Primarily visualization

tones). The ability to perceive sound and play with it in one's mind is clearly relevant to musicians. For example, Beethoven was able to compose great music even after he was nearly completely deaf because he could still imagine what his compositions would sound like. Few cognitive batteries measure such abilities (although the WJ R and WJ III did).

Auditory processing is unusual because clinicians are primarily interested in one of its narrow abilities rather than the broad domain as a whole. Clinicians usually are interested in phonological processing because of its strong connections to learning to decode words (Nelson et al., 2012; Torgesen et al., 1997; Wagner & Torgesen, 1987). Deficits in phonological processing can increase the risk of developing dyslexia (Peng et al., 2019, 2022).

The primary measures of phonological processing in the WJ V are Sound Blending and Segmentation, which form the Phonological Awareness cluster. The Nonsense Word Repetition, Sound Reversal, Sound Deletion, and Sound Substitution tasks are supplemental measures that can isolate very specific kinds of phonological processing deficits. With the exception of Nonsense Word Repetition, all of these tests require holding sounds in working memory and manipulating them, which often means that test scores must be interpreted in conjunction with other measures of working memory. Of interest, however, is the finding that Nonsense Word Repetition's loading on working memory is even stronger than its loading on Ga.

In the WJ V, the tests and clusters measuring auditory processing are all contained in the Virtual Test Library (VTL; see Rapid Reference 2.4).

Working Memory (Gwm)

Working memory is the ability to hold information in immediate awareness, usually while processing it in some way. Working memory allows people to juggle ideas in their mind while they reason through complex problems (Ackerman et al., 2005; Fry & Hale, 1996, 2000;

Rapid Reference 2.4

WJ V Auditory Processing (Ga) Tests

- **Sound Blending (VTL):** Phonological processing
- **Segmentation (VTL):** Phonological processing
- **Nonsense Word Repetition (VTL):** Phonological processing; also requires working memory (Gwm)
- **Sound Reversal (VTL):** Phonological processing; may also require working memory (Gwm)
- **Sound Deletion (VTL):** Phonological processing may also require working memory (Gwm)
- **Sound Substitution (VTL):** Phonological processing may also require working memory (Gwm)

Kail, 2007). Being able to hold and process information simultaneously makes it possible to participate in dynamic, two-way conversations (Keidser et al., 2015). Deficits in working memory capacity make it difficult to listen to a lecture and take notes at the same time (Bui & Myerson, 2014). Working memory facilitates predictive inferences while reading complex passages (Calvo, 2005). Strong working memory ability allows people to perform multistep math problems without becoming distracted (Tolar et al., 2009; Ünal et al., 2022), particularly with longer word problems.

The working memory system contains several narrow abilities. Memory span tasks measure short-term storage of information and make no additional processing demands. The storage of visual and auditory information corresponds to distinct abilities, but examinees often enhance their performance in one modality by forming a second representation of the information in the other. For example, people put names to visual stimuli in a visual memory span task. People also visualize auditory stimuli (e.g., they visualize numbers that are presented orally). Thus, it is not always possible to cleanly distinguish between these abilities.

On the WJ V, Memory for Words is a relatively pure measure of auditory memory span (see Rapid Reference 2.5). Sentence Repetition is less pure because better comprehension skills make it possible to perform better on longer sentences. What Sentence Repetition lacks in purity, it makes up for in ecological validity. Working memory did not evolve to help us hold onto lists of disconnected words. Among other things, it evolved to help us understand and process long sentences we hear.

Nonsense Word Repetition is also an auditory span test, but one that requires strong phonological processing ability to hear and repeat made-up nonsense words.

At the core of working memory capacity is the ability to direct the focus of attention to accomplish a mental task. Unfortunately, attentional control cannot be measured directly. In general, it is measured in the context of a task in which there are distractions or memory burdens. Complex span tests require examinees to hold information while processing it, a feat

Rapid Reference 2.5

WJ V Working Memory (Gwm) Tests

- **Verbal Attention (COG):** Auditory working memory capacity
- **Numbers Reversed (COG):** Auditory working memory capacity
- **Animal-Number Sequencing (COG):** Auditory working memory capacity
- **Visual Working Memory (COG):** Visual memory span
- **Memory for Words (VTL):** Auditory memory span
- **Sentence Repetition (VTL):** Auditory memory span
- **Nonsense Word Repetition (VTL):** Auditory memory span; requires strong Ga (phonological processing) skills (see Rapid Reference 2.4)

that requires attentional control. Although attentional control is central to working memory performance, it is an important component of other kinds of performance as well. For example, attentional control is manifested in tasks with little to no memory load (e.g., Symbol Inhibition). For this reason, measures of attentional control in the context of a complex span task are referred to as tests of working memory capacity. That is, they test the functioning of the working memory system as a whole, rather than isolating parts of the system.

Auditory complex span tests on the WJ V include Verbal Attention, Numbers Reversed, and Animal-Number Sequencing. Visual Working Memory is a complex span measure in the visual modality.

Learning Efficiency (Gl)

Learning efficiency[2] is the rate at which new information is acquired. In theory, learning efficiency is the speed at which any kind of information, easy or hard, can be learned. In practice, learning efficiency is measured using material that is easy for anyone to understand, given enough time. If learning efficiency were tested with material that was difficult, then the test would not be applicable for many people. There are three primary narrow abilities in this domain: associative memory, list learning, and meaningful memory. As the WJ V lacks any measures of list learning, only associative memory and meaningful memory are discussed here (see Rapid Reference 2.6).

Associative memory *Associative memory* is the efficiency with which one learns arbitrary pairings of stimuli. Associative memory is relevant in learning math facts (e.g., the stimulus 6×7 is paired with the answer 42). Although skilled readers sound out unfamiliar words at first, with enough repetitions, associative memory allows for recognizing them lexically (i.e., as sight words), which is more efficient than sounding each word out every time.

The Visual-Auditory Learning test is a structured learning task in which examinees learn rebus-word pairs one at a time. The test has a degree of ecological validity in that it was designed to simulate how well someone can learn to read a new writing system. The test is

Rapid Reference 2.6

WJ V Learning Efficiency/Long-Term Storage (Gl) Tests

- **Story Recall (COG):** Meaningful memory (listening)
- **Story Comprehension (COG/ACH):** Meaningful memory (listening)
- **Reading Recall (ACH):** Meaningful memory (reading)
- **Visual-Auditory Learning (COG):** Associative memory; also measures fluid reasoning (Gf), visual processing (Gv), and working memory (Gwm) at various ages.

[2] In the WJ V, learning efficiency is called *long-term storage*.

not a pure measure of associative learning because the rebus-word pairs are not entirely arbitrary. That is, there is an underlying logic to which rebuses are paired with which words such that astute examinees can make informed guesses about the correct answer even before being told what a rebus means. In addition, the rebus-word pairs are not presented in a random order; they are presented as well-structured sentences. Thus, examinees with strong fluid reasoning can make predictive inferences about the next answer, even if the rebus-word pair is not fully memorized. Thus, Visual-Auditory Learning is an associative memory test that is also, to some degree, a crystallized and fluid reasoning test. Because rebuses are visual stimuli, Gv is also involved via the narrow ability of visual memory. The technical manual suggests that Visual-Auditory Memory has a complex pattern of relationships with Gf, Gv, Gl, and Gwm at different ages. Thus, the test can inform how well a person can learn a new script but is not an unambiguous measure of any one broad ability.

Meaningful Memory *Meaningful memory* is the efficiency with which one acquires meaningful units of knowledge, often presented in a narrative. The distinction between listening ability and meaningful memory is, by nature, fuzzy, but listening ability tests can be made more difficult by increasing the difficulty of the material to be learned, whereas meaningful memory tests can be made more difficult by increasing the amount of material to be learned. In meaningful memory tests, all of the information should be easy enough for most examinees to learn, if given enough time and repeated learning opportunities.

Meaningful memory tests have obvious ecological validity. We care about how much information a person can take in by listening to an instructor or a conversation partner. Narratives are the primary mechanism by which we teach and learn much of what we know.

The WJ V has three measures of meaningful memory. Story Recall is the most straightforward of the three. Examinees listen to stories and repeat them back as best they can, preferably verbatim. In the Story Comprehension test, examinees listen to stories and then answer a series of questions that assess their understanding of the stories. This format emphasizes a mixture of listening ability and meaningful memory. The Reading Recall test is analogous to Story Recall, but instead of listening to the stories, the examinee reads the stories silently to themselves before retelling the story in detail. A comparison of Reading Recall and Story Recall can be informative. Obviously, Reading Recall performance will be lower for examinees with reading difficulties; however, the difference between the two tests is not just that one is a recording and one is text. One is presented at the pace set by the recording, and the other is self-paced. Thus, Reading Recall allows for a motivated examinee with good executive functions to pause and plan how to remember passages better. Story Recall allows for no such planning, and examinees get one opportunity to listen and remember.

Retrieval Fluency (Gr)

Memory retrieval fluency (Gr), the speed at which memories are retrieved, has long been an important marker of neuropsychological dysfunction. As people enter late adulthood, their speech tends to slow, and pauses, *ah*s, and *um*s become more frequent. Within the Gr domain, there is a primary distinction between convergent and divergent retrieval.

Convergent retrieval In convergent memory retrieval fluency tests (sometimes referred to as *rapid automatized naming*, RAN, or *naming facility*), one measures the speed at which a person can give a single correct answer (e.g., how quickly one can name a series of objects). Rapid automatized naming (RAN) is a well-established long-term predictor of arithmetic math fact fluency and reading fluency (Balhinez & Shaul, 2019; Georgiou et al., 2021; Hoff et al., 2023; Psyridou et al., 2024). In the WJ V, Rapid Picture Naming, Rapid Letter Naming, Rapid Phoneme Naming, Rapid Quantity Naming, and Rapid Number Naming are all measures of RAN (see Rapid Reference 2.7).

RAN tests correlate more strongly with processing speed tests than with tests of divergent retrieval. Thus, it is not yet clear whether RAN should be reclassified as a verbal processing speed ability. RAN, however, clearly requires memory retrieval whereas most processing speed tests do not. Perhaps processing speed is a fundamental ability that underlies memory retrieval fluency.

Divergent retrieval Divergent memory retrieval fluency tests measure the number of correct answers one can give to a prompt that has many correct answers (e.g., words that end in *z*, ice cream flavors, items one might find in a kitchen). Divergent memory fluency is not creativity itself, but it serves as an important aid to creative idea production (Beaty & Kenett, 2023; Benedek et al., 2023; Said-Metwaly et al., 2024; Silvia et al., 2013). There is strong evidence linking divergent memory fluency with employment status and work performance after a traumatic brain injury (Aliaga et al., 2024).

Rapid Reference 2.7

WJ V Retrieval Fluency (Gr) Tests

- **Semantic Word Retrieval (COG):** Divergent retrieval; ideational fluency
- **Phonemic Word Retrieval (COG):** Divergent retrieval; word fluency
- **Rapid Picture Naming (VTL):** Convergent retrieval (RAN); also processing speed (Gs)
- **Rapid Letter Naming (VTL):** Convergent retrieval (RAN); also processing speed (Gs)
- **Rapid Phoneme Naming (VTL):** Convergent retrieval (RAN); also processing speed (Gs) and auditory processing (Ga)
- **Rapid Number Naming (VTL):** Convergent retrieval (RAN); also processing speed (Gs)
- **Rapid Quantity Naming (VTL):** Convergent retrieval (RAN); also processing speed (Gs) and visual processing (Gv)

Semantic Word Retrieval is a measure of *ideational fluency*, the ability to produce a series of examples within a particular category (e.g., names, countries, items for sale at a hardware store). Phonemic Word Retrieval is a measure of *word fluency*, the ability to produce words starting or ending with a specific sound.

Processing Speed (Gs)

Processing speed is the ability to perform simple processing tasks in a rapid sequence. Tests of this ability often require making simple judgments as to whether two objects are the same or different, sorting items by initial letter, or searching for items that share a similar feature (e.g., find all the words on a page that contain the letter *e*).

Processing speed is thought to be a primary basis for other abilities, including working memory, retrieval fluency, and fluid reasoning (Fry & Hale, 1996; Mashburn et al., 2023; Tourva et al., 2016; Tourva & Spanoudis, 2020). Processing speed is a strong marker of injury severity after a traumatic brain injury (Rommelse et al., 2020), and it is the ability that naturally declines more than any other as adults age (Salthouse, 1996). Processing speed is a strong predictor of fluency in reading, writing, and calculation (Cormier et al., 2017; Gerst et al., 2021; Peng et al., 2019, 2022).

In the WJ V, Number-Pattern Matching and Letter-Pattern Matching are measures of the Gs narrow ability *perceptual speed* (see Rapid Reference 2.8). Symbol Inhibition clearly measures Gs, but it is not yet clear which narrow ability it measures. This is not the WJ V's fault. The narrow abilities within Gs are poorly understood, and, thus, many Gs tests

Rapid Reference 2.8

WJ V Processing Speed (Gs) Tests

- **Number-Pattern Matching (COG):** Perceptual speed
- **Letter-Pattern Matching (COG):** Perceptual speed
- **Symbol Inhibition (COG):** New test in WJ V; unclear which narrow Gs ability is measured but likely a mixed measure of processing speed (Gs), working memory (Gwm)–attentional control, and visual processing (Gv)
- **Math Facts Fluency (ACH):** Mixed measure of Gs and math skills
- **Magnitude Comparison (ACH):** Mixed measure of Gs and math skills
- **Word Reading Fluency (ACH):** Mixed measure of Gs and reading skills
- **Sentence Reading Fluency (ACH):** Mixed measure of Gs and reading skills
- **Letter Writing Fluency (ACH):** Mixed measure of Gs and writing skills
- **Sentence Writing Fluency (ACH):** Mixed measure of Gs and writing skills
- **RAN tests (VTL):** Primarily retrieval fluency (Gr) with Gs

are hard to classify. Fortunately, there is not yet a strong reason to distinguish sharply among narrow abilities within Gs. What usually matters is the overall performance in the Gs domain.

Academic fluency measures (Magnitude Comparison, Math Facts Fluency, Word Reading Fluency, Sentence Reading Fluency, Letter Writing Fluency, and Sentence Writing Fluency) are mixed measures of processing speed and academic skills. In general, cognitive measures of processing speed are invoked as an explanation of academic fluency deficits.

Comprehension-Knowledge (Gc)

Crystallized intelligence (Gc) is referred to as *Comprehension-Knowledge* in the WJ V, which is a more descriptive term for what Gc actually is. As the compound term *Comprehension-Knowledge* implies, Gc has two closely interrelated intermediate ability groups, which in CHC theory are referred to as *language development* and *general verbal knowledge.*

Language development At the core of Gc is *language development,* or the ability to *understand* and communicate with others. Speech-language pathologists refer to the ability to comprehend language as *receptive language* and the ability to use language to communicate as *expressive language*, respectively. Language is core to Gc because language is the medium by which knowledge is communicated and learned.

Because Carroll's primary area of scholarship over many decades was in language abilities, the language development component of Gc has greater elaboration than most other ability domains in CHC theory. The WJ V does not attempt to measure all aspects of language, but it covers the aspects of language that are most important for adaptive functioning and problem solving (see Rapid Reference 2.9).

Verbal analogies have a long-venerated paradigm in which examinees complete analogies with verbal concepts (e.g., *Horse* is to *big* as *mouse* is to ____). The Verbal Analogies test requires that the examinee understand the meaning of individual words; however, the emphasis is not on the difficulty of the vocabulary but on understanding how the verbal concepts interrelate. Analogical reasoning allows abstract ideas to be applied across contexts.

The WJ V Technical Manual (LaForte et al., 2025) demonstrates that the Verbal Analogies test loads primarily with Gc tests but has a strong secondary loading on Gf, in part because analogical reasoning is a core feature of fluid reasoning. Should we discount Verbal Analogies because it is not a pure measure of Gc or of Gf? No, . . .and for the same reason that we should not discount hurdling on the basis that it is a pure measure of neither running nor jumping. Likewise, we do not discount reading comprehension on the basis that it is not a pure measure of either reading or comprehension (See what we did there? We defended the use of Verbal Analogies with verbal analogies!). Analogical reasoning with verbal concepts is an important skill worth measuring in its own right, and it informs interpretation of scores on other language tests and other reasoning tests.

Rapid Reference 2.9

WJ V Comprehension-Knowledge (Gc) Tests

- **Oral Vocabulary (COG):** Vocabulary/lexical knowledge
- **Verbal Analogies (COG):** Vocabulary; also fluid reasoning (Gf)–induction
- **Picture Vocabulary (ACH):** Vocabulary/lexical knowledge
- **Academic Vocabulary (ACH):** Vocabulary/lexical knowledge
- **Story Comprehension (COG/ACH):** Listening ability, but primarily learning efficiency (Gl)
- **Story Recall (COG):** Listening ability, but primarily learning efficiency (Gl)
- **Oral Comprehension (ACH):** Listening ability
- **Passage Comprehension (ACH):** Listening ability, but primarily reading (Grw)
- **Oral Language Samples (ACH):** Communication ability
- **General Information (COG):** General verbal knowledge
- **Academic Facts (ACH):** General verbal knowledge

Vocabulary Because vocabulary (sometimes called *lexical knowledge*) is relatively easy to measure and is of central importance to communication, it is included in almost every intelligence battery that measures Gc. A good vocabulary test item avoids specialized vocabulary that is useful only in specific contexts. A vocabulary test item should only be included if knowledge of it would enhance nearly anyone's ability to communicate or make fine-grained distinctions that are valued in a society. The WJ V has several measures of vocabulary that allow for understanding different aspects of vocabulary and for measuring vocabulary among people with expressive language difficulties.

Oral Vocabulary requires that a person give synonyms and antonyms for words presented orally and on a tablet screen. Picture Vocabulary requires examinees to name objects in pictures. Both tests allow for one-word answers, which, compared to tests requiring full-sentence responses, makes them better suited for people with expressive language difficulties. Academic Vocabulary tests knowledge of vocabulary terms taught explicitly in school rather than terms that a person would experience in everyday settings. The General Information test functions mostly as a test of vocabulary referring to physical objects (e.g., What would you do with a caliper? Where would you find a sump pump?).

Listening ability Receptive language, the ability to understand spoken, written, and/or nonverbal language, is fundamental to making one's way in a society. Often, the ability to understand spoken language (i.e., speech) proves especially vital. There is no pure culture-free way of measuring listening ability because cultural assumptions and connotations are embedded in all speech utterances. The WJ V has multiple measures of listening ability that vary in terms of format, complexity, and length of utterance. Listening ability tests are typically mixed measures of language comprehension, short-term working memory, and long-term memory.

Story Comprehension and Story Recall are intended as tests of the meaningful memory facet of long-term memory/learning efficiency (Gl), but meaningful memory is, by its nature, entangled with listening ability. There is no way to measure retention of meaningful stories without also measuring the ability to comprehend. Story Recall requires examinees to retell a story, preferably verbatim. Story Comprehension requires examinees to answer questions that test their understanding of stories they have just heard. Although Story Recall emphasizes memory retention and Story Comprehension emphasizes narrative comprehension, both tests require both abilities.

Oral Comprehension ingeniously minimizes memory demands by presenting a single sentence with a word missing. Because examinees need only remember a single sentence and say a single word that makes sense in the context of the sentence, memory demands (and language demands) are much reduced. Oral Comprehension, by design, is exactly analogous to Passage Comprehension, which is the same format except that the sentences with missing words are presented as text rather than orally. A person who scores low on both tests likely has difficulty understanding language across modalities. A person who scores high on Oral Comprehension but low on Passage Comprehension and Letter-Word Identification likely does not have a language comprehension problem but a reading decoding problem. A person who scores high on Passage Comprehension but low on Oral Comprehension might have difficulty processing speech in real time but, with self-paced reading, can understand language well. Of course, score differences in two tests are merely suggestive. Confident interpretation always requires additional confirmatory information, often obtained via follow-up testing.

Communication ability Expressive language, the ability to communicate one's thoughts, wants, and intentions to others, is as important as receptive language. The Oral Language Samples test requires examinees to express a word or complete a sentence that satisfies a verbal prompt (sometimes accompanied by an image).

General verbal knowledge What is acquired and communicated with language is *verbal knowledge*, which allows for efficient problem-solving. Rather than each of us having to figure things out on our own, we can communicate and learn from each other. Remembering a learned solution is much more efficient than wrestling with a problem and waiting for insight to strike.

Whereas the language domain has a more finite and circumscribed list of narrow abilities, the list of verbal knowledge domains is, necessarily, open-ended. New knowledge domains come into being all the time (e.g., computer programming, financial literacy, and the history of K-pop). Domains in the outer periphery of specialized knowledge are termed Domain-specific knowledge (Gkn). Gkn might be important in a specific context (e.g., debugging in the COBOL programming language), but such knowledge would never be tested in a verbal knowledge measure of Gc. General verbal knowledge test items consist of knowledge that would be highly valued for any member of a society to have (e.g., how to safely prepare food, principles on which one's system of government is founded, defining moments of cultural history).

On the WJ V, the Academic Facts test is the most direct measure of general verbal knowledge, measuring knowledge of math, science, and the humanities. Because these subjects are taught explicitly in school, the interpretation of an examinee's score is contingent on the examinee's educational opportunities.

The General Information test is also a measure of general knowledge, particularly about objects found in everyday settings.

Quantitative Knowledge–Numeracy (Gq)

Strictly speaking, quantitative knowledge is not really a separate broad ability. It is an important domain within Gc. In centuries past, it would have been considered the province of specialists and would have been one of many specialized domains within Gkn; however, mathematics is considered to be so important in a modern society that it is now taught to every student in every school.

There is an emerging literature on presumably innate cognitive abilities that facilitate our ability to perceive and process basic aspects of quantity (Amland et al., 2025; Dehaene, 1997). The WJ V Number Sense and Magnitude Comparison tests are measures of some of these fundamental abilities to estimate size, quantity, position, and volume.

Mathematics skills can be viewed in terms of basic calculation skills (Calculation), calculation fluency (Math Facts Fluency and Magnitude Comparison), and applied problem solving with math (Applied Problems and Math Problem Identification) (see Rapid Reference 2.10).

Reading/Writing–Literacy (Grw)

Like numeracy, literacy is not really a broad ability in its own right. It is a facet of acquired knowledge that sits squarely in the Gc domain. Before literacy was commonplace, it would have been the province of specialists—scribes and elite administrators.

Rapid Reference 2.10

WJ V Quantitative Knowledge (Gq) Tests

- **Calculation (ACH):** Calculation skills
- **Math Facts Fluency (ACH):** Fluency
- **Magnitude Comparison (ACH):** Fluency
- **Applied Problems (ACH):** Calculation skills
- **Math Problem Identification (ACH):** Calculation skills
- **Number Sense (ACH):** Number Sense
- **Rapid Quantity Naming (ACH):** Number Sense

Rapid Reference 2.11

WJ V Reading and Writing (Grw) Tests

Domain	Reading	Writing
Letters	Letter-Word Identification (ACH)	Letter Writing Fluency (ACH)
Nonsense Words	Word Attack (ACH)	Spelling of Sounds (ACH)
Words	Letter-Word Identification (ACH)	Spelling (ACH)
Accuracy	Oral Reading (ACH) Sentence Reading Fluency (ACH)	Sentence Writing Accuracy (ACH)
Fluency	Sentence Reading Fluency Word Reading Fluency	Sentence Writing Fluency (ACH)
Sentences	Passage Comprehension (ACH) Paragraph Reading Comprehension (ACH) Reading Recall (ACH)	Written Language Samples (ACH)

Today, literacy is so important that it is the primary task for students to master in their first few years of schooling.

Although reading and writing are clearly different tasks, the cognitive skills that underlie them are intertwined such that factor analysis does not cleanly separate reading abilities from writing abilities. Rather, the skills seem to sort themselves by whether they have to do with word-level decoding/spelling, sentence-level comprehension/composition, and reading/writing fluency.

The WJ V has a carefully selected set of reading and writing tests that measure skills related to letters, nonsense words, real words, sentences, and higher-order comprehension with paragraphs (see Rapid Reference 2.11).

TEST YOURSELF

1. **Spearman hypothesized the existence of a general factor of intelligence because he needed a way to explain the positive correlations among all cognitive abilities. True or False?**
2. **Why did Spearman eventually recognize the existence of group factors (i.e., broad and narrow abilities)?**

3. **Which of the following is *not* true?**
   (A) Fluid intelligence generates new knowledge, and crystallized intelligence contains previously obtained knowledge.
   (B) Carroll's factor-analytic work proved that fluid intelligence is synonymous with general intelligence.
   (C) Fluid intelligence begins to decline in early adulthood, whereas crystallized intelligence tends to increase into late adulthood.
   (D) A primary difference between the Horn/Cattell Gf-Gc theory and the Carroll Three-Stratum theory is the absence or presence, respectively, of a general intelligence (g) factor at the apex.
4. **On which of the following WJ V tests would we expect an examinee's score to be most impacted from being fatigued or intoxicated?**
   (A) Oral Vocabulary
   (B) General Information
   (C) Matrices
   (D) Oral Comprehension
5. **Why are fluid reasoning measures and visual-spatial processing tests often hard to distinguish?**
6. **What is auditory processing, and how does it differ from language comprehension?**
7. **What is the difference between divergent and convergent memory retrieval?**
8. **Each WJ V test can be mapped to one distinct broad and narrow CHC ability. True or False?**
9. **Which of the following pairs of WJ V tests might be *most* useful to help determine why a 2nd-grade student is having difficulty sounding out words?**
   (A) Sound Blending and Segmentation
   (B) Letter-Word Identification and Word Attack
   (C) Word Reading Fluency and Sentence Reading Fluency
   (D) Memory for Words and Sentence Repetition
10. **Which of the following is a WJ V test with high ecological validity?**
   (A) Nonsense Word Repetition
   (B) Sentence Repetition
   (C) Rapid Phoneme Naming
   (D) Sound Deletion

ANSWERS

1. **True.**
2. Groups of related abilities correlated with each other more highly than could be explained by a general factor.
3. **B.** While Carroll noted that fluid intelligence and general intelligence were highly statistically correlated, he did not believe that they were synonymous.
4. **C.** Fluid reasoning (Gf) abilities are generally more vulnerable to toxins, disease, and brain injury than are crystallized (Gc) abilities.

5. Many fluid reasoning tests use visual item formats similar to visual-spatial tests. Fluid reasoning tests often require examinees to use visual processing to solve reasoning problems. Visual-spatial tests can sometimes be solved via reasoning rather than by visual-spatial processing.
6. Auditory processing is the ability to perceive and manipulate information obtained via sound (e.g., pitch and rhythm). Language comprehension does not fall under the auditory processing domain. Auditory processing does facilitate discrimination among speech sounds, which is a precursor to understanding which words have been spoken.
7. Divergent retrieval is finding many answers to an open-ended question. Convergent retrieval is finding the correct answer to a closed-ended question.
8. **False.** Although many tests clearly measure distinct broad and narrow abilities, many WJ V tests measure aspects of multiple CHC abilities.
9. **A.** Sound Blending and Segmentation, along with Sound Reversal, Sound Deletion, and Sound Substitution, are useful WJ V tests for identifying phonological processing deficits, which can make it difficult for a student to decode words.
10. **B.** The test task in Sentence Repetition approximates the working memory demands of everyday conversations.

REFERENCES

Ackerman, P. L. (2018). Intelligence-as-process, personality, interests, and intelligence-as-knowledge: A framework for adult intellectual development. In D. P. Flanagan & E. M. McDonough (Eds.), *Contemporary intellectual assessment: Theories, tests, and issues* (4th ed., pp. 225–241). The Guilford Press.

Ackerman, P. L., Beier, M. E., & Boyle, M. O. (2005). Working memory and intelligence. *Psychological Bulletin, 131*(1), 30–60.

Adcock, C. J., & Webberley, M. (1971). Primary mental abilities. *The Journal of General Psychology, 84*(2), 229–243. https://doi.org/10.1080/00221309.1971.9711309

Aliaga, Á., Bracho, M. J., Romero, M., Saldías, M. J., Jofré, X., & Salas, C. (2024). The contribution of executive functions to the process of return to work after brain injury: A systematic review. *Neuropsychological Rehabilitation, 34*(5), 619–648. https://doi.org/10.1080/09602011.2023.2224031

Allen, J. L., & Mayer, J. D. (2022). Personal intelligence is evident in the sophistication of people's narratives about personality. *Journal of Intelligence, 10*(3), 56. https://doi.org/10.3390/jintelligence10030056

Amland, T., Grande, G., Scherer, R., Lervåg, A., & Melby-Lervåg, M. (2025). Cognitive factors underlying mathematical skills: A systematic review and meta-analysis. *Psychological Bulletin, 151*(1), 88–129. https://doi.org/10.1037/bul0000457

Bajpai, S., Upadhayay, A. D., Banerjee, J., Chakrawarthy, A., Chatterjee, P., Lee, J., & Dey, A. B. (2022). Discrepancy in fluid and crystallized intelligence: An early cognitive marker of dementia from the LASI-DAD cohort. *Dementia and Geriatric Cognitive Disorders Extra, 12*(1), 51–59. https://doi.org/10.1159/000520879

Balhinez, R., & Shaul, S. (2019). The relationship between reading fluency and arithmetic fact fluency and their shared cognitive skills: A developmental perspective. *Frontiers in Psychology, 10*. https://doi.org/10.3389/fpsyg.2019.01281

Bardach, L., Lohmann, J., Horstmann, K. T., Zitzmann, S., & Hecht, M. (2023). From intellectual investment trait theory to dynamic intellectual investment trait and state theory: Theory extension, methodological advancement, and empirical illustration. *Journal of Research in Personality*, 104445. https://doi.org/10.1016/j.jrp.2023.104445

Beaty, R. E., & Kenett, Y. N. (2023). Associative thinking at the core of creativity. *Trends in Cognitive Sciences*, *27*(7), 671–683. https://doi.org/10.1016/j.tics.2023.04.004

Beauducel, A., Brocke, B., & Liepmann, D. (2001). Perspectives on fluid and crystallized intelligence: Facets for verbal, numerical, and figural intelligence. *Personality and Individual Differences*, *30*(6), 977–994.

Benedek, M., Beaty, R. E., Schacter, D. L., & Kenett, Y. N. (2023). The role of memory in creative ideation. *Nature Reviews Psychology*, *2*(4), 246–257. https://doi.org/10.1038/s44159-023-00158-z

Biesok, A., Ziegler, M., Montag, C., & Nenchev, I. (2024). Adding a piece to the puzzle? The allocation of figurative language comprehension into the CHC model of cognitive abilities. *Journal of Intelligence*, *12*(3), 29. https://doi.org/10.3390/jintelligence12030029

Blair, C. (2006). How similar are fluid cognition and general intelligence? A developmental neuroscience perspective on fluid cognition as an aspect of human cognitive ability. *Behavioral and Brain Sciences*, *29*(2), 109–125. https://doi.org/10.1017/S0140525X06009034

Blanch, A., & Blanco, E. (2025). Fluid-crystallised abilities and academic achievement in secondary education and university. *Educational Psychology*, *1–18*. https://doi.org/10.1080/01443410.2025.2497319

Brewster, B. (1882). Portfolio. *The Yale Literary Magazine*, *47*(5), 201–205.

Buckley, J., Seery, N., & Canty, D. (2019). Spatial cognition in engineering education: Developing a spatial ability framework to support the translation of theory into practice. *European Journal of Engineering Education*, *44*(1–2), 164–178. https://doi.org/10.1080/03043797.2017.1327944

Bui, D. C., & Myerson, J. (2014). The role of working memory abilities in lecture note-taking. *Learning and Individual Differences*, *33*, 12–22. https://doi.org/10.1016/j.lindif.2014.05.002

Callis, Z., Gerrans, P., Walker, D. L., & Gignac, G. E. (2023). The association between intelligence and financial literacy: A conceptual and meta-analytic review. *Intelligence*, *100*, 101781. https://doi.org/10.1016/j.intell.2023.101781

Calvo, M. G. (2005). Relative contribution of vocabulary knowledge and working memory span to elaborative inferences in reading. *Learning and Individual Differences*, *15*(1), 53–65. https://doi.org/10.1016/j.lindif.2004.07.002

Carroll, J. B. (1941). A factor analysis of verbal abilities. *Psychometrika*, *6*(5), 279–307. https://doi.org/10.1007/BF02288585

Carroll, J. B. (1978). How shall we study individual differences in cognitive abilities?—Methodological and theoretical perspectives. *Intelligence*, *2*(2), 87–115. https://doi.org/10.1016/0160-2896(78)90002-8

Carroll, J. B. (1979). Psychometric approaches to the study of language abilities. In C. J. Fillmore, D. Kempler, & W. S.-Y. Wang (Eds.), *Individual differences in language ability and language behavior* (pp. 13–31). Elsevier. https://doi.org/10.1016/B978-0-12-255950-1.50008-1

Carroll, J. B. (1989). The Carroll model: A 25-year retrospective and prospective view. *Educational Researcher, 18*(1), 26–31. https://doi.org/10.3102/0013189X018001026

Carroll, J. B. (1993). *Human cognitive abilities: A survey of factor-analytic studies.* Cambridge University Press. https://doi.org/10.1017/cbo9780511571312

Carroll, J. B. (2003). The higher-stratum structure of cognitive abilities: Current evidence supports g and about ten broad factors. In H. Nyborg (Ed.), *The scientific study of general intelligence: Tribute to Arthur R. Jensen* (pp. 5–22). Pergamon.

Cattell, R. B. (1943). The measurement of adult intelligence. *Psychological Bulletin, 40*(3), 153–193. https://doi.org/10.1037/h0059973

Cattell, R. B. (1971). *Abilities: Its structure, growth and action.* Houghton Mifflin.

Cattell, R. B. (1987). *Intelligence: Its structure, growth and action.* Elsevier.

Chang, T.-Y., Cha, O., & Gauthier, I. (2024). A general ability for judging simple and complex ensembles. *Journal of Experimental Psychology: General, 153*(6), 1517–1536. https://doi.org/10.1037/xge0001582

Cormier, D. C., McGrew, K. S., Bulut, O., & Funamoto, A. (2017). Revisiting the relations between the WJ-IV measures of Cattell-Horn-Carroll (CHC) cognitive abilities and reading achievement during the school-age years. *Journal of Psychoeducational Assessment, 35*(8), 731–754. https://doi.org/10.1177/0734282916659208

Das, J. P., Kirby, J., & Jarman, R. F. (1975). Simultaneous and successive synthesis: An alternative model for cognitive abilities. *Psychological Bulletin, 82*, 87–103. https://doi.org/10.1037/h0076163

Dehaene, S. (1997). *The number sense: How the mind creates mathematics.* Oxford University Press.

Ekstrom, R. B., French, J. W., Harman, H. H., & Dermen, D. (1976). *Kit of factor-referenced cognitive tests.* Educational Testing Service.

Ericsson, K. A. (2017). Expertise and individual differences: The search for the structure and acquisition of experts' superior performance. *WIREs Cognitive Science, 8*(1–2), e1382. https://doi.org/10.1002/wcs.1382

Ericsson, K. A., & Kintsch, W. (1995). Long-term working memory. *Psychological Review, 102*(2), 211–245. https://doi.org/10.1037/0033-295X.102.2.211

Flanagan, D. P., McGrew, K. S., & Ortiz, S. O. (2000). *The Wechsler Intelligence Scales and Gf-Gc theory: A contemporary approach to interpretation.* Allyn & Bacon.

French, J. W., Ekstrom, R. B., & Price, L. A. (1963). Manual for kit of reference tests for cognitive factors (revised 1963). *Educational Testing Service.* https://doi.org/10.21236/ad0410915

Fry, A. F., & Hale, S. (1996). Processing speed, working memory, and fluid intelligence: Evidence for a developmental cascade. *Psychological Science, 7*(4), 237–241. https://doi.org/10.1111/j.1467-9280.1996.tb00366.x

Fry, A. F., & Hale, S. (2000). Relationships among processing speed, working memory, and fluid intelligence in children. *Biological Psychology, 54*(1), 1–34.

Gardner, H. (1983). *Frames of mind.* Basic Books.
Geiger, M., Olderbak, S. G., & Wilhelm, O. (2024). "Show me what you got": The nomological network of the ability to pose facial emotion expressions. *Journal of Intelligence, 12*(3), 27. https://doi.org/10.3390/jintelligence12030027
Georgiou, G. K., Inoue, T., & Parrila, R. (2021). Do reading and arithmetic fluency share the same cognitive base? *Frontiers in Psychology, 12,* 709448. https://doi.org/10.3389/fpsyg.2021.709448
Gerst, E. H., Cirino, P. T., Macdonald, K. T., Miciak, J., Yoshida, H., Woods, S. P., & Gibbs, M. C. (2021). The structure of processing speed in children and its impact on reading. *Journal of Cognition and Development, 22*(1), 84–107. https://doi.org/10.1080/15248372.2020.1862121
Guilford, J. P. (1967). *The nature of human intelligence.* McGraw-Hill.
Guttman, L. (1954). A new approach to factor analysis: The radex. In P. F. Lazarsfeld (Ed.), *Mathematical thinking in the social sciences* (pp. 258–348). Free Press.
Guttman, R., & Greenbaum, C. W. (1998). Facet theory: Its development and current status. *European Psychologist, 3*(1), 13–36. https://doi.org/10.1027//1016-9040.3.1.13
Hall, G. S. (1882). The education of the will. *The Princeton Review, 2,* 306–325.
Hart, B., & Spearman, C. E. (1912). General ability, its existence and nature. *British Journal of Psychology, 5*(1), 51–84. https://doi.org/10.1111/j.2044-8295.1912.tb00055.x
Hawkins, J. (2004). *On intelligence.* Times Books.
Hawkins, J. (2021). *A thousand brains: A new theory of intelligence* (1st ed.). Basic Books.
Hawkins, J., & Ahmad, S. (2016). Why neurons have thousands of synapses: A theory of sequence memory in neocortex. *Frontiers in Neural Circuits, 10.* https://doi.org/10.3389/fncir.2016.00023
Hoff, D., Amland, T., Melby-Lervåg, M., Lervåg, A., & Protopapas, A. (2023). Early rapid naming longitudinally predicts shared variance in reading and arithmetic fluency. *Journal of Experimental Child Psychology, 231,* 105656. https://doi.org/10.1016/j.jecp.2023.105656
Horn, J. L. (1980). Concepts of intellect in relation to learning and adult development. *Intelligence, 4*(4), 285–317. https://doi.org/10.1016/0160-2896(80)90025-2
Horn, J. L. (1982). The theory of fluid and crystallized intelligence in relation to concepts of cognitive psychology and aging in adulthood. In R. I. M. Craik & S. Trehub (Eds.), *Aging and cognitive processes* (pp. 237–278). Plenum Press.
Horn, J. L. (1985). Remodeling old models of intelligence. In B. B. Wolman (Ed.), *Handbook of intelligence* (pp. 267–300). Wiley.
Horn, J. L. (2007). Spearman, g, expertise, and the nature of human cognitive capability. In P. C. Kyllonen, R. D. Roberts, & L. Stankov (Eds.), *Extending intelligence.* Routledge.
Horn, J. L., & Blankson, N. (2005). Foundations for better understanding of cognitive abilities. In D. P. Flanagan & P. L. Harrison (Eds.), *Contemporary intellectual assessment: Theories, tests, and issues* (2nd ed., pp. 41–68). Guilford Press.

Horn, J. L., & Cattell, R. B. (1967). Age differences in fluid and crystallized intelligence. *Acta Psychologica, 26,* 107–129. https://doi.org/10.1016/0001-6918(67)90011-X

Horn, J. L., & McArdle, J. J. (2007). Understanding human intelligence since Spearman. In R. Cudeck & R. C. MacCallum (Eds.), *Factor analysis at 100: Historical developments and future directions* (pp. 767–782). Routledge.

Humphreys, L. G. (1962). The organization of human abilities. *American Psychologist, 17*(7), 475–483. https://doi.org/10.1037/h0041550

Jensen, A. R. (1998). *The g factor: The science of mental ability.* Praeger.

Johnson, W., & Bouchard, T. J. (2005). The structure of human intelligence: It is verbal, perceptual, and image rotation (VPR), not fluid and crystallized. *Intelligence, 33*(4), 393–416. https://doi.org/10.1016/j.intell.2004.12.002

Kail, R. V. (2007). Longitudinal evidence that increases in processing speed and working memory enhance children's reasoning. *Psychological Science, 18*(4), 312–313. https://doi.org/10.1111/j.1467-9280.2007.01895.x

Keidser, G., Best, V., Freeston, K., & Boyce, A. (2015). Cognitive spare capacity: Evaluation data and its association with comprehension of dynamic conversations. *Frontiers in Psychology, 6.* https://doi.org/10.3389/fpsyg.2015.00597

Kievit, R. A., Lindenberger, U., Goodyer, I. M., Jones, P. B., Fonagy, P., Bullmore, E. T., The Neuroscience in Psychiatry Network, & Dolan, R. J. (2017). Mutualistic coupling between vocabulary and reasoning supports cognitive development during late adolescence and early adulthood. *Psychological Science, 28*(10), 1419–1431. https://doi.org/10.1177/0956797617710785

Kvist, A. V., & Gustafsson, J. E. (2008). The relation between fluid intelligence and the general factor as a function of cultural background: A test of Cattell's investment theory. *Intelligence, 36*(5), 422–436.

LaForte, E. M., Daily, D., & McGrew, K. S. (2025). *Technical manual.* Woodcock-Johnson V. Riverside Assessments, LLC.

Lakin, J. M., & Gambrell, J. L. (2012). Distinguishing verbal, quantitative, and figural facets of fluid intelligence in young students. *Intelligence, 40*(6), 560–570.

Lubinski, D. (2010). Spatial ability and STEM: A sleeping giant for talent identification and development. *Personality and Individual Differences, 49*(4), 344–351.

Marshalek, B., Lohman, D. F., & Snow, R. E. (1983). The complexity continuum in the radex and hierarchical models of intelligence. *Intelligence, 7*(2), 107–127.

Mashburn, C. A., Barnett, M. K., & Engle, R. W. (2023). Processing speed and executive attention as causes of intelligence. *Psychological Review.* https://doi.org/10.1037/rev0000439

Mayer, J. D., Caruso, D. R., Sitarenios, G., & Escobar, M. R. (2024). How many emotional intelligence abilities are there? An examination of four measures of emotional intelligence. *Personality and Individual Differences, 219,* 112468. https://doi.org/10.1016/j.paid.2023.112468

McGrew, K. S. (1997a). Analysis of the major intelligence batteries according to a proposed comprehensive Gf-Gc framework. In D. P. Flanagan, J. L. Genshaft, & P. L. Harrison (Eds.), *Contemporary intellectual assessment: Theories, tests, and issues* (pp. 151–179). Guilford Press.

McGrew, K. S. (1997b). Analysis of the major intelligence batteries according to a proposed comprehensive Gf-Gc framework. In D. P. Flanagan, J. L. Genshaft, & P. L. Harrison (Eds.), *Contemporary intellectual assessment: Theories, tests, and issues* (pp. 151–179). Guilford Press.

McGrew, K. S. (2005). The Cattell-Horn-Carroll theory of cognitive abilities: Past, present, and future. In D. P. Flanagan & P. L. Harrison (Eds.), *Contemporary intellectual assessment. Theories, tests, and issues* (2nd ed., pp. 136–181). Guilford Press.

McGrew, K. S. (2009). CHC theory and the human cognitive abilities project: Standing on the shoulders of the giants of psychometric intelligence research. *Intelligence, 37*(1), 1–10. https://doi.org/10.1016/j.intell.2008.08.004

McGrew, K. S. (2023). Carroll's Three-Stratum (3S) cognitive ability theory at 30 years: Impact, 3S-CHC theory clarification, structural replication, and cognitive–achievement psychometric network analysis extension. *Journal of Intelligence, 11*(2), 32. https://doi.org/10.3390/jintelligence11020032

McGrew, K. S., & Flanagan, D. P. (1998). *The intelligence test desk reference (ITDR): Gf-Gc cross-battery assessment.* Allyn & Bacon.

Nelson, J. M., Lindstrom, J. H., Lindstrom, W., & Denis, D. (2012). The structure of phonological processing and its relationship to basic reading. *Exceptionality, 20*(3), 179–196. https://doi.org/10.1080/09362835.2012.694612

Peng, P., Fuchs, D., Fuchs, L. S., Elleman, A. M., Kearns, D. M., Gilbert, J. K., Compton, D. L., Cho, E., & Patton, S. (2019). A longitudinal analysis of the trajectories and predictors of word reading and reading comprehension development among at-risk readers. *Journal of Learning Disabilities, 52*(3), 195–208. https://doi.org/10.1177/0022219418809080

Peng, P., Zhang, Z., Wang, W., Lee, K., Wang, T., Wang, C., Luo, J., & Lin, J. (2022). A meta-analytic review of cognition and reading difficulties: Individual differences, moderation, and language mediation mechanisms. *Psychological Bulletin, 148*(3–4), 227–272. https://doi.org/10.1037/bul0000361

Psyridou, M., Koponen, T., Tolvanen, A., Aunola, K., Lerkkanen, M.-K., Poikkeus, A.-M., & Torppa, M. (2024). Early prediction of math difficulties with the use of a neural networks model. *Journal of Educational Psychology, 116*(2), 212–232. https://doi.org/10.1037/edu0000835

Reynolds, M. R., Keith, T. Z., Flanagan, D. P., & Alfonso, V. C. (2013). A cross-battery, reference variable, confirmatory factor analytic investigation of the CHC taxonomy. *Journal of School Psychology, 51*(4), 535–555.

Rommelse, N., Luman, M., & Kievit, R. (2020). Slow processing speed: A cross-disorder phenomenon with significant clinical value, and in need of further methodological scrutiny. *European Child & Adolescent Psychiatry, 29*(10), 1325–1327. https://doi.org/10.1007/s00787-020-01639-9

Said-Metwaly, S., Taylor, C. L., Camarda, A., & Barbot, B. (2024). Divergent thinking and creative achievement—How strong is the link? An updated meta-analysis. *Psychology of Aesthetics, Creativity, and the Arts, 18*(5), 869–881. https://doi.org/10.1037/aca0000507

Salthouse, T. A. (1996). The processing-speed theory of adult age differences in cognition. *Psychological Review, 103*(3), 403–428. https://doi.org/10.1037/0033-295X.103.3.403

Scherrer, V., Breit, M., & Preckel, F. (2024). Crystallized intelligence, fluid intelligence, and need for cognition: Their longitudinal relations in adolescence. *Journal of Intelligence, 12*(11), 104. https://doi.org/10.3390/jintelligence12110104

Schneider, W. J., & McGrew, K. S. (2012). The Cattell-Horn-Carroll model of intelligence. In D. P. Flanagan & P. L. Harrison (Eds.), *Contemporary intellectual assessment: Theories, tests, and issues* (3rd ed., pp. 99–144). Guilford Press. https://psycnet.apa.org/record/2012-09043-004

Schneider, W. J., & McGrew, K. S. (2018). The Cattell-Horn-Carroll theory of cognitive abilities. In D. P. Flanagan & E. M. McDonough (Eds.), *Contemporary intellectual assessment: Theories, tests, and issues* (4th ed., pp. 73–130). Guilford Press. https://www.guilford.com/books/Contemporary-Intellectual-Assessment/Flanagan-McDonough/9781462552030

Schneider, W. J., & McGrew, K. S. (2019). Process overlap theory is a milestone achievement among intelligence theories. *Journal of Applied Research in Memory and Cognition, 8*(3), 273–276. https://doi.org/10.1016/j.jarmac.2019.06.006

Schneider, W. J., Mayer, J. D., & Newman, D. A. (2016). Integrating hot and cool intelligences: Thinking broadly about broad abilities. *Journal of Intelligence, 4*(1), 1–25. https://doi.org/10.3390/jintelligence4010001

Silvia, P. J., Beaty, R. E., & Nusbaum, E. C. (2013). Verbal fluency and creativity: General and specific contributions of broad retrieval ability (Gr) factors to divergent thinking. *Intelligence, 41*(5), 328–340. https://doi.org/10.1016/j.intell.2013.05.004

Spearman, C. E. (1904). "General intelligence," objectively determined and measured. *The American Journal of Psychology, 15*(2), 201–292. https://doi.org/10.2307/1412107

Spearman, C. E. (1923). *The nature of "intelligence" and the principles of cognition.* Macmillan.

Spearman, C. E. (1927). *The abilities of man: Their nature and measurement.* MacMillan. https://doi.org/10.1038/120181a0

Sternberg, R. J. (1985). *Beyond IQ: A triarchic theory of human intelligence.* Cambridge University Press.

Thorsen, C., Gustafsson, J., & Cliffordson, C. (2014). The influence of fluid and crystallized intelligence on the development of knowledge and skills. *British Journal of Educational Psychology, 84*(4), 556–570. https://doi.org/10.1111/bjep.12041

Thurstone, L. L. (1931). Multiple factor analysis. *Psychological Review, 38*(5), 406–427. https://doi.org/10.1037/h0069792

Thurstone, L. L. (1934). The vectors of mind. *Psychological Review, 41*(1), 1–34. https://doi.org/10.1037/h0075959

Thurstone, L. L. (1935). *The vectors of mind: Multiple-factor analysis for the isolation of primary traits.* University of Chicago Press. https://doi.org/10.1037/10018-000

Thurstone, L. L. (1938). *Primary mental abilities*. University of Chicago Press.
Thurstone, L. L. (1940). Experimental study of simple structure. *Psychometrika*, *5*(2), 153–168. https://doi.org/10.1007/BF02287873
Thurstone, L. L. (1950). Some primary abilities in visual thinking. *Proceedings of the American Philosophical Society*, *94*(6), 517–521.
Tolar, T. D., Lederberg, A. R., & Fletcher, J. M. (2009). A structural model of algebra achievement: Computational fluency and spatial visualisation as mediators of the effect of working memory on algebra achievement. *Educational Psychology*, *29*(2), 239–266. https://doi.org/10.1080/01443410802708903
Torgesen, J. K., Wagner, R. K., Rashotte, C. A., Burgess, S., & Hecht, S. (1997). Contributions of phonological awareness and rapid automatic naming ability to the growth of word-reading skills in second-to fifth-grade children. *Scientific Studies of Reading*, *1*(2), 161–185. https://doi.org/10.1207/s1532799xssr0102_4
Tourva, A., & Spanoudis, G. (2020). Speed of processing, control of processing, working memory and crystallized and fluid intelligence: Evidence for a developmental cascade. *Intelligence*, *83*, 101503. https://doi.org/10.1016/j.intell.2020.101503
Tourva, A., Spanoudis, G., & Demetriou, A. (2016). Cognitive correlates of developing intelligence: The contribution of working memory, processing speed and attention. *Intelligence*, *54*, 136–146. https://doi.org/10.1016/j.intell.2015.12.001
Tucker-Drob, E. M., Brandmaier, A. M., & Lindenberger, U. (2019). Coupled cognitive changes in adulthood: A meta-analysis. *Psychological Bulletin*, *145*(3), 273–301. https://doi.org/10.1037/bul0000179
Tucker-Drob, E. M., De La Fuente, J., Köhncke, Y., Brandmaier, A. M., Nyberg, L., & Lindenberger, U. (2022). A strong dependency between changes in fluid and crystallized abilities in human cognitive aging. *Science Advances*, *8*(5), eabj2422. https://doi.org/10.1126/sciadv.abj2422
Ünal, Z. E., Forsberg, A., Geary, D. C., & Cowan, N. (2022). The role of domain-general attention and domain-specific processing in working memory in algebraic performance: An experimental approach. *Journal of Experimental Psychology: Learning, Memory, and Cognition*, *48*(3), 348–374. https://doi.org/10.1037/xlm0001117
Unsworth, N. (2024). Variation in general retrieval ability in semantic and autobiographical fluency tasks. *Intelligence*, *105*, 101837. https://doi.org/10.1016/j.intell.2024.101837
Uttal, D. H., Miller, D. I., & Newcombe, N. S. (2013). Exploring and enhancing spatial thinking links to achievement in science, technology, engineering, and mathematics? *Current Directions in Psychological Science*, *22*(5), 367–373.
Vernon, P. E. (1950). *The structure of human abilities*. Wiley.
von Stumm, S., & Ackerman, P. L. (2013). Investment and intellect: A review and meta-analysis. *Psychological Bulletin*, *139*(4), 841–869. https://doi.org/10.1037/a0030746
Wagner, R. K., & Torgesen, J. K. (1987). The nature of phonological processing and its causal role in the acquisition of reading skills. *Psychological Bulletin*, *101*(2), 192–212. https://doi.org/10.1037/0033-2909.101.2.192

Walker, D. L., Palermo, R., & Gignac, G. E. (2024). General figure and face-specific closure ability: Predictors of trait-autism? *Current Psychology, 43*(2), 1179–1189. https://doi.org/10.1007/s12144-023-04351-4

Wang, L., & Carr, M. (2020). Understanding the relationship between spatial ability and mathematics achievement through the lens of information processing theory. *North American Journal of Psychology, 22*(2), 173–192.

Watrin, L., Schroeders, U., & Wilhelm, O. (2022). Structural invariance of declarative knowledge across the adult lifespan. *Psychology and Aging, 37*(3), 283–297. https://doi.org/10.1037/pag0000660

Weiss, S., & Wilhelm, O. (2022). Is flexibility more than fluency and originality? *Journal of Intelligence, 10*(4), 96. https://doi.org/10.3390/jintelligence10040096

Weiss, L. G., Keith, T. Z., Zhu, J., & Chen, H. (2013a). WAIS-IV and clinical validation of the four- and five-factor interpretative approaches. *Journal of Psychoeducational Assessment, 31*(2), 94–113. https://doi.org/10.1177/0734282913478030

Weiss, L. G., Keith, T. Z., Zhu, J., & Chen, H. (2013b). WISC-IV and clinical validation of the four-and five-factor interpretative approaches. *Journal of Psychoeducational Assessment, 31*(2), 114–131. https://doi.org/10.1177/0734282913478032

Wilhelm, O., & Kyllonen, P. (2021). To predict the future, consider the past: Revisiting Carroll (1993) as a guide to the future of intelligence research. *Intelligence, 89*, 101585. https://doi.org/10.1016/j.intell.2021.101585

Woodcock, R. W. (1993). An information processing view of the Gf-Gc theory. *Journal of Psychoeducational Assessment, 11*, 80–102. Psychoeducational Corporation

Woodcock, R. W., & Johnson, M. B. (1977). *Woodcock-Johnson Psycho-Educational Battery*. Riverside Assessments, LLC.

Woodcock, R. W., & Johnson, M. B. (1989). *Woodcock-Johnson Psycho-Educational Battery–revised*. Riverside Assessments, LLC.

Woodcock, R. W., McGrew, K. S., & Mather, N. (2001). *Woodcock-Johnson III*. Riverside Assessments, LLC.

Woodcock, R. W., Maricle, D. E., Miller, D. C., & McGill, R. J. (2018). Functional Cattell-Horn-Carroll nomenclature for practical applications. In *Contemporary intellectual assessment: Theories, tests, and issues* (4th ed., pp. 901–911). Guilford Press.

Three

GENERAL ADMINISTRATION PROCEDURES

Proper administration of the WJ V requires training, study, and practice. Although individuals in a wide range of professions can learn the actual procedures for administering the test, a higher degree of skill is required to interpret the results or to test individuals who have special needs or specific disabilities; some examiners can adequately administer a test but may need help interpreting and accurately explaining the results. Only properly trained individuals should interpret the results of standardized tests, especially in high-stakes situations such as making decisions for special education eligibility.

Standards applicable to testing have been developed through a collaborative effort of three professional organizations: the American Educational Research Association (AERA), the American Psychological Association (APA), and the National Council on Measurement in Education (NCME). These standards are published in the *Standards for Educational and Psychological Testing* (AERA, APA, & NCME, 2014). The WJ V authors adhered to these standards during the development of the WJ V. It is your responsibility to be familiar with, and adhere to, the relevant standards when administering and interpreting the WJ V tests.

It is seldom, if ever, necessary to administer all of the WJ V tests to one person. For example, if an individual was referred for a reading evaluation, you may only want to administer the tests that are related to reading performance from the WJ V Achievement (ACH) battery and the WJ V Virtual Test Library (VTL). In addition, you may wish to administer several tests from the WJ V Cognitive (COG) battery that are related to reading performance. Selective testing tables, presented in Figures 3.1 and 3.2, illustrate which WJ V tests need to be administered to obtain the various cluster scores.

Essentials of WJ V™ Assessment, First Edition. Erica M. LaForte, Nancy Mather, and W. Joel Schneider.

			General Intelligence Clusters			CHC Broad Ability Clusters								CHC Narrow Ability and Clinical Clusters						
	CHC Broad Ability	Test	General Intellectual Ability (GIA)	Brief Intellectual Ability (BIA)	Gf-Gc Composite	Comprehension-Knowledge (Gc)	Fluid Reasoning (Gf)	Auditory Working Memory Capacity (Gwm)	Cognitive Processing Speed (Gs)	Retrieval Fluency (Gr)	Long-Term Storage (Gl)	Visual Processing (Gv)	Phonological Awareness (Ga)	Phonological Manipulation (Ga)	Auditory Memory Span (Gwm)	Cognitive Efficiency (CE)	Phonemic Retrieval Fluency (Gr)	RAN–Reading (Gs, Gr)	RAN–Math (Gs, Gr)	Single Tests
COG Standard Tests	Gc	Oral Vocabulary	■	■	■	■														
	Gf	Matrices	■	■	■		■													
	Gv	Spatial Relations	■									■								
	Gl	Story Recall	■								■									
	Gr	Semantic Word Retrieval	■							■										
	Gwm	Verbal Attention	■	■				■								■				
	Gs	Number-Pattern Matching	■						■							■				
	Gc, Gf	Verbal Analogies	■		■	■														
	Gf	Analysis-Synthesis			■		■													
	Gv	Block Rotation										■								
	Gl	Story Comprehension									■									
	Gr	Phonemic Word Retrieval								■							■			
	Gwm	Numbers Reversed						■												
	Gs	Letter-Pattern Matching							■											
COG Extended Tests	Gc	General Information																		■
	Gf	Concept Formation																		■
	Gq, Gf	Number Series																		■
	Gv, Gf	Visual-Auditory Learning																		■
	Gwm, Gv	Visual Working Memory																		■
	Gs	Symbol Inhibition																		■
Virtual Test Library	Ga, Gwm	Nonsense Word Repetition																		■
	Gs, Gr	Rapid Picture Naming																■		
	Gwm	Animal-Number Sequencing																		■
	Ga	Sound Reversal																		■
	Gs, Gr	Rapid Letter Naming																■		
	Gwm, Gf	Understanding Directions																		■
	Ga	Sound Blending											■							
	Gr, Ga	Rapid Phoneme Naming															■	■		
	Gwm	Memory for Words													■					
	Ga	Segmentation											■							
	Gs, Gr	Rapid Number Naming																	■	
	Gwm	Sentence Repetition													■					
	Ga	Sound Deletion												■						
	Gs, Gv	Rapid Quantity Naming																	■	
	Ga	Sound Substitution												■						

Figure 3.1 WJ V COG and VTL Selective Testing Table

Woodcock-Johnson, 2025 / with permission of Riverside Insights

	CHC Broad Ability	Test	Oral Language Clusters: Oral Language (Gc)	Oral Language Clusters: Listening Comprehension (Gc)	Oral Language Clusters: Oral Expression (Gc, Gl)	Oral Language Clusters: Vocabulary (Gc)	Reading Clusters: Brief Reading (Grw)	Reading Clusters: Basic Reading Skills (Grw)	Reading Clusters: Reading Fluency (Grw)	Reading Clusters: Reading Comprehension (Grw)	Math Clusters: Brief Math (Gq)	Math Clusters: Math Calculation Skills (Gq)	Math Clusters: Number Concepts (Gq)	Math Clusters: Math Problem Solving (Gq)	Writing Clusters: Brief Writing (Grw)	Writing Clusters: Basic Writing Skills (Grw)	Writing Clusters: Spelling Skills (Grw, Ga)	Writing Clusters: Written Expression (Grw)	Cross-Domain Achievement Clusters: Broad Achievement (Grw, Gq, Gs)	Cross-Domain Achievement Clusters: Academic Skills/Brief Achievement (Grw, Gq)	Cross-Domain Achievement Clusters: Academic Fluency (Gs)	Cross-Domain Achievement Clusters: Academic Applications (Grw, Gq)	Cross-Domain Achievement Clusters: Academic Knowledge (Gc)	Cross-Domain Achievement Clusters: Phoneme-Grapheme Knowledge (Grw, Ga)	CHC Broad Ability Cluster: Phonological Awareness (Ga)	CHC Narrow Ability and Clinical Clusters: Phonological Manipulation (Ga)	CHC Narrow Ability and Clinical Clusters: Auditory Memory Span (Gwm)	CHC Narrow Ability and Clinical Clusters: RAN–Reading (Gs, Gr)	CHC Narrow Ability and Clinical Clusters: RAN–Math (Gs, Gr)	Single Tests
ACH Standard Tests	Gc	Picture Vocabulary	■		■	■																								
ACH Standard Tests	Grw	Letter-Word Identification					■	■											■	■										
ACH Standard Tests	Gq	Calculation									■	■							■	■										
ACH Standard Tests	Grw	Spelling														■	■		■	■										
ACH Standard Tests	Gc	Oral Comprehension	■	■																										
ACH Standard Tests	Grw, Ga	Word Attack						■																■						
ACH Standard Tests	Gs, Gq	Math Facts Fluency										■							■		■									
ACH Standard Tests	Grw	Sentence Writing Accuracy													■	■														
ACH Standard Tests	Grw, Gc	Passage Comprehension					■			■									■			■								
ACH Standard Tests	Gq	Applied Problems									■			■					■			■								
ACH Standard Tests	Gs, Grw	Sentence Reading Fluency							■										■		■									
ACH Standard Tests	Grw	Written Language Samples													■			■	■			■								
ACH Standard Tests	Gl, Gc	Oral Language Samples	■		■																									
ACH Standard Tests	Gs, Grw	Sentence Writing Fluency																■	■		■									
ACH Standard Tests	Grw, Gc	Paragraph Reading Comprehension								■																				
ACH Standard Tests	Gl	Story Comprehension	■	■																										
ACH Standard Tests	Gs, Grw	Word Reading Fluency							■																					
ACH Standard Tests	Gq, Gf	Math Problem Identification												■																
ACH Extended Tests	Gs, Gq	Magnitude Comparison											■																	
ACH Extended Tests	Gq	Number Sense											■																	
ACH Extended Tests	Ga, Grw	Spelling of Sounds															■							■						
ACH Extended Tests	Grw	Oral Reading																												■
ACH Extended Tests	Grw, Gl	Reading Recall																												■
ACH Extended Tests	Gc	Academic Vocabulary				■																	■							
ACH Extended Tests	Gc	Academic Facts																					■							
ACH Extended Tests	Gs	Letter Writing Fluency																												■
Virtual Test Library	Ga, Gwm	Nonsense Word Repetition																												■
Virtual Test Library	Gs, Gr	Rapid Picture Naming																										■		
Virtual Test Library	Gwm	Animal-Number Sequencing																												■
Virtual Test Library	Ga	Sound Reversal																												■
Virtual Test Library	Gs, Gr	Rapid Letter Naming																										■		
Virtual Test Library	Gwm, Gf	Understanding Directions																												■
Virtual Test Library	Ga	Sound Blending																							■					
Virtual Test Library	Gr, Ga	Rapid Phoneme Naming																										■		
Virtual Test Library	Gwm	Memory for Words																									■			
Virtual Test Library	Ga	Segmentation																							■					
Virtual Test Library	Gs, Gr	Rapid Number Naming																											■	
Virtual Test Library	Gwm	Sentence Repetition																									■			
Virtual Test Library	Ga	Sound Deletion																								■				
Virtual Test Library	Gs, Gv	Rapid Quantity Naming																											■	
Virtual Test Library	Ga	Sound Substitution																								■				

Figure 3.2 WJ V ACH and VTL Selective Testing Table

Woodcock-Johnson, 2025 / with permission of Riverside Insights

PREPARING TO TEST

The Testing Environment

Prior to testing, select a testing room that is quiet, comfortable, and has adequate lighting and ventilation. Ideally, only you and the examinee should be in the room. Ensure that the room has a desk or table and two chairs, one of which is an appropriate size for the examinee. Further, ensure that the seating arrangement prevents your laptop screen from being visible to the examinee and allows space for you to use your mouse. The best seating arrangement is one in which you sit diagonally across from the examinee at the corner of a table. Another possible arrangement is to sit directly across the table. With this arrangement, the table must be narrow and low enough so you can see and point to the examinee's Response Booklet if necessary.

Testing Materials

You will need the following materials to administer and score the WJ V:

- A Mac or Windows laptop with 8GB RAM or more (for optimal performance), screen resolution of 1920 × 1080 or higher, and a high-speed internet connection (consult the publisher's website at www.riversideinsights.com for current hardware and browser requirements)
- A silent mouse
- An iPad 8th Generation or newer with a minimum screen size of 10.2 in. and iOS 16 or higher
- A Response Booklet and at least two sharpened pencils, if you will be administering any ACH tests that require written responses (see Rapid Reference 3.1).
- A scoring guide, if you will be administering any of the tests that require you to score the examinee's written responses (see Rapid Reference 3.2).

Setting Up Your Test Session on *Riverside Score*®

All WJ V tests are administered on the *Riverside Score*® digital platform. Before any testing can begin, you must log in to the *Riverside Score*® platform and complete the steps to set up your test assignment. This section describes the steps for adding an examinee, creating a Test Set, assigning the Test Set to the examinee, and printing a Response Booklet. It is best to complete these steps prior to the time the examinee arrives for testing.

Log in to *Riverside Score*®. On the Examinees menu, select Add Examinee. Enter the examinee's name, gender, and date of birth. Optionally, you can use the Demographics/Programs and User Identified Fields tabs to add other examinee information. Then save the examinee's record.

Next, you will create a Test Set that includes the tests you will administer to the examinee. On the Test Sets menu, select Create New Test Set. On this screen, you can select tests to administer to the examinee in either of the following ways:

- On the Clusters tab, select from among the available clusters. When a cluster is selected, the tests that contribute to the cluster will be added to the Test Set.

- On the All Tests tab, select from among the available tests. The test(s) you include will be added to the Test Set in the order you select them.

DON'T FORGET

Test Sets can be assigned to multiple examinees. For example, if there are specific tests you use often, you can save those tests into a custom Test Set. You can add tests to a Test Set at any time by selecting the Edit icon next to the Test Set name on the Test Sets tab. The *Riverside Score*® platform provides some default Test Sets. For example, the General Intellectual Ability (GIA) Test Set contains the 8 tests that comprise the GIA cluster, and the Dyslexia Test Set contains 19 tests that are often included as part of a dyslexia evaluation. If you add tests to a default Test Set, you must save the new Test Set with a unique name.

After you finish selecting clusters and/or individual tests to administer, you can rearrange the order of the tests within your Test Set, if desired. Then save the Test Set with a unique name. The *Riverside Score*® platform provides an estimate of the amount of time it will take you to administer all of the tests in your Test Set.

CAUTION

The administration time estimates provided by *Riverside Score*® are based on the average administration times across all examinees in the WJ V norming sample. The estimates include *only* the actual test administration time; they do *not* include the time for setting up the test session, taking breaks between tests, or scoring examinee responses in the Response Booklet. Testing times can vary dramatically depending on the examinee's age, ability, and other characteristics. If you are relying on the time estimates provided by *Riverside Score*® to schedule your test session, allow an appropriate margin of error around the estimated administration time. For instance, younger children may take more time to get acclimated to the test activities and may require more frequent breaks between tests, and older or higher-ability examinees may need to take more items to reach a ceiling on some tests. Both of these factors could result in longer-than-average administration times.

Next, you will assign the newly created Test Set to the examinee. On the Examinee Management page, locate the examinee's name and click the Create Test Assignment icon.

- Confirm that the details for the examinee are correct, and then click Next.
- Use the drop-down menu to locate the Test Set you created in the prior step (or select from among any of your other previously saved Test Sets), and then click Next.
- Use the Education drop-down to select the examinee's current grade (for an examinee currently in Kindergarten through 12th grade) or the examinee's highest level of education (for an adult examinee). This selection will direct the platform to the appropriate starting point for each test during administration. By default, the platform uses August 16 as the school year start date and May 15 as the school year

end date to assign the tenth-of-school-year value. You can override these defaults by adjusting the dates in the School Year Start Date and School Year End Date boxes.

- After you have selected the education level, you can select either grade- or age-based starting points. You can also override the default starting point to a lower or higher age or grade. You can change this starting point selection for any test during the testing session.
- Finally, you can opt to capture a voice recording of the test session using the Voice Capture toggle. The voice recording allows you to review the examinee's oral responses after administration is complete and, if necessary, confirm the item scores you assigned. This is especially useful for tests such as Semantic Word Retrieval and Phonemic Word Retrieval, where the examinee may speak quickly, and for tests where you need to double-check the examinee's pronunciation. The voice recording will be saved on the platform for 90 days after you first generate a score report; then, it will be permanently deleted.

CAUTION

Voice recordings may be considered an education record under the Family Educational Rights and Privacy Act (FERPA). Before enabling the Voice Capture feature on the WJ V platform, be aware of your organization's rules about student data privacy under FERPA.

After you make your selections, save the test assignment and review the details. If you are ready to begin testing, you can launch the assignment from this screen or click Close to begin testing later. If you choose to begin testing later, simply click on the examinee's name on your Dashboard to launch the session.

Printing a Response Booklet Several WJ V ACH tests require the examinee to write their responses in a Response Booklet. Rapid Reference 3.1 contains a list of ACH tests that require a Response Booklet. Full-color versions of Response Booklets are available for purchase from the publisher (www.riversideinsights.com). Alternatively, you may print a grayscale version of the Response Booklet on your own printer. To print a Response Booklet, navigate to the Resources tab of *Riverside Score®* and select *Tests of Achievement Response Booklet* under the WJ V Materials heading. Page 1 of the Response Booklet includes a Table of Contents; select the page(s) that you want to print in your print dialog box. At a minimum, print page 1 of the Response Booklet and all the pages for any tests you are planning to administer; however, if you think that you might administer additional tests later, it is more convenient to print the entire Response Booklet before you begin testing than to print additional pages later.

Follow the instructions provided by the publisher on the Resources tab of *Riverside Score®* for printing and assembling the Response Booklet (see Caution box). Treat the Response Booklet as secure test material and do not share it with anyone outside of the evaluation team.

Rapid Reference 3.1

WJ V ACH Tests Requiring a Response Booklet

- Calculation
- Spelling
- Math Facts Fluency
- Sentence Writing Accuracy
- Applied Problems (for scratch paper only)
- Written Language Samples
- Sentence Writing Fluency
- Math Problem Identification (for scratch paper only)
- Spelling of Sounds
- Letter Writing Fluency

CAUTION

If you opt to print Response Booklets from your own printer, follow these guidelines to ensure the validity of your test results:

- Make sure your printer has sufficient ink so that your Response Booklet pages are legible and not faded.
- Print on only the front side of each sheet of paper; do not select double-sided printing.
- Print pages in portrait mode at 100% scale; do not try to fit multiple pages on a single sheet of paper.
- Staple the sheets together in the upper-left corner.

For more detailed instructions on printing and assembling Response Booklets, log into the WJ V platform at www.riversidescore.com and navigate to the Resources tab.

Accessing scoring guides Some WJ V tests require you to consult a scoring guide to assign scores to the examinee's written responses (see Rapid Reference 3.2). These scoring guides are available as downloadable PDF files on the Resources tab of *Riverside Score*®. If you will be administering these WJ V tests often, you may consider printing copies of the scoring guides and keeping them in a secure location for regular use.

The Math Facts Fluency Scoring Guide was designed so that if it is printed onto a transparency, you can lay it over the Response Booklet and see the correct response for each item immediately to the left of the examinee's written response.

Rapid Reference 3.2

WJ V Tests Requiring a Scoring Guide

- Math Facts Fluency
- Sentence Writing Accuracy
- Written Language Samples
- Sentence Writing Fluency
- Letter Writing Fluency

DON'T FORGET

Keys for Preparing to Administer the WJ V:

- Ensure that your hardware and software meet the minimum requirements, and that you have a stable high-speed internet connection.
- Log in to the *Riverside Score®* platform to create an examinee record, create a Test Set (if necessary), and assign the Test Set to the examinee prior to starting the test session.
- If necessary, confirm that you have a Response Booklet (purchased from the publisher or printed locally from the *Riverside Score®* platform).
- If necessary, confirm that you have the appropriate scoring guides (downloadable from the *Riverside Score®* platform).
- Select an appropriate location for the test session.

Establishing and Maintaining Rapport

In most instances, you will have little difficulty establishing a good relationship with the examinee. Often, examiners begin the test session with a short period of conversation, discussing something of interest to the person, such as what the person enjoys doing in leisure time or what sports the student plays. When you launch the test session on *Riverside Score®*, the platform provides a short introduction to the testing interface on the iPad that you can present to the examinee. Do not begin testing until the examinee seems relatively at ease. If the examinee appears to be overly tired, sick, or disinterested, do not attempt testing.

Throughout the test session, encourage responses when items are difficult. If the examinee appears to be struggling with an item, you can say, *Would you like to take a guess on that one?* During the test session, keep the examinee engaged by providing encouragement and praising the examinee's effort. However, take care to avoid revealing whether the examinee's answers are correct or incorrect unless the test instructions call for corrective feedback. For example, do not say *good* after correct responses or pause longer after incorrect responses as if waiting for the examinee to change a response.

NAVIGATING THE WJ V DIGITAL TEST INTERFACE

> **CAUTION**
>
> - Be careful not to reveal the correct answers to test items.
> - Do not indicate whether a response is correct or incorrect, unless the test item's instructions allow feedback.
> - Provide encouragement throughout the administration, not just when the examinee answers correctly or incorrectly.

Riverside Score® provides the digital interface for administration and scoring the WJ V tests. The examiner's laptop and the examinee's iPad are connected through the devices' browsers over a high-speed Wi-Fi network. Begin a test session by logging in to the *Riverside Score®* administration platform from your laptop's browser. Create an examinee record, save the clusters or individual tests to be administered into a Test Set, and assign the Test Set to the examinee. Upon launching the test session, you will be prompted to connect the iPad to the session by scanning the QR code on your laptop screen. When the iPad is connected to the session, you can begin administering the first test in your Test Set.

During the test session, the examinee will see and/or hear item stimuli from the iPad. The Examiner's View on your laptop screen contains the test administration instructions, scoring keys, audio play interface (for tests requiring audio prompts), and timer (for timed tests). Additionally, you can view the contents of the examinee's iPad screen directly from your laptop in the Examinee's View panel of your laptop's interface. Figure 3.3 shows the *Riverside Score®* WJ V examiner's test interface, and the following sections describe these interface features.

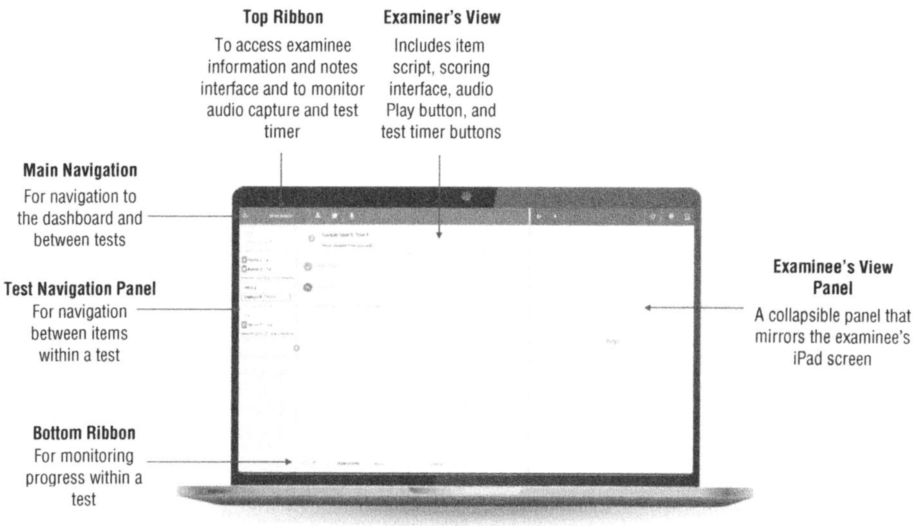

Figure 3.3 *Riverside Score®* WJ V Examiner's Test Interface

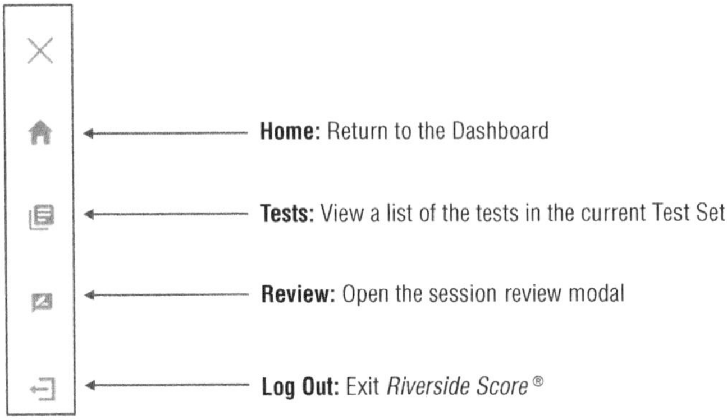

From the *Woodcock-Johnson*® V Copyright © 2025, by Riverside Assessments, LLC. All rights reserved. Used with permission of the publisher.

Figure 3.4 Main Navigation Menu

Main Navigation Menu

Figure 3.4 shows the Main Navigation menu options. Click the Main Navigation icon in the upper-left corner of your laptop screen at any time during test administration to view these options:

- **Home.** If you click this option during a test, you will exit the test and return to your Dashboard. Note that if you exit a timed test (such as Math Facts Fluency or Letter-Pattern Matching) while the test timer is running, the test will end and will not be considered a valid administration. If you click Home at any time *during* a test, the platform will ask you to confirm that you do, indeed, want to exit the test session.
- **Tests.** Clicking this option opens the Tests panel, where you can see a list of the tests in your current Test Set. An icon to the left of each test name indicates the test's status (Not Started, In Progress, or Complete). There are also warning icons to indicate if a test has one or more scoring errors (for example, an item score that is missing) or whether the test needs to be scored later (in the case of tests that are scored after administration, such as Math Facts Fluency or Written Language Samples). If you want to change the order of test administration after the test session has started, you may skip any test that has a status of Not Started or In Progress by clicking the "x" icon to the right of the test; later, you may click the icon again to restore the test to your Test Set.
- **Review.** Use this option to launch the test session review modal. Here, you can review test items that you flagged during administration, see tests and items that

CAUTION

Exiting a timed test while the timer is running by clicking Home or selecting a different test from the Tests option in the Main Navigation menu will end the test and you will not be able to return to it.

require score entry or score error resolution, enter Test Session Observations, and write notes about the test session.

- **Log Out.** Clicking this option will log you out of the *Riverside Score®* platform.

Top Ribbon

The Top Ribbon (Figure 3.5) contains several features to orient you to the current test. The test name appears on the far left, next to the Main Navigation icon. Roll your cursor over the Examinee icon to see the examinee's name, date of birth, age, and grade (if applicable). Click the Notes icon to enter item, test, or session-level notes at any time during the test administration. The Voice Capture icon glows when audio is being captured, and the Timer icon glows and displays a counter when the timer is running.

Bottom Ribbon

The Bottom Ribbon (Figure 3.6) contains useful tools for test administration.

- **Information icon.** At any time during the administration of a test, you may access the Test Overview by clicking the Information ("i") icon from the Bottom Ribbon (see Figure 3.3). If you click on the Information icon *during* a test, the Test Overview will display as a pop-up modal on your screen but will not affect what the examinee sees on the iPad.
- **Flag icon.** Click this icon at any time during test administration to flag the item for later review. Clicking this icon will also open the Notes window, where you can type observational notes about the examinee's response or behavior. Flagged items will appear as a list in your Review modal after testing, and you may return to them to confirm the examinee's score, listen to the voice recording, or review any notes you entered during the test.
- **Item Score Indicator.** This indicator displays the score that was assigned to the examinee's response—in most cases, a 1 for correct or a 0 for incorrect. For tests

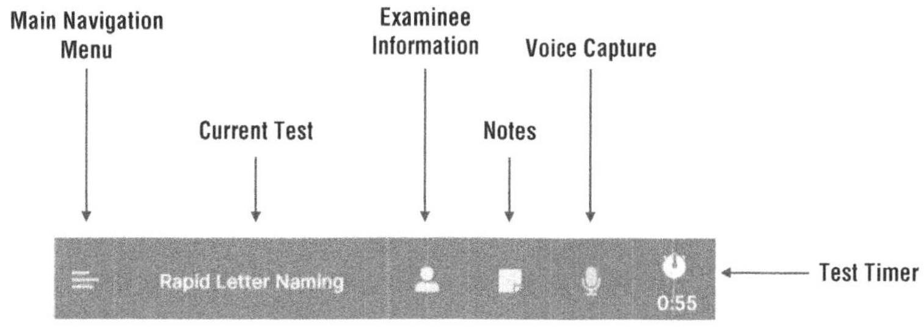

Figure 3.5 Top Ribbon

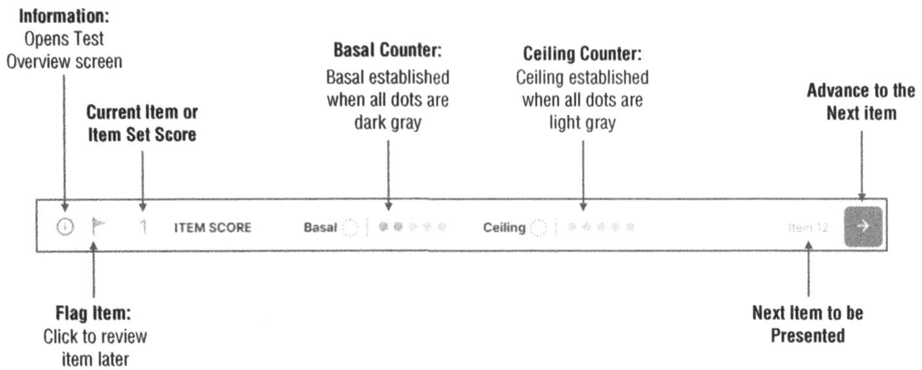

Figure 3.6 Bottom Ribbon

with multiple-point items (e.g., Story Recall, Semantic Word Retrieval), the Item Score Indicator shows the number of points the examinee earned on the story or item. For tests on which examinee errors, and not correct responses, are counted (e.g., Visual-Auditory Learning, the RAN tests), the Item Score Indicator displays the number of errors the examinee made on the story or item set.

- **Basal and Ceiling Counters.** For tests that use basal and ceiling rules, these counters track the examinee's progress toward obtaining a basal and a ceiling. The number of dots on these counters represents the basal and ceiling rule for the test (e.g., if the basal and ceiling rule is 5, each counter will have 5 dots). Each time the examinee correctly answers an item that contributes to the basal, a dot changes from gray to green (dark gray in figure) on the Basal Counter. If the examinee answers an item incorrectly before the basal is met, the counter resets and begins counting again when the examinee answers a lower-numbered item correctly. When the Basal Counter displays all green (dark gray in figure) dots, the basal is established and testing proceeds forward. The Ceiling Counter displays a red dot (light gray in figure) for each successive *incorrect* response. When the ceiling has been established (i.e., when the Ceiling Counter displays all red dots [light gray in figure]), the test ends.
- **Next button.** Click the Next button to advance to the next item, story, or item set during testing. To prevent advancing past an unadministered or unscored item, the Next button is not active until the current item has been scored. Once a score has been assigned to the current item, the text to the left of the Next button shows the item number of the next item that will be displayed. Note that this is not always a higher-numbered item or story. In cases where the examinee does not establish a basal and needs to test backward, or in cases where the examinee is routed to an easier set of items, the item number displayed to the left of the Next button may be a lower-numbered item or item set. In lieu of clicking the Next button, you can also use the N key on your keyboard to advance to the next item or item set during test administration.

Examiner's View

The Examiner's View contains the information you will need to administer and score each test item. During administration, the item script, or the instructions you need to read aloud to the examinee, are printed in bold, blue type (gray bold text in figure); other instructions are presented in black type. The item scoring interface varies by test. For some tests, the examinee taps responses on the iPad and the platform assigns a score to each item. For other tests, you will use your mouse to click the word or words the examinee says; the platform assigns a score of correct or incorrect to the selected response. For some tests where the examinee provides an oral response (e.g., Oral Vocabulary, Picture Vocabulary, or Passage Comprehension), the most common correct and incorrect responses collected during the WJ V norming study are included in the Correct and Incorrect keys (see Figure 3.7). Select the option that matches the examinee's response. If the examinee's response is not among those listed in the item keys, use the Other-1 or Other-0 option to score the item correct or incorrect. Optionally, you can type the examinee's response in the Other text field for later review.

Many items include I Don't Know and No Response options. If the examinee says *I don't know*, or doesn't respond at all, you may select from these options. The platform will automatically assign a score of 0 to the item.

For tests with audio stimuli, the Play button is embedded into the item text field; simply click Play to present the item to the examinee (see Figure 3.8). For tests with timers, the Start Timer button is embedded into the item text field (see Figure 3.9). Read the instructions orally to the examinee, and then click the button to start the timer.

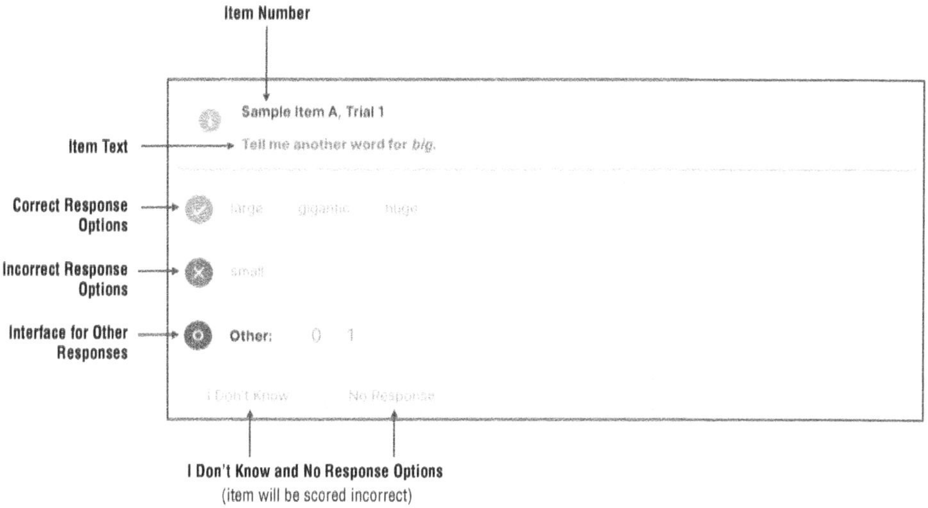

Figure 3.7 Examiner's View

Figure 3.8 Audio-Recorded Item Stimulus

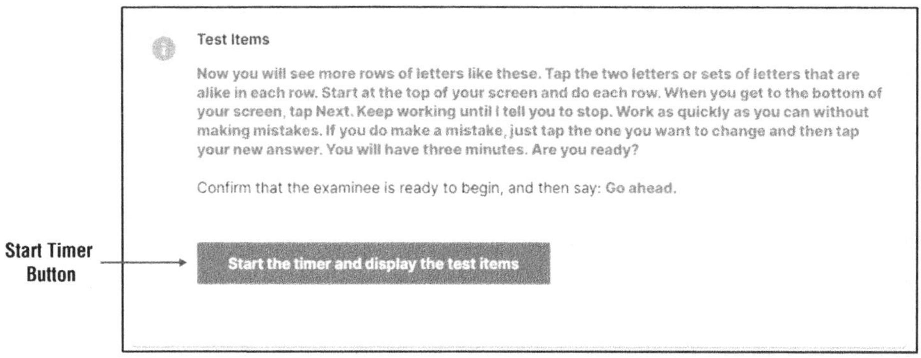

Figure 3.9 A Timed Test

> **DON'T FORGET**
>
> **Examiner's View Reminders:**
>
> - Item administration instructions, scoring interface, audio recordings, and test timers are built into the *Riverside Score®* interface.
> - Read all text printed in bold, blue type (gray bold text in figure) aloud; follow instructions printed in black type.
> - The item scoring interface varies depending on the test.

Test Navigation Panel

During test administration, the Test Navigation panel (Figure 3.10) orients you to the test items by displaying numbered item cards. The icon on each item card displays the item number (e.g., Item 1, Sample Item A) and the item's status—not administered, in progress, or administered. Administered item numbers appear in bold type. Cards for items that were scored correct display a check mark, and cards for items that were scored incorrect display a "X." For tests with age- or grade-based starting points, the Starting Point indicator displays above the card for the first item, or item set, that was administered.

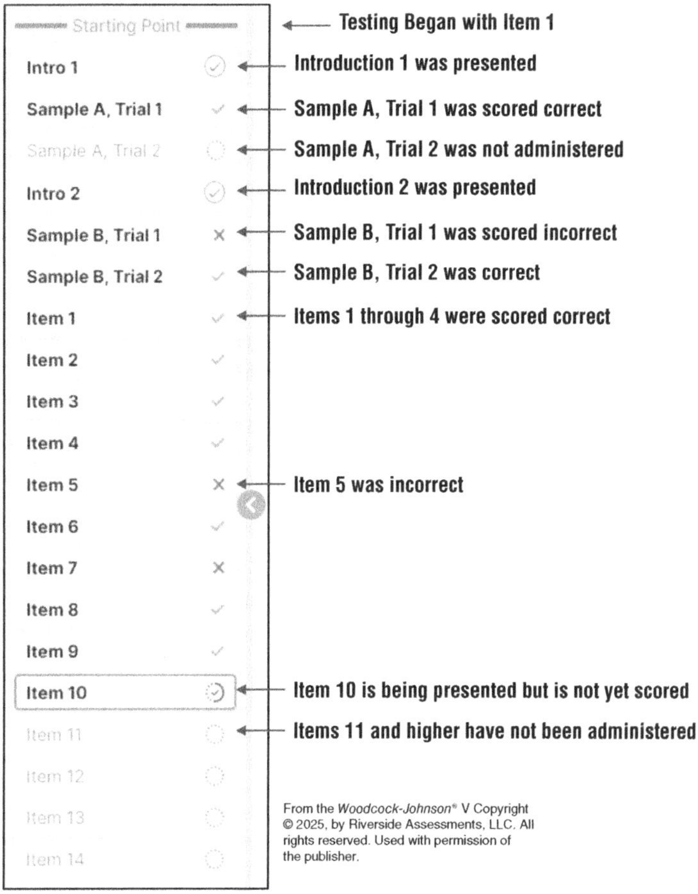

Figure 3.10 Test Navigation Panel

At any time during testing, you can roll your cursor over an item card to see a brief description of the item and the score that was assigned to the examinee's response (e.g., 1 or 0). You can also return to a previously administered item by clicking on the item card. This is useful if, for example, the examinee changes their response to an item after you have advanced to the next item. In this scenario, use the Test Navigation panel, and not your browser's back button, to return to the previous item.

If you change the examinee's response to a previously administered item from correct to incorrect and the change "breaks" an established basal, the platform will establish a new basal before continuing to test forward. Consider the example of a third-grade student who begins testing with Item 10 on Applied Problems. The examinee answers Items 10–14 correctly (establishing a basal), so the platform advances to Item 15. Before responding to Item 15, the examinee asks to change their answer to Item 14. You use your Test Navigation panel to return to Item 14 and change the examinee's response, and the item is now incorrect. Instead of advancing forward to Item 15, the platform will route to Item 19. If the examinee answers Item 19 correctly, the platform will route to Item 16 and then continue testing forward.

Likewise, if the examinee self-corrects on a previously administered item that contributed to a ceiling, the platform will continue to test forward until the examinee responds incorrectly to the required number of items to establish a ceiling.

Examinee's View Panel

The Examinee's View panel (See Figure 3.11) of your test interface displays a duplicate of the iPad screen. Using the features built into the Examinee's View, you can:

- **View the item stimuli.** At any time during the test, the Examinee's View displays exactly what the examinee is seeing on their iPad. This eliminates the need for you to look back and forth between your laptop screen and the iPad screen.
- **Point to stimuli on the iPad.** When you take control of the iPad and drag your cursor over the Examinee's View on your laptop screen, a pointer tool appears on the examinee's iPad in the same location as your cursor; this enables you to point to item stimuli on the examinee's iPad directly from your laptop. For items that require you to point to visual stimuli on the examinee's iPad, the tablet control defaults to activated. For other items, you can click the Activate/Deactivate Tablet Control icon to turn your control on and off. For example, if the examinee asks to change their response to an item on the Block Rotation test, you can take control of the iPad and click the examinee's original responses to deselect them.
- **Hide or show the iPad Screen.** Click the Hide/Show iPad Screen icon to hide the contents of the iPad screen from the examinee. Click the icon again to re-display the stimuli. This feature is useful for situations when an examinee may be distracted by visual stimuli while listening to test instructions.
- **Check the Wi-Fi connection.** Roll your cursor over the Check Wi-Fi Connection icon to confirm that your test session connection is stable.
- **Expand or collapse the Examinee's View.** If you need more space on your laptop screen, you can collapse the Examinee's View using the icon at the top right-hand corner of the panel. Click the icon again to expand the Examinee's View.

DON'T FORGET

The WJ V platform on *Riverside Score®* contains many useful features to make test administration easier and more efficient.

- The platform keeps track of the examinee's progress toward establishing a basal and a ceiling, and automatically navigates to the next item or item set that should be administered—even if it is a lower-numbered item or item set.

- You can use the N key on your keyboard to advance to the next item or item set during test administration. Some examiners find this to be less cumbersome than rolling their mouse down to the Next button on each screen.
- The Test Navigation panel orients you to the examinee's progress in the current test by showing which items have been administered and the scores that were assigned. You can return to any previously administered item by clicking the corresponding item card in this panel.
- When control of the iPad is activated and you roll your cursor over the Examinee's View, the examinee sees a pointer tool on the iPad in the location of your cursor. Use this feature to point to visual stimuli on the iPad or, if necessary, to deselect the examinee's tapped response in the event they ask to change an answer.

ADMINISTRATION BASICS

The goal of standardized testing is to see how well a person can perform tasks when given instructions identical to those presented to individuals in the norm sample. For this reason, present each item to the examinee *exactly* as described in the item's instructions; read oral prompts exactly as they are written and point to item stimuli when instructed to do so. Before testing a client or student, you should become familiar enough with the digital administration platform and the WJ V test content to administer and score the test items

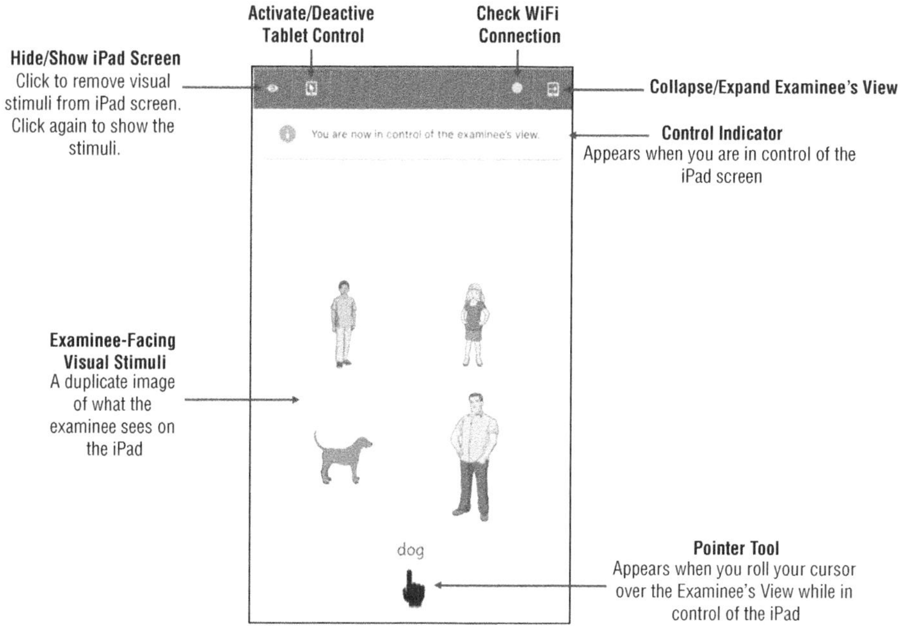

Figure 3.11 Examinee's View Panel

accurately and fluently. Use the resources provided on the *Riverside Score®* platform, including content guides and administration tutorials, to familiarize yourself with the test content and digital platform. Administer several practice tests to individuals of different ages, treating them as if they were actual administrations. Strive for administrations that are both exact and brisk.

Avoid unnecessary conversation during tests that may slow down the administration or distract the examinee from the test tasks. Advance to the next item immediately upon completion of each item. If necessary, take short breaks *between* tests; do not stop for a break *during* a test.

The platform displays a Test Overview screen before each test begins. The Test Overviews contain information and reminders about administering and scoring each test. For example, the Test Overview will tell you whether the test uses audio-recorded item stimuli, whether it is timed (and if so, the test time limit), and whether you are allowed to repeat an item prompt if the examinee requests it.

DON'T FORGET

Exact Administration:

- Present each item *exactly* as written.
- Use the resources on *Riverside Score®* to become familiar with the test administration, scoring, and digital interface.
- Practice administering each test several times before conducting an administration with a client or student.
- Review the Test Overview screen for helpful reminders about administration and scoring before starting each test.

Brisk Administration:

- Advance to the next item *immediately* after completing each item.
- Do not stop and visit during a test.

Estimating Testing Time

The amount of time that it takes to administer the WJ V depends upon the number of tests that are administered, and on the individual examinee's age, ability, and speed of responding. The *Riverside Score®* platform provides an estimate of total testing time when you create a Test Set. The estimated testing time is based on the average testing times across all ages in the WJ V norming sample. Your examinee may take more time or less time depending on individual characteristics. Schedule your test session with enough time that you will not need to rush the examinee through the tests. If you are administering a large number of tests, consider breaking up the testing across multiple days.

Order of Test Administration

You may administer the WJ V tests in any order; however, when possible you should try to alternate test tasks to keep the examinee engaged and focused. For instance, if you are administering several tests from the WJ V ACH battery, you might alternate reading, math, and writing tests. Avoid administering two timed tests (such as Letter Pattern Matching and Number Pattern Matching) or two tests involving sustained writing (such as Written Language Samples and Sentence Writing Accuracy) in a row. Also, consider the likes and dislikes of the examinee. For example, if a student struggles with math, separate the administration of the math tests with other tests that may be less difficult. In addition, you may discontinue testing between the administration of any two tests and resume on another day, if needed.

You can specify the order of test administration when you create a Test Set by clicking and dragging the tests up or down in the Test Set Creation modal. Alternatively, you can change the order of test administration at any time during the testing session by accessing the Tests option from the Main Navigation menu and selecting the test to administer next from among the tests in your Test Set.

> **DON'T FORGET**
>
> You may administer the WJ V tests in any order, but alternate test tasks when possible to keep the examinee engaged. You can specify the administration order of the tests when you create a Test Set. You can also change the order of test administration during the test session. To do this, use the Tests option from the Main Navigation menu and click the "x" icon(s) next to the test name(s) to skip one or more unadministered tests in your Test Set. When you are ready to administer the test(s) later, you can click the icon(s) again to enable the test(s).

General Guidelines for Item Administration and Scoring

To ensure that the information you glean from the examinee's scores on the WJ V is valid and accurately reflects the examinee's abilities, adhere to the standardized administration procedures throughout the test session. Follow all instructions on each item screen exactly; when prompted, read all bold, blue text (gray bold text in figure) verbatim. Do not paraphrase, translate, or change any words on spoken instructions. On some tests, you may repeat an item if the examinee requests it; on other tests, you may not repeat an item prompt. Refer to the Test Overviews within the *Riverside Score*® platform to determine whether you are allowed to repeat an item.

Learn the pronunciation of all the words in all test items prior to administering the WJ V for the first time. Pronounce all words printed in bold, blue type (gray bold text in figure) correctly to maintain standardized administration procedures. On the Letter-Word Identification, Word Attack, and Oral Reading tests, the examinee reads words, nonsense words, or passages, and you must determine whether the examinee's pronunciation is correct. Therefore, you must know the correct pronunciation for all items on these tests. The *Riverside Score*®

platform contains pronunciation guides and audio clips demonstrating the correct pronunciation for all difficult words on the test; study these materials so that you are comfortable and familiar with all the words you will encounter during administration. Do not penalize an examinee on any test item for articulation errors or for regional or dialectical speech variations.

For items that are examiner-scored, the scoring criteria are included with each item. Follow the scoring criteria exactly; do not give the examinee the benefit of the doubt if the answer is only partially correct or is not exactly the response listed in the Correct key. On some items, if the examinee provides a partially correct response, when you click that response in the item scoring key, the platform will prompt you to query the examinee for more details (e.g., *Tell me another word*, or *Tell me more.*) In those cases, score the next response the examinee provides. When the examinee gives more than one response to an item (for example, in cases where the examinee changes their response later), always score the *last* response given, even if it changes the item score from correct to incorrect.

Several WJ V tests are timed; these tests are discussed later in this chapter. When administering items on untimed tests, allow a reasonable amount of time for the examinee to respond to an item and then suggest moving on to the next item. For some items, the platform will alert you when 30 or 60 seconds have passed as a reminder to keep the testing pace brisk. In these instances, disregard the alert if the examinee is still actively engaged in solving the problem. Some tests, however, include item time *limits* of 30 or 60 seconds; if the examinee has not responded within the time limit, the platform will instruct you to score the item as No Response and advance immediately to the next item.

CAUTION

Possible Administration Errors:

- Not following standardized administration procedures
- Providing an examinee with too much assistance
- Not querying when indicated
- Being too lenient or stringent when scoring responses
- Not enforcing item time limits when provided

DON'T FORGET

Keys to Competent Administration:

- Know the correct pronunciation of all test items.
- Be fluent in administration.
- If the examinee gives more than one response to an item, score the last response given.
- Do not penalize for errors due to articulation or for regional or dialectical speech differences.

Suggested Starting Points

Most WJ V tests contain a range of items that are appropriate for different examinee ability levels, from preschool children through college-educated adults. An examinee would rarely, if ever, encounter all of the items on a test. Suggested Starting Points (SSPs) help to reduce testing time by identifying an appropriate starting item for each examinee based on their age or grade. Depending on the selections you make when you assign a Test Set to an examinee, the platform will use either the examinee's age or their current grade as the basis for the default SSPs. If you suspect that the examinee is performing above or below their age or grade level, you may override the platform-assigned default age- or grade-level SSP and select a higher or lower age or grade level. For example, an individual who is low functioning may need to begin with an easier item than indicated by their present age or grade placement to avoid frustration; in contrast, an individual who is higher-functioning or gifted can start testing with a more difficult item to avoid spending time on items that are too easy. The platform offers the option to edit the starting point each time you launch a new test; this way, you can use information about the examinee's performance from earlier tests to adjust the starting point on later tests.

> **DON'T FORGET**
>
> The *Riverside Score*® platform will select a default starting point based on your examinee's age or grade level, but you can change or override it at any time during testing.

Tests Administered with Basal and Ceiling Rules

Because most WJ V tests include items spanning a wide range of difficulty, many items on the tests may be too easy or too difficult for an examinee. The purpose of basal and ceiling rules is to limit the set of items administered to only those that are appropriately matched to the examinee's ability, thereby avoiding items that are much too easy (i.e., lower-numbered items) or much too difficult (i.e., higher-numbered items). Not all WJ V tests use basal and ceiling rules; however, for those that do, the platform implements the basal and ceiling rules automatically. Rapid Reference 3.3 lists the WJ V tests that use basal and ceiling rules for administration, and the number of items needed to obtain the basal and ceiling.

When you administer a test that uses basal and ceiling rules, the platform will present an appropriate first item based on the examinee's default age or education/grade level SSP. If you choose to override the default SSP before you launch the test, the platform will select an item that is appropriate for the age or grade level you specified. By design, the first item administered should be relatively easy for a typical examinee at the selected SSP level.

A basal is established when the examinee correctly answers a series of 4, 5, or 6 (depending on the test) items in a row and no lower-numbered items were administered, *or* when the examinee is administered Item 1. When a basal is established, the platform assigns scores of 1 (correct) to all unadministered items below the basal; these are items that the examinee would have been very likely to answer correctly if they *had*

Rapid Reference 3.3

Tests with Basal and Ceiling Rules

WJ V COG Tests	
Oral Vocabulary	5 items
Spatial Relations	5 items
Verbal Attention	5 items
Verbal Analogies	5 items
Numbers Reversed	4 items
General Information	4 items
Number Series	4 items
WJ V ACH Tests	
Picture Vocabulary	5 items
Calculation	5 items
Spelling	5 items
Oral Comprehension	5 items
Applied Problems	5 items
Math Problem Identification	5 items
Number Sense	5 items
Academic Vocabulary	5 items
Academic Facts	5 items
WJ V VTL Tests	
Nonsense Word Repetition	6 items
Sound Reversal	5 items
Sound Blending	5 items
Memory for Words	4 items

been administered. If the examinee does not correctly answer enough items in a row to obtain a basal right away, the platform will present easier items until a basal is obtained or until Item 1 has been administered. (Note that younger examinees may begin the test with Item 1; for these examinees, Item 1 *is* the basal.) The Basal Counter, located on the Bottom Ribbon of the examiner interface (see Figure 3.6), tracks progress toward the basal.

A ceiling is established when the examinee incorrectly answers a series of 4, 5, or 6 (depending on the test) items in a row and no higher-numbered items administered are correct, *or* when the highest-numbered item on the test is administered. When a ceiling is established, the platform assigns scores of 0 to any higher-numbered unadministered items; these are items that the examinee would have been very likely to answer incorrectly if they had been administered. The Ceiling Counter, located on the Bottom Ribbon of the examiner interface (see Figure 3.6), tracks progress toward the ceiling; the test ends when a ceiling is obtained or when the highest-numbered item on the test is administered.

DON'T FORGET

You do not need to track or compute basal and ceilings; the *Riverside Score*® platform will determine the order of item presentation until a basal and ceiling are established. When the platform calculates the test score at the end of a test, it automatically assigns scores of 1 (correct) to all unadministered items below the basal and scores of 0 (incorrect) to all unadministered items above the ceiling.

Tests Administered with Item Blocks

Several WJ V tests are administered using item blocks. On these tests, the examinee is administered one or more *sets* of items ("blocks") and takes *all* the items in those blocks. Block-administered tests often contain passages, stories, or distinct sets of items for which basal and ceiling administration rules would not be appropriate. Rapid Reference 3.4 lists the WJ V tests that are administered using item blocks.

When you administer a test that uses item blocks, the platform presents an appropriate initial block of items based on the examinee's default SSP. If you choose to override the default SSP before you launch the test, the platform will select an item block that is appropriate for the age or grade level you specified. Typically, the first block of items administered should be relatively easy for a typical examinee at the selected SSP level.

After you administer the initial item block, the platform evaluates the examinee's performance on the item block against the continuation requirements to determine whether to present an additional block of easier or more difficult items, or whether the test should end.

DON'T FORGET

For tests administered with item blocks, the *Riverside Score*® platform automatically ends the test when the examinee fails to meet the continuation requirements at the end of a block.

Tests Administered with Blocks and Basal and Ceiling Rules

Some WJ V tests are administered with a combination of item blocks and basal and ceiling rules. The items on these tests are grouped into blocks, with significant differences in test tasks between the blocks. The highest (i.e., most difficult) block of items is administered

Rapid Reference 3.4

Tests with Item Blocks

WJ V COG Tests:

- Matrices
- Story Recall
- Analysis-Synthesis*
- Story Comprehension
- Concept Formation**
- Visual-Auditory Learning*
- Visual Working Memory*

WJ V ACH Tests:

- Sentence Writing Accuracy
- Written Language Samples
- Oral Language Samples
- Paragraph Reading Comprehension
- Story Comprehension
- Reading Recall
- Spelling of Sounds
- Oral Reading

WJ V VTL Tests:

- Understanding Directions
- Segmentation
- Sound Deletion
- Sound Substitution

* All examinees begin with Block A and proceed forward.

** Examinees begin testing with either Block A or Block B and proceed forward.

using basal and ceiling rules *within the block*, whereas examinees who encounter any earlier block(s) will be administered all the items in the block, in order. For examinees who encounter the highest item block on each of these tests, the first item in the block is treated as the lowest-numbered item for purposes of establishing a basal. Rapid Reference 3.5 contains information about the tests that are administered using both block and basal/ceiling administration rules.

Two examples using the Letter-Word Identification test illustrate how basal and ceiling rules are used within these block-administered tests. The first student, a typical 5-year-old, starts testing with Block A (Items 1–4). The student meets the continuation requirements at the end of Block A and advances to Block B (Items 5–13). The student meets the continuation

Rapid Reference 3.5

Tests with a Combination of Item Blocks and Basal/Ceiling Rules

WJ V COG Test	**Blocks**	**Basal/Ceiling Rule**
Block Rotation	A, B*	6 items
WJ V ACH Tests	**Blocks**	**Basal/Ceiling Rule**
Letter-Word Identification	A, B, C*	6 items
Word Attack	A, B, C*	6 items
Passage Comprehension	A, B*	5 items
WJ V VTL Tests	**Blocks**	**Basal/Ceiling Rule**
Animal-Number Sequencing	A, B*	4 items
Sentence Repetition	A, B*	4 items

* Basal and ceiling rules apply within this block.

requirements at the end of Block B and advances to Block C (Items 14–89), which is administered with basal and ceiling rules. For purposes of establishing a basal on Block C, Item 14 is treated as the lowest-numbered item. Testing continues from Item 14 until the examinee meets the ceiling rule (i.e., the 6 highest-numbered administered items incorrect), at which time the test ends. The second student, a typical 16-year-old, begins testing with Item 60 in Block C. Testing continues until the student obtains a basal (i.e., the 6 lowest-numbered administered items correct, or Item 14) and a ceiling.

The *Riverside Score*® platform presents an appropriate first block of items based on the examinee's default age- or grade-level SSP. If you choose to override the default SSP before you launch the test, the platform selects an item block that is appropriate for the age or grade level you specified. The platform then evaluates the examinee's performance at the end of the first block and determines if additional block(s) of items should be administered or if the test should end.

DON'T FORGET

For tests that use a combination of block administration and basal/ceiling rules, the Riverside Score platform will determine the item block(s) to be administered. If the last block in the test is administered, the platform will administer items until a basal and a ceiling have been established within that block.

Tests Requiring a Response Booklet

You will need a WJ V Response Booklet for several tests in the WJ V ACH; Rapid Reference 3.6 lists these tests. You can purchase full-color Response Booklets directly from the publisher

Rapid Reference 3.6

WJ V ACH Tests Requiring the Response Booklet

Calculation
Spelling
Math Facts Fluency
Sentence Writing Accuracy
Applied Problems*
Written Language Samples
Sentence Writing Fluency
Math Problem Identification*
Spelling of Sounds
Letter Writing Fluency

* Provides workspace for solving problems.

(www. riversidescore.com) or you can print grayscale versions from your office printer. Follow the instructions on the Resources tab of the *Riverside Score®* platform to print and assemble the Response Booklets locally. When the platform directs you to do so during the test administration, hand the examinee the Response Booklet and a pencil. When presenting the instructions or administering sample items, do not let the examinee study the test items.

If necessary, remind the examinee to turn the page when they reach the bottom of each Response Booklet page. If the examinee makes an error while working in the Response Booklet, encourage them to cross out, rather than erase, the error.

For the Applied Problems and Math Problem Identification tests, the Response Booklet provides a blank page for the examinee to work the presented problems. Often, an analysis of the way the examinee approaches math problems provides insights into their mathematical understanding.

Tests Requiring Scoring Guides

For some tests that require the Response Booklet, you will use a scoring guide to score the examinee's written responses in the Response Booklet after the test administration is complete (see Rapid Reference 3.2). After you determine the number of points the examinee earned for each page or block of items in the Response Booklet, enter these totals in the *Riverside Score®* when prompted by the platform. Do not attempt to score these tests while the examinee is writing responses. Instead, wait until the test or session is over and then use the scoring guide to assign item scores. The scoring guides for the writing tests contain detailed criteria for assigning scores to the examinee's written responses and, in most cases, contain actual examples of correct and incorrect responses gathered from examinees during the WJ V norming study. Even after you are familiar with the WJ V test items, do not attempt to score the examinee's responses without consulting the scoring guide.

Note that on the Written Language Samples test, the platform may require you to administer additional items based on the examinee's score from the first block(s) of items administered. For this reason, score the examinee's responses to Written Language Samples and enter them in the platform before the examinee leaves the testing room, if possible.

CAUTION

Do not attempt to score the Math Facts Fluency, Sentence Writing Accuracy, Written Language Samples, Sentence Writing Fluency, or Letter Writing Fluency tests without consulting the scoring guides, even after you become familiar with the test items.

Timed Tests

Several WJ V tests require the examinee to complete as many items or provide as many responses as they can within a specific time limit. For these tests, the *Riverside Score®* platform contains built-in timers. For some timed tests, the items are presented on the iPad and the examinee responds by tapping responses. For other tests, the examinee writes responses in the Response Booklet. Still other tests require the examinee to provide oral responses. Rapid Reference 3.7 lists the tests, response formats, and time limits for the timed tests.

Tests with Audio-Recorded Prompts

Several WJ V tests contain item stimuli that are presented from an audio recording (see Rapid Reference 3.8). For these tests, the audio play interface is integrated into each item presentation screen on the *Riverside Score®* platform (see Figure 3.8). When administering items from the audio recording, click the Play button in the Examiner's View to present the item. The audio prompt will play from the examinee's iPad speaker. Each audio prompt is preceded by a single beep and followed by two beeps. After the two beeps, look expectantly at the examinee for a response.

Before administering a test with audio-recorded item prompts, use the controls included on the *Riverside Score®* platform to set the iPad's volume to a comfortable level.

DOCUMENTING QUALITATIVE INFORMATION

In addition to offering scores that reflect an examinee's current level of functioning, a standardized assessment like the WJ V can also provide comprehensive qualitative insights into the examinee's approaches, strategies, attention, and other related factors. The *Riverside Score®* platform provides several features to document these types of qualitative information.

Item-, Test-, and Test Set-Level Notes

It is often helpful to write notes that contain questions about specific items or tests or general observations about the examinee's behaviors or error patterns during the test session. The Riverside Score platform contains fields to document notes at the Item, Test,

Rapid Reference 3.7

Timed Test Formats and Time Limits

WJ V COG Tests	Response Format	Time Limit
Semantic Word Retrieval	Oral	1 minute for each item
Number-Pattern Matching	iPad Tap	3 minutes
Phonemic Word Retrieval	Oral	1 minute for each item
Letter-Pattern Matching	iPad Tap	3 minutes
Symbol Inhibition	iPad Tap	1 minute for each item set
WJ V ACH Tests	**Response Format**	**Time Limit**
Math Facts Fluency	Written	3 minutes
Sentence Reading Fluency	iPad Tap	3 minutes
Sentence Writing Fluency	Written	5 minutes
Word Reading Fluency	iPad Tap	3 minutes
Magnitude Comparison	iPad Tap	2 minutes
Letter Writing Fluency	Written	30 seconds for each trial
WJ V VTL	**Response Format**	**Time Limit**
Rapid Picture Naming	Oral	1 minute
Rapid Letter Naming	Oral	1 minute
Rapid Phoneme Naming	Oral	1 minute
Rapid Number Naming	Oral	1 minute
Rapid Quantity Naming	Oral	1 minute

and Test Set levels. You can access the notes fields at any time during testing by clicking the Notes icon on the Top Ribbon, or by clicking the Flag icon in the Bottom Ribbon. Then select Item, Test, or Test Set from the drop-down menu. Type your notes and click the Save icon. At the end of the test session, the platform will prompt you to review your notes so that you can resolve any outstanding questions prior to submitting the session for scoring. For example, if an examinee provides a response that you are unsure how to score, you may include an item-level note to remind yourself to come back to the item later to resolve the scoring question. Additionally, your notes about the examinee's response

Rapid Reference 3.8

Tests Containing Audio-Recorded Item Prompts

WJ V COG Tests:

- Oral Vocabulary
- Story Recall
- Verbal Attention
- Story Comprehension
- Numbers Reversed

WJ V ACH Tests:

- Oral Comprehension
- Sentence Writing Accuracy
- Story Comprehension
- Spelling of Sounds

WJ V VTL Tests:

- Nonsense Word Repetition
- Animal-Number Sequencing
- Understanding Directions
- Sound Blending
- Memory for Words
- Sentence Repetition
- Sound Deletion
- Sound Substitution

patterns and questions the examinee asks during the test session can be useful when writing your evaluation report. For example, you might note that a first-grade examinee has difficulty with short vowel sounds on the Letter-Word Identification and Word Attack tests. Noting these types of specific details about the examinee's errors and response styles during the test session may assist you with making specific recommendations and planning an instructional program.

Response Style and Behaviors Checklists

Because standardized testing occurs in a one-on-one setting, you can gain valuable insights by noting the examinee's response style and behaviors in reaction to the specific tasks of each test. *Riverside Score*® provides an optional qualitative checklist at the end of each test. When you select statements that describe the examinee's testing behaviors from the checklist, those statements can be included in the score report. Information you document using these checklists can provide important insights about how the individual completed

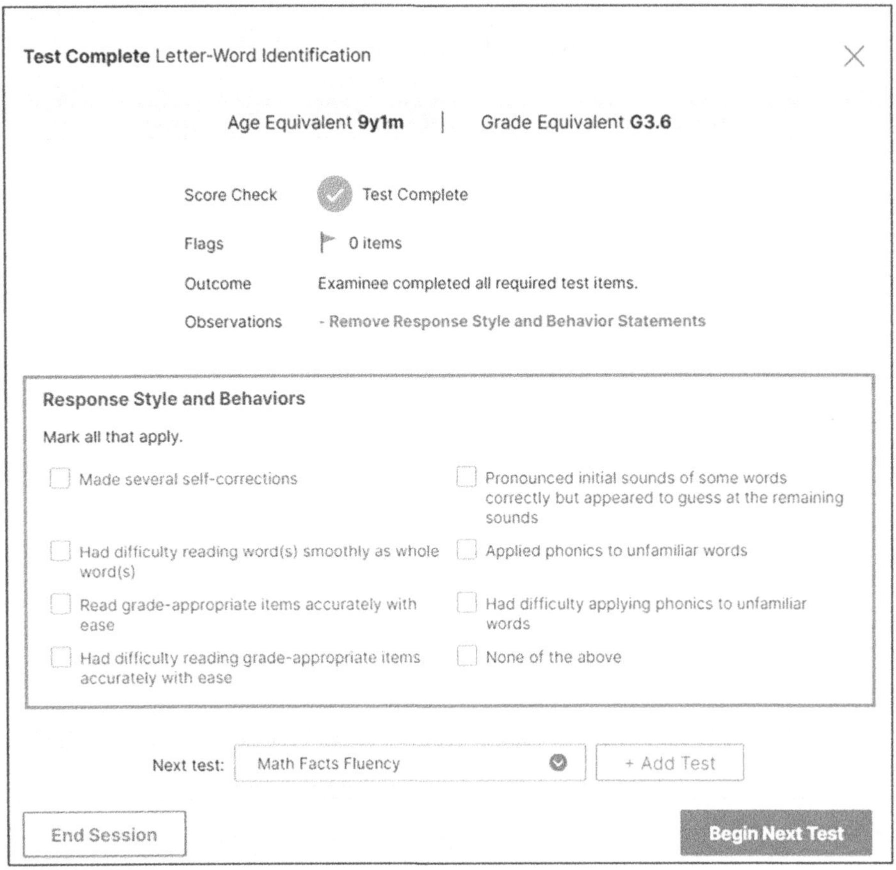

Figure 3.12 Response Style and Behaviors Checklist for Letter-Word Identification

the test tasks. For example, on the Letter-Word Identification test, you may observe that the examinee had difficulty reading words smoothly, read grade-appropriate words with ease, or had difficulty applying phonics to unfamiliar words. The Response Style and Behaviors Checklists are unique to each test. As an example, Figure 3.12 contains the Response Style and Behaviors Checklist for Letter-Word Identification.

Test Session Observations

When you have completed administration of all tests in the Test Set and prior to generating a score report, *Riverside Score®* presents a set of Test Session Observations on which you may rate the examinee's overall behaviors, demeanor, and attitude during the testing session. The last two items provide a place for you to indicate if you believe the test to be a fair assessment of the examinee's abilities, and whether you made any changes to the standardized administration procedures that might invalidate the score interpretations from the session. Figure 3.13 shows the Test Session Observations interface in the review workflow, and Rapid Reference 3.9 shows the statements provided for each of the drop-down selections in the Test Session Observations. These items are optional; however, if you choose to complete them, the information can be included in the score report.

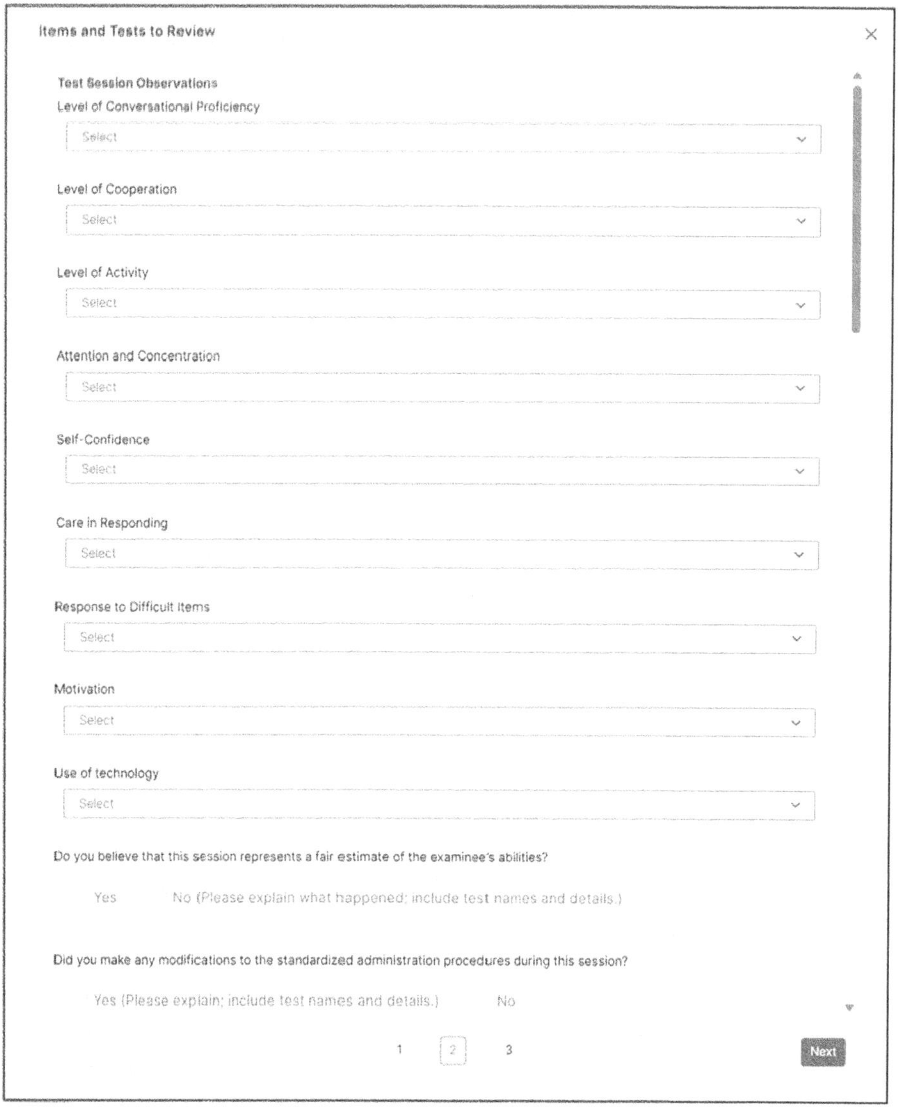

Figure 3.13 Test Session Observations

Rapid Reference 3.9

Test Session Observation Statements

Level of Conversational Proficiency:

- Very advanced; initiated and sustained conversations
- Advanced
- Typical for age/grade
- Provided basic responses to conversation questions but rarely initiated questions/conversations
- Limited
- Very limited

Level of Cooperation:

- Was exceptionally cooperative throughout the examination
- Was cooperative (typical for age/grade)
- Was uncooperative at times
- Was uncooperative throughout the examination

Level of Activity:

- Seemed lethargic
- Activity level was appropriate (typical for age/grade)
- Appeared fidgety or restless
- Was overly active for age/grade; had difficulty remaining still/seated during tasks

Attention and Concentration:

- Displayed good attention throughout
- Was attentive to tasks (typical for age/grade)
- Appeared distracted some of the time
- Needed directions or items repeated
- Was frequently inattentive and distracted
- Required frequent examiner redirection/prompts to remain focused on tasks

Self-Confidence:

- Appeared confident and self-assured
- Appeared at ease and comfortable (typical for age/grade)
- Appeared hesitant or unsure when providing responses to tasks
- Appeared tense or worried at times
- Appeared overly anxious

Care in Responding:

- Responded deliberately and assuredly
- Responded deliberately but carefully (typical for age/grade)
- Responded too quickly at times

- Responded slowly and hesitantly
- Responded impulsively and carelessly
- Attempted to begin tasks before hearing instructions/expectations in their entirety

Response to Difficult Items:

- Persevered on difficult items
- Generally persisted on difficult items (typical for age/grade)
- Attempted difficult items but gave up easily
- Made random guesses
- Required examiner encouragement to attempt and complete tasks that appeared difficult
- Would not try difficult items

Motivation:

- Was highly engaged with tasks
- Was engaged with tasks even when uncertain
- Was generally engaged with tasks (typical for age/grade)
- Was somewhat resistant to tasks
- Was resistant to tasks

Do you believe that this session represents a fair estimate of the examinee's abilities?

- Yes
- No (Please explain what happened; include test names and details.

Did you make any modifications to the standardized administration procedures during this session?

- Yes (Please explain; include test names and details.)
- No

DON'T FORGET

- The Item-, Test-, and Session-Level Notes fields are provided for you to use during the test session.
- Use the test-level Response Style and Behaviors Checklists at the end of each test to document the examinee's strategies in response to the specific test tasks.
- Use the Test Session Observations to document observational data regarding the examinee's response style, level of effort, attention, persistence, level of cooperation, and conversational proficiency throughout the testing session.

TESTING INDIVIDUALS WITH SPECIAL NEEDS

At times, you may need to adapt the standard test procedures in order to accommodate an individual who has specific limitations. *Accommodations* are changes in the standardized procedures that allow an examinee to demonstrate their abilities, but do not change the measurement of the construct or the interpretation of the test scores. In contrast, *modifications* are changes to the standardized test procedures that change the measurement of the construct and invalidate the test scores (American Educational Research Association [AERA], American Psychological Association [APA], and National Council on Measurement in Education [NCME], 2014). Familiarity with the test items and the constructs measured by each WJ V test is essential for understanding when accommodations are appropriate for examinees with specific access issues. Describe all accommodations in the session notes and in the test report. Because any change to standardized administration procedures may compromise the validity of the test score interpretations, use caution when interpreting the results. Three broad classes of individuals often require accommodations in the assessment process: young children or preschoolers, English learners (ELs), and individuals with disabilities.

DON'T FORGET

The term *accommodation* is used to denote changes with which the comparability of scores is retained, and the term ***modification*** is used to denote changes that affect the construct measured by the test (AERA et al., 2014, p. 58).

CAUTION

For norm-based score interpretations, any modification that changes the construct will invalidate the norms for score interpretations (AERA et al., 2014, p. 61).

Modifying standardized procedures for an examinee with a particular disability is inappropriate when the purpose of a test is to diagnose the presence and degree of that disability (AERA et al., 2014). For example, allowing a student who is being evaluated for reading fluency difficulties additional time to complete tasks on a timed reading test will limit the test's utility for determining the extent of the reading weakness.

Preschool Examinees

Some young children are uncomfortable with unfamiliar adults and may perform better if a parent is nearby. If a parent will be present during the test session, briefly explain the testing process and the importance of not assisting the child on any item before actual testing begins. Initially, some children may be shy and refuse to speak to a stranger. If a child still refuses to speak after several rapport-building activities (such as interacting with a puppet), discontinue testing and try again at a later date.

Some WJ V tests are more useful than others for assessing preschool children. For example, some tests require the examinee to have academic skills that generally do not emerge until formal schooling begins. See Rapid References 1.7 and 1.8 for the recommended age range for each WJ V test.

Possible accommodations when testing preschool children include:

- Allowing a parent to remain in the room but not directly in view of the child.
- Allowing the child to sit on a parent's lap if separation is not possible.
- Providing breaks between tests.
- Varying the activity level of tasks (e.g., fine-motor activity, oral activity).
- Providing reinforcements (e.g., stickers, snacks).
- Sitting on the floor with the child when administering the tests.
- Maintaining a fun, interesting, and appropriate testing pace.

English Learners (ELs)

Before using the WJ V (or any English test) with a student whose first language is not English, determine the individual's English proficiency and language dominance. The vocabulary and syntax used in the test instructions may be too complex for some individuals who are just learning English. Although the test instructions are controlled for complexity, in some cases, you may need to provide further explanation of the task. Note and explain this modification of the standardized testing procedures in the evaluation report because, in some cases, you will need to interpret the scores with caution.

The *Standards for Educational and Psychological Testing* (AERA et al., 2014) state that tests "should be administered in the language that is most relevant and appropriate to the test purpose" and provide guidance for testing examinees in their nonnative language:

> Test users should take into account the linguistic and cultural characteristics and relative language proficiencies of examinees who are bilingual or use multiple languages. Identifying the most appropriate language(s) for testing also requires close consideration of the context and purpose for testing. Except in cases where the purpose of testing is to determine the test taker's level of proficiency in a particular language, the test takers should be tested in the language in which they are most proficient. (p. 69)

Possible accommodations when testing ELs include:

- Using English words that may be more familiar to the individual when presenting test Introductions.
- Providing supplemental practice or reviewing test directions to enhance understanding.

CAUTION

Do not modify standardized procedures when measuring some aspect of an individual's English language ability (i.e., reading, writing, listening, or speaking skills). Do not translate test items into another language. When available, use a test in the individual's primary language.

Individuals with Disabilities

In modifying test procedures and interpreting test results for individuals with disabilities, be sensitive to the limitations that different impairments may impose on an individual's abilities and behavior. Some tests cannot be administered to individuals with profound impairments; you will need to determine the most appropriate tests on a case-by-case basis.

Hearing impairments When testing an examinee with hearing impairment:

- Be sure hearing aids are worn and functioning.
- Use the examinee's mode of communication (e.g., American Sign Language, Signed English, written responses).
- Use an interpreter if you are not proficient in the examinee's mode of communication.

Visual impairments When testing an examinee with visual impairment:

- Adjust the brightness and contrast on the iPad screen.
- Make environmental modifications (e.g., position a lamp to provide additional light or dimmed illumination).
- Allow the examinee to alter the position of the iPad.

Physical impairments When testing an examinee with physical impairment:

- Provide rest periods or breaks during the testing session to prevent fatigue.
- Modify the response mode when necessary. For example, if the examinee is unable to tap on the iPad for a test that requires tapping responses (such as Matrices or Block Rotation), the examinee may provide their responses orally (e.g., *A and C*). You can either take control of the Examinee's View and select the responses with your cursor or use the scoring interface in the Examiner's View to select Correct or Incorrect.
- When appropriate, allow use of special equipment (e.g., keyboard instead of a pencil for writing responses).

CAUTION

Use extreme caution when interpreting scores from timed tests (e.g., Letter-Pattern Matching, Magnitude Comparison) if you allow the examinee to respond orally. The change to response mode will likely impact the response time for each item, potentially resulting in deflated scores.

Learning disabilities and reading disabilities In many instances, the purpose of the WJ V assessment is to determine the severity of an impairment in learning or reading; therefore, accommodations are usually not provided on the WJ V tests for students who struggle with learning or reading. Although an accommodation may improve performance, the resulting score would not be an accurate reflection of a person's capabilities. Clearly, you would not want to read the reading test items to an individual with reading difficulties, as the main purpose of the evaluation is to determine the extent and severity of the reading problem, not to measure oral language comprehension. The goal of the evaluation is to determine an individual's unique pattern of strengths and weaknesses and then to use this assessment data to suggest appropriate classroom accommodations and recommend possible teaching strategies and interventions.

Behavioral disorders/attention-deficit/hyperactivity disorder Clinical expertise is needed to assess children with behavior or attention difficulties. You can often use specific behavioral management techniques that will increase the likelihood of compliance. It is a good idea to become familiar with the typical classroom behaviors of students who exhibit severe attention or behavior challenges prior to conducting an assessment. You will need to determine whether the test results provide a valid representation of the individual's present performance level. When evaluating a student with challenging behaviors, attempt to determine the effects of the problem behaviors on the assessment process and how the behaviors affect performance. For example, Robert, a third-grade student with severe behavioral challenges, completed three items on the Written Language Samples test. He then refused to write any more sentences, stating that he hated writing and had to do too much in school anyway. The examiner tried to encourage Robert, but he was adamant that he was not doing any more. In this situation, the test results would not be representative of Robert's writing abilities, but they do suggest how his behavior affects his school performance.

DON'T FORGET

Reminders About Modifying Standardized Procedures:

- Use professional judgment on a case-by-case basis when using modifications.
- Modifying standardized procedures may invalidate the normative interpretation of test results.
- Note any modifications in the report.

CONFIDENTIALITY OF TEST MATERIALS

Test security, which includes careful storing of the materials and protecting test content, is the responsibility of test users. Keep your *Riverside Score®* login credentials secure and do not share them with anyone. Do not leave the Response Booklets unattended where others may see them and look at the test items. During a discussion of the test results, you may generally describe the types of items included but avoid disclosing specific test content. Use examples similar to the test items without revealing the actual test items.

The issue of test confidentiality is also important. Do not share test content or results with curious nonprofessionals or make materials available for public inspection. During testing or after testing has been completed, do not inform an examinee of whether answers are correct or incorrect and do not explain the correct answers to any of the questions. For example, it would not be appropriate to show a student how to solve a problem on the Calculation test after the test session was complete. Occasionally, individuals will request information. Usually, you will be able to recognize whether it is appropriate or inappropriate to supply the requested information. If you should not supply the requested information, respond with a comment such as, "I'm not supposed to share that information."

CAUTION

Disclosing specific test content can invalidate future administrations. As noted in the *WJ V Examiner's Manual*, the WJ V is not to be used in programs that require disclosure of questions or answers.

TEST YOURSELF

1. **You must administer all of the tests in the Standard Batteries before using the tests in the Extended Batteries. True or False?**
2. **For which of the following tests is it imperative that you know the pronunciation of all the items on the test? (Select all that apply.)**
   (A) Oral Vocabulary
   (B) Letter-Word Identification
   (C) Oral Reading
   (D) Word Attack
3. **Which of the following tests contain audio-recorded item prompts? (Select all that apply.)**
   (A) Spelling of Sounds
   (B) Spelling
   (C) Oral Vocabulary
   (D) Sound Reversal
4. **Which test is *not* timed?**
   (A) Sentence Reading Fluency
   (B) Semantic Word Retrieval
   (C) Oral Comprehension
   (D) Magnitude Comparison
5. **Which test does *not* require the use of the Response Booklet?**
   (A) Spelling
   (B) Matrices
   (C) Applied Problems
   (D) Sentence Writing Fluency
6. **Which of the following apply when using the Response Booklet? (Select all that apply.)**
   (A) If you are printing the Response Booklet on your office printer, print on only one side of the paper.
   (B) Remind the examinee to erase their mistakes.

(C) Allow the examinee to skip around on the page, but do not allow them to turn the page until instructed.
(D) Score the examinee's responses to Written Language Samples and Sentence Writing Accuracy during the test.
(E) Score the examinee's responses to Spelling of Sounds and Calculation during the test.

7. **You may select age- or grade-based suggested starting points, but once you select a default starting point, you cannot change it later. True or False?**
8. **The WJ V may be used if an individual has physical or sensory impairments. True or False?**
9. **It is okay to share a student's specific responses to test items if their parent requests it. True or False?**
10. **You are testing a fifth-grade student on Memory for Words, which has a basal and ceiling rule of 4. The student started testing with Item 6, and answered the first 7 questions (Items 6–12) correctly. Before you present Item 13, she asks if she could change her response to an earlier item (Item 8). You use the Test Navigation panel to return to Item 8, and the student gives a new, but incorrect, answer. What should you do?**
    (A) Change the Item 8 score from correct to incorrect and then use the Test Navigation panel to return to Item 13.
    (B) Change the Item 8 score from correct to incorrect and then click Next. The platform will automatically route to Item 4 to establish a new basal.
    (C) Change the Item 8 score from correct to incorrect and then use the Back button on your browser to return to Item 13.
    (D) Do not change the score for Item 8 because the student answered it correctly the first time.

ANSWERS

1. **False.** The WJ V tests can be administered in any order. You can arrange the tests into your desired order when you are creating a Test Set. Alternatively, you can skip tests during the test session and come back to them later.
2. **B, C, and D.**
3. **A and C.**
4. **C.**
5. **B.**
6. **A and E.**
7. **False.** You can select either age- or grade-based suggested starting points, and you can change the starting point for any test during the testing session.
8. **True.** The WJ V tests can be used with individuals who have disabilities such as motor, visual, or hearing impairments. Document any deviations from standardized testing procedures and note them in your report; scores should be interpreted with caution.
9. **False.** In most cases, it is not acceptable to share the content of individual test items with a parent or other nonprofessional. Maintain security of the test content at all times.
10. **B.** When an examinee changes a response that "breaks" a basal, the platform will immediately route to a lower-numbered item to establish a new basal. Do not use the Back button on your browser to navigate between test items.

REFERENCE

American Educational Research Association [AERA], American Psychological Association [APA], & National Council on Measurement in Education [NCME]. (2014). *Standards for educational and psychological testing.* American Educational Research Association.

Four

WJ V COGNITIVE TEST ADMINISTRATION

This chapter provides an overview of the administration procedures for the WJ V Cognitive tests. Whether you are just learning the WJ V or need a review of certain tests, this chapter can serve as a guide or refresher. At the end of the chapter, there is a Test Yourself quiz. After studying or reviewing the test administration procedures in this chapter, you may wish to do a practice administration of each test.

Before administering each test on the digital platform, review the Administration Overview screen for administration and scoring reminders, and consult the Things to Know panel to see if the test is timed or uses audio recordings.

ORAL VOCABULARY

Oral Vocabulary (Rapid Reference 4.1) is a measure of vocabulary knowledge (Gc). It is administered in two parts (i.e., subtests). In the first part, Synonyms, the examinee listens to words from an audio recording and provides synonyms. In the second part, Antonyms, the examinee listens to words from an audio recording and provides antonyms. Oral Vocabulary is recommended for ages 5 and older. It contributes to the General Intellectual Ability (GIA), Brief Intellectual Ability (BIA), Gf-Gc Composite, and Comprehension-Knowledge (Gc) clusters.

Administration. To obtain scores for this test, administer both subtests. Always administer Synonyms immediately before Antonyms. On each subtest, all examinees begin with Sample Items A and B and are then routed to an appropriate starting item.

Essentials of WJ V™ Assessment, First Edition. Erica M. LaForte, Nancy Mather, and W. Joel Schneider.

Rapid Reference 4.1

Key Administration Points for Oral Vocabulary

- Recommended for ages 5 and older.
- Know the correct pronunciations for all words on the test.
- Use the Suggested Starting Point or select a different starting point.
- Always administer Antonyms immediately after Synonyms.
- On both Synonyms and Antonyms, administer Sample Item A orally, and administer Sample Item B and all test items from the audio recording.
- Score as correct responses that differ only in verb tense or number (singular/plural).
- Score as incorrect responses that become a different part of speech.
- Query the examinee's response when instructed by the platform.

Present Sample Item A orally, and present Sample Item B and all test items from the audio recording. You may opt to administer all items orally if the examinee appears to have difficulty understanding the audio-recorded item prompts. If you administer the item prompts orally, be certain that you know the correct pronunciation of all the stimulus words.

Unless noted, accept only one-word responses. If an examinee provides a two-word response, ask for a one-word answer. On Antonyms, if the examinee says the item preceded by *non-* or *un-*, ask for another answer unless otherwise indicated in the scoring key.

Accept words that differ from the correct response in verb tense (e.g., *standing* for *stand*), possessive case (e.g., *dad's* for *dad*), or number (e.g., *foot* for *feet* or *strangers* for *stranger*). Score a response as incorrect if it differs from the correct response in the part of speech (for example, if it substitutes *shape*, a noun, for *shaping* a verb). Do not penalize the examinee for mispronunciations resulting from articulation errors, dialect variations, or regional speech patterns.

The platform alerts you after 30 seconds if you have not selected a response from the scoring key. Encourage the examinee to respond. If the examinee is not actively engaged, click No Response and advance to the next item.

You may repeat an item if the examinee requests it.

Some items require you to query certain examinee responses. Read the query prompt exactly as it appears on the screen and then score the examinee's next response.

Each subtest ends when the examinee reaches a ceiling of five consecutive items incorrect, or when Item 25 (Synonyms) or Item 30 (Antonyms) is administered.

Item scoring. For each item, click the word in the scoring key that matches the examinee's response. If the examinee says a word that does not appear in the scoring key, use the Other–1 option for a correct response or the Other–0 option for an incorrect response. Optionally, you can also type the examinee's response into the Other text field for later analysis. The platform assigns 1 point for correct responses and 0 points for incorrect responses. If you click I Don't Know or No Response, the item is scored incorrect (0 points).

Possible administration errors. Possible administration errors include mispronouncing the words when administering the items orally and not querying when the examinee's response requires it.

MATRICES

Matrices (Rapid Reference 4.2) is a measure of fluid reasoning (Gf). It requires the examinee to identify the piece that completes a 2 × 2 or 3 × 3 figural matrix. To be correct, the examinee's response must complete the matrix both horizontally and vertically. For some 3 × 3 matrices, the correct response completes the matrix horizontally, vertically, and diagonally. Matrices is recommended for ages 6 and older. It contributes to the GIA, BIA, Gf-Gc Composite, and Fluid Reasoning (Gf) clusters.

Administration. This test includes animated video introductions; play each video introduction only one time. All examinees start with Introduction 1. Examinees in Preschool to Grade 6 then begin testing with Block A (2 × 2 matrices; Items 1–8), while examinees in Grade 7–12 and all adults begin testing with Block B (2 × 2 matrices; Items 9–16). The examinee is routed to an appropriate second block of Items (A, C, or D) based on their score from the first block administered, or the test ends for examinees who started with Block A but did not meet the continuation requirements. For examinees who are routed to Block C (3 × 3 matrices; Items 17–24) or Block D (3 × 3 matrices; Items 25–32), administer Introduction 2 and Sample Items A and B.

Item 1 and Sample Items A and B contain animated error feedback; when examinees select an incorrect response to any of these items, the platform automatically plays the feedback video.

Examinees respond to each item on this test by tapping one of the four response options (labeled A through D) on their iPad screen. If the examinee wishes to change a response, instruct them to tap the option again to deselect it, and then tap a different response.

Rapid Reference 4.2

Key Administration Points for Matrices

- Recommended for ages 6 and older.
- Use the Suggested Starting Point or select a different starting point.
- Play each introduction video only one time.
- The examinee can tap a response again to deselect it.
- Follow the prompts provided by the platform for item time limits.

An examinee who has motor impairments or other difficulties with tapping may respond by saying the letter that corresponds to their selection. If the examinee provides oral responses, you can either take control of the iPad on the Examinee's View and click the examinee's response or click Correct in the scoring interface. The green icon on the Examinee's View indicates the correct response.

During administration of this test, examinees sometimes tap to highlight responses they are considering; be careful not to advance the screen until you are certain the examinee has finished responding. If necessary, say: *Are you finished?* or wait for the examinee to look up at you before advancing to the next item.

The platform alerts you if the examinee has not responded after 30 seconds for items in Blocks A and B, and after 60 seconds for items in Blocks C and D. Encourage the examinee to respond. If the examinee is not actively engaged in solving the matrix after prompting, click No Response and advance to the next item.

The test ends when the examinee either does not meet the continuation requirements after Block A, or when the examinee has completed two blocks of items.

Item scoring. Based on the examinee's tapped response, the platform scores each item as correct (1 point) or incorrect (0 points).

Possible administration error. A possible administration error includes allowing the examinee additional time to solve the matrix after the platform displays the 30- or 60-second prompt.

SPATIAL RELATIONS

Spatial Relations (Rapid Reference 4.3) is a measure of visual processing (Gv) that requires the examinee to identify the pieces that go together to form a complete shape. Correct pieces can be rotated but not flipped. Spatial Relations is recommended for ages 4 and older. It contributes to the GIA and Visual Processing (Gv) clusters.

Administration. All examinees begin with Introduction 1. Sample Items A and B are presented to all examinees to ensure that the examinee understands the test task. Examinees in Preschool to Grade 5 begin testing with Item 1, whereas those in Grades 6 to 12 are first routed to Sample Item C and then begin testing with Item 11.

Rapid Reference 4.3

Key Administration Points for Spatial Relations

- Recommended for ages 4 and older.
- Use the Suggested Starting Point or select a different starting point.
- The examinee can tap a response again to deselect it.
- On items with three pieces, if the examinee taps only two pieces, say "*And what else?*" up through Item 29.

The sample items provide feedback for correct and incorrect responses.

Examinees respond to each item on this test by tapping response options (labeled A through F) on their iPad screen. If the examinee wishes to change a response, instruct them to tap the option again to deselect it, and then tap a different response. An examinee who has motor impairments or other difficulties with tapping may respond by saying the letters that correspond to their selections. If the examinee provides oral responses, you can either take control of the iPad on the Examinee's View and click the examinee's responses or click Correct in the scoring interface. The green icons on the Examinee's View indicate the correct responses.

During administration of this test, examinees sometimes tap to highlight responses they are considering; be careful not to advance the screen until you are certain the examinee has finished responding. If necessary, say: *Are you finished?* or wait for the examinee to look up at you before advancing to the next item.

Most items on this test require the examinee to select two pieces; some later items require the examinee to select three pieces. On puzzles that have three pieces, if the examinee taps only two pieces, say: *And what else*? up through Item 29; do not provide this prompt on subsequent items. The examinee may tap the pieces in any order.

The test ends when the examinee reaches a ceiling of five consecutive items incorrect or when Item 35 is administered.

Item scoring. Based on the examinee's tapped responses, the platform scores each item correct (1 point) or incorrect (0 points). All required pieces must be tapped for the item to be scored correct.

Possible administration errors. Possible administration errors include not presenting the sample item feedback and not asking *And what else?* if the examinee identifies only two pieces when there are three.

STORY RECALL

Story Recall (Rapid Reference 4.4) is a measure of long-term storage (Gl). The examinee listens to stories from an audio recording and then retells the stories with as much detail as possible. Story Recall is recommended for ages 4 and older. It contributes to the GIA and Long-Term Storage (Gl) clusters.

Administration. The platform suggests an appropriate starting block. Examinees in Preschool to Grade 1 begin with Block A (Stories 1 and 2); examinees in Grades 2–5 begin with Block B (Stories 3 and 4); examinees in Grades 6–8 begin with Block D (Stories 5 and 6); and examinees in Grades 9–12 and all adults begin with Block D (Stories 7 and 8).

Press the Play button to present the story from the audio recording. When the story ends, the examinee hears two beeps and then begins retelling the story in as much detail as they can remember. The examinee does *not* need to recall the elements in the correct order.

As the examinee recalls the details in the story, click to select the correctly recalled elements. An element is correctly recalled if the examinee says the word(s) in bold type. Accept a response that is a synonym of the bold word (e.g., *houses* for *homes*), as long as the response preserves the meaning of the word. If a bold word is a proper name, accept any reasonable

Rapid Reference 4.4

Key Administration Points for Story Recall

- Recommended for ages 4 and older.
- Use the Suggested Starting Point or select a different starting point.
- Play each story only one time.
- Words in bold type must be recalled exactly with a few exceptions (synonyms, e.g., *houses* for *homes*; different verb tenses, e.g., *go* for *going*; singular or plural, e.g., *bubbles* for *bubble*; a derivation of a name, e.g., *Douglas* for *Doug*; or the addition/removal of possessive case, e.g., *dad's* for *dad*).
- Times and numbers (e.g., *two o'clock, fifty*) must be recalled *exactly*.
- The elements may be recalled in any order.

derivation of the name (e.g., *Douglas* for *Doug*). Accept words that differ in verb tense (e.g., *go* for *going*) or possessive case (e.g., *dad's* for *dad*). If the bold word is singular (e.g., *bubble*), accept a plural response (e.g., *bubbles*), and vice-versa. However, if a bold word is a time or number (e.g., *two o'clock* or *fifty*), the examinee must recall the time or number *exactly* to receive credit. Do not penalize the examinee for mispronunciations resulting from articulation errors, dialect variations, or regional speech patterns.

If the examinee does not respond after the two beeps, say: *Tell me anything about the story you remember.* Do not replay any of the stories. Based on the examinee's score from the first two stories that were administered, the examinee will be routed to an easier or more difficult block of stories, or the test ends. In most cases, an examinee will hear a maximum of four stories (two blocks); however, in rare cases, an examinee may hear six stories (three blocks) before the test ends.

You may opt to administer the stories orally if the examinee appears to have difficulty understanding the audio-recorded stories. If you administer the stories orally, read the stories *exactly* as they are presented on the screen, at the same pace and with the same inflection as the audio-recorded stories.

Item scoring. The platform assigns 1 point for every correctly recalled bold element. If you are unsure whether you scored the story correctly, you may review the test's audio capture prior to submitting the test set for reporting.

Possible administration errors. Possible administration errors include not scoring the elements correctly and playing a story more than one time.

SEMANTIC WORD RETRIEVAL

Semantic Word Retrieval (Rapid Reference 4.5) is a measure of retrieval fluency (Gr). The examinee says as many words as possible that fit into a semantic category. There are three items, each with a 1-minute time limit. Semantic Word Retrieval is recommended for ages 4 and older. It contributes to the GIA and Retrieval Fluency (Gr) clusters.

Rapid Reference 4.5

Key Administration Points for Semantic Word Retrieval

- Recommended for ages 4 and older.
- Administer all three items.
- Do not count duplicate responses as correct.
- Do not ask the examinee to repeat a response.
- Accept variations of a word as correct.
- If you accidentally click the plus button for an incorrect response, click the minus button to remove the response from the count of correct responses.

Administration. Administer all three items to all examinees. For each item, use the Start Timer button to start the timer; the platform will alert you and the examinee when 1 minute is up. Allow the examinee to work for the full minute on each item; do not stop the timer early.

Count each unique correct response one time by clicking the plus (+) button on your screen. Use the minus (–) button to adjust the score if you inadvertently click the plus button too many times. Do *not* use the minus button to count incorrect responses.

CAUTION

Do not click the minus button for incorrect responses.

For Item 1 (foods and drinks), accept brand names of foods or drinks (e.g., *Coke®*, *Spaghetti-Os®*). Also accept different variations of the same type of food or drink (e.g., *Swiss cheese, cheddar cheese, American cheese*). For Item 2 (names of people), accept variations of the same name (e.g., *Bob, Bobby, Robert*) and familial relationships (e.g., *mom, mommy, ma*). For Item 3 (animals), accept variations of the same type of animal (e.g., *bear, grizzly bear, black bear, polar bear*).

Do not count duplicate words within an item; for example, if the examinee says *giraffe* two times, click the + button only one time. If you cannot remember whether the examinee has already said a word, do not stop the examinee to ask if the word was already named; you can review the voice recording later to check your scoring accuracy, and—if necessary—you can adjust the score then.

Do not penalize the examinee for mispronunciations resulting from articulation errors, dialect variations, or regional speech patterns.

If the examinee pauses for 10 seconds, say: *Go ahead. Say the words as quickly as you can.* However, do not provide this prompt if the examinee appears to be engaged in thinking of words.

Item scoring. For each correct response, click the plus (+) button. In the event you click the plus button too many times, click the minus (–) button to adjust the score. Do not use the minus (–) button to record incorrect responses. The platform computes

DON'T FORGET

After you complete testing, you can review the voice recording for any test to ensure that you scored all the items accurately. The voice recordings are deleted from the *Riverside Score®* platform 90 days after you first generate a score report.

the total score by adding the number of correct responses across the three items.

Possible administration errors. Possible administration errors include failing to give credit for variations of correct responses, counting duplicate responses as correct, and using the minus (−) button for incorrect responses.

VERBAL ATTENTION

Verbal Attention (Rapid Reference 4.6) is a measure of attention and memory (Gwm). The examinee hears a series of animals and numbers and then answers a specific question about the sequence of information. Verbal Attention is recommended for ages 4 and older. It contributes to the GIA, BIA, Auditory Working Memory Capacity (Gwm), and Cognitive Efficiency (CE) clusters.

Administration. The platform suggests an appropriate starting item. Examinees in Preschool to Grade 3 begin with Sample Items A and B and Item 1. Examinees in Grades 4 through 12 and all adults begin with Sample C and Item 7.

Administer Samples B and C and all test items from the audio recording. You may opt to administer all items orally if the examinee appears to have difficulty understanding the audio-recorded item prompts. If you administer the item prompts orally, say them exactly as they are presented on the audio recording, at a rate of one word per second. Drop your voice slightly at the end of each series so the examinee knows that the series has ended. After the series of animals and numbers is presented, read the test question orally to the examinee.

You may repeat the sample items, but do not repeat any of the test items.

The test ends when the examinee reaches a ceiling of five consecutive items incorrect or when Item 36 is administered.

Rapid Reference 4.6

Key Administration Points for Verbal Attention

- Recommended for ages 4 and older.
- Use the Suggested Starting Point or select a different starting point.
- Administer Sample Item A orally and administer Sample Items B and C and all test items from the audio recording.
- Other than the sample items, do not replay or repeat any of the test items.

Item scoring. For each item, click the option in the scoring key that matches the examinee's response. If the examinee provides an incorrect response, click Incorrect. The platform assigns 1 point for correct responses and 0 points for incorrect responses. For items that specify a particular order, the response must be in that order to be counted as correct.

Possible administration errors. Possible administration errors include giving credit for an item where order is specified but the response is in the wrong order or playing an item more than one time.

NUMBER-PATTERN MATCHING

Number-Pattern Matching (Rapid Reference 4.7) is a measure of perceptual speed (Gs). The examinee taps on the two identical numbers in a row of six. The test has a 3-minute time limit. Number Pattern Matching is recommended for ages 4 and older. It contributes to the GIA, Cognitive Processing Speed (Gs), and Cognitive Efficiency (CE) clusters.

Administration. All examinees begin with Introduction 1, followed by Sample Items A and B. On the sample items, use your cursor to point to the row of numbers on the Examinee's View and read the item text orally to the examinee. Both sample items include feedback for correct and incorrect responses. If the examinee responds incorrectly to the first trial of Sample Item A or B, use your cursor to point to the correct responses on the Examinee's View while reading the corrective feedback. For examinees who do not respond correctly to both Sample Items A and B, even after corrective feedback, the test ends. All other examinees proceed to the Practice Exercise.

Read the Practice Exercise instructions orally to the examinee, and then click the Start Practice Exercise button to display the Practice Exercise on the examinee's iPad screen. If the examinee does not respond in 5 seconds, encourage a response. If necessary, remind the examinee to tap Done when finished.

Rapid Reference 4.7

Key Administration Points for Number-Pattern Matching

- Recommended for ages 4 and older.
- The platform will end the test if an examinee does not have 2 correct on Sample Items A and B, or if the examinee has a score of 3 or fewer correct on the Practice Exercise.
- If necessary, provide corrective feedback for examinee errors on the sample items and the Practice Exercise.
- If necessary, remind the examinee to tap Next to continue to the next screen.
- If the examinee starts skipping around, remind them to work row by row.
- If the examinee appears to disengage from the task for more than 5 seconds, say: *Go ahead and choose the two that are alike.*
- The test ends after 3 minutes or when the examinee completes all nine screens.

If the examinee makes errors on the Practice Exercise, use your cursor to deselect the examinee's incorrect response(s) on the Examinee's View and follow the script to provide corrective feedback. Allow the examinee *one attempt* to correct each error and then instruct the examinee to tap Done when finished. Do not allow the examinee more than one opportunity to correct an error and do not explain the correct response(s). Examinees who tap the correct responses in 4 or more rows in the Practice Exercise advance to the test items; for all other examinees, the test ends.

For examinees who advance to the test items, read the instructions orally to the examinee, and then click the button to start the timer and display the test items on the examinee's iPad screen. Allow the examinee the full 3 minutes to work. If necessary, remind the examinee to tap Next at the bottom of each screen to advance to the next screen. Encourage the examinee to respond to all items on each screen and not to skip around. To prevent the examinee from accidentally advancing through an entire screen of items, the Next button will not become active until the examinee taps at least one number in six rows.

If the examinee pauses for more than 5 seconds or appears disengaged from the task during the test, say *Go ahead and choose the two that are alike*; however, do not provide this reminder if the examinee appears to be thinking.

This test has nine screens of items. The platform will alert you and the examinee when 3 minutes are up. Allow the examinee to work for the full 3 minutes; do not stop the timer early. Most examinees will not complete all nine screens; however, if the examinee finishes before the 3-minute timer is up, the test will end when the examinee taps Done on the last screen.

Item scoring. The platform assigns 1 point for each correct pair, and 0 points for each row that is skipped, incorrect, or incomplete.

Possible administration errors. Possible administration errors include not providing the corrective feedback for errors on Sample Items A and B and the Practice Exercise and not reminding the examinee to work row by row if they appear to be skipping items.

VERBAL ANALOGIES

Verbal Analogies (Rapid Reference 4.8) is a measure of comprehension-knowledge (Gc) and fluid reasoning (Gf). The examinee hears an incomplete analogy and provides a word that completes the analogy. Verbal Analogies is recommended for ages 4 and older. It contributes to the GIA, Gf-Gc Composite, and Comprehension-Knowledge (Gc) clusters.

Administration. All examinees begin with Sample Items A and B. Examinees in Preschool to Grade 1 then begin testing with Item 1, and examinees in Grade 2 begin testing with Item 4. All other examinees are administered Sample Item C and are then routed to an appropriate starting item; examinees in Grades 3–6 begin with Item 9, examinees in Grades 7–12 and some adults begin with Item 12, and college-educated adults begin with Item 16.

Unless noted, accept only one-word responses. If an examinee provides a two-word response, ask for a one-word answer.

Rapid Reference 4.8

Key Administration Points for Verbal Analogies

- Recommended for ages 4 and older.
- Use the Suggested Starting Point or select a different starting point.
- Administer Sample Item A orally and administer Sample Item B and all test items from the audio recording.
- Score as correct responses that differ only in verb tense or number (singular/plural).
- Score as incorrect responses that become a different part of speech.
- Query the examinee's response when instructed by the platform.

Accept words that differ from the correct response in verb tense (e.g., *swimming* for *swims*), possessive (e.g., *dad's* for *dad*), or number (e.g., *foot* for *feet* or *puppies* for *puppy*). Score a response as incorrect if it differs from the correct response in the part of speech (for example, if it substitutes *shaping*, a noun, for *shape*, a verb). Do not penalize the examinee for mispronunciations resulting from articulation errors, dialect variations, or regional speech patterns.

The platform alerts you after 30 seconds if you have not selected a response from the scoring key. Encourage the examinee to respond. If the examinee is not actively engaged, click No Response and advance to the next item.

You may repeat an item if the examinee requests it.

Some items require you to query certain examinee responses. Read the query prompt exactly as it appears on the screen and then score the examinee's next response.

The test ends when the examinee reaches a ceiling of five consecutive items incorrect or when Item 35 is administered.

Item scoring. For each item, click the word in the scoring key that matches the examinee's response. If the examinee says a word that does not appear in the scoring key, use the Other–1 option for a correct response or the Other–0 option for an incorrect response. Optionally, you can also type the examinee's response into the Other text field for later analysis. The platform assigns 1 point for correct responses and 0 points for incorrect responses. If you click I Don't Know or No Response, the item is scored incorrect (0 points).

Possible administration errors. Possible administration errors include mispronouncing the words when administering the items orally and not querying when the examinee's response requires it.

ANALYSIS-SYNTHESIS

Analysis-Synthesis (Rapid Reference 4.9) is a controlled-learning measure of fluid reasoning (Gf). The examinee learns how to use a key to solve color puzzles and then uses deductive reasoning to determine the missing color(s) in puzzle. The rules are taught via

Rapid Reference 4.9

Key Administration Points for Analysis-Synthesis

- Recommended for ages 5 and older.
- Use the Suggested Starting Point or select a different starting point.
- Play each video introduction only one time.
- To maintain the controlled learn aspect of this test, all sample items contain animated corrective feedback for incorrect responses. For Items 1–28, you provide feedback for correct *and* incorrect responses. Always read corrective feedback *exactly* as it appears on your screen.
- Do not provide *any* feedback for Items 29–35.
- Query the examinee's response when instructed by the platform.
- Follow the prompts provided by the platform for item time limits.

animated introductions and are enforced by the feedback that is provided to the examinee on the sample items and test items. The items become more difficult as more color combinations are added to the key. Analysis-Synthesis is recommended for ages 5 and older. It contributes to the Gf-Gc Composite and Fluid Reasoning (Gf) clusters.

Administration. All examinees begin with the Color Pretest. The purpose of the Color Pretest is to determine whether the examinee is able to name colors and to rule out color vision deficiency that would prevent the examinee from being able to distinguish between the colors in the puzzles. For each Color Pretest item, the examinee taps the squares that correspond to the color you say. For examinees who do not pass the Color Pretest, the test ends and no score is assigned. Examinees who pass the Color Pretest proceed to Introduction 1.

This test includes animated video introductions; play each introduction video only one time.

To maintain the controlled learning aspect of this test, all sample items contain animated error feedback; when an examinee responds incorrectly to any of these items, the platform automatically plays the feedback video. Acknowledge correct responses on all sample items by saying, *That's right* or *That's correct*, or—for Sample Item C—by reading the feedback script provided on your screen verbatim.

On test Items 1–28, provide oral feedback to the examinee for both correct and incorrect responses. The feedback script for incorrect responses is provided by the platform. Read the feedback *exactly* as it appears on your screen and, if applicable, use your cursor to point to the puzzle on the Examinee's View. Acknowledge correct responses to Items 1–28 by saying, *That's right* or *That's correct*. Do not provide any feedback for correct or incorrect responses on Items 29–35.

Some items require you to query certain examinee responses. Read the query prompt exactly as it appears on the screen and then score the examinee's next response.

The platform alerts you after 30 seconds for Items 1–25 and after 60 seconds for Items 26–35 if you have not selected a response from the scoring key. When this happens, say: *Let's do another one*. Then click No Response and advance to the next item.

Testing continues through Item 35 unless the examinee does not meet the continuation requirements after Item 7, 19, 25, or 31.

Item scoring. Click the option in the scoring key that matches the examinee's response. If the examinee provides an incorrect response, click Incorrect. The platform assigns 1 point for correct responses and 0 points for incorrect responses. If you click I Don't Know or No Response, the item is scored incorrect (0 points).

Possible administration errors. Possible administration errors include playing an animated introduction more than one time, not reading feedback *exactly* as it appears on your screen, not providing the required feedback for correct and incorrect responses up through Item 28, providing feedback on Items 29–35, and allowing the examinee additional time to respond after the platform displays the 30- or 60-second prompt.

BLOCK ROTATION

Block Rotation (Rapid Reference 4.10) is a measure of visual processing (Gv). It requires the examinee to identify the two rotated block patterns (from among five options) that match the target block pattern. Block Rotation is recommended for ages 4 and older. It contributes to the Visual Processing (Gv) cluster.

Administration. This test includes animated video introductions; play each video introduction only one time. Examinees in preschool to Grade 2 start with Introduction 1, followed by Sample Item A, Introduction 2, Sample Item B, and Introduction 3, and then begin testing with Block A (Items 1–9). Examinees in Grades 3–12 and all adults start with Introduction 4, followed by Sample Item C, Introduction 5, and Sample Item B, and then begin testing with Block B (Items 10–28).

Sample Items A, B, and C contain animated error feedback; when an examinee selects an incorrect response to any of these items the platform automatically plays the feedback video.

Rapid Reference 4.10

Key Administration Points for Block Rotation

- Recommended for ages 4 and older.
- Use the Suggested Starting Point or select a different starting point.
- Play each introduction video only one time.
- The examinee can tap a response again to deselect it.
- Block B (Items 10–28) uses basal and ceiling rules. Examinees who do not have at least 4 correct after obtaining a ceiling on Block B will be administered all items (1–9) in Block A.

The examinee responds to each item on this test by tapping two of the five response options (labeled A, B, C, D, and E) on their iPad screen. If the examinee wishes to change a response, instruct them to tap the option again to deselect it, and then tap a different response. An examinee who has motor impairments or other difficulties with tapping may respond by saying the letters that correspond to their selections. If the examinee provides oral responses, you can either take control of the iPad on the Examinee's View and click the examinee's response or click Correct in the scoring interface. The green icons on the Examinee's View indicate the correct responses.

During administration of this test, examinees sometimes tap to highlight responses they are considering; be careful not to advance the screen until you are certain the examinee has finished responding. If necessary, say: *Are you finished?* or wait for the examinee to look up at you before advancing to the next item.

The platform alerts you when 30 seconds are up for items in Block B. Encourage the examinee to respond. If the examinee is not actively engaged in responding after prompting, click No Response and advance to the next item.

Block B (Items 10–28) is administered with basal and ceiling rules. Examinees who are administered Block B must obtain a basal (Item 10) and a ceiling (six consecutive items incorrect or Item 28) within Block B. Examinees who are administered Block B but have a score of fewer than 4 points after a ceiling is obtained are routed to Block A, unless it was already administered.

Item scoring. Based on the examinee's tapped responses, the platform scores each item correct (1 point) or incorrect (0 points).

Possible administration errors. Possible administration errors include playing the introduction videos more than one time, allowing the examinee additional time to work after the platform displays the 30-second prompt, and not confirming that the examinee is finished responding before advancing to the next item.

DON'T FORGET

Story Comprehension is also included in the Listening Comprehension and Oral Language clusters in the Achievement battery.

STORY COMPREHENSION

Story Comprehension (Rapid Reference 4.11) is a measure of listening comprehension and long-term storage (Gl). The examinee hears a short passage or story from an audio recording and then answers literal and inferential comprehension questions. Story Comprehension is the only test in the WJ V that contributes to clusters in both the Cognitive and Achievement batteries. Story Comprehension is recommended for ages 6 and older. In the Cognitive battery, it contributes to the Long-Term Storage (Gl) cluster.

Administration. Examinees in preschool to Grade 2 start with Sample Items A and B. If an examinee does not respond correctly to at least one trial of Sample Items A and B,

Rapid Reference 4.11

Key Administration Points for Story Comprehension

- Recommended for ages 6 and older.
- Use the Suggested Starting Point or select a different starting point.
- Read the stories in Sample Items A and B orally and play all other stories from the audio recording.
- Read or play each story only one time.
- Read all comprehension questions orally only one time.
- Query the examinee's response when instructed by the platform.

the test ends. Otherwise, the examinee proceeds to Block A (Stories 1–4). Examinees who have at least 6 points on Block A proceed to Block B (Stories 5–7).

All other examinees are administered two blocks of stories. Examinees in Grades 3–5 begin testing with Block B (Stories 5–7). Examinees in Grades 6 to 8 begin testing with Block C (Stories 8–10). Examinees in Grades 9–12 and all adults begin testing with Block D (Stories 11–13). Based on the score from the first block of stories, the platform routes each examinee to an appropriate (easier or more difficult) second block of stories.

Play all stories from the audio recording. Confirm the examinee is ready before clicking the Play button for each story. You may opt to present the stories orally if the examinee appears to have difficulty understanding the audio-recorded stories. If you present the stories orally, read them with the same inflection as the audio-recorded passages. Be certain that you know the correct pronunciation of all the words in the stories. Do not replay or repeat any story on this test.

Read each comprehension question clearly and with inflection. Read each question only one time.

Some items require you to query certain examinee responses. Read the query prompt exactly as it appears on the screen and then score the examinee's next response.

Item scoring. For each item, select the examinee's response from the scoring key or click Incorrect. Some items allow any reasonable response; use your professional judgment to determine if the examinee's response is correct. If you click I Don't Know or No Response, the item is scored incorrect (0 points).

Possible administration errors. Possible administration errors include replaying a story or repeating a comprehension question and not querying when the examinee's response requires it.

PHONEMIC WORD RETRIEVAL

Phonemic Word Retrieval (Rapid Reference 4.12) is a measure of retrieval fluency (Gr). The examinee says as many words as possible that start with specific phonemes. There are three items, each with a 1-minute time limit. Phonemic Word Retrieval is recommended

Rapid Reference 4.12

Key Administration Points for Phonemic Word Retrieval

- Recommended for ages 5 and older.
- Administer all three items.
- Pronounce letters between slashes as the letter sound. Be careful not to add a schwa sound.
- Do not count duplicate responses as correct.
- Do not ask the examinee to repeat a response.
- If you accidentally click the plus button for an incorrect response, click the minus button to remove the response from the count of correct responses.

for ages 5 and older. It contributes to the Retrieval Fluency (Gr) and Phonemic Retrieval Fluency (Gr) clusters.

Administration. Administer all three items to all examinees. When you read the prompt for each item, pronounce the letter between slashes (i.e., /t/ for Item 1, /m/ for Item 2, and /b/ for Item 3) as the sound the letter makes, not the name of the letter. Be careful not to add a schwa sound to the phoneme (e.g., for Item 2, pronounce /m/ as *mm* and not as *mə-muh*).

For each item, use the Start Timer button to start the timer; the platform will alert you and the examinee when 1 minute is up. Allow the examinee to work for the full minute on each item; do not stop the timer early.

Count each unique correct response one time by clicking the plus (+) button on your screen. Use the minus (−) button to adjust the score if you inadvertently click the plus button too many times. Do *not* use the minus button to count incorrect responses.

For all items, if the examinee says the example word from the item instructions (i.e., *milk* for Item 1, *top* for Item 2, or *boy* for Item 3), do not count the word as correct. For Item 2 (/t/), do not count words that begin with the /th/ sound as correct.

Do not count duplicate words within an item; for example, if the examinee says *tiger* two times, click the + button only one time. If you cannot remember whether the examinee has already said a word, do not stop the examinee to ask if the word was already named; you can review the voice recording later to check your scoring accuracy, and—if necessary—you can adjust the score then.

Do not penalize the examinee for mispronunciations resulting from articulation errors, dialect variations, or regional speech patterns.

If the examinee pauses for 10 seconds, say: *Go ahead. Say the words as quickly as you can.* However, do not provide this prompt if the examinee appears to be engaged in thinking of words.

Item scoring. For each correct response, click the plus (+) button. In the event you click the plus button too many times, click the minus (−) button to adjust the score. Do not use the minus (−) button to record incorrect responses. The platform computes the total score by adding the number of correct responses across the three items.

Possible administration errors. Possible administration errors include mispronouncing the letter sounds when you read the item instructions, counting duplicate responses as correct, and using the minus (−) button for incorrect responses.

CAUTION

Do not click the minus button for incorrect responses.

NUMBERS REVERSED

Numbers Reversed (Rapid Reference 4.13) is a measure of auditory working memory (Gwm). The examinee hears a series of numbers and then repeats the numbers in reverse order. Numbers Reversed is recommended for ages 5 and older. It contributes to the Auditory Working Memory Capacity (Gwm) cluster.

Administration. The platform suggests an appropriate starting item. Examinees in Preschool to Grade 4 begin with Sample Item A and Item 1, examinees in Grade 5–12 and average-ability adults begin with Sample Item B and Item 6, and above-average adults begin with Sample Items C and D and Item 11. The platform evaluates the examinee's performance after Sample Items B and C; examinees who do not respond correctly to the sample item in two trials are routed back to the prior sample item, unless it was already administered. This ensures that each examinee begins testing at an appropriately difficult test item.

Administer Sample Items A, B, and C, and Items 1–10 orally. Administer Sample Item D and Items 11–34 from the audio recording. You may opt to administer all items orally if the examinee appears to have difficulty understanding the audio-recorded item prompts. If you administer the item prompts orally, say them exactly as they are presented on the audio recording, at a rate of one number per second. Drop your voice slightly at the end of each series so the examinee knows that the series has ended.

Rapid Reference 4.13

Key Administration Points for Numbers Reversed

- Recommended for ages 5 and older.
- Use the Suggested Starting Point or select a different starting point.
- Administer Sample Items A, B, and C and Items 1–10 orally, and administer Sample Item D and Items 11–34 from the audio recording.
- Other than the sample items, do not replay or repeat any of the test items.

If an examinee responds incorrectly to the first trial of a sample item, read the corrective feedback before advancing to the second trial. The platform provides corrective feedback for Items 1, 6, and 11 if the examinee says the numbers exactly as they were presented instead of saying them in reverse order. If this happens, read the corrective feedback before advancing to the next item.

You may repeat the sample items, but do not repeat any of the test items.

The test ends when the examinee reaches a ceiling of five consecutive items incorrect or when Item 34 is administered.

Item scoring. For each item, click the option in the scoring key that matches the examinee's response. If the examinee provides an incorrect response, click Incorrect. The platform assigns 1 point for correct responses and 0 points for incorrect responses.

Possible administration errors. Possible administration errors include not reading corrective feedback when it is provided or repeating an item prompt.

LETTER-PATTERN MATCHING

Letter-Pattern Matching (Rapid Reference 4.14) is a measure of perceptual speed (Gs). The examinee taps on the two identical letters or letter patterns in a row of six. The test has a 3-minute time limit. Letter-Pattern Matching is recommended for ages 4 and older. It contributes to the Cognitive Processing Speed (Gs) cluster.

Administration. All examinees begin with Introduction 1, followed by Sample Items A and B. On the sample items, use your cursor to point to the row of letters on the Examinee's View and read the item text orally to the examinee. Both sample items include feedback for correct and incorrect responses. If the examinee responds incorrectly to the first trial of Sample Item A or B, use your cursor to point to the correct responses on the Examinee's View while reading the corrective feedback. For examinees who do not respond

Rapid Reference 4.14

Key Administration Points for Letter-Pattern Matching

- Recommended for ages 4 and older.
- The platform will end the test if an examinee does not have 2 correct on Sample Items A and B, or if the examinee has a score of 3 or fewer correct on the Practice Exercise.
- If necessary, provide corrective feedback for examinee errors on the sample items and the Practice Exercise.
- If necessary, remind the examinee to tap Next to continue to the next screen.
- If an examinee starts skipping around, remind them to work row by row.
- If the examinee appears to disengage from the task for more than 5 seconds, say: *Go ahead and choose the two that are alike.*
- The test ends after 3 minutes or when the examinee completes all 10 screens.

correctly to both Sample Items A and B, even after corrective feedback, the test ends. All other examinees proceed to the Practice Exercise.

Read the Practice Exercise instructions orally to the examinee, and then click the Start Practice Exercise button to display the Practice Exercise on the examinee's iPad screen. If the examinee does not respond in 5 seconds, encourage a response. If necessary, remind the examinee to tap Done when finished.

If the examinee makes errors on the Practice Exercise, use your cursor to deselect the examinee's incorrect response(s) on the Examinee's View and follow the script to provide corrective feedback. Allow the examinee *one attempt* to correct each error and then instruct the examinee to tap Done when finished. Do not allow the examinee more than one opportunity to correct an error and do not explain the correct response(s). Examinees who tap the correct responses in 4 or more rows of the Practice Exercise advance to the test items; for all other examinees, the test ends.

For examinees who advance to the test items, read the instructions orally to the examinee, and then click the button to start the timer and display the test items on the examinee's iPad screen. Allow the examinee the full 3 minutes to work. If necessary, remind the examinee to tap Next at the bottom of each screen to advance to the next screen. Encourage the examinee to respond to all items on each screen and not to skip around. To prevent the examinee from accidentally advancing through an entire screen of items, the Next button will not become active until the examinee taps at least one letter or letter combination in six rows.

If the examinee pauses for more than 5 seconds or appears disengaged from the task during the test, say *Go ahead and choose the two that are alike*; however, do not provide this reminder if the examinee appears to be thinking.

This test has 10 screens of items. The platform will alert you and the examinee when 3 minutes are up. Allow the examinee to work for the full 3 minutes; do not stop the timer early. Most examinees will not complete all 10 screens; however, if the examinee finishes before the 3-minute timer is up, the test will end when the examinee taps Done on the last screen.

Item scoring. The platform assigns 1 point for each correct pair, and 0 points for each row that is skipped, incorrect, or incomplete.

Possible administration errors. Possible administration errors include not providing the corrective feedback for errors on Sample Items A and B and the Practice Exercise and not reminding the examinee to work row by row if they appear to be skipping items.

GENERAL INFORMATION

General Information (Rapid Reference 4.15) is a measure of comprehension-knowledge (Gc). It is administered in two parts (i.e., subtests). In the first part, Where, the examinee answers questions that begin with *Where would you find ...*. In the second part, What, the examinee answers questions that begin with *What would you do with ...*. General Information is recommended for ages 5 and older. It does not contribute to any WJ V clusters.

Rapid Reference 4.15

Key Administration Points for General Information

- Recommended for ages 5 and older.
- Know the correct pronunciations for all words on the test.
- Use the Suggested Starting Point or select a different starting point.
- Always administer What immediately after Where.
- Query the examinee's response when instructed by the platform.

Administration. Before administering this test, make sure you know the correct pronunciation of all the words in the item prompts. If you are unsure about a pronunciation, consult a standard dictionary or the Item Pronunciation Guide on the Resources tab of the *Riverside Score®* platform.

To obtain scores for this test, administer both subtests. Always administer Where immediately before What. The platform suggests an appropriate starting item for each subtest. On Where, examinees in Preschool to Grade 6 begin with Item 1, examinees in Grades 7–12 and average adults begin with Item 6, and college-educated adults begin with Item 12. On What, examinees in Preschool to Kindergarten begin with Item 1, examinees in Grades 1–3 begin with Item 4, examinees in Grades 4–6 begin with Item 6, examinees in Grades 7–9 begin with Item 8, and examinees in Grades 10–12 and all adults begin with Item 11.

You may repeat an item if the examinee requests it. When administering the What subtest, if an examinee responds with a "where" response, repeat the item using the complete sentence *What would people usually do with a ____?* Do not give this prompt more than one time.

Some items require you to query certain examinee responses. Read the query prompt exactly as it appears on the screen and then score the examinee's next response.

Do not penalize the examinee for mispronunciations resulting from articulation errors, dialect variations, or regional speech patterns.

Each subtest ends when the examinee reaches a ceiling of four consecutive items incorrect, or when Item 23 (Where) or Item 22 (What) is administered.

Item scoring. For each item, click the word in the scoring key that matches the examinee's response. If the examinee says a word that does not appear in the scoring key, use the Other–1 option for a correct response or the Other–0 option for an incorrect response. Optionally, you can also type the examinee's response into the Other text field for later analysis. The platform assigns 1 point for correct responses and 0 points for incorrect responses. If you click I Don't Know or No Response, the item is scored incorrect (0 points).

Possible administration errors. Possible administration errors include mispronouncing the words when administering the items and not querying when the examinee's response requires it.

CONCEPT FORMATION

Concept Formation (Rapid Reference 4.16) is a controlled learning measure of fluid reasoning (Gf). The examinee learns rules for classifying colored shapes into groups and then uses inductive reasoning to state the rule(s) that describe how the colored shapes are grouped within each item. The rules are taught via animated introductions and are enforced by the feedback provided to the examinee on the sample items and test items. The items become more difficult as the examinee learns more rules and must decide which rule(s) apply to each puzzle. Concept Formation is recommended for ages 6 and older. It does not contribute to any WJ V cluster.

Administration. Examinees in Preschool to Grade 6 start with Introduction 1 and Sample Item A and then begin testing with Item 1, while examinees in Grade 2–12 and all adults start with Introduction 2 and Sample Items C, D, and E. Examinees who start with Introduction 2 and score fewer than 2 points on Sample Items C, D, and E (even after corrective feedback), are routed back to Sample Item A and Item 1, while all other examinees proceed to Item 6.

This test includes animated video introductions; play each introduction video only one time.

On Sample Items A and B and Items 1–5, the examinee responds by tapping their selection on the iPad screen. For all other items, the examinee provides an oral response. Accept reasonable synonyms for the correct response. For example, if the correct response is *little*, accept *littler*, *small*, or *smaller*, and if the correct response is *two* accept *pair* or *double*. If the examinee persists in using a synonym, adapt the feedback script appropriately to use that synonym to avoid confusing the examinee. For example, if the examinee consistently says *large* instead of *big* throughout the test and then provides an incorrect

Rapid Reference 4.16

Key Administration Points for Concept Formation

- Recommended for ages 6 and older.
- Use the Suggested Starting Point or select a different starting point.
- Play each video introduction only one time.
- To maintain the controlled learning aspect of this test, all sample items and Item 1 contain animated corrective feedback for incorrect responses. For Items 2–35, you provide feedback for correct *and* incorrect responses. Always read item response feedback *exactly* as it appears on your screen.
- Do not provide *any* feedback for Items 36–40.
- Accept reasonable synonyms for correct responses (e.g., *small* for *little*). If the examinee persists in using a synonym throughout the test, adapt the corrective feedback to use the same word.
- Query the examinee's response when instructed by the platform.
- Follow the prompts provided by the platform for item time limits.

response to Item 30, you should change the feedback to say: *That answer should be large* rather than *That answer should be big*.

To maintain the controlled learning aspect of this test, Item 1 and Sample Items A through H contain animated error feedback; when an examinee responds incorrectly to any of these items, the platform automatically plays the feedback video. On Items 2–35, you provide oral feedback to the examinee for both correct and incorrect responses. The feedback script for incorrect responses for items 2–35 is provided by the platform. Other than the exception noted above for reasonable synonyms, read the feedback *exactly* as it appears on your screen and, if applicable, use your cursor to point to the puzzle on the Examinee's View. If the examinee provides a correct response on Items 2–35, say: *That's right* or *That's correct*. Do not provide any feedback for correct or incorrect responses on Items 36–40.

Some items require you to query certain examinee responses. Read the query prompt exactly as it appears on the screen and then score the examinee's next response.

The platform alerts you after 30 seconds for Items 6–26 and after 60 seconds for Items 27–40 if you have not selected a response from the scoring key. When this happens, say: *Let's do another one*. Then click No Response and advance to the next item.

Testing continues through Item 40 unless the examinee does not meet the continuation requirements after Item 11, 20, or 29.

Item scoring. Sample Items A and B and Items 1–5 require the examinee to tap their responses. Based on the examinee's responses, the platform scores each item as correct (1 point) or incorrect (0 points). For all other items, click the option in the scoring key that matches the examinee's response. If the examinee provides an incorrect response, click Incorrect. The platform assigns 1 point for correct responses and 0 points for incorrect responses. If you click I Don't Know or No Response, the item is scored incorrect (0 points).

Possible administration errors. Possible administration errors include playing an animated introduction more than one time, not reading feedback *exactly* as it appears on your screen, not providing the required feedback for correct and incorrect responses up through Item 35, providing feedback on Items 36–40, not accepting reasonable synonyms for correct responses, and allowing the examinee additional time to respond after the platform displays the 30- or 60-second prompt.

NUMBER SERIES

Number Series (Rapid Reference 4.17) is a measure of quantitative reasoning (Gq) and fluid reasoning (Gf). The examinee sees a series of numbers and must determine the missing number that completes the underlying pattern. Number Series is recommended for ages 4 and older. It does not contribute to any WJ V cluster.

Administration. Make sure that the examinee has scratch paper and a pencil before administering this test.

All examinees start with Sample Item A. Examinees in preschool to kindergarten then proceed to Item 1, while examinees in Grades 1–2 proceed to Item 6. Examinees in Grades

Rapid Reference 4.17

Key Administration Points for Number Series

- Recommended for ages 4 and older.
- Use the Suggested Starting Point or select a different starting point.
- If the examinee does not respond after 30 seconds (Items 1–22) or 60 seconds (Items 23–40), select No Response and advance to the next item.

3–12 and all adults proceed from Sample Item A directly to Sample Item B. Then, examinees in Grade 3 begin testing with Item 10, examinees in Grades 4–5 begin testing with Item 12, and examinees in Grades 6–12 and all adults begin testing with Item 14.

The sample items provide feedback for correct and incorrect responses.

The platform alerts you after 30 seconds for Items 1–22 and after 60 seconds for Items 23–40 if you have not selected a response from the scoring key. Encourage the examinee to respond. If the examinee still does not respond, click No Response and advance to the next item.

The test ends when the examinee reaches a ceiling of four consecutive items incorrect or when Item 40 is administered.

Item scoring. For each item, click the word in the scoring key that matches the examinee's response. If you click I Don't Know or No Response, the item is scored incorrect (0 points).

Possible administration errors. Possible administration errors include not providing scratch paper, not reading the feedback on the sample items, and allowing the examinee to work past the item's time limit.

VISUAL-AUDITORY LEARNING

Visual-Auditory Learning (Rapid Reference 4.18) is a controlled-learning measure of visual processing (Gv) and fluid reasoning (Gf). The examinee learns to associate specific words and pictures, and then "reads" sentences that are formed by the pictures. The examiner teaches the examinee the word–picture relationships by pointing to each picture and saying its name orally and then enforces the relationships by providing immediate oral feedback if the examinee makes an error while "reading" a story. Visual-Auditory Learning is recommended for ages 4 and older. It does not contribute to any WJ V cluster.

Administration. All examinees begin with Introduction 1. Read the Introduction text orally to the examinee. Then, when you use your cursor to hover *under* the first picture on the Examinee's View, the name of the picture (*cowboy*) will display above the picture on the Examinee's View of your screen, and the examinee will see your cursor as a pointer icon on their iPad screen. Read the word orally and then pause to allow the examinee to say the word. Then move *immediately* to the next picture. Repeat this for each picture, pausing after you name the picture so the examinee can repeat the word you say.

Rapid Reference 4.18

Key Administration Points for Visual-Auditory Learning

- Recommended for ages 4 and older.
- On the Introductions, use your cursor to hover under each picture on the Examinee's View as you read the word orally. Pause to allow the examinee to say the word and then move immediately to the next word. Do not repeat any words or help the examinee learn the picture-word associations.
- On each test story, run your cursor under the words on the Examinee's View as the examinee is reading the story. If the examinee makes an error, skips a word, or pauses for 5 seconds, immediately say the word and click it to mark it as an error. Then move your cursor to the next word.
- Do not accept synonyms.
- Be careful not to obscure the examinee's view of the pictures with your cursor.
- On Story 7, score certain words as two separate parts.

After the examinee repeats the name of the last picture, immediately advance to Story 1. Use your cursor to hover on the word (*cowboy*) for the first picture of Story 1 and say: *What does this say?* Pause for the examinee to say *cowboy*, and then immediately move your cursor to the next picture. If the examinee says the wrong word or does not respond in 5 seconds, say *cowboy*, click the word to score it as an error, and then immediately move your cursor to the next word. Continue this process for all pictures in Story 1, using your cursor to point to each word. When it is clear that the examinee understands the task, you can move your cursor below the words (and the pointer will then disappear from the examinee's iPad screen). However, if the examinee skips a word or makes an error, *immediately* say the word and click on it to score it as an error. If the examinee does not make any errors, click the All Correct button before advancing to Introduction 2.

CAUTION

When administering Visual-Auditory Learning, be careful not to obscure the examinee's view of the pictures with your cursor. On the Introduction screens, hover your cursor under each picture to see the picture's name. On the test stories, run your cursor under the words on the Examinee's View as the examinee names the pictures. If the examinee makes an error on a test story, immediately click the word to score it as an error and say the word, then move your cursor to the next word. When you are hovering over a word or clicking to select a word as an error on a test story, your cursor will appear as a pointer icon on the examinee's iPad. This visual feedback, combined with the oral correction you provide, maintains the controlled learning aspect of this test.

The test contains seven introduction/story pairs. On each introduction, read the first picture name to the examinee, pause for the examinee to say the word, and then move your cursor *immediately* to the next picture. Do not repeat any words unless the examinee misunderstands you or does not hear a word. Do not talk about the pictures or give the examinee any additional help to learn the words or to form associations between the pictures and their names. Do not allow the examinee additional time to learn the picture names on the introductions.

The examinee learns 4 picture names each on Introductions 1–6. On Introduction 7, the examinee learns the pictures for *–s* and *–ing*. Read the text in the black tooltip exactly as it appears. When pronouncing /s/ and /z/, say the sounds (i.e., *ss* and *zz*) and not the letter names. Be careful not to add a schwa sound by saying *sə or zə (suh or zuh)*.

On the test stories, the examinee must say the exact word for each picture; do not accept synonyms. Do not penalize the examinee for mispronunciations resulting from articulation errors, dialect variations, or regional speech patterns. For words composed of two symbols on Story 7 (e.g., *ride…ing*, *horse…s*), score each part of the word separately. If the examinee makes an error on the first part of the word, correct the error without saying the second part. For example, if the word is *tree…s* and the examinee says, *horses*, say *tree* and click the word to mark it as an error, but do not say *s* or mark it as an error.

Testing continues through Story 7 unless the examinee fails to meet the continuation requirements after Stories 2, 4, or 6.

Item scoring. The platform assigns 1 point for each picture the examinee correctly names and 0 points for each picture the examinee skips or names incorrectly. If the examinee says *I don't know* or refuses to name any symbols, you can click the I Don't Know button or the No Response button to score the entire story incorrect (0 points).

Possible administration errors. Possible administration errors include not reading the picture names accurately or not pausing to allow the examinee to repeat each word on the Introductions, not *immediately* correcting errors or skipped pictures on the test stories, obscuring the examinee's view of the pictures on the iPad with your cursor, not correctly naming the /s/ and /z/ sounds on Introduction 7, and not scoring or providing feedback for each part of the word separately in Story 7.

VISUAL WORKING MEMORY

Visual Working Memory (Rapid Reference 4.19) is a measure of visual-spatial working memory (Gwm) and visual processing (Gv). The examinee sees a random pattern of dots for a fixed time interval. Then, the examinee must hold the location of the dots in active memory while responding to a simple (unscored) distractor task. Finally, the examinee must recall the locations of the dots on the screen. Visual Working Memory is recommended for ages 6 and older. It does not contribute to any WJ V cluster.

Administration. There are two training phases and a test phase in this test. During the first training phase, Sample Items A and B teach the examinee to recall the locations of

Rapid Reference 4.19

Key Administration Points for Visual Working Memory

- Recommended for ages 6 and older.
- Read all instructions and corrective feedback *exactly* as they appear on your screen.
- If necessary, allow the examinee to respond orally to the distractor task and use your cursor to click Yes or No on the Examinee's View.
- Confirm that the examinee is ready before advancing to the Presentation screen for each test item.
- If necessary, encourage responses from the examinee on the Distractor and Response screens.

dots on the screen (the test task). Read the text for Sample Items A and B orally to the examinee and use your cursor to point where instructed on the Examinee's View. If the examinee makes an error on either sample item, read the corrective feedback *exactly* as it appears on your screen. For examinees who fail both sample items, the test ends. All other examinees proceed to the second training phase.

In the second training phase, the examinee is taught to distinguish whether two simple stick figures are the same or different (the distractor task). After a series of demonstration items, the examinee responds to four practice items by tapping Yes if the stick figures are the same, and No if the stick figures are different. Read the text for the demonstration and practice items orally to the examinee and use your cursor to point where instructed on the Examinee's View.

If an examinee exhibits difficulty distinguishing the Yes and No buttons, allow them to respond orally by saying *Yes* or *No* for the distractor task and use your cursor to select the corresponding button on the Examinee's View.

If the examinee makes an error on any practice item, read the corrective feedback *exactly* as it appears on your screen. For examinees who respond correctly to fewer than two of the four practice items, the test ends. All other examinees proceed to Sample Item C, which combines the test task with the distractor task, and then to test Item 1.

Each test item has three parts: A Presentation screen, a Distractor screen, and a Response screen. Confirm that the examinee is ready before advancing to the Presentation screen for each item. The platform displays the Presentation screen for a fixed number of seconds (5 seconds for Items 1–7 and 10 seconds for Items 8–10), and then immediately displays the Distractor screen. If necessary, prompt the examinee to respond to the distractor task by saying, *Are these the same?* The examinee's response on the Distractor screen does not impact the test score.

If the examinee does not appear engaged in tapping the location of the dots on the Response screen, say: *Where was (were) the dot (dots)?* If necessary, remind the examinee to tap Done on the Response screen.

Testing continues through Item 10 unless the examinee does not meet the continuation requirement after Item 2.

Item scoring. The platform computes a score (0–8) points for the Response Screen of each item using the following equation:

$$\left(\frac{8i}{i+o}\right)\times\left(1-\frac{Z}{Z+Y}\right),$$

where i is the number of boxes the examinee correctly tapped, o is the number of boxes the examinee incorrectly skipped, Y is the number of boxes the examinee correctly skipped, and Z is the number of boxes the examinee incorrectly tapped. The 8 in the first term standardizes all the item scores to range from 0 to 8. The platform then sums the 0–8 scores across all administered items.

Possible administration errors. Possible administration errors include not reading all instructions and item text exactly, not providing the corrective feedback on the sample items and practice items, and not confirming that the examinee is ready before advancing to each item.

SYMBOL INHIBITION

Symbol Inhibition (Rapid Reference 4.20) is a measure of processing speed (Gs) that requires the executive functions of inhibitory and attentional control. The examinee sees one or more target shapes at the top of the screen and must work as quickly as possible to tap all the shapes on the screen that do *not* match the target shape(s). Symbol Inhibition is recommended for ages 7 and older. It does not contribute to any WJ V cluster.

Administration. All examinees start with Sample Items A and B. For examinees who do not respond correctly to either Sample Item A or B, even after corrective feedback, the test ends. All other examinees proceed to the Practice Exercise.

Read the Practice Exercise instructions orally to the examinee, and if applicable, use your cursor to point to shapes on the Examinee's View. Then click the Start Practice Exercise button to start the 30-second timer and display the Practice Exercise on the examinee's iPad screen. The examinee should work across each row and tap every shape that is *not* a blue

Rapid Reference 4.20

Key Administration Points for Symbol Inhibition

- Recommended for ages 7 and older.
- Read all instructions *exactly* as they appear on your screen.
- If an examinee starts skipping around, remind them to work row by row.
- If necessary, remind the examinee to tap Next to continue to the next screen.

triangle (the target shape). If the examinee begins skipping around, say: *Remember, work one row at a time. Do the whole row before going to the next row.* If necessary, remind the examinee to tap Done when they finish the last row. For examinees who score fewer than 4 points out of 8 on the Practice Exercise (see Item Scoring rules below for the calculation of the 0–8 score), the test ends. All other examinees proceed to Item Set 1.

This test contains three item sets, each with a 1-minute time limit. Item Set 1 contains eight screens of items with one target shape. Item Set 2 contains five screens of items with two target shapes. Item Set 3 contains five screens of items with three target shapes. For each item set, orally read the instructions to the examinee and then click the Start Timer button to start the timer and display the first screen of items on the examinee's iPad. The platform will alert you and the examinee when 1 minute is up. Allow the examinee to work for the full minute on each item set; do not stop the timer early.

When the examinee taps a shape, the iPad responds with a slight flash of the tapped shape but does not keep the shape highlighted; for this reason, the examinee will not be able to see which shapes they have already tapped. The platform shows a black cursor along the left edge of the screen to orient the examinee to the row they are working on. As soon as the examinee taps one shape in the next row, the cursor moves down. The examinee should complete each row in order, from the top of the screen to the bottom of the screen. Do not allow the examinee to skip around between rows. If necessary, remind the examinee to click Next at the bottom of each screen.

The test ends when the examinee completes the last screen of items on Item Set 3, or when the 1-minute timer on Item Set 3 runs out, whichever comes first.

Item scoring. The platform computes a score (0–8) points for each screen using the following equation:

$$\left(\frac{8Y}{Y+Z}\right)\times\left(1-\frac{o}{o+i}\right)\times\left(\frac{(Y+Z+i+o)}{24}\right),$$

where Y is the number of shapes the examinee correctly skipped, Z is the number of shapes the examinee incorrectly tapped, i is the number of shapes the examinee correctly tapped, and o is the number of shapes the examinee incorrectly skipped. The 8 in the first term standardizes all the item scores to range from 0 to 8, and the last term adjusts the screen score to account for rows that the examinee skips or does not reach on a screen before the timer runs out.

The platform then sums the 0–8 scores across all administered screens on all three item sets.

Possible administration errors. Possible administration errors include not reading all instructions and item text exactly, allowing the examinee to skip around between rows, and not reminding the examinee to tap Next at the end of each screen if necessary.

TEST YOURSELF

1. **On both Semantic Word Retrieval and Phonemic Word Retrieval, if the examinee repeats a word, you should click the minus button to score it as incorrect. True or false?**
2. **On which of the following tests can you accept synonyms as correct responses?**
   (A) Visual-Auditory Learning
   (B) Concept Formation
   (C) Both A and B
   (D) None of the above.
3. **On the Symbol Inhibition test, the examinee should:**
   (A) Tap all the shapes that are different from the one(s) at the top of the screen.
   (B) Tap all the shapes that are the same as the one(s) at the top of the screen.
   (C) Tap the shapes that are round and square.
   (D) Tap the shapes that are not round or square.
4. **If the examinee requests that you repeat a test item on Verbal Attention, you may:**
   (A) Click the Play button to repeat the audio-recorded prompt.
   (B) Read the item stem orally to the examinee.
   (C) A or B
   (D) None of the above.
5. **On Story Recall, the examinee must repeat the story elements back in the correct order to be scored correct. True or false?**
6. **If an examinee asks to change their responses on a Spatial Relations test item, you may (select all that apply):**
   (A) Tell the examinee to tap the pictures again to deselect them.
   (B) Use the refresh button on your browser to reset the item.
   (C) Take control of the iPad and click the pictures on the Examinee's View to deselect them.
   (D) Tell the examinee that they are not allowed to change their response.
7. **Because Analysis-Synthesis is a controlled learning test, you should:**
   (A) Acknowledge all correct responses.
   (B) Provide feedback on all incorrect responses.
   (C) Both A and B
   (D) Acknowledge correct responses and provide feedback for incorrect responses, except for Items 29–35.
8. **On Phonemic Word Retrieval Item 2 (words that begin with the /t/ sound), the examinee says: *top, Tom, take, them, these, tell, take*. How many correct responses should you count?**
   (A) 6
   (B) 5
   (C) 3
   (D) 2

9. **On the Oral Vocabulary test, if an examinee says a word that is not listed in the answer key, what should you do?**
   (A) Score the response incorrect because the words listed in the Correct key are the only acceptable responses.
   (B) Say: *Tell me another word.*
   (C) Use your professional judgment to score the response correct (0) or incorrect (1).
   (D) Type the word into the Other text field but leave the item unscored; return to it later to see if the examinee provides a different response.

10. **Which of the following is *not* true about Visual Working Memory?**
   (A) The *Riverside Score* platform automatically advances to the Distractor screen after a fixed time on the Presentation Screen.
   (B) After the test ends, the platform calculates the score for the Response screens by counting the number of boxes the examinee correctly tapped and skipped and subtracts 1 point for each Distractor item the examinee answered incorrectly.
   (C) If an examinee cannot read, you may allow them to orally respond *Yes* or *No* to the distractor items and use your cursor to click the corresponding button on the Examinee's View.
   (D) If an examinee does not understand the tasks after the first or second training phase, the test will end, and the examinee will not see live items.

ANSWERS

1. **False.** Do not click the minus button for incorrect responses. You should click the minus (−) button *only* to adjust the score if you accidentally click the plus (+) button too many times.
2. **B.** Concept Formation. For example, if the correct response is *little* and the examinee says *small*, *smaller*, or *littler*, accept the response as correct.
3. **A.** In the Symbol Inhibition test, a measure of attention and inhibitory control, the examinee should quickly tap all the pictures that are *not* the same as the target pictures at the top of the screen.
4. **D.** None of the above. Verbal Attention is a measure of short-term working memory, so you should not repeat any test items.
5. **False.** On Story Recall, the examinee may recall the elements in any order.
6. **A or C.** An examinee can change their response to a Spatial Relations item by tapping the pictures again to deselect them. Alternatively, you can use your cursor to take control of the iPad and click the pictures in the Examinee's View to deselect them. Clicking the refresh button on your browser will not remove the selected responses and is not a recommended action.
7. **D.** Provide feedback about whether a response is correct or incorrect on Items 1–28, but do not provide any feedback for correct *or* incorrect responses on Items 29–35.
8. **C.** The examinee said three correct words: *Tom*, *take*, and *tell*. Do not count *top* as a correct response because it is the example word. Do not count *them* and *these* as correct responses because they begin with the /th/ sound, not the /t/ sound. Do not give credit for the examinee's repeat of the word *take*.

9. **C.** The scoring keys provide the most common correct and incorrect responses that were given during the norming study. If the examinee says a word that is not included in the list of correct or incorrect responses, use your professional judgment to decide if the response is correct or incorrect, and then use the Other–1 or Other–0 options to assign a score. Optionally, you can type the examinee's response into the text field for later review. The platform will not allow you to advance to the next item until you have assigned an item score.
10. **B.** The Distractor items on Visual Working Memory do not contribute to the test score.

Five

WJ V ACHIEVEMENT TEST ADMINISTRATION

This chapter provides an overview of the administration procedures for the WJ V Achievement tests. Whether you are just learning the WJ V or need a review of certain tests, this chapter can serve as a guide or refresher. At the end of the chapter, there is a Test Yourself quiz. After studying or reviewing the test administration procedures in this chapter, you may wish to do a practice administration of each test.

Before administering each test on the digital platform, review the Administration Overview screen for administration and scoring reminders, and consult the Things to Know panel to see if the test is timed, uses audio recordings, or requires a Response Booklet.

PICTURE VOCABULARY

Picture Vocabulary (Rapid Reference 5.1) is a comprehension-knowledge (Gc) measure of expressive vocabulary. The examinee orally names pictures. Picture Vocabulary is recommended for ages 4 and older. It contributes to the Oral Language, Oral Expression, and Vocabulary clusters.

Administration. The platform suggests an appropriate starting item. Examinees in preschool begin with Item 1, examinees in Kindergarten to Grade 1 begin with Item 10, examinees in Grades 2–3 begin with Item 14, examinees in Grades 4–5 begin with Item 16, examinees in Grades 6–9 begin with Item 18, examinees in Grades 10–12 and average-ability adults begin with Item 22, and above-average adults begin with Item 28.

Essentials of WJ V™ Assessment, First Edition. Erica M. LaForte, Nancy Mather, and W. Joel Schneider.

Rapid Reference 5.1

Key Administration Points for Picture Vocabulary

- Recommended for ages 4 and older.
- Use the Suggested Starting Point or select a different starting point.
- Query the examinee's response when instructed by the platform.

Read each item orally and, when instructed, use your cursor to point to the picture, or the specific part of the picture, on the Examinee's View.

You may repeat an item if the examinee requests it.

Some items require you to query certain examinee responses. Read the query prompt exactly as it appears on the screen and then score the examinee's next response.

The test ends when the examinee reaches a ceiling of five consecutive items incorrect or when Item 47 is administered.

Item scoring. For each item, click the word in the scoring key that matches the examinee's response. If the examinee says a word that does not appear in the scoring key, use the Other–1 option for a correct response or the Other–0 option for an incorrect response. Optionally, you can also type the examinee's response into the Other text field for later analysis. The platform assigns 1 point for correct responses and 0 points for incorrect responses. If you click I Don't Know or No Response, the item is scored incorrect (0 points).

Possible administration errors. Possible administration errors include not pointing to the picture, or a specific part of the picture, when instructed and not querying when the examinee's response requires it.

LETTER-WORD IDENTIFICATION

Letter-Word Identification (Rapid Reference 5.2) is a measure of word reading (Grw). The early items measure pre-reading tasks such as letter identification and letter naming. Later items require single-word identification and single-word reading; the examinee does not need to know the meaning of the words. Letter-Word Identification is recommended for ages 4 and older. It contributes to the Brief Reading, Basic Reading Skills, Broad Achievement, and Academic Skills/Brief Achievement clusters.

Administration. Before administering this test, make sure you know the correct pronunciation of all the words. If you are unsure about a pronunciation, consult a standard dictionary or the Item Pronunciation Guide on the Resources tab of the *Riverside Score*® platform.

Examinees in preschool to kindergarten begin testing with Block A (Items 1–4). Examinees who score at least 1 correct on Block A advance to Block B (Items 5–15). The test ends for examinees with scores of fewer than 2 points after Block A or fewer than 10 points after Blocks A and B. All other examinees in preschool to kindergarten then advance

Rapid Reference 5.2

Key Administration Points for Letter-Word Identification

- Recommended for ages 4 and older.
- Know the correct pronunciation for all test items.
- Use the Suggested Starting Point or select a different starting point.
- If necessary, remind the examinee to read the words smoothly. Score an item incorrect if the examinee pronounces the word letter by letter or phoneme by phoneme.
- Block C (Items 16–89) uses basal and ceiling rules. Examinees who do not have at least 5 correct on Block C are administered all items (1–15) in Blocks A and B, unless they were already administered.

to Item 16 (Block C). Examinees in Grades 1–12 and all adults begin testing with an appropriate item in Block C (Items 16–89).

On Items 1–4 (Block A), the examinee taps the letter you say (from among six options). Block B (Items 5–15) contains two different item types: on Items 5–13, the examinee sees a letter on the screen and names the letter, and on Items 14–15, the examinee taps the word you say (from among four options). On Block C, the examinee reads single words orally.

To be scored correct, the examinee must read the word smoothly. If the examinee reads the word letter by letter or phoneme by phoneme, and then says it smoothly, score the item as correct. (Many examinees need to employ decoding strategies to read unfamiliar words, and this should not be penalized.) However, if the examinee reads the word phoneme by phoneme but then fails to read it smoothly, instruct them to say the word aloud smoothly. Provide this instruction only one time during the test. If an examinee's last response to an item is not read smoothly after that, score it incorrect.

Do not penalize the examinee for mispronunciations resulting from articulation errors, dialect variations, or regional speech patterns.

The platform alerts you when 10 seconds are up on each item. Encourage the examinee to respond. If the examinee is not actively engaged in responding after prompting, click No Response and advance to the next item.

Block C (Items 16–89) is administered with basal and ceiling rules. Examinees who are administered Block C must obtain both a basal (six consecutive items correct or Item 16) and a ceiling (six consecutive items incorrect or Item 89) within Block C. Examinees who begin testing within Block C but have a score of fewer than 5 points are administered all items in Blocks A and B, unless they were already administered.

Item scoring. Items 1–4 in Block A and Items 14–15 in Block B require the examinee to tap their responses. Based on the examinee's responses, the platform scores each item as correct (1 point) or incorrect (0 points). For all other items, select Correct or Incorrect. The platform assigns 1 point for correct responses and 0 points for incorrect responses. If you click I Don't Know or No Response, the item is scored incorrect (0 points).

You can review the voice recording of this test later on *Riverside Score®* to analyze the examinee's errors. Error analysis on this test can provide valuable insights into the examinee's knowledge of phoneme–grapheme relationships.

Possible administration errors. Possible administration errors include not knowing the correct pronunciation of all words on the test and not reminding the examinee to read the words smoothly if they read the words letter by letter or phoneme by phoneme.

CALCULATION

Calculation (Rapid Reference 5.3) is a measure of quantitative reasoning (Gq). The examinee works problems requiring math operations that are presented in a paper Response Booklet. Calculation is recommended for ages 6 and older. It contributes to the Brief Math, Math Calculation Skills, Broad Achievement, and Academic Skills/Brief Achievement clusters.

Administration. Make sure the examinee has the Calculation Response Booklet and a pencil before administering this test. This test has two forms; make sure you have the correct form of the Response Booklet.

Examinees in preschool to Grade 1 start with Sample Items A and B and then begin testing with Item 1. For examinees who do not respond correctly to both Sample Items A and B, the test ends.

All other examinees begin with an appropriate starting item: Item 7 for Grade 2, Item 11 for Grade 3, Item 15 for Grade 4, Item 19 for Grades 5–6, Item 23 for Grades 7–8, and Item 27 for Grades 9–12 and all adults.

Read the Introduction orally, and if necessary, help the examinee locate the appropriate starting item in the Response Booklet.

As the examinee completes each item in the Response Booklet, assign a score to the item by clicking the option in the scoring key that matches the examinee's response. If necessary, remind the examinee to work the problems in order. If the examinee skips an

Rapid Reference 5.3

Key Administration Points for Calculation

- Recommended for ages 6 and older.
- Make sure the examinee has the Calculation Response Booklet and a pencil.
- Use the Suggested Starting Point or select a different starting point.
- If the examinee skips an item in the Response Booklet, click No Response and then advance to the next item. Do not allow the examinee to skip around randomly on the Response Booklet page.
- Watch the item numbers on your screen. If the platform skips backward or forward, direct the examinee to the appropriate item in the Response Booklet.

item, click No Response and direct the examinee to the next item. Because the platform displays the items in a defined order on your screen, do *not* allow the examinee to skip around randomly on the Response Booklet page.

Pay close attention to the item numbers on your screen; the platform may skip back to an easier item to obtain a basal. If this happens, point to the appropriate item in the Response Booklet and say: *Do this one.*

If the examinee shows their work but you are unsure about their final response, ask the examinee to circle their answer.

Do not penalize the examinee for poorly formed or reversed numbers; however, if the examinee transposes numbers (e.g., if the examinee writes *13* instead of *31*), score the item incorrect.

The test ends when the examinee reaches a ceiling of five consecutive items incorrect or when Item 42 is administered.

Item scoring. For each item, click the option in the scoring key that matches the examinee's response. If the examinee provides an incorrect response, click Incorrect. The platform assigns 1 point for correct responses and 0 points for incorrect responses. If you click I Don't Know or No Response, the item is scored incorrect (0 points).

Possible administration errors. Possible administration errors include not providing the Calculation Response Booklet, not directing the examinee to the appropriate item in the Response Booklet, and allowing the examinee to skip around randomly on the Response Booklet page.

SPELLING

Spelling (Rapid Reference 5.4) is a measure of writing (Grw). The examinee writes letters or words that are orally dictated by the examiner. Spelling is recommended for ages 5 and older. It contributes to the Basic Writing Skills, Spelling Skills, Broad Achievement, and Academic Skills/Brief Achievement clusters.

Rapid Reference 5.4

Key Administration Points for Spelling

- Recommended for ages 5 and older.
- Make sure the examinee has the Spelling Response Booklet and a pencil.
- Know the correct pronunciation for all test items.
- Use the Suggested Starting Point or select a different starting point.
- Instruct the examinee to write the words in the Response Booklet in the order they are presented.
- Do not penalize for poor handwriting unless it is illegible.
- Accept a letter reversal unless it forms a different letter.

Administration. Before administering this test, make sure you know the correct pronunciation of all the words in the item prompts. Pronunciation for the more difficult items is provided on the item screen. If you are unsure about a pronunciation, consult a standard dictionary.

Make sure the examinee has the Spelling Response Booklet and a pencil before administering this test. This test has two forms; make sure you have the correct form of the Response Booklet.

The platform suggests an appropriate starting item. Examinees in preschool to Grade 1 begin with Item 1, examinees in Grade 2 begin with Item 7, examinees in Grade 3 begin with Item 15, examinees in Grades 4–5 begin with Item 20, examinees in Grade 6 begin with Item 24, examinees in Grades 7–8 begin with Item 30, examinees in Grades 9–12 and average adults begin with Item 33, and above-average adults begin with Item 43.

Read each item prompt orally, stressing the italicized words. Instruct the examinee to write their first word on the first line of the Spelling Response Booklet, and to use the other lines in order. Items 5 and 6 contain visual stimuli on the iPad; direct the examinee's attention to the screen during the administration of those items.

The platform may skip back to an easier item to obtain a basal. If this happens, you do not need to alert the examinee because the lines in the Spelling Response Booklet do not contain item numbers.

Encourage the examinee to print responses instead of writing them in cursive, but do not penalize for cursive responses. Do not penalize the examinee for poor handwriting unless it is illegible. Accept reversed letters unless the reversal forms a different letter (e.g., a reversed *b* becomes a *d* and is counted as an error). Unless the scoring key specifies a case, accept upper- or lowercase letters.

You may repeat an item if the examinee requests it.

The test ends when the examinee reaches a ceiling of five consecutive items incorrect or when Item 60 is administered.

Item scoring. For each item, click the option in the scoring key that matches the examinee's response. If the examinee provides an incorrect response, click Incorrect. The platform assigns 1 point for correct responses and 0 points for incorrect responses. If you click I Don't Know or No Response, the item is scored incorrect (0 points).

Possible administration errors. Possible administration errors include not knowing the correct pronunciation of all words on the test, penalizing for poor handwriting that is still legible, and accepting letter reversals if they form different letters.

ORAL COMPREHENSION

Oral Comprehension (Rapid Reference 5.5) is a measure of comprehension-knowledge (Gc). The examinee hears a short passage and supplies a missing word. Oral Comprehension is recommended for ages 4 and older. It contributes to the Oral Language and Listening Comprehension clusters.

Rapid Reference 5.5

Key Administration Points for Oral Comprehension

- Recommended for ages 4 and older.
- Use the Suggested Starting Point or select a different starting point.
- Administer Sample Items A and B orally and administer Sample Items B and C and all test items from the audio recording.
- Score responses that become a different part of speech incorrect.
- Unless otherwise noted in the scoring key, if the examinee provides a two-word response, ask for a one-word answer.

Administration. Examinees in preschool to kindergarten start with Sample Items A through D and then begin testing with Item 1. All other examinees start with Sample Items C and D and are then routed to an appropriate starting item. Administer Sample Items A and B orally; administer Sample Items C and D and all test items from the audio recording.

You may opt to administer all items orally if the examinee appears to have difficulty understanding the audio-recorded item prompts. If you administer the item prompts orally, read the passages with the same inflection as the audio-recorded passages. Be certain that you know the correct pronunciation of all the words in the passages.

Unless noted, accept only one-word responses. If an examinee provides a two-word response, ask for a one-word answer.

Score a response as incorrect if it differs from the correct response in the part of speech (for example, if it substitutes *cleaning*, a verb, for *clean*, an adjective). Do not penalize the examinee for mispronunciations resulting from articulation errors, dialect variations, or regional speech patterns.

Do not repeat any item on this test.

Some items require you to query certain examinee responses. Read the query prompt exactly as it appears on the screen and then score the examinee's next response.

The test ends when the examinee reaches a ceiling of five consecutive items incorrect or when Item 33 is administered.

Item scoring. For each item, click the word in the scoring key that matches the examinee's response. If the examinee says a word that does not appear in the scoring key, use the Other–1 option for a correct response or the Other–0 option for an incorrect response. Optionally, you can also type the examinee's response into the Other text field for later analysis. The platform assigns 1 point for correct responses and 0 points for incorrect responses. If you click I Don't Know or No Response, the item is scored incorrect (0 points).

Possible administration errors. Possible administration errors include mispronouncing the words when administering the items orally and not querying when the examinee's response requires it.

WORD ATTACK

Word Attack (Rapid Reference 5.6) is a measure of nonsense word reading (Grw). The early items measure identification of single phonemes, blends, and digraphs. Later items require the examinee to apply phonics and structural analysis skills to pronounce nonsense words. Word Attack is recommended for ages 5 and older. It contributes to the Basic Reading Skills and Phoneme–Grapheme Knowledge clusters.

Administration. Before administering this test, make sure you know the correct pronunciation of all the nonsense words. Pronunciation for the more difficult items is provided on the item screen. If you are unsure about a pronunciation, consult the Item Pronunciation Guide on the Resources tab of the *Riverside Score*® platform.

Examinees in preschool to Grade 2 start with the Introduction and Sample Item A and then begin testing with Block A (Items 1–3). Examinees with 3 correct on Block A advance to Block B (Items 4–10). The test ends for examinees who have 2 or fewer points after Block A or 3 or fewer points after Blocks A and B. All other examinees in preschool to Kindergarten then advance to Sample Item B and Item 11 (Block C). Examinees in Grades 1–12 and all adults start with Sample Item B and then begin testing with an appropriate item in Block C (Items 11–62).

On Items 1–3 (Block A), the examinee sees a letter and says the letter sound. Score the item incorrect if the examinee names the letter instead of saying the letter sound, but do not penalize the examinee if they add a schwa sound (e.g., if the examinee says *muh* instead of *mm* for /m/). On Items 4–10 (Block B), the examinee sees a blend (e.g., *sw*) or digraph (e.g., *ay*) and says the sound the letters make together. On Items 11–62 (Block C), the examinee reads nonsense words orally.

On the Introduction and the Sample Item A corrective feedback, make sure to pronounce the letter between the slashes (e.g., /t/) as the letter *sound* and not the letter *name.*

To be scored correct, the examinee must read the nonsense word smoothly. If the examinee reads the nonsense word letter by letter or phoneme by phoneme, and then says it

Rapid Reference 5.6

Key Administration Points for Word Attack

- Recommended for ages 5 and older.
- Know the correct pronunciation for all test items.
- Use the Suggested Starting Point or select a different starting point.
- If necessary, remind the examinee to read the nonsense words smoothly. Do not score an item as correct if the examinee pronounces the nonsense word letter by letter or phoneme by phoneme.
- Block C (Items 16–89) uses basal and ceiling rules. Examinees who do not have at least 3 correct on Block C are administered all items (1–11) in Blocks A and B, unless they were already administered.

smoothly, score the item as correct. (Many examinees need to employ decoding strategies to read unfamiliar words, and this should not be penalized.) However, if the examinee reads the nonsense word phoneme by phoneme but then fails to read it smoothly, instruct them to say the word aloud smoothly. Provide this instruction only one time during the test. If an examinee's last response to an item is not read smoothly after that, score it incorrect.

Do not penalize the examinee for mispronunciations resulting from articulation errors, dialect variations, or regional speech patterns.

The platform alerts you when 10 seconds are up on each item. Encourage the examinee to respond. If the examinee is not actively engaged in responding after prompting, click No Response and advance to the next item.

Block C (Items 11–62) is administered with basal and ceiling rules. Examinees who are administered Block C must obtain both a basal (six consecutive items correct or Item 11) and a ceiling (six consecutive items incorrect or Item 62) within Block C. Examinees who are administered Block C but do not score at least 3 points are routed back to Block A and are administered all items in Blocks A and B, unless they were already administered.

Item scoring. Score each item by clicking Correct or Incorrect. On Items 1–10, if the examinee says the letter names, click Says Letter Names and then read the corrective feedback. The platform assigns 1 point for correct responses and 0 points for incorrect responses. If you click I Don't Know or No Response, the item is scored incorrect (0 points).

You can review the voice recording of this test later on *Riverside Score*® to analyze the examinee's errors. Error analysis on this test can provide valuable insights into the examinee's knowledge of phoneme–grapheme relationships.

Possible administration errors. Possible administration errors include not knowing the correct pronunciation of all nonsense words on the test and not reminding the examinee to read the words smoothly if they read the nonsense words letter by letter or phoneme by phoneme.

CAUTION

When administering Math Facts Fluency, be careful not to display the Response Booklet pages containing the Practice Exercise or the test items to the examinee before the platform instructs you to do so. If the examinee can see the items in the Response Booklet while you are reading the instructions and before you start the timer, the test score will be invalid because the examinee will have had extra time to think about their answers.

MATH FACTS FLUENCY

Math Facts Fluency (Rapid Reference 5.7) is a cognitive processing speed (Gs) and quantitative knowledge (Gq) measure of automaticity with math facts. Working in a Response Booklet, the examinee solves simple addition, subtraction, and multiplication problems. The test has a 3-minute time limit. Math Facts Fluency is recommended for ages 6 and older. It contributes to the Math Calculation Skills, Broad Achievement, and Academic Fluency clusters.

Administration. Make sure the examinee has the Math Facts Fluency Response Booklet

Rapid Reference 5.7

Key Administration Points for Math Facts Fluency

- Recommended for ages 6 and older.
- Make sure the examinee has the Math Facts Fluency Response Booklet and a pencil, but do not allow the examinee to see the Practice Item or test item content until the platform instructs you to do so.
- The platform will end the test if an examinee does not have at least 1 correct on the Practice Exercise.
- If necessary, remind the examinee to cross out, and not erase, any answer they want to change.
- If an examinee starts skipping around, remind them to work row by row.
- If the examinee appears to disengage from the task for more than 5 seconds, say: *Go ahead. Work as quickly as you can.*
- The test ends after 3 minutes or when the examinee completes both pages of the test items.
- Score all test items *after* the test is complete using the Math Facts Fluency Scoring Guide. Do not attempt to score test items during the administration.

and a pencil before administering this test. This test has two forms; make sure you have the correct form of the Response Booklet.

Examinees in preschool to Grade 1 begin with the Practice Exercise. Turn to the page of the Response Booklet containing Math Facts Fluency Introduction 1. Read the Practice Exercise instructions orally to the examinee, and then click the button to start the 20-second timer. If the examinee completes all 5 Practice Items in fewer than 20 seconds, click the blue timer button to stop the timer. Click in the Practice Exercise score entry field to activate the scoring key and check the examinee's written responses. Enter the number correct (0–5) for the Practice Exercise in the score entry field. Examinees who correctly respond to 1 or more items in the Practice Exercise advance to the test items; otherwise, the test ends.

Examinees in Grades 2–12 and all adults skip the Practice Exercise and begin with the test items.

To administer the test items, turn to the page of the Response Booklet containing Math Facts Fluency Introduction 2. Read the instructions orally to the examinee, and then click the button to start the 3-minute timer when the examinee turns to the first page of test items.

Do not assist the examinee with any items or remind the examinee to watch the signs.

If the examinee pauses for more than 5 seconds or appears disengaged from the task during the test, say: *Go ahead. Work as quickly as you can.* However, do not provide this reminder if the examinee appears to be thinking.

Because it takes more time, do not allow the examinee to erase any responses. If the examinee begins to erase a response, remind them to just cross out their first answer and write their new one.

The examinee may skip an item that they do not know; however, if the examinee begins skipping around the page, remind them to work row by row. If necessary, remind the examinee to turn the page when they reach the bottom of the first page of math problems.

The platform will alert you when 3 minutes are up. Most examinees will not complete all test items; however, if the examinee finishes before the 3-minute timer is up, click the blue timer button to stop the timer.

Item scoring. Do not score the examinee's responses to the test items until after the administration is complete. Using the Math Facts Fluency Scoring Guide, check the examinee's written responses and note any errors. Do not penalize the examinee for poorly formed or reversed numbers. Count the number of correct responses in each row of the Response Booklet and write the totals in the shaded column. Then sum the row totals to obtain the pages 4 and 5 totals and enter these values in the Math Facts Fluency score entry fields on *Riverside Score®*.

DON'T FORGET

The Math Facts Fluency Scoring Guide is located on the Resources tab of Riverside Score. You can view it on screen, or you can print it out and make a transparency to simplify scoring this test.

Possible administration errors. Possible administration errors include allowing the examinee to see the Practice Item and test item content before the platform instructs you to do so, allowing the examinee to skip around on the page, not reminding the examine to cross out responses instead of erasing them, scoring the examinee's responses during the timed portion of the test, and not correctly summing the number of correct responses on pages 4 and 5 of the Response Booklet.

SENTENCE WRITING ACCURACY

Sentence Writing Accuracy (Rapid Reference 5.8) is a measure of basic writing skills (Grw). The examinee writes sentences dictated from an audio recording. Responses are scored on four dimensions: dictation accuracy, spelling, capitalization, and punctuation. Sentence Writing Accuracy is recommended for ages 6 and older. It contributes to the Brief Writing and Basic Writing Skills clusters.

Administration. Make sure the examinee has the Sentence Writing Accuracy Response Booklet and a pencil before administering this test. You will need the Sentence Writing Accuracy Scoring Guide, available on the Resources tab of *Riverside Score,* to score the examinee's responses after testing is complete. This test has two forms; make sure you have the correct form of the Response Booklet and scoring guide.

This test is administered in item blocks. Block A contains Items 1–5, Block B contains Items 6–15, and Block C contains Items 16–20. The platform suggests an appropriate

Rapid Reference 5.8

Key Administration Points for Sentence Writing Accuracy

- Recommended for ages 6 and older.
- Make sure the examinee has the Sentence Writing Accuracy Response Booklet and a pencil.
- Use the Suggested Starting Point or select a different starting point.
- Administer all items from the audio recording.
- Score the examinee's response to Sample Item A *immediately* using the dictation accuracy, spelling, capitalization, and punctuation scoring criteria on the platform.
- Score all test items *after* the test is complete. Do not attempt to score test items during the administration.
- After testing is complete, compare the examinee's written responses to the criteria and examples in the Sentence Writing Accuracy Scoring Guide and assign a score of 1 (correct) or 0 (incorrect) for each dimension (dictation accuracy, spelling, capitalization, and punctuation). Sum the scores for all items in the block across each dimension and enter the totals in the appropriate fields in the Review modal on the *Riverside Score* platform.
- If necessary, the platform will prompt you to relaunch the test and administer a second block of items.

block of items based on the examinee's grade or age. After you administer the item block, the test ends. Then, use the Sentence Writing Accuracy Scoring Guide to score each response correct or incorrect on the dimensions of dictation accuracy, spelling, capitalization, and punctuation.

CAUTION

Based on the examinee's total score from the first Block of items administered, the platform *may* prompt you to administer an additional block of items. If this happens, you will not be able to generate a report for this test until the additional items are administered. If you know that it will not be possible or convenient to schedule an additional testing session with the examinee, score the examinee's responses to this test *immediately* after the test ends, while the examinee is still present with you. This is a good opportunity to give the examinee a short break. However, if you know that you can easily schedule an additional testing session within a few days, you may wait to score their responses to this test until the testing session is complete.

Examinees in preschool to Grade 2 start with the Introduction and Sample Item A. Read the introduction orally and then administer Sample Item A from the audio recording. Immediately score the examinee's written response to Sample Item A as correct or incorrect on the dimensions of dictation accuracy, spelling, capitalization, and punctuation. If necessary, click the "i" icon in the Sample Item A scoring interface for access to the scoring rubric for each scoring dimension. If you select I Don't Know or No Response, the platform will assign scores of 0 to all four dimensions. If the examinee makes an error on any of the four scoring dimensions on Sample Item A, read the corrective feedback to the examinee before advancing to the second trial. If the examinee does not score at least 1 point on either trial of Sample Item A, the test ends. Otherwise, the examinee proceeds to Block A (Items 1–5). If the examinee has 17 or more points on Block A after scoring, the platform will prompt you to relaunch the test and administer Block B.

Examinees in Grades 3–8 begin testing with Block B (Items 6–15). If the examinee has fewer than 5 points or more than 35 points on Block B after scoring, the platform will prompt you to relaunch the test and administer another block of items (Block A or Block C).

Examinees in Grades 9–12 and all adults begin testing with Block C. If the examinee has fewer than 5 points on Block C after scoring, the platform will prompt you to relaunch the test and administer Block B.

Administer all test items from the audio recording. You may opt to administer all items orally if the examinee appears to have difficulty understanding the audio-recorded item prompts. If you administer the item prompts orally, read the sentences with the same inflection as the audio-recorded passages. Be certain that you know the correct pronunciation of all the words in the sentences.

Encourage the examinee to print responses instead of writing them in cursive, but do not penalize for cursive responses. Do not penalize the examinee for poor handwriting unless it is illegible.

You may repeat an item if the examinee requests it.

Item scoring. Use the Sentence Writing Accuracy Scoring Guide (available on the Resources tab of *Riverside Score*) to score the examinee's written responses *after* the test is complete. Except for Sample Item A, do *not* attempt to score the examinee's written responses during the administration. This test has two forms; make sure that you use the scoring guide that corresponds to the form of the test you administered.

For each item, compare the examinee's response to the criteria and examples in the scoring guide to determine whether the examinee's response is correct (1) or incorrect (0) on the dimensions of dictation accuracy, spelling, capitalization, and punctuation. Write the 1 or 0 score for each dimension in the corresponding D, S, C, and P boxes to the right of each item in the Response Booklet. Sum the score for each scoring dimension across all items in the block and write the totals in the Total boxes at the bottom of the page.

CAUTION

Even if you are an experienced examiner and have administered this test before, do not attempt to score the items on this test without using the Sentence Writing Accuracy Scoring Guide. The scoring guide contains detailed criteria for scoring each dimension and includes example responses from real examinees, along with a rationale for the scores assigned to each response.

To enter the examinee's scores on the *Riverside Score®* platform, launch the Review workflow. Under Items and Tests to Review, click the link for Sentence Writing Accuracy to launch the score entry modal. Transfer the dictation accuracy, spelling, capitalization, and punctuation dimension totals from the Response Booklet to the score entry fields on the platform. Then click Submit.

Possible administration errors. Possible administration errors include attempting to score test items during the administration, not using the scoring guide to score the examinee's written responses after testing is complete, not correctly applying the scoring criteria for each dimension (dictation accuracy, spelling, capitalization, and punctuation), penalizing the examinee for poor handwriting that is still legible, and not administering an additional block of items if the platform prompts you to do so.

PASSAGE COMPREHENSION

Passage Comprehension (Rapid Reference 5.9) is a measure of reading (Grw) and comprehension-knowledge (Gc). The examinee reads a short passage and supplies a missing word that makes sense in the context of the passage. Passage Comprehension is recommended for ages 5 and older. It contributes to the Brief Reading, Reading Comprehension, Broad Achievement, and Academic Applications clusters.

Administration. Examinees in preschool to Grade 1 begin with Block A (Items 1–7). For examinees who score fewer than 4 points on Block A, the test ends; all other examinees continue to Item 8 (Block B). Examinees in Grade 2 and up begin with Sample Item A and are then routed to an appropriate starting item in Block B.

The examinee reads each passage on their iPad screen silently. If the examinee reads aloud, encourage them to read silently, but do not require it. Do not help the examinee read any words on this test.

Unless noted, accept only one-word responses. If an examinee provides a two-word response, ask for a one-word answer.

Rapid Reference 5.9

Key Administration Points for Passage Comprehension

- Recommended for ages 5 and older.
- Use the Suggested Starting Point or select a different starting point.
- Score responses that become a different part of speech incorrect.
- Unless otherwise noted in the scoring key, if the examinee provides a two-word response, ask for a one-word answer.
- Block B (Items 8–38) uses basal and ceiling rules. Examinees who do not have at least 5 correct on Block B are administered all items (1–7) in Block A.

Score a response as incorrect if it differs from the correct response in the part of speech (for example, if it substitutes *reader*, a noun, for *read*, a verb). Do not penalize the examinee for mispronunciations resulting from articulation errors, dialect variations, or regional speech patterns.

Some items require you to query certain examinee responses. Read the query prompt exactly as it appears on the screen and then score the examinee's next response.

Block B (Items 8–38) is administered with basal and ceiling rules. Examinees who are administered Block B must obtain both a basal (six consecutive items correct or Item 8) and a ceiling (six consecutive items incorrect or Item 38) within Block B. Examinees who are administered Block B but have a score of fewer than 5 points are routed to Block A.

Item scoring. For each item, click the word in the scoring key that matches the examinee's response. If the examinee says a word that does not appear in the scoring key, use the Other–1 option for a correct response or the Other–0 option for an incorrect response. Optionally, you can also type the examinee's response into the Other text field for later analysis. The platform assigns 1 point for correct responses and 0 points for incorrect responses. If you click I Don't Know or No Response, the item is scored incorrect (0 points).

Possible administration errors. Possible administration errors include not querying when the examinee's response requires it and helping the examinee to read words on the test.

APPLIED PROBLEMS

Applied Problems (Rapid Reference 5.10) is a quantitative reasoning (Gq) measure of an examinee's ability to solve practical math problems. The examinee hears math story problems, some of which are accompanied by visual stimuli, and responds orally. Applied Problems is recommended for ages 4 and older. It contributes to the Brief Math, Math Problem Solving, Broad Achievement, and Academic Applications clusters.

Administration. Make sure the examinee has the Applied Problem Worksheet from the Response Booklet and a pencil before administering this test.

The platform suggests an appropriate starting item. Examinees in preschool begin with Item 1, examinees in Kindergarten to Grade 1 begin with Item 5, examinees in Grades

Rapid Reference 5.10

Key Administration Points for Applied Problems

- Recommended for ages 4 and older.
- Use the Suggested Starting Point or select a different starting point.
- Query the examinee's response when instructed by the platform.
- If a unit label appears with a correct response in the scoring key, the examinee must provide the unit label to receive credit.
- You may repeat an item if the examinee requests it.

2–3 begin with Item 10, examinees in Grade 4 begin with Item 14, examinees in Grades 5–6 begin with Item 16, examinees in Grades 7–10 begin with Item 18, examinees in Grades 11–12 and average-ability adults begin with Item 20, and above-average adults begin with Item 22.

Read each item orally and, if instructed, use your cursor to point to the stimulus, or the specific part of the stimulus, on the Examinee's View.

Some items require the examinee to tap their response on the iPad screen.

If a unit label (e.g., inches, pounds, dollars) appears with a correct response in the scoring key, the examinee *must* say the unit label to receive credit. If a unit label is not included in the scoring key, it is not required; however, if the examinee provides a correct response with an appropriate unit label, score the item as correct. If an examinee provides an *incorrect* unit label for an item that does *not* require a label, score the item incorrect.

Some items require you to query certain examinee responses. Read the query prompt exactly as it appears on the screen and then score the examinee's next response.

You may repeat an item if the examinee requests it.

The platform alerts you after 30 seconds if you have not selected a response from the scoring key or if the examinee has not yet tapped a response (for items that require the examinee to tap). Encourage the examinee to respond. If the examinee still does not respond, click No Response and advance to the next item.

The test ends when the examinee reaches a ceiling of five consecutive items incorrect or when Item 48 is administered.

Item scoring. For each item, click the option in the scoring key that matches the examinee's response. If the examinee provides an incorrect response, click Incorrect. The platform assigns 1 point for correct responses and 0 points for incorrect responses. Some items require the examinee to tap their responses. Based on the examinee's responses, the platform scores each item as correct (1 point) or incorrect (0 points). If you click I Don't Know or No Response, the item is scored incorrect (0 points).

Possible administration errors. Possible administration errors include giving credit for responses that are missing the required unit label and not querying when the examinee's response requires it.

SENTENCE READING FLUENCY

Sentence Reading Fluency (Rapid Reference 5.11) is a measure of cognitive processing speed (Gs) and reading (Grw). The examinee reads simple sentences and taps Yes if the sentence is true, and No if the sentence is false. The test has a 3-minute time limit. Sentence Reading Fluency is recommended for ages 5 and older. It contributes to the Reading Fluency, Broad Achievement, and Academic Fluency clusters.

Administration. All examinees begin with Introduction 1, followed by Sample Items A and B. On the sample items, use your cursor to point to the sentence on the Examinee's View and read the item text orally to the examinee. Both sample items include feedback for correct and incorrect responses. If the examinee responds incorrectly to the first trial of

Rapid Reference 5.11

Key Administration Points for Sentence Reading Fluency

- Recommended for ages 5 and older.
- The platform will end the test if an examinee does not have 2 correct on Sample Items A and B, or if the examinee has a score of 2 or fewer correct on the Practice Exercise.
- If necessary, provide corrective feedback for examinee errors on the sample items and the Practice Exercise.
- If necessary, remind the examinee to tap Next to continue to the next screen.
- If an examinee starts skipping around, remind them to work row by row.
- If the examinee appears to disengage from the task for more than 5 seconds, say: *Go ahead.*
- The test ends after 3 minutes or when the examinee completes all 12 screens.

Sample Item A or B, use your cursor to point to the correct response (Yes or No) on the Examinee's View while reading the corrective feedback. For examinees who do not respond correctly to both Sample Items A and B, even after corrective feedback, the test ends. All other examinees proceed to the Practice Exercise.

Read the Practice Exercise instructions orally to the examinee, and then click the Start Practice Exercise button to display the Practice Exercise on the examinee's iPad screen. If the examinee does not respond in 5 seconds, encourage a response. If necessary, remind the examinee to tap Done when finished.

If the examinee makes errors on the Practice Exercise, use your cursor to deselect the examinee's incorrect response(s) on the Examinee's View and follow the script to provide corrective feedback. Allow the examinee *one attempt* to correct each error and then instruct the examinee to tap Done when finished. Do not allow the examinee more than one opportunity to correct an error and do not explain the correct response(s). Examinees who tap the correct responses for three or more sentences on the Practice Exercise advance to the test items; for all other examinees, the test ends.

For examinees who advance to the test items, read the instructions orally to the examinee, and then click the button to start the timer and display the test items on the examinee's iPad screen. Allow the examinee the full 3 minutes to work. If necessary, remind the examinee to tap Next at the bottom of each screen to advance to the next screen. Encourage the examinee to respond to all items on each screen and not to skip around. To prevent the examinee from accidentally advancing through an entire screen of items, the Next button will not become active until the examinee taps responses for at least six pairs of numerical values.

If the examinee pauses for more than 5 seconds or appears disengaged from the task during the test, say: *Go ahead*; however, do not provide this reminder if the examinee appears to be thinking. Do *not* help the examinee read any words on the test.

This test has 12 screens of items. The platform will alert you and the examinee when 3 minutes are up. Allow the examinee to work for the full 3 minutes; do not stop the timer early. Most examinees will not complete all 12 screens; however, if the examinee finishes before the 3-minute timer is up, the test will end when the examinee taps Done on the last screen.

Item scoring. The platform assigns 1 point for each correct response and 0 points for each sentence that is skipped; the platform subtracts 1 point for each incorrect response.

Possible administration errors. Possible administration errors include not providing the corrective feedback for errors on Sample Items A and B and the Practice Exercise, not reminding the examinee to work row by row if they appear to be skipping items, and helping the examinee to read words on the test.

CAUTION

Do not administer Sentence Reading Fluency to an individual who cannot read. Although the platform enforces minimum score requirements to advance to the test items, a nonreader who responds randomly could still meet the continuation requirements by chance. In that case, the test score would not be an accurate reflection of the examinee's reading ability.

WRITTEN LANGUAGE SAMPLES

Written Language Samples (Rapid Reference 5.12) is a measure of written expression (Grw). The examinee writes 1- or 2-word or full-sentence responses to prompts read orally by the examiner, some of which are accompanied by visual stimuli. Full-sentence responses are scored for ideation but are not penalized for errors in spelling and mechanics. Written

Rapid Reference 5.12

Key Administration Points for Written Language Samples

- Recommended for ages 5 and older.
- Make sure the examinee has the Written Language Samples Response Booklet and a pencil.
- Use the Suggested Starting Point or select a different starting point.
- Score the examinee's responses to items in Block A *immediately* using the scoring criteria on the platform.
- Score items in Blocks B through E *after* the test is complete. Do not attempt to score Block B through E test items during the administration.
- After testing is complete, compare the examinee's written responses to the criteria and examples in the Written Language Samples Scoring Guide and assign a score of 2, 1, or 0 to each item. Sum the scores for all items in the block(s) and enter the total(s) in the appropriate field(s) in the Review modal on the *Riverside Score* platform.
- If necessary, the platform will prompt you to relaunch the test and administer an additional block of items.

Language Samples is recommended for ages 5 and older. It contributes to the Brief Writing, Written Expression, Broad Achievement, and Academic Applications clusters.

Administration. Make sure the examinee has the Written Language Samples Response Booklet and a pencil before administering this test. You will need the Written Language Samples Scoring Guide, available on the Resources tab of *Riverside Score*, to score the examinee's responses to items in Blocks B through E after testing is complete. This test has two forms; make sure you have the correct form of the Response Booklet and scoring guide.

This test is administered in item blocks. Block A contains Items 1–5, Block B contains Items 6–10, Block C contains Items 11–15, Block D contains Items 16–20, and Block E contains Items 21–25. The platform suggests an appropriate block of items based on the examinee's grade or age. With the exception of Block A (which is scored during testing), use the Written Language Samples Scoring Guide to assign a score of 2, 1, or 0 points to each written response after the test ends.

CAUTION

Based on the examinee's total score from the administered items, the platform *may* prompt you to administer an additional block of items. If this happens, you will not be able to generate a report for this test until the additional items are administered. If you know that it will not be possible or convenient to schedule an additional testing session with the examinee, score the examinee's responses to this test *immediately* after the test ends, while the examinee is still present with you. This is a good opportunity to give the examinee a short break. However, if you know that you can easily schedule an additional testing session within a few days, you may wait to score their responses to this test until the testing session is complete.

Examinees in preschool to Grade 2 begin testing with Block A. Read each item orally, and then immediately score the examinee's written response as correct or incorrect using the scoring criteria in the item's scoring interface. If the examinee does not score at least 3 correct on Block A, the test ends. Otherwise, the examinee advances to Block B (Items 6–10). After Block B, the test ends. Use the Writing Samples Scoring Guide to score each response 2 points, 1 point, or 0 points. If the examinee has 14 or more points on Blocks A and B after scoring, the platform will prompt you to relaunch the test and administer Block C.

Examinees in Grades 3–6 are administered Blocks B and C (Items 6–15), and then the test ends. If the examinee has 0 points or more than 19 points on Blocks B and C after scoring, the platform will prompt you to relaunch the test and administer another block of items (Block A or Block D).

Examinees in Grades 7–12 and average-ability adults are administered Blocks C and D (Items 11–20), and then the test ends. If the examinee has 0 points or more than 19 points on Blocks C and D after scoring, the platform will prompt you to relaunch the test and administer another block of items (Block B or Block E).

Above-average adults are administered Blocks D and E (Items 16–25), and then the test ends. If the examinee has 0 points in Blocks D and E after scoring, the platform will prompt you to relaunch the test and administer Block C.

Some items in this test require the examinee to use stimulus words or a stimulus phrase in their response. When the stimulus word(s) are printed in the response booklet, the examinee must include the word(s) in their written response. If the examinee writes the response around the printed stimulus words but does not actually rewrite the words, say: *Remember to write the words* (insert words) *in your sentence.*

Encourage the examinee to print responses instead of writing them in cursive, but do not penalize for cursive responses. Do not penalize the examinee for poor handwriting unless it is illegible.

You may repeat an item if the examinee requests it.

Item scoring. Except for Block A items, use the Written Language Samples Scoring Guide (available on the Resources tab of *Riverside Score*) to score the examinee's written responses to the test items *after* the test is complete. Do *not* attempt to score the examinee's written responses to items in Blocks B through E during the test administration. This test has two forms; make sure that you use the scoring guide that corresponds to the form of the test you administered.

CAUTION

Even if you are an experienced examiner and have administered this test before, do not attempt to score the items in Blocks B through E without using the Written Language Samples Scoring Guide. The scoring guide contains detailed criteria for scoring each item and includes example responses from real examinees, along with a rationale for the score assigned to each response.

For each item, compare the examinee's response to the criteria and examples in the scoring guide to determine whether the examinee's response should be scored 2 points, 1 point, or 0 points. Write the score for each item in the box to the right of the item in the Response Booklet. Sum the scores across all items in the block and write the total in the box at the bottom of the page.

To enter the examinee's scores on the *Riverside Score*® platform, launch the Review workflow. Under Items and Tests to Review, click the link for Written Language Samples to launch the score entry modal. Transfer the block score(s) from the Response Booklet to the appropriate score entry field(s) on the platform. Then click Submit.

Possible administration errors. Possible administration errors include attempting to score test items from Blocks B through E during the administration, not using the scoring guide to score the examinee's written responses after testing is complete, not correctly applying the scoring criteria, penalizing the examinee for poor handwriting that is still legible, and not administering an additional block of items if the platform prompts you to do so.

ORAL LANGUAGE SAMPLES

Oral Language Samples (Rapid Reference 5.13) is a measure of oral expression (Gl, Gc). The examinee responds orally (with a single word or a full sentence) to prompts read orally by the examiner, some of which are accompanied by visual stimuli. Oral Language Samples is recommended for ages 4 and older. It contributes to the Oral Language and Oral Expression clusters.

Administration. This test is administered in item blocks. Block A contains five items that require the examinee to provide two words that finish a sentence. Block B contains five items that require the examinee to provide simple, full-sentence oral responses to prompts. Block C contains 12 items that require the examinee to formulate detailed, full-sentence oral responses to prompts. The platform suggests an appropriate block of items based on the examinee's grade or age.

Examinees in preschool to Kindergarten start with Introduction 2 and Sample Item A. Read the introduction and sample item text orally to the examinee, using your cursor to point to the pictures on the Examinee's View when instructed. Sample Item A includes feedback for correct and incorrect responses. All examinees then proceed to the Block A test items, regardless of their score on Sample Item A. Examinees who score at least 4 correct on Block A advance to Block B.

Examinees in Grades 1–2 start with Introduction 3 and Sample Item B. Read the introduction and sample item text orally to the examinee, using your cursor to point to the picture on the Examinee's View when instructed. Sample Item B includes feedback for correct and incorrect responses. All examinees then proceed to the Block B test items, regardless of their score on Sample Item B. Examinees who score at least 4 correct on Block B advance to Introduction 4, Sample Item C, and Block C, while

Rapid Reference 5.13

Key Administration Points for Oral Language Samples

- Recommended for ages 4 and older.
- Use the Suggested Starting Point or select a different starting point.
- Score the examinee's responses to items in Blocks A and B as correct or incorrect.
- For items in Block C, assign a score of 2, 1, or 0 to each of the examinee's responses, using the scoring criteria and examples on the platform.
- For items that require a complete sentence, if necessary, remind the examinee to say a complete sentence or to say only one sentence. Provide these reminders only one time.
- For responses that require the examinee to use a stimulus word or words, if necessary, remind the examinee to use all the words and not to change any of the words. Provide these reminders only one time.

examinees who score 3 or fewer points on Block B are routed back to Introduction 2, Sample Item A, and Block A.

Examinees in Grades 3–12 and all adults start with Introduction 4 and Sample Item C. Read the introduction and sample item text orally to the examinee, using your cursor to point to the picture on the Examinee's View when instructed. Sample Item C includes feedback for 2-, 1-, and 0-point responses. All examinees then proceed to the Block C test items, regardless of their score on Sample Item C.

Block A and B items are scored correct (1 point) or incorrect (0 points). Block C items are scored 2, 1, or 0 points using the scoring criteria provided for each item on the platform. Be sure to read the scoring criteria for an item carefully before assigning a score to an examinee's response.

For Block C items, hover your cursor over the Examples icon to see example responses for each score category. Generally, the examinee must provide a complete sentence that satisfies the prompt requirements to score 1 or 2 points. With some minor exceptions, what typically differentiates 2-point responses from 1-point responses is the level of detail the examinee provides in the sentence. Responses that are not a complete sentence, are multiple sentences, or do not meet the prompt requirements (for example, not using all three stimulus words in the sentence) are generally scored 0.

> **CAUTION**
>
> Be careful not to be too harsh or lenient in scoring the examinee's responses. Make sure that you are familiar with the scoring criteria and are able to assess whether an examinee's response meets the minimum item requirements. The example 2-point, 1-point, and 0-point responses provided on the platform for Block C items are responses that examinees provided for those items during the WJ V norming study.

For items that require the examinee to say a complete sentence, if an examinee responds with an incomplete sentence, score the item incorrect/0 points and say: *Remember to say a complete sentence.* If an examinee says two sentences, say: *Remember to say just one sentence.* If an item requires the examinee to use three words in a sentence and they do not say all the required words in their response, score the item incorrect/0 points and say: *Remember to use all the words.* If the examinee changes a stimulus word in any way, score the item incorrect/0 points and say: *Remember, do not change the word(s) in any way.* Only give any of these reminders one time during the test.

Some items require you to query certain examinee responses. Read the query prompt exactly as it appears on the screen and then score the examinee's next response.

Do not penalize the examinee for mispronunciations resulting from articulation errors, dialect variations, or regional speech patterns. Do not penalize the examinee for grammar errors, unless the error makes the sentence uninterpretable.

You may repeat an item if the examinee requests it.

Item scoring. For each item in Blocks A and B, click the option in the scoring key that matches the examinee's response. The platform assigns 1 point for correct responses and 0 points for incorrect responses. For Block C, use the scoring criteria and examples on the platform to assign a score of 2, 1, or 0 points to the examinee's response. If you click I Don't Know or No Response, the item is scored incorrect (0 points).

Possible administration errors. Possible administration errors include not reading item prompts and corrective feedback verbatim, not pointing to the picture when the instructions require pointing, not querying when the examinee's response requires it, and not following the scoring criteria exactly when assigning scores to the examinee's responses.

SENTENCE WRITING FLUENCY

Sentence Writing Fluency (Rapid Reference 5.14) is a measure of cognitive processing speed (Gs) and writing (Grw). Using the three words provided, the examinee writes short sentences about stimulus pictures. The test has a 5-minute time limit. Sentence Writing Fluency is recommended for ages 7 and older. It contributes to the Written Expression, Broad Achievement, and Academic Fluency clusters.

Administration. Make sure the examinee has the Sentence Writing Fluency Response Booklet and a pencil before administering this test. This test has two forms; make sure you have the correct form of the Response Booklet. Open the Response Booklet to the page containing the Demonstration and sample items.

Rapid Reference 5.14

Key Administration Points for Sentence Writing Fluency

- Recommended for ages 7 and older.
- Make sure the examinee has the Sentence Writing Fluency Response Booklet and a pencil, but do not allow the examinee to see the sample item or test item content until the platform instructs you to do so.
- The platform will end the test if an examinee does not have at least 2 correct on Sample Items A through C.
- If necessary, remind the examinee to cross out, and not erase, any answer they want to change.
- If an examinee starts skipping around, remind them to work item by item.
- If the examinee appears to disengage from the task for more than 5 seconds, say: *Go ahead. Work as quickly as you can.*
- The platform will prompt you to end the test after 2 minutes if the examinee has not written at least one correct sentence; for all other examinees, the test ends after 5 minutes or when the examinee completes all the test items.
- Score the examinee's responses after testing is complete.
- Do not penalize for poor handwriting unless it is illegible.

CAUTION

When administering Sentence Writing Fluency, be careful not to display the Response Booklet pages containing the Practice Exercise or the test items to the examinee before the platform instructs you to do so. If the examinee can see the items in the Response Booklet while you are reading the instructions and before you start the timer, the test score will be invalid because the examinee will have had extra time to think about their answers.

All examinees start with the Demonstration and Sample Items A, B, and C. All sample items include feedback for incorrect responses. For examinees who do not respond correctly to at least 2 sample items, even after corrective feedback, the test ends. Otherwise, the examinee proceeds to the test items.

To administer the test items, read the instructions orally to the examinee, and then click the button to start the 5-minute timer when the examinee turns to the first page of test items.

You may read any word on this test if the examinee requests it.

Encourage the examinee to print responses instead of writing them in cursive, but do not penalize for cursive responses.

If the examinee writes the three stimulus words but does not use them in a sentence, say: *Remember to use the three words in a complete sentence.* Give this instruction only one time during the test.

If the examinee pauses for more than 5 seconds or appears disengaged from the task during the test, say: *Go ahead. Work as quickly as you can.* However, do not provide this reminder if the examinee appears to be thinking.

Because it takes more time, do not allow the examinee to erase any responses. If the examinee begins to erase a response, remind them to just cross out their first answer and write their new one.

The examinee may skip an item that they do not know; however, if the examinee begins skipping around the page, remind them to work item by item. If necessary, remind the examinee to turn the page when they reach the bottom of each page.

Some very young or low-ability examinees may pass the sample items but have difficulty completing the test task independently. If this happens, the platform allows you to end the test early to avoid unnecessary frustration for the examinee. If you notice that the examinee is struggling to write complete sentences or is refusing to engage in the task, watch for the 2-minute alert on your screen and click Stop Timer if the examinee has not written at least 1 correct sentence.

For all other examinees, the platform will alert you when 5 minutes are up. Most examinees will not complete all test items; however, if the examinee finishes before the 5-minute timer is up, click the timer button to stop the timer.

Item scoring. Do not score the examinee's responses to the test items until after the administration is complete. Assign 1 point for each complete sentence that includes all three stimulus words. The words do not have to be used in the same order they appear on the Response Booklet page. Assign 0 points to a response if the examinee did not use all three words, changed any words, or did not write a complete sentence. Do not penalize the examinee for poor handwriting unless it is illegible. Do not penalize for errors in spelling, punctuation, or capitalization.

Stimulus words that are miscopied or misspelled can still receive credit if the word has not changed tense, number, part of speech, or become a different word, and the examinee wrote a reasonable, complete sentence. For example, if an examinee wrote *The foot is litle*, the misspelling of *little* would not be penalized, but if the examinee wrote *small* instead of *little* the response would be incorrect. As long as the sentence contains the three stimulus words and is meaningful, score awkward sentences and sentences with the understood subject "you" as correct. Sentences that use alternate characters, such as an ampersand (&) or a plus sign (+) for the word or an abbreviation like "w/" instead of the word *with* are scored correct if the response meets all other criteria. If the examinee omits a word that is critical to the sentence's meaning, score the response as incorrect. Do not penalize for an accidental omission of a less meaningful word (e.g., *a*, *the*, *an*) in a sentence, unless it is one of the three stimulus words.

Count the number of correct sentences the examinee wrote on pages 2 through 6 of the Response Booklet and enter the totals in the Sentence Writing Fluency score entry fields on *Riverside Score*®.

Possible administration errors. Possible administration errors include allowing the examinee to see the test item content before the platform instructs you to do so, penalizing for spelling or mechanics errors, scoring an item correct if the examinee changes or omits one or more of the stimulus words, and not correctly summing the number of correct responses on pages 2 through 6 of the Response Booklet.

PARAGRAPH READING COMPREHENSION

Paragraph Reading Comprehension (Rapid Reference 5.15) is a measure of reading (Grw) and comprehension-knowledge (Gc). The examinee reads a short passage or story and then answers literal and inferential comprehension questions. Paragraph Reading Comprehension is recommended for ages 6 and older. It contributes to the Reading Comprehension cluster.

Administration. The platform suggests an appropriate starting block. Examinees in preschool to Grade 1 start with Block A (Stories 1–2), examinees in Grade 2 start with Block B (Stories 3–4), examinees in Grade 3 start with Block C (Stories 5–6), and examinees in Grades 4–12 and all adults start with Block D (Stories 7–8).

The platform evaluates the examinee's score after each block of stories and routes the examinee to an easier or more difficult block (up to a maximum of three blocks) or ends the test for examinees who do not meet continuation requirements.

The examinee reads each story on their iPad screen silently. If the examinee reads aloud, encourage them to read silently, but do not require it. Do not help the examinee read any words in the stories. If necessary, instruct the examinee to tap Done when they finish reading the story.

Rapid Reference 5.15

Key Administration Points for Paragraph Reading Comprehension

- Recommended for ages 6 and older. Use the Suggested Starting Point or select a different starting point.
- Do not help the examinee read any words.
- Read all comprehension questions orally. You may repeat a comprehension question if an examinee requests it.
- Query the examinee's response when instructed by the platform.

Each comprehension question is presented on the examinee's screen, under the story. Read the comprehension questions clearly and with inflection. You may repeat a comprehension question if an examinee requests it.

Some items require you to query certain examinee responses. Read the query prompt exactly as it appears on the screen and then score the examinee's next response.

Item scoring. For each item, select the examinee's response from the scoring key or click Incorrect. Some items allow any reasonable response; use your professional judgment to determine if the examinee's response is correct. If you click I Don't Know or No Response, the item is scored incorrect (0 points).

Possible administration errors. Possible administration errors include helping the examinee read words in the stories and not querying when the examinee's response requires it.

STORY COMPREHENSION

Story Comprehension (Rapid Reference 5.16) is a measure of listening comprehension and long-term storage (Gl). The examinee hears a short passage or story from an audio recording and then answers literal and inferential comprehension questions. Story Comprehension is the only test in the WJ V that is included in both the Cognitive and Achievement batteries. Story Comprehension is recommended for ages 6 and older. In the Achievement battery, it contributes to the Oral Language and Listening Comprehension clusters.

Administration. Examinees in preschool to Grade 2 start with Sample Items A and B. If an examinee does not respond correctly to at least one trial of Sample Items A and B, the test ends. Otherwise, the examinee proceeds to Block A (Stories 1–4). Examinees who have at least 6 points on Block A proceed to Block B (Stories 5–7).

All other examinees are administered two blocks of stories. Examinees in Grades 3–5 begin testing with Block B (Stories 5–7).

DON'T FORGET

Story Comprehension is also part of the Long-Term Storage (Gl) cluster in the Cognitive battery.

Rapid Reference 5.16

Key Administration Points for Story Comprehension

- Recommended for ages 6 and older.
- Use the Suggested Starting Point or select a different starting point.
- Read the stories in Sample Items A and B orally and play all other stories from the audio recording.
- Read or play each story only one time.
- Read all comprehension questions orally only one time.
- Query the examinee's response when instructed by the platform.

Examinees in Grades 6–8 begin testing with Block C (Stories 8–10). Examinees in Grades 9–12 and all adults begin testing with Block D (Stories 11–13). Based on the score from the first block of stories, the platform routes each examinee to an appropriate (easier or more difficult) second block of stories.

Play all stories from the audio recording. Confirm the examinee is ready before clicking the Play button for each story. You may opt to present the stories orally if the examinee appears to have difficulty understanding the audio-recorded stories. If you present the stories orally, read them with the same inflection as the audio-recorded passages. Be certain that you know the correct pronunciation of all the words in the stories. Do not replay or repeat any story on this test.

Read each comprehension question clearly and with inflection. Read each question only one time.

Some items require you to query certain examinee responses. Read the query prompt exactly as it appears on the screen and then score the examinee's next response.

Item scoring. For each item, select the examinee's response from the scoring key or click Incorrect. Some items allow any reasonable response; use your professional judgment to determine if the examinee's response is correct. If you click I Don't Know or No Response, the item is scored incorrect (0 points).

Possible administration errors. Possible administration errors include replaying a story or repeating a comprehension question and not querying when the examinee's response requires it.

WORD READING FLUENCY

Word Reading Fluency (Rapid Reference 5.17) is a measure of cognitive processing speed (Gs) and reading (Grw). The examinee reads four words in a row and taps the two words that have a semantic relationship. The test has a 3-minute time limit. Word Reading Fluency is recommended for ages 6 and older. It contributes to the Reading Fluency cluster.

Rapid Reference 5.17

Key Administration Points for Word Reading Fluency

- Recommended for ages 6 and older.
- The platform will end the test if an examinee does not have 2 correct on Sample Items A and B, or if the examinee has a score of 1 or 0 correct on the Practice Exercise.
- If necessary, provide corrective feedback for examinee errors on the sample items and the Practice Exercise.
- If necessary, remind the examinee to tap Next to continue to the next screen.
- If an examinee starts skipping around, remind them to work row by row.
- If the examinee appears to disengage from the task for more than 5 seconds, say: *Go ahead and choose two.*
- The test ends after 3 minutes or when the examinee completes all nine screens.

Administration. All examinees begin with Introduction 1, followed by Sample Items A and B. On the sample items, use your cursor to point to the words on the Examinee's View and read the item text orally to the examinee. Both sample items include feedback for correct and incorrect responses. If the examinee responds incorrectly to the first trial of Sample Item A or B, use your cursor to point to the two words that go together on the Examinee's View while reading the corrective feedback. For examinees who do not respond correctly to both Sample Items A and B, even after corrective feedback, the test ends. All other examinees proceed to the Practice Exercise.

Read the Practice Exercise instructions orally to the examinee, and then click the Start Practice Exercise button to display the Practice Exercise on the examinee's iPad screen. If the examinee does not respond in 5 seconds, encourage a response. If necessary, remind the examinee to tap Done when finished.

If the examinee makes errors on the Practice Exercise, use your cursor to deselect the examinee's incorrect response(s) on the Examinee's View and follow the script to provide corrective feedback. Allow the examinee *one attempt* to correct each error and then instruct the examinee to tap Done when finished. Do not allow the examinee more than one opportunity to correct an error and do not explain the correct response(s). Examinees who tap the correct responses in two or more rows on the Practice Exercise advance to the test items; for all other examinees, the test ends.

For examinees who advance to the test items, read the instructions orally to the examinee, and then click the button to start the timer and display the test items on the examinee's iPad screen. Allow the examinee the full 3 minutes to work. If necessary, remind the examinee to tap Next at the bottom of each screen to advance to the next screen. Encourage the examinee to respond to all items on each screen and not to skip around. To prevent the examinee from accidentally advancing through an entire screen of items, the Next button will not become active until the examinee taps at least one letter or letter combination in six rows.

> **CAUTION**
>
> Do not administer Word Reading Fluency to an individual who cannot read. Although the platform enforces minimum score requirements to advance to the test items, a nonreader who responds randomly could still meet the continuation requirements by chance. In that case, the test score would not be an accurate reflection of the examinee's reading ability.

If the examinee pauses for more than 5 seconds or appears disengaged from the task during the test, say: *Go ahead and choose two words*; however, do not provide this reminder if the examinee appears to be thinking. Do *not* help the examinee read any words on the test.

This test has nine screens of items. The platform will alert you and the examinee when 3 minutes are up. Allow the examinee to work for the full 3 minutes; do not stop the timer early. Most examinees will not complete all nine screens; however, if the examinee finishes before the 3-minute timer is up, the test will end when the examinee taps Done on the last screen.

Item scoring. The platform assigns 1 point for each correct pair and 0 points for each row that is skipped, incorrect, or incomplete.

Possible administration errors. Possible administration errors include not providing the corrective feedback for errors on Sample Items A and B and the Practice Exercise, not reminding the examinee to work row by row if they appear to be skipping items, and helping the examinee to read words on the test.

MATH PROBLEM IDENTIFICATION

Math Problem Identification (Rapid Reference 5.18) is a measure of quantitative reasoning (Gq) and fluid reasoning (Gf). The examinee hears unsolvable math problems read orally by the examiner, sometimes accompanied by a visual stimulus, and must state why the problem cannot be solved. Math Problem Identification is recommended for ages 5 and older. It contributes to the Math Problem Solving cluster.

> ***Rapid Reference 5.18***
>
> **Key Administration Points for Math Problem Identification**
>
> - Recommended for ages 5 and older.
> - Make sure the examinee has the Math Problem Identification Worksheet and a pencil.
> - Use the Suggested Starting Point or select a different starting point.
> - Read the feedback for correct and incorrect responses on Sample Items A and B, and if necessary, read the feedback for incorrect responses on Sample Items C and D.
> - Query the examinee's response when instructed by the platform.
> - You may repeat an item if the examinee requests it.

Administration. Make sure the examinee has the Math Problem Identification Worksheet from the Response Booklet and a pencil before administering this test.

Examinees in preschool to Grade 5 start with Sample Items A and B and are then routed to an appropriate starting point: Item 1 for examinees in preschool to Grade 1, Item 5 for examinees in Grades 2–3, and Item 8 for examinees in Grades 4–5. For examinees who do not respond correctly to either Sample Item A or B, even after corrective feedback, the test ends.

Examinees in Grades 6–12 and all adults start with Sample Items C and D and are then routed to an appropriate starting point: Item 11 for examinees in Grades 6–8, Item 15 for examinees in Grades 9–12 and average adults, and Item 22 for above-average adults.

Read each item orally and, when instructed, use your cursor to point to the stimulus, or the specific part of the stimulus, on the Examinee's View.

Read the feedback for correct and incorrect responses on Sample Items A and B. If an examinee responds incorrectly to the first trial of Sample Item C or D, read the corrective feedback before advancing to the second trial.

Some items require you to query certain examinee responses. Read the query prompt exactly as it appears on the screen and then score the examinee's next response. For items without queries, if the examinee simply states that a math problem is wrong (e.g., if the examinee says, *That is not the correct answer*) but does not say what is missing or what makes it incorrect, say: *Tell me what is wrong with the problem.*

Allow the examinee a reasonable amount of time to work on each item and then encourage the examinee to respond. If the examinee is not actively engaged, click No Response and say: *Let's do another one.* Then advance to the next item.

You may repeat an item if the examinee requests it.

The test ends when the examinee reaches a ceiling of five consecutive items incorrect or when Item 47 is administered.

Item scoring. For each item, click the response in the scoring key that most closely matches the examinee's response. If the examinee's response does not match or closely resemble a response in the scoring key, click Incorrect. The platform assigns 1 point for correct responses and 0 points for incorrect responses. If you click I Don't Know or No Response, the item is scored incorrect (0 points).

Possible administration errors. Possible administration errors include not providing the examinee with the Math Problem Identification worksheet and a pencil; not pointing to the picture, or a specific part of the picture, when instructed; not reading the feedback, if provided, on sample items; and not querying when the examinee's response requires it.

MAGNITUDE COMPARISON

Magnitude Comparison (Rapid Reference 5.19) is a measure of cognitive processing speed (Gs) and quantitative knowledge (Gq). The examinee evaluates pairs of numerical values (shape groups, numerals, fractions, or decimals) and taps the value that is greater. The test

Rapid Reference 5.19

Key Administration Points for Magnitude Comparison

- Recommended for ages 4 and older.
- The platform will end the test if an examinee does not have 2 correct on Sample Items A and B, or if the examinee has a score of 3 or fewer correct on the Practice Exercise.
- If necessary, provide corrective feedback for examinee errors on the sample items and the Practice Exercise.
- If necessary, remind the examinee to tap Next to continue to the next screen.
- If an examinee starts skipping around, remind them to work row by row.
- If the examinee appears to disengage from the task for more than 5 seconds, say: *Go ahead.*
- The test ends after 3 minutes or when the examinee completes all 12 screens.

has a 2-minute time limit. Magnitude Comparison is recommended for ages 4 and older. It contributes to the Number Concepts cluster.

Administration. All examinees begin with Introduction 1, followed by Sample Items A and B. On the sample items, use your cursor to point to two numerical values on the Examinee's View and read the item text orally to the examinee. Both sample items include feedback for correct and incorrect responses. If the examinee responds incorrectly to the first trial of Sample Item A or B, use your cursor to point to the correct response on the Examinee's View while reading the corrective feedback. For examinees who do not respond correctly to both Sample Items A and B, even after corrective feedback, the test ends. All other examinees proceed to the Practice Exercise.

Read the Practice Exercise instructions orally to the examinee, and then click the Start Practice Exercise button to display the Practice Exercise on the examinee's iPad screen. If the examinee does not respond in 5 seconds, encourage a response. If necessary, remind the examinee to tap Done when finished.

If the examinee makes errors on the Practice Exercise, use your cursor to deselect the examinee's incorrect response(s) on the Examinee's View and follow the script to provide corrective feedback. Allow the examinee *one attempt* to correct each error and then instruct the examinee to tap Done when finished. Do not allow the examinee more than one opportunity to correct an error and do not explain the correct response(s). Examinees who select correct responses for four or more pairs of numerical values on the Practice Exercise advance to the test items; for all other examinees, the test ends.

For examinees who advance to the test items, read the instructions orally to the examinee, and then click the button to start the timer and display the test items on the examinee's iPad screen. Allow the examinee the full 2 minutes to work. If necessary, remind the examinee to tap Next at the bottom of each screen to advance to the next screen. Encourage the examinee to respond to all items on each screen and not to skip around.

To prevent the examinee from accidentally advancing through an entire screen of items, the Next button will not become active until the examinee taps responses for at least six pairs of numerical values.

If the examinee pauses for more than 5 seconds or appears disengaged from the task during the test, say: *Go ahead and tap the one that has more*; however, do not provide this reminder if the examinee appears to be thinking.

This test has 12 screens of items. The platform will alert you and the examinee when 2 minutes are up. Allow the examinee to work for the full 2 minutes; do not stop the timer early. Most examinees will not complete all 12 screens; however, if the examinee finishes before the 2-minute timer is up, the test will end when the examinee taps Done on the last screen.

Item scoring. The platform assigns 1 point for each correct pair and 0 points for each pair that is skipped; the platform subtracts 1 point for each incorrect response.

Possible administration errors. Possible administration errors include not providing the corrective feedback for errors on Sample Items A and B and the Practice Exercise and not reminding the examinee to work row by row if they appear to be skipping items.

NUMBER SENSE

Number Sense (Rapid Reference 5.20) is a measure of quantitative reasoning (Gq). The examinee orally answers questions that assess math vocabulary and numerical comparisons or estimations of size, quantity, position, and volume. Some questions are accompanied by visual stimuli. Number Sense is recommended for ages 5 and older. It contributes to the Number Concepts cluster.

Administration. This test contains items that require the examinee to make estimations. For this reason, do *not* provide the examinee with scratch paper or a pencil for this test.

The platform suggests an appropriate starting item. Examinees in preschool to Kindergarten begin with Item 1, examinees in Grades 1–2 begin with Item 4, examinees

Rapid Reference 5.20

Key Administration Points for Number Sense

- Recommended for ages 5 and older.
- Use the Suggested Starting Point or select a different starting point.
- Query the examinee's response when instructed by the platform.
- If the examinee begins counting on estimation items, remind them to estimate.
- If a unit label appears with a correct response in the scoring key, the examinee must provide the unit label to receive credit.
- You may repeat an item if the examinee requests it.

in Grades 3–4 begin with Item 8, examinees in Grades 5–6 begin with Item 13, examinees in Grades 7–8 begin with Item 16, examinees in Grades 9–10 begin with Item 18, and examinees in Grades 11–12 and all adults begin with Item 20.

Read each item orally and, if instructed, use your cursor to point to the stimulus, or the specific part of the stimulus, on the Examinee's View.

Some items require the examinee to tap their response on the iPad screen.

Some items require the examinee to estimate a quantity. If the examinee begins counting, say: *Do not count. Just guess how many.* Some items require you to query certain examinee responses. Read the query prompt exactly as it appears on the screen and then score the examinee's next response.

If a unit label (e.g., inches, pounds, dollars) appears with a correct response in the scoring key, the examinee *must* say the unit label to receive credit. If a unit label is not included in the scoring key, it is not required; however, if the examinee provides a correct response with an appropriate unit label, score the item as correct. If an examinee provides an *incorrect* unit label for an item that does *not* require a label, score the item incorrect.

You may repeat an item if the examinee requests it.

The test ends when the examinee reaches a ceiling of five consecutive items incorrect or when Item 42 is administered.

Item scoring. For each item, click the option in the scoring key that matches the examinee's response. If the examinee provides an incorrect response, click Incorrect. The platform assigns 1 point for correct responses and 0 points for incorrect responses. Some items require the examinee to tap their responses. Based on the examinee's responses, the platform scores each item as correct (1 point) or incorrect (0 points). If you click I Don't Know or No Response, the item is scored incorrect (0 points).

Possible administration errors. Possible administration errors include providing the examinee with scratch paper, not pointing to the picture when the instructions require pointing, and not querying when the examinee's response requires it.

SPELLING OF SOUNDS

Spelling of Sounds (Rapid Reference 5.21) is a measure of phonological awareness (Ga) and writing (Grw). The examinee writes dictated letter sounds or nonsense words that conform to regular English spelling patterns. Spelling of Sounds is recommended for ages 6 and older. It contributes to the Spelling Skills and Phoneme–Grapheme Knowledge clusters.

Administration. Make sure the examinee has the Spelling of Sounds Response Booklet and a pencil before administering this test.

Examinees in preschool to Grade 1 start with Sample Items A and B. If an examinee does not respond correctly to at least one trial of Sample Item A or B, the test ends. Otherwise, the examinee proceeds to Block A (Items 1–5). Examinees who score at least 3 points on Block A proceed to Block B (Items 6–23).

Examinees in Grades 2–12 and all adults start with Sample Items C and D. If an examinee does not respond correctly to at least one trial of Sample Items C and D, the platform

Rapid Reference 5.21

Key Administration Points for Spelling of Sounds

- Recommended for ages 6 and older.
- Make sure the examinee has the Spelling of Sounds Response Booklet and a pencil.
- Use the Suggested Starting Point or select a different starting point.
- Administer Sample Items A–D and Items 1–5 orally and administer all other items from the audio recording.
- On Sample Items A and B and Items 1–5, pronounce letters between slashes as the letter sound.
- Instruct the examinee to write the words in the Response Booklet in the order they are presented.
- If necessary, remind the examinee to say the sound or nonsense word before writing their response. Do not correct the examinee if they mispronounce the sound or word.

routes the examinee back to Sample Item A. Otherwise, the examinee proceeds to Block B (Items 6–23). Examinees who score fewer than 3 points on Block B are routed back to Sample Item A. Examinees who score more than 15 points on Block B proceed to Block C (Items 24–28). For all other examinees, the test ends after Block B.

Administer all sample items and Items 1–5 orally and administer all other items from the audio recording. When you present the item prompts for Sample Items A and B and Items 1–5, pronounce the letters between slashes as the sound the letter makes, not the name of the letter. Be careful not to add a schwa sound to the phoneme (e.g., pronounce /t/ as a short, or clipped, *t* sound and not as *tuh*, and pronounce /m/ as *mm* and not as *muh*).

You may opt to administer Items 6–28 orally if the examinee appears to have difficulty understanding the audio-recorded item prompts. If you administer the item prompts orally, pronounce each item exactly as it is presented on the audio recording.

The test instructions require the examinee to say each sound or nonsense word before writing their response. This has no impact on the item scoring, but it does provide qualitative information. If the examinee mispronounces the item, do not correct the examinee or repeat the item. Note the mispronunciation and then compare it to the written response to obtain instructional insights. For example, if an examinee pronounces the nonsense word *foy* as *voy* and then proceeds to spell the word as *voy*, it may suggest that the examinee has difficulty discriminating between the /f/ and /v/ sounds (unvoiced and voiced consonants), rather than difficulties with spelling. If necessary, remind the examinee to say the sound or nonsense word before writing their response.

Instruct the examinee to write their first word on the first line of the Spelling Response Booklet, and to use the other lines in order.

Encourage the examinee to print responses instead of writing them in cursive, but do not penalize for cursive responses. Do not penalize the examinee for poor handwriting unless it is illegible. Accept reversed letters unless the reversal forms a different letter (e.g., a reversed *b* becomes a *d* and should be counted as an error). Accept upper- or lowercase letters.

You may repeat an item if the examinee requests it.

Item scoring. For each item, click the option in the scoring key that matches the examinee's response. If the examinee provides an incorrect response, click Incorrect. The platform assigns 1 point for correct responses and 0 points for incorrect responses. If you click I Don't Know or No Response, the item is scored incorrect (0 points).

Possible administration errors. Possible administration errors include not providing the Spelling of Sounds Response Booklet, mispronouncing the letter sounds when you read the item instructions, and penalizing the examinee for mispronouncing the sound or word.

ORAL READING

Oral Reading (Rapid Reference 5.22) is a measure of reading (Grw). It requires the examinee to orally read sentences that increase in difficulty. Oral Reading is recommended for ages 6 and older. It does not contribute to any WJ V cluster.

Administration. Before administering this test, make sure you know the correct pronunciation of all the words. If you are unsure about a pronunciation, consult a standard dictionary or the Item Pronunciation Guide on the Resources tab of the *Riverside Score*® platform.

This test is administered in item blocks. Each item block contains a story comprised of several sentences. Although the sentences are not presented in paragraph form, they

Rapid Reference 5.22

Key Administration Points for Oral Reading

- Recommended for ages 6 and older.
- Use the Suggested Starting Point or select a different starting point.
- Click any word the examinee mispronounces or omits to mark it as an error.
- If the examinee substitutes a different word for a presented word, click the word to select it as an error.
- If the examinee transposes words, click both words to select them as errors.
- If necessary, remind the examinee to read carefully, not quickly.
- You may conduct an error analysis later by reviewing the voice recording.
- Do not help the examinee read any words.

are organized around a specific content theme. Block A contains Story 1, Block B contains Story 2, Block C contains Story 3, Block D contains Story 4, Block E contains Story 5, and Block F contains Story 6. The platform suggests an appropriate starting block based on the examinee's grade or age.

Examinees in Grades 1–2 start with Introduction 1 and Block A. Examinees in Grades 3–12 and all adults start with Introduction 2 and Block C. Based on the score from each administered block, the platform routes the examinee to an appropriate (easier or more difficult) next block. Testing continues until the examinee does not meet the continuation requirements.

As the examinee reads each story on their iPad aloud, click to select any word on which the examinee makes an error. Possible error types are:

- **Mispronunciations.** The examinee mispronounces a word (e.g., the examinee says *storm* instead of *storing*; however, do not penalize the examinee for mispronunciations resulting from articulation errors, dialect variations, or regional speech patterns).
- **Omissions.** The examinee skips one or more words. If the examinee skips an entire sentence, mark all words in the sentence as errors.
- **Substitution.** The examinee substitutes a presented word with a different word.
- **Transpositions.** The examinee switches the order of the presented words. If this happens, select both words as errors.
- **Hesitations.** The examinee hesitates for 3 or more seconds on a word. If this happens, select the word as an error and say: *Go on to the next word.*

If the examinee self-corrects on any word already selected as an error, click the word again to deselect it. Do *not* count the following as errors:

- Repetitions (i.e., the examinee says the same word twice in a row)
- Additions or insertions (Note that this rule is different from the WJ IV scoring rules.)

Some examinees may read quickly, making it difficult to score their responses. If the examinee is reading too quickly, say: *Remember to read carefully, not quickly.* If necessary, you may ask the examinee to pause at the end of each sentence if you need additional time to score their responses.

Do not help the examinee read any words on this test.

DON'T FORGET

On the WJ V, you do not need to document the specific error types when you are administering Oral Reading. However, a qualitative analysis of error types can be useful for understanding the examinee's reading difficulties. You can review the voice recording later to conduct an error analysis and—if necessary—you can also check your scoring accuracy at that time. The voice recordings are deleted from the *Riverside Score*® platform 90 days after you first generate a score report.

Item scoring. The platform assigns a score of 2 points for each sentence the examinee reads with no errors, 1 point for each sentence with 1 error, and 0 points for each sentence with 2 or more errors.

Possible administration errors. Possible administration errors include not knowing the correct pronunciation of all words on the test; helping the examinee to read words; not selecting mispronunciations, omissions, substitutions, and hesitations as errors; and not selecting both words as errors if the examinee transposes words.

READING RECALL

Reading Recall (Rapid Reference 5.23) is a measure of reading (Grw) and long-term storage (Gl). It requires the examinee to read stories and then retell the stories with as much detail as possible. Reading Recall is recommended for ages 6 and older. It does not contribute to any WJ V cluster.

Administration. All examinees begin with Introduction 1. The examinee is then routed to an appropriate block of stories. Examinees in Preschool to Grade 1 begin with Block A (Stories 1 and 2); examinees in Grades 2–4 begin with Block B (Stories 3 and 4); examinees in Grades 5–8 begin with Block D (Stories 5 and 6); and examinees in Grades 9–12 and all adults begin with Block D (Stories 7 and 8).

The examinee reads each story on their iPad screen silently. If the examinee reads aloud, encourage them to read silently, but do not require it. Do not help the examinee read any words on this test. When the examinee is finished reading the story, they tap Done and then begin retelling the story in as much detail as they can remember. The examinee does *not* need to recall the elements in the correct order.

As the examinee recalls the details in the story, click to select the correctly recalled elements. An element is correctly recalled if the examinee says the word(s) in bold type. Accept a response that is a synonym of the bold word (e.g., *cash* for *money*), as long as the

Rapid Reference 5.23

Key Administration Points for Reading Recall

- Recommended for ages 6 and older.
- Use the Suggested Starting Point or select a different starting point.
- Play each story only one time.
- Words in bold type must be recalled exactly with a few exceptions (e.g., synonyms, e.g., *kitty* for *cat*; different verb tenses, e.g., *jumping* for *jump*; singular or plural, e.g., *neighbor* for *neighbors*; a derivation of a name, e.g., *Joey* for *Joe*; or the addition/removal of possessive case, e.g., *Francisco* for *Francisco's*).
- Numbers (e.g., *forty*) must be recalled *exactly*.
- The elements may be recalled in any order.

response preserves the meaning of the word. If a bold word is a proper name, accept any reasonable derivation of the name (e.g., *Joey* for *Joe*). Accept words that differ in verb tense (e.g., *jumping* for *jump*) or possessive (e.g., *Francisco* for *Francisco's*). If the bold word is singular (e.g., *puppet*), accept a plural response (e.g., *puppets*), and vice versa. However, if a bold word is a number (e.g., *forty*), the examinee must recall the number *exactly* to receive credit. Do not penalize the examinee for mispronunciations resulting from articulation errors, dialect variations, or regional speech patterns.

If the examinee does not respond after reading the story, say: *Tell me anything about the story you remember.* Based on the examinee's total score from the first two stories administered, the examinee will be routed to an easier or more difficult block of stories, or the test will end. In most cases, an examinee will hear a maximum of four stories (two blocks); however, in rare cases, an examinee may hear six stories (three blocks) before the test ends.

Item scoring. The platform assigns 1 point for every correctly recalled bold element. If you are unsure whether you scored the story correctly, you may review the test's audio capture prior to submitting the test set for reporting.

Possible administration errors. Possible administration errors include helping the examinee to read words and not scoring the elements correctly.

ACADEMIC VOCABULARY

Academic Vocabulary (Rapid Reference 5.24) is a comprehension-knowledge (Gc) measure of vocabulary in academic domains. The examinee answers questions read orally by the examiner from the academic domains of science, mathematics, and the humanities. Academic Vocabulary is recommended for ages 5 and older. It contributes to the Academic Knowledge cluster.

Administration. The platform suggests an appropriate starting item. Examinees in preschool to Grade 2 begin with Item 1, examinees in Grades 3–4 begin with Item 4, examinees in Grades 5–6 begin with Item 8, examinees in Grades 7–12 and average-ability adults begin with Item 10, and above-average adults begin with Item 15.

Unless noted, accept only one-word responses. If an examinee provides a two-word response, ask for a one-word answer. Do not penalize the examinee for mispronunciations resulting from articulation errors, dialect variations, or regional speech patterns.

You may repeat an item if the examinee requests it.

Rapid Reference 5.24

Key Administration Points for Academic Vocabulary

- Use the Suggested Starting Point or select a different starting point.
- Query the examinee's response when instructed by the platform.
- Recommended for ages 5 and older.

Some items require you to query certain examinee responses. Read the query prompt exactly as it appears on the screen and then score the examinee's next response.

The test ends when the examinee reaches a ceiling of five consecutive items incorrect or when Item 36 is administered.

Item scoring. For each item, click the word in the scoring key that matches the examinee's response. If the examinee says a word that does not appear in the scoring key, use the Other–1 option for a correct response or the Other–0 option for an incorrect response. Optionally, you can also type the examinee's response into the Other text field for later analysis. The platform assigns 1 point for correct responses and 0 points for incorrect responses. If you click I Don't Know or No Response, the item is scored incorrect (0 points).

Possible administration errors. Possible administration errors include mispronouncing the words when administering the items orally and not querying when the examinee's response requires it.

ACADEMIC FACTS

Academic Facts (Rapid Reference 5.25) is a measure of comprehension-knowledge (Gc) in academic domains. The examinee answers questions read orally by the examiner from the academic domains of science, mathematics, and the humanities. Academic Facts is recommended for ages 5 and older. It contributes to the Academic Knowledge cluster.

Administration. The platform suggests an appropriate starting item. Examinees in preschool to Kindergarten begin with Item 1, examinees in Grades 1–2 begin with Item 6, examinees in Grades 3–4 begin with Item 9, examinees in Grades 5–6 begin with Item 13, examinees in Grades 7–12 and average adults begin with Item 16, and above-average adults begin with Item 20.

Unless noted, accept only one-word responses. If an examinee provides a two-word response, ask for a one-word answer. Do not penalize the examinee for mispronunciations resulting from articulation errors, dialect variations, or regional speech patterns.

You may repeat an item if the examinee requests it.

Some items require you to query certain examinee responses. Read the query prompt exactly as it appears on the screen and then score the examinee's next response.

Rapid Reference 5.25

Key Administration Points for Academic Facts

- Recommended for ages 5 and older.
- Use the Suggested Starting Point or select a different starting point.
- Query the examinee's response when instructed by the platform.

The test ends when the examinee reaches a ceiling of five consecutive items incorrect or when Item 44 is administered.

Item scoring. For each item, click the word in the scoring key that matches the examinee's response. If you click I Don't Know or No Response, the item is scored incorrect (0 points).

Possible administration errors. Possible administration errors include mispronouncing the words when administering the items orally and not querying when the examinee's response requires it.

LETTER WRITING FLUENCY

Letter Writing Fluency (Rapid Reference 5.26) is a speeded (Gs) measure of letter writing automaticity. It requires the examinee to write the letters of the alphabet as quickly as possible, first from memory and then by copying from a printed model. Each item has a 30-second time limit. Letter Writing Fluency is recommended for examinees ages 4–9. While it can be administered to an examinee of any age, it will only provide normative scores for examinees in this age range. It does not contribute to any WJ V cluster.

Administration. Make sure the examinee has the Letter Writing Fluency Response Booklet and a pencil before administering this test. You will need the Letter Writing Fluency Scoring Guide, available on the Resources tab of *Riverside Score*®, to score the examinee's responses.

Administer Items 1 and 2 to all examinees. For each item, read the instructions orally to the examinee and then click the Start Timer button to start the 30-second timer. The platform will alert you when 30 seconds are up. If the examinee finishes writing all the letters before the time is up, click Stop Timer.

On Item 1, the examinee does *not* need to write the letters in alphabetical order. If the examinee pauses for more than 2 seconds, say: *Just write all the letters you know.*

Rapid Reference 5.26

Key Administration Points for Letter Writing Fluency

- Recommended for ages 4 to 9; this test produces normative scores for *only* ages 4 to 9.
- Make sure the examinee has the Letter Writing Fluency Response Booklet and a pencil.
- Administer both items.
- If necessary on Item 1, encourage the examinee to write any letters they know.
- If necessary, remind the examinee to cross out, and not erase, any letter they want to change.
- Score all test items *after* the test is complete using the Letter Writing Fluency Scoring Guide. Do not attempt to score the test items during the administration.

If the examinee struggles further, you can suggest that they write the letters in their name. On Item 2, the examinee should write the letters in alphabetical order as shown in the model.

The examinee can write either upper- or lowercase letters.

Because it takes more time, do not allow the examinee to erase any letters. If the examinee begins to erase a letter, remind them to just cross out their first letter and write their new one.

Item scoring. Do not score the examinee's responses to the test items until after the administration is complete. For each item, assign 1 point for each unique, recognizable letter of the alphabet. On Item 2 only, assign 0 points to any letter not in alphabetical order when reading from left to right. If the examinee writes the same letter more than one time, score only the first occurrence and ignore the other(s) when reading from left to right. Score both uppercase and lowercase letters as correct if they are recognizable. Assign 0 points for letters that are reversed, inverted, or illegible. Refer to the examples in the Letter Writing Fluency Scoring Guide for scoring guidance.

Count the number of correct letters (0–26) on each item in the Response Booklet and write the totals in the Totals boxes at the bottom of each page. To enter the examinee's scores on the *Riverside Score*® platform, launch the Review workflow. Under Items and Tests to Review, click the link for Letter Writing Fluency to launch the score entry modal. Transfer the Item 1 and Item 2 totals from the Response Booklet to the score entry fields on the platform. Then click Submit.

Possible administration errors. Possible administration errors include not reminding the examinee to cross out letters instead of erasing, giving credit for duplicate letters, giving credit for letters written out of order on Item 2, and not penalizing for reversed, inverted, or illegible letters.

TEST YOURSELF

1. Which test has a 5-minute limit?

(A) Sentence Reading Fluency
(B) Math Facts Fluency
(C) Sentence Writing Fluency
(D) Word Reading Fluency

2. Which test does *not* require a Response Booklet?

(A) Applied Problems
(B) Math Problem Identification
(C) Math Facts Fluency
(D) Word Attack
(E) Spelling of Sounds

3. **Which of the following are *true* about the administration of the Calculation test? (Select all that apply.)**
   (A) You may allow the examinee to work independently to solve the problems in the Response Booklet because this test is scored after the administration is complete.
   (B) You should instruct the examinee to work the problems in order in the Response Booklet while you follow along and score each item as correct or incorrect in the *Riverside Score*® platform.
   (C) If the examinee skips an item, click Next to advance to the next item.
   (D) If the examinee skips an item, click No Response.
4. **On Oral Reading, the sentence is *A tree's age may be determined by its growth rings.* The examinee reads the sentence as follows: *A tree's age may be detrimental to its growth rings.* How many errors should you mark?**
   (A) 4
   (B) 3
   (C) 2
   (D) 1
5. **On Math Facts Fluency, you can either score the examinee's responses while they are working or wait until the test is over to score the responses. True or false?**
6. **On which test might the *Riverside Score*® platform prompt you to administer more items after you enter the examinee's item scores?**
   (A) Written Language Samples
   (B) Sentence Writing Fluency
   (C) Calculation
   (D) Spelling of Sounds
7. **While you are administering the Spelling of Sounds item *grunches*, the examinee says *glunches* and then writes *glunches*. You should score the response correct because the examinee wrote the word the way they heard it. True or false?**
8. **Which of the following tests does *not* require you to use a separate scoring guide to assign scores to the examinee's responses?**
   (A) Sentence Writing Fluency
   (B) Written Language Samples
   (C) Math Facts Fluency
   (D) Math Problem Identification
9. **On Sentence Writing Fluency, the words are *cone*, *looks*, and *good*. The examinee writes: *that cone looked good*. How should you score the response?**
   (A) Correct.
   (B) Incorrect because the examinee did not use the words in the correct order.
   (C) Incorrect because the examinee changed the word *looks* to *looked*.
   (D) Incorrect because the examinee did not capitalize the first word of the sentence.

10. In which of the following scenarios is it *acceptable* to help an examinee read a word?

(A) On Word Reading Fluency, during the Practice Exercise.

(B) On Sentence Writing Fluency, if the examinee asks for help reading a stimulus word on a test item.

(C) On Paragraph Reading Comprehension, when the examinee is reading the passage.

(D) On Oral Reading, if the examinee has reached items beyond their reading level.

11. On Letter Writing Fluency Item 1, if the examinee writes both an upper-case *T* and a lower-case t, you should:

(A) Score 2 points for the letter *t*.

(B) Score 1 point for the letter *t*.

(C) Score 0 points for the letter *t*.

12. On Passage Comprehension, if the examinee reads aloud, you should remind them to read silently, but do not penalize them for reading aloud. True or false?

ANSWERS

1. **C.** Sentence Writing Fluency has a 5-minute limit; however, you may stop the timer to end the test after 2 minutes if the examinee has not written at least one correct sentence.
2. **D.** Word Attack does not require a Response Booklet.
3. **B and D.** On the Calculation test, the examinee works the problems in the Response Booklet in order, while you follow along and score each item correct or incorrect. Do not allow the examinee to skip around. If the examinee skips one item, select No Response and advance to the next item. In some cases, the platform may skip back to an easier item. If this happens, point to the appropriate item in the Response Booklet and say: Do this one.
4. **C.** The examinee made two errors: (a) they substituted detrimental for determined; and (b) they substituted the word *to* for by.
5. **False.** You should not attempt to score the examinee's responses during the test. Instead, wait until you have finished administering the test and then use the Math Facts Fluency Scoring Guide to score the responses.
6. **A.** Based on the examinee's score on the Written Language Samples items that were administered, the platform may prompt you to administer an additional block of items. For this reason, it is a good idea to score the examinee's responses while they are still present, especially if it will not be possible or convenient to schedule an additional testing session.
7. **False.** Even if the examinee writes the word exactly as they pronounce it, score the item incorrect if it does not match the correct spelling in the scoring key. If an examinee consistently mispronounces the words on this test, it might provide qualitative information about the examinee's ability to differentiate speech sounds.
8. **D.** Math Problem Identification does not require you to use a separate scoring guide.
9. **C.** In Sentence Writing Fluency, the examinee must not change any of the stimulus words. They do *not* need to use the words in the same order they are presented, and you should not penalize for capitalization, spelling, or punctuation errors.

10. **B.** You may read any word the examinee asks for help with on Sentence Writing Fluency. Do not help the examinee with words on the Word Reading Fluency Practice Exercise, since one purpose of the Practice Exercise is to determine whether the examinee can read well enough to take the test. Do not help the examinee with *any* words on reading tests, such as Paragraph Reading Comprehension or Oral Reading.
11. **B.** Count each letter only one time. The examinee may write in upper- or lower-case. Do not assign an extra point if the examinee writes a letter both ways.
12. **True.** On tests that require the examinee to read passages, such as Passage Comprehension, Paragraph Reading Comprehension, and Reading Recall, encourage the examinee to read silently but do not penalize the examinee for reading aloud.

Six

WJ V VIRTUAL TEST LIBRARY TEST ADMINISTRATION

This chapter provides an overview of the administration procedures for the WJ V Virtual Test Library tests. Whether you are just learning the WJ V or need a review of certain tests, this chapter can serve as a guide or refresher. At the end of the chapter, there is a Test Yourself quiz. After studying or reviewing the test administration procedures, you may wish to do a practice administration of each test.

Before administering each test on the digital platform, review the Administration Overview screen for administration and scoring reminders, and consult the Things to Know panel to see if the test is timed or uses audio recordings.

NONSENSE WORD REPETITION

Nonsense Word Repetition (Rapid Reference 6.1) is a measure of auditory processing (Ga) and auditory working memory capacity (Gwm). The examinee hears a nonsense word and then repeats it verbatim. Nonsense Word Repetition is recommended for ages 4 and older. It does not contribute to any WJ V cluster.

Administration. Before administering this test, make sure you know the correct pronunciations for the nonsense words in Items 1–4. A phonetic pronunciation guide is included with each item.

All examinees start with Sample Items A and B and are then routed to an appropriate starting point: Item 1 for examinees in preschool to Grade 1, Item 5 for examinees in Grades 2–6, and Item 10 for examinees in Grades 7–12 and all adults.

Essentials of WJ V™ Assessment, First Edition. Erica M. LaForte, Nancy Mather, and W. Joel Schneider.

Rapid Reference 6.1

Key Administration Points for Nonsense Word Repetition

- Recommended for ages 4 and older.
- Use the Suggested Starting Point or select a different starting point.
- Administer Sample Items A and B and Items 1–4 orally and administer Items 5–33 from the audio recording.
- Other than the sample items, do not replay or repeat any of the test items.
- If necessary, remind the examinee to say the nonsense words smoothly.
- Score an item correct if the examinee repeats the sounds in the nonsense word exactly but changes the emphasis on syllables.

Administer Sample Items A and B and Items 1–4 orally. Administer Items 5–33 from the audio recording. You may opt to administer Items 5–14 orally if the examinee appears to have difficulty understanding the audio-recorded item prompts. If you administer the item prompts orally, use the phonetic pronunciation guide provided with each item to say it exactly as it is presented on the audio recording. Because they are difficult to pronounce correctly, do *not* attempt to administer Items 15–33 orally.

If an examinee responds incorrectly to the first trial of a sample item, read the corrective feedback before advancing to the second trial.

You may repeat the sample items, but do not repeat any of the test items.

To be scored correct, the examinee must say the nonsense word smoothly. If the examinee says the word phoneme by phoneme and then says it smoothly, score the item as correct. However, if the examinee says the word phoneme by phoneme but then fails to say it smoothly, instruct them to say the word aloud smoothly. Provide this instruction only one time during the test. If the examinee does not say the word smoothly after that, score it incorrect.

Examinees must repeat the sounds in each nonsense word exactly, but do not need to stress the syllables exactly as they were stressed in the item prompt. If you are unsure whether the examinee repeated the sounds in the nonsense word exactly, do not ask the examinee to say it again. If the examinee has not obtained a basal, score the item incorrect; otherwise, score it correct. Flag the item for later review. You can review the voice recording on *Riverside Score®* to check your scoring accuracy.

Do not penalize the examinee for mispronunciations resulting from articulation errors, dialect variations, or regional speech patterns.

The test ends when the examinee reaches a ceiling of six consecutive items incorrect or when Item 33 is administered.

Item scoring. For each item, click the option in the scoring key that matches the examinee's response. If the examinee provides an incorrect response, click Incorrect. The platform assigns 1 point for correct responses and 0 points for incorrect responses. If you click I Don't Know or No Response, the item is scored incorrect (0 points).

Possible administration errors. Possible administration errors include not reading corrective feedback when it is provided, repeating a test item, or scoring an item incorrect if the examinee said the sounds correctly but stressed different syllables.

RAPID PICTURE NAMING

Rapid Picture Naming (Rapid Reference 6.2) is a measure of cognitive processing speed (Gs) and retrieval fluency (Gr). The examinee sees pictures on the screen and says the names of as many pictures as possible in 1 minute. Rapid Picture Naming is recommended for ages 4 and older. It contributes to the Rapid Automatized Naming (RAN)-Reading (Gs, Gr) cluster.

Administration. All examinees start with Sample Item A. Read the Sample A instructions to the examinee, and then click on any words the examinee says incorrectly or skips. If an examinee incorrectly names or skips any pictures, use your cursor to point to the picture(s) on the Examinee's View and read the corrective feedback before advancing to the second trial. For examinees who do not correctly name all five pictures in two trials of Sample Item A, the test ends. All other examinees proceed to the test items.

This test contains 8 item sets. Each item set contains 3 rows of 5 pictures each (15 total pictures per screen). Read the introduction to the test items and then click Next to display the first set of items on the examinee's iPad and say: *Go ahead.*

As the examinee names the pictures, use your cursor to follow along and roll over the words in your scoring interface. If the examinee says an incorrect picture name or skips a picture, click the word to score that picture incorrect. If the examinee self-corrects, click the word again to score it correct.

If the examinee starts naming the pictures down the screen instead of across the rows, say: *Remember to work across the row.* If the examinee pauses for 2 seconds and does not appear engaged in the task, say: *Do the next one.* However, be careful not to give this prompt if the examinee appears to be focused on the task, to avoid distracting the examinee.

Rapid Reference 6.2

Key Administration Points for Rapid Picture Naming

- Recommended for ages 4 and older.
- This test has a 1-minute time limit.
- Click on any picture the examinee skips or says incorrectly to mark it as an error.
- If the examinee pauses for 2 seconds and does not appear to be engaged in the task, say: *Do the next one.*
- Do not ask the examinee to repeat a response.
- Tap N on your keyboard when the examinee says the last word on the screen to *immediately* advance to the next item set.

When the examinee reaches the last picture on each screen, *immediately* click Next or use the hotkey N on your computer keyboard to advance the screen. The item sets alternate between a light gray and dark gray background color to visually cue the examinee that the screen has changed.

Do not penalize the examinee if they say a synonym or reasonable alternative word, such as *cap* for *hat* or *puppy* for *dog*.

If you are unsure whether the examinee named a picture, do not stop the examinee to ask. You can review the voice recording later to check your scoring accuracy, and—if necessary—you can adjust the score then.

Do not penalize the examinee for mispronunciations resulting from articulation errors, dialect variations, or regional speech patterns.

When the 1-minute timer runs out or when the examinee completes Item Set 8, say: *Stop.* If the examinee is still naming pictures when the timer runs out, the platform will prompt you to click the last word the examinee said. Then, it will prompt you to click on any errors that were not marked before the timer ran out. This is to ensure that the platform can accurately compute the score for a partially completed item set.

CAUTION

The Rapid Automatized Naming (RAN) tests are scored based on the examinee's accuracy *and* speed. To avoid a delay in advancing the screen (which can deflate the examinee's score), *immediately* advance the screen when the examinee names the last picture in each item set. Instead of clicking Next, you can tap the N key on your keyboard to quickly advance the screen. A good strategy is to use your dominant hand to follow along the scoring interface with your mouse while resting the pointer finger of your nondominant hand on your keyboard's N key. This way, you can quickly advance the screen when the examinee finishes each item set.

Item scoring. Click on any words the examinee names incorrectly or skips. The platform assigns 1 point for each picture the examinee names correctly and 0 points for each picture the examinee skips or names incorrectly.

Possible administration errors. Possible administration errors include not providing corrective feedback if the examinee makes an error on Sample Item A, not marking errors or skipped pictures incorrect, and not advancing the screen *immediately* when the examinee names the last picture.

ANIMAL-NUMBER SEQUENCING

Animal-Number Sequencing (Rapid Reference 6.3) is a measure of auditory working memory (Gwm). The examinee hears an intermingled series of animals and numbers and then says the animals in order followed by the numbers in order. Animal-Number Sequencing is recommended for ages 5 and older. It does not contribute to any WJ V cluster.

Administration. All examinees begin with Introduction 1 and Sample Item A. Examinees in preschool to Grade 3 then proceed to Introduction 2, Sample Item B, and Block A (Items 1–6), while examinees in Grades 4–12 and all adults proceed to Introduction 3 and Sample Item C and then begin testing with Item 7 (Block B). For examinees who have fewer than 4 correct after Block A, the test ends.

Rapid Reference 6.3

Key Administration Points for Animal-Number Sequencing

- Recommended for ages 5 and older.
- Use the Suggested Starting Point or select a different starting point.
- Administer Sample Item A orally and administer Sample Items B and C and all test items from the audio recording.
- You may repeat sample items, but do not replay or repeat any of the test items.
- The examinee must say the animals first, in order, followed by the numbers, in order, to receive credit.
- Block B uses basal and ceiling rules. Examinees who do not have at least 4 correct on Block B are administered Block A, unless it was already administered.

Administer Sample Items B and C and all test items from the audio recording. You may opt to administer all items orally if the examinee appears to have difficulty understanding the audio-recorded item prompts. If you administer the item prompts orally, say them exactly as they are presented on the audio recording, at a rate of one word per second. Drop your voice slightly at the end of each series so the examinee knows that the series has ended.

The examinee must say the animals first in order, followed by the numbers in order, to receive credit. If the examinee says the digits first, click Says Digits First and then read the corrective feedback.

You may repeat the sample items, but do not repeat any of the test items.

Block B (Items 7–31) is administered with basal and ceiling rules. Examinees who are administered Block B must obtain a basal (Item 7) and a ceiling (4 consecutive items incorrect or Item 31) within Block B. Examinees who are administered Block B but have a score of fewer than 4 points after a ceiling is obtained are routed back to Block A, unless it was already administered.

Item scoring. For each item, click the option in the scoring key that matches the examinee's response. If the examinee provides another incorrect response, click Incorrect. The platform assigns 1 point for correct responses and 0 points for incorrect responses.

Possible administration errors. Possible administration errors include giving credit for an item where the examinee says the words in the wrong order or playing an item more than one time.

SOUND REVERSAL

Sound Reversal (Rapid Reference 6.4) is a measure of phonological awareness (Ga). The examinee hears a word and says the sounds in reverse order to form a new word. Sound Reversal is recommended for ages 7 and older. It does not contribute to any WJ V cluster.

Administration. All examinees begin with Sample Item A. Examinees in preschool to Grade 8 then proceed to Item 1, while examinees in Grades 9–12 and all adults proceed to Item 5.

Rapid Reference 6.4

Key Administration Points for Sound Reversal

- Recommended for ages 7 and older.
- Use the Suggested Starting Point or select a different starting point.
- Administer all items orally.
- Pronounce letters between slashes as the letter sound. Be careful not to add a schwa sound.
- If necessary, remind the examinee to say the word smoothly.

When you present the Introduction and the item prompt for Sample Item A, pronounce the letters between slashes as the sound the letter makes, not the name of the letter. Be careful not to add a schwa sound to the phoneme (e.g., pronounce /n/ as *nn* and not as nuh).

If an examinee responds incorrectly to the first trial of Sample Item A, read the corrective feedback before advancing to the second trial.

You may repeat an item if the examinee requests it.

To be scored correct, the examinee must say the word smoothly. If the examinee says the word sound by sound or phoneme by phoneme and then says it smoothly, score the item as correct. However, if the examinee says the word sound by sound or phoneme by phoneme but then fails to say it smoothly, instruct them to say the word aloud smoothly. Provide this instruction only one time during the test. If the examinee does not say a word smoothly after that, score it incorrect.

Do not penalize the examinee for mispronunciations resulting from articulation errors, dialect variations, or regional speech patterns.

The test ends when the examinee reaches a ceiling of 5 consecutive items incorrect or when Item 20 is administered.

Item scoring. For each item, click the option in the scoring key that matches the examinee's response. If the examinee provides an incorrect response, click Incorrect. The platform assigns 1 point for correct responses and 0 points for incorrect responses. If you click I Don't Know or No Response, the item is scored incorrect (0 points).

Possible administration errors. Possible administration errors include mispronouncing the letter sounds when you read the Introduction and Sample Item A, not reading corrective feedback when it is provided, and scoring words the examinee pronounces sound by sound or phoneme by phoneme correct.

RAPID LETTER NAMING

Rapid Letter Naming (Rapid Reference 6.5) is a measure of cognitive processing speed (Gs) and retrieval fluency (Gr). The examinee sees letters on the screen and says the names of as many letters as possible in 1 minute. Rapid Letter Naming is recommended for ages 4 and older. It contributes to the RAN-Reading (Gs, Gr) cluster.

Rapid Reference 6.5

Key Administration Points for Rapid Letter Naming

- Recommended for ages 4 and older.
- This test has a 1-minute time limit.
- Click on any letter the examinee skips or says incorrectly to mark it as an error.
- If the examinee pauses for 2 seconds and does not appear to be engaged in the task, say: *Do the next one.*
- Do not ask the examinee to repeat a response.
- Tap N on your keyboard when the examinee says the last letter on the screen to *immediately* advance to the next item set.

Administration. All examinees start with Sample Item A. Read the Sample A instructions to the examinee, and then click on any letters the examinee says incorrectly or skips. If an examinee incorrectly names or skips any letters, use your cursor to point to the letter(s) on the Examinee's View and read the corrective feedback before advancing to the second trial. For examinees who do not correctly name all 5 letters in two trials of Sample Item A, the test ends. All other examinees proceed to the test items.

This test contains 8 item sets. Each item set contains 3 rows of 5 letters each (15 total letters per screen). Read the introduction to the test items and then click Next to display the first set of items on the examinee's iPad and say: *Go ahead.*

As the examinee names the letters, use your cursor to follow along and roll over the letters in your scoring interface. If the examinee says an incorrect letter name or skips a letter, click the letter to score it incorrect. If the examinee self-corrects, click the letter again to score it correct.

If the examinee starts naming the letters down the screen instead of across the rows, say: *Remember to work across the row.* If the examinee pauses for 2 seconds and does not appear engaged in the task, say: *Do the next one.* However, be careful not to give this prompt if the examinee appears to be focused on the task, to avoid distracting the examinee.

When the examinee reaches the last letter on each screen, *immediately* click Next or use the hotkey N on your computer keyboard to advance the screen. The item sets alternate between a light gray and dark gray background color to visually cue the examinee that the screen has changed.

If you are unsure whether the examinee named a letter, do not stop the examinee to ask. You can review the voice recording later to check your scoring accuracy, and—if necessary—you can adjust the score then.

Do not penalize the examinee for mispronunciations resulting from articulation errors, dialect variations, or regional speech patterns.

When the 1-minute timer runs out or when the examinee completes Item Set 8, say: *Stop.* If the examinee is still naming letters when the timer runs out, the platform will prompt you to click the last letter the examinee said. Then, it will prompt you to click on any errors that were not marked before the timer ran out. This is to ensure that the platform can accurately compute the score for a partially completed item set.

Item scoring. Click on any letters that the examinee names incorrectly or skips. The platform assigns 1 point for each letter the examinee names correctly and 0 points for each letter the examinee skips or names incorrectly.

Possible administration errors. Possible administration errors include not providing corrective feedback if the examinee makes an error on Sample Item A, not marking errors or skipped letters incorrect, and not advancing the screen *immediately* when the examinee names the last letter.

UNDERSTANDING DIRECTIONS

Understanding Directions (Rapid Reference 6.6) is a measure of working memory (Gwm) and fluid reasoning (Gf). The examinee sees a picture for 10 seconds and then responds to oral or audio-recorded prompts to tap specific elements in the picture. Understanding Directions is recommended for ages 4 and older. It does not contribute to any WJ V cluster.

Administration. This test is administered in item blocks. Block A contains Picture 1, Block B contains Pictures 2 and 3, Block C contains Pictures 4 and 5, and Block D contains Picture 6. All examinees start with Introduction 1, and then the platform suggests an appropriate starting block based on the examinee's grade or age.

Examinees in preschool begin testing with Introduction 2 and Block A. For examinees with fewer than 7 correct after Block A, the test ends. Otherwise, the examinee proceeds to Introduction 3 and Block B.

Examinees in Kindergarten to Grade 3 begin testing with Introduction 3 and Block B. Examinees in Grades 4–12 and all adults begin testing with Introduction 5 and Block C. Based on the score from the first block of pictures administered, the platform routes each examinee to an appropriate (easier or more difficult) second block of pictures.

Rapid Reference 6.6

Key Administration Points for Understanding Directions

- Recommended for ages 4 and older.
- Use the Suggested Starting Point or select a different starting point.
- On the introduction for each picture, advance the screen when the platform alerts you that 10 seconds have passed. Do not allow the examinee additional time to review the picture.
- Use the Clear Examinee's Response button if the examinee asks to redo an item, but do *not* replay the audio prompt.
- If necessary, remind the examinee to tap Done when they have finished responding.

On the introduction to each picture, read the text exactly as it appears on your screen. The platform will alert you when 10 seconds have passed. When this happens, advance to the first item. Do not allow the examinee additional time to review the picture.

Administer all items from the audio recording. You may opt to administer all items orally if the examinee appears to have difficulty understanding the audio-recorded item prompts. If you administer the item prompts orally, read them with the same inflection as the audio-recorded prompts.

The examinee responds to the item prompts by tapping elements on their iPad screen. The locations of the examinee's taps appear on the Examinee's View as numbered icons. Evaluate the location and order of each numbered icon to determine whether the examinee's response is correct or incorrect. If the examinee makes a mistake and asks to change it, use the Clear Examinee's Response button and say: *Go ahead and do it again,* but do *not* repeat the item prompt.

If the examinee begins tapping their response before the audio-recorded item prompt says, *Go,* say: *Remember, do not tap until you hear the word "Go."* Clear the examinee's response and allow a second attempt if the examinee requests it, but do *not* repeat the item prompt.

In some cases, if the examinee's finger lingers on the iPad after they make a tap, the platform may register multiple taps. If this happens, do not mark the multiple taps as errors and do not ask the examinee to repeat their response. Score the response as though only one tap registered. However, if an examinee clearly taps twice in the same location, mark the response incorrect.

Some items require you to query certain examinee responses. Read the query prompt exactly as it appears on the screen and then score the examinee's next response.

If necessary, remind the examinee to tap Done when they have finished responding.

Do not repeat any item prompt on this test.

Item scoring. Compare the location and order of the examinee's taps to the scoring key. Score the item correct if the examinee taps all required elements in the correct order. Score the item incorrect if the examinee taps the elements in the wrong order, skips one or more required elements, or taps an incorrect element.

Possible administration errors. Possible administration errors include allowing the examinee more than 10 seconds to view each picture, replaying item prompts, not clearing the examinee's responses when they ask to start over, and not following the scoring criteria exactly when assigning scores to the examinee's responses.

SOUND BLENDING

Sound Blending (Rapid Reference 6.7) is a measure of phonological awareness (Ga). The examinee hears word parts, and then phonemes, and blends them together to say the whole word smoothly. Sound Blending is recommended for ages 4 and older. It contributes to the Phonological Awareness (Ga) cluster.

Rapid Reference 6.7

Key Administration Points for Sound Blending

- Recommended for ages 4 and older.
- Use the Suggested Starting Point or select a different starting point.
- Administer Sample Item A orally and administer Sample Item B and all test items from the audio recording.
- Other than the sample items, do not replay or repeat any of the test items.
- If necessary, remind the examinee to say the word smoothly.

Administration. All examinees begin with Sample Items A and B. Examinees in preschool to Grade 1 are then routed to Item 1, examinees in Grades 2–6 are routed to Item 4, and examinees in Grades 7–12 and all adults are routed to Item 8.

Present Sample Item A orally. Present Sample Item B and all test items from the audio recording. You may opt to present Items 1–16 orally if the examinee appears to have difficulty understanding the audio-recorded item prompts. If you administer the item prompts orally, use the phonetic pronunciation guide provided with each item to say it exactly as it is presented on the audio recording, pausing slightly between each sound. Because they are difficult to pronounce correctly, do *not* attempt to administer Items 17–30 orally.

If an examinee responds incorrectly to the first trial of Sample Item A or B, read the corrective feedback before advancing to the second trial.

You may repeat the sample items, but do not repeat any of the test items.

To be scored correct, the examinee must say the word smoothly. If the examinee repeats the word sound by sound and then says it smoothly, score the item correct. However, if the examinee says the word sound by sound but then fails to say it smoothly, instruct them to say the word aloud smoothly. Provide this instruction only one time during the test. If the examinee does not say a word smoothly after that, score it incorrect.

Do not penalize the examinee for mispronunciations resulting from articulation errors, dialect variations, or regional speech patterns.

The test ends when the examinee reaches a ceiling of 5 consecutive items incorrect or when Item 30 is administered.

Item scoring. For each item, click the option in the scoring key that matches the examinee's response. If the examinee provides an incorrect response, click Incorrect. The platform assigns 1 point for correct responses and 0 points for incorrect responses. If you click I Don't Know or No Response, the item is scored incorrect (0 points).

Possible administration errors. Possible administration errors include not reading corrective feedback when it is provided and scoring words the examinee pronounces sound by sound or phoneme by phoneme correct.

RAPID PHONEME NAMING

Rapid Phoneme Naming (Rapid Reference 6.8) is a measure of cognitive processing speed (Gs), retrieval fluency (Gr), and auditory processing (Ga). The examinee sees letters on the screen and says as many letter sounds as possible in 1 minute. Rapid Phoneme Naming is recommended for ages 6 and older. It contributes to the RAN-Reading (Gs, Gr) cluster.

Administration. All examinees start with Introduction 1 and Sample Items A and B. On Introduction 1, pronounce the letters between slashes as the sounds the letters make, not the letter names. Be careful not to add a schwa sound to the phonemes (e.g., pronounce /m/ as *mm* and not as *muh*). On Samples A and B, click on any phonemes the examinee says incorrectly or skips. If an examinee incorrectly names or skips any phonemes, use your cursor to point to the phoneme(s) on the Examinee's View and read the corrective feedback before advancing to the second trial. For examinees who do not correctly name all six phonemes in two trials of Sample Items A and B, the test ends. All other examinees proceed to the test items.

This test contains 8 item sets. Each item set contains 2 rows of 5 phonemes each (10 total phonemes per screen). Read the introduction to the test items and then click Next to display the first set of items on the examinee's iPad and say: *Go ahead.*

As the examinee names the phonemes, use your cursor to follow along and roll over the phonemes in your scoring interface. If the examinee says an incorrect phoneme or skips a phoneme, click the phoneme to score it incorrect. If the examinee self-corrects, click the phoneme again to score it correct.

If the examinee says the letter name instead of the letter sound, click to score the phoneme as an error. If the examinee adds a schwa sound to a phoneme (e.g., if the examinee pronounces /m/ as *muh* instead of *mm*), do not count the phoneme as an error.

Rapid Reference 6.8

Key Administration Points for Rapid Phoneme Naming

- Recommended for ages 6 and older.
- This test has a 1-minute time limit.
- Click on any phoneme the examinee skips or says incorrectly to mark it as an error. If the examinee says the letter name instead of the letter sound, mark the phoneme incorrect.
- Do not mark phonemes incorrect if the examinee adds a schwa sound (e.g., if the examinee says *muh* instead of *mm* for the phoneme /m/).
- If the examinee pauses for 2 seconds and does not appear to be engaged in the task, say: *Do the next one.*
- Do not ask the examinee to repeat a response.
- Tap N on your keyboard when the examinee says the last phoneme on the screen to *immediately* advance to the next item set.

CAUTION

Although you demonstrate the correct pronunciations of the phonemes when you read Introduction 1 and (if applicable) the corrective feedback for Sample Items A and B, the examinee may still add a schwa sound to a phoneme (e.g., by saying *muh* instead of *mm* for the phoneme /m/) during the timed portion of the test. If this happens, do not mark the phoneme as an error and do not correct the examinee's pronunciation.

If the examinee starts naming the phonemes down the screen instead of across the rows, say: *Remember to work across the row.* If the examinee pauses for 2 seconds and does not appear engaged in the task, say: *Do the next one.* However, be careful not to give this prompt if the examinee appears to be focused on the task, to avoid distracting the examinee.

When the examinee reaches the last phoneme on each screen, *immediately* click Next or use the hotkey N on your computer keyboard to advance the screen. The item sets alternate between a light gray and dark gray background color to visually cue the examinee that the screen has changed.

If you are unsure whether the examinee named a phoneme, do not stop the examinee to ask. You can review the voice recording later to check your scoring accuracy, and—if necessary—you can adjust the score then.

Do not penalize the examinee for mispronunciations resulting from articulation errors, dialect variations, or regional speech patterns.

When the 1-minute timer runs out or when the examinee completes Item Set 8, say: *Stop.* If the examinee is still naming phonemes when the timer runs out, the platform will prompt you to click the last phoneme the examinee said. Then, it will prompt you to click on any errors that were not marked before the timer ran out. This is to ensure that the platform can accurately compute the score for a partially completed item set.

Item scoring. Click on any phoneme the examinee says incorrectly or skips. The platform assigns 1 point for each phoneme the examinee says correctly and 0 points for each phoneme the examinee skips or says incorrectly.

Possible administration errors. Possible administration errors include not pronouncing the phonemes correctly on Introduction 1, not providing corrective feedback if the examinee makes an error on Sample Item A or B, not marking a phoneme correct if the examinee says the letter name and not the letter sound, marking a phoneme incorrect if the examinee adds a schwa sound, and not advancing the screen *immediately* when the examinee says the last phoneme.

MEMORY FOR WORDS

Memory for Words (Rapid Reference 6.9) is a measure of auditory working memory capacity (Gwm). The examinee hears a series of words and must repeat them back in the same order. Memory for Words is recommended for ages 4 and older. It contributes to the Auditory Memory Span (Gwm) cluster.

Rapid Reference 6.9

Key Administration Points for Memory for Words

- Recommended for ages 4 and older.
- Use the Suggested Starting Point or select a different starting point.
- Administer Sample Item A orally and administer Sample Item B and all test items from the audio recording.
- Other than the sample items, do not replay or repeat any of the test items.
- The examinee must repeat the words in the same order but can substitute a similar sounding or a rhyming word.

Administration. All examinees begin with Sample Items A and B. Examinees in preschool to Grade 2 then proceed to Item 1, while examinees in Grades 3–12 and all adults proceed to Item 6.

Administer Sample Item A orally. Administer Sample Item B and all test items from the audio recording. You may opt to administer all items orally if the examinee appears to have difficulty understanding the audio-recorded item prompts. If you administer the item prompts orally, say them exactly as they are presented on the audio recording, at a rate of one word per second. Drop your voice slightly at the end of each series so the examinee knows that the series has ended.

If an examinee responds incorrectly to the first trial of a sample item, read the corrective feedback before advancing to the second trial.

You may repeat the sample items, but do not repeat any of the test items.

The examinee must say the words in the correct order, but does not need to say the exact words; if the examinee says a word that is close in pronunciation (e.g., musk for must) or rhymes with the correct word (e.g., *just* for *must* or *mark* for *dark*), score the response correct.

Do not penalize the examinee for mispronunciations resulting from articulation errors, dialect variations, or regional speech patterns.

The test ends when the examinee reaches a ceiling of 4 consecutive items incorrect or when Item 25 is administered.

Item scoring. For each item, click the option in the scoring key that matches the examinee's response. If the examinee provides an incorrect response, click Incorrect. The platform assigns 1 point for correct responses and 0 points for incorrect responses. If you click I Don't Know or No Response, the item is scored incorrect (0 points).

Possible administration errors. Possible administration errors include not reading corrective feedback when it is provided, repeating an item prompt, or scoring a different but similar word or rhyming word as incorrect.

SEGMENTATION

Segmentation (Rapid Reference 6.10) is a measure of phonological processing (Ga). The examinee hears a word and breaks it apart into parts or phonemes. Segmentation is recommended for ages 4 and older. It contributes to the Phonological Awareness (Ga) cluster.

Administration. This test is administered in blocks of items. Items 1–5 (Block A) require the examinee to break apart a compound word into separate words. Items 6–13 (Block B) require the examinee to break apart whole words into separate syllables. Items 14–26 (Block C) require the examinee to break apart whole words into separate sounds, or phonemes.

Examinees in preschool to Kindergarten start with Sample Items A and B. If an examinee does not respond correctly to at least one trial of Sample Items A and B, the test ends. Otherwise, the examinee begins testing with Block A. Examinees who score at least 3 points on Block A proceed to Sample Items C and D and Block B.

Examinees in Grade 1 start with Sample Items C and D. If an examinee does not respond correctly to at least one trial of Sample Items C and D, the platform routes the examinee back to Sample Item A. Otherwise, the examinee begins testing with Block B. Examinees who score 5 or fewer points on Block B are routed to Sample Items A and B and Block A, while examinees who score at least 6 points on Block B are routed to Sample Items E and F and Block C.

Examinees in Grades 2–12 and all adults start with Sample Items E and F. If an examinee does not respond correctly to at least one trial of Sample Items E and F, the platform routes the examinee back to Sample Item C. Otherwise, the examinee begins testing with Block C. Examinees who score 3 or fewer points on Block C are routed to Sample Items C and D and Block B. For examinees who score 4 or more correct on Block C, the test ends.

When you present the item prompts for Sample Items E and F, pronounce the letters between slashes as the sound the letter makes, not the name of the letter. Be careful not to

Rapid Reference 6.10

Key Administration Points for Segmentation

- Recommended for ages 4 and older.
- Use the Suggested Starting Point or select a different starting point.
- Administer all items orally.
- For Sample Items E and F, pronounce letters between slashes as the letter sounds. Be careful not to add a schwa sound.
- For items in Block B, accept any reasonable segmentation that has the correct number of syllables.
- For items in Block C, the examinee must say *all* of the sounds to receive credit.

add a schwa sound to the phoneme (e.g., pronounce /t/ as a short, or clipped, *t* sound and not as *tuh*, and pronounce /m/ as *mm* and not as *muh*).

If an examinee responds incorrectly to the first trial of any sample item, read the corrective feedback before advancing to the second trial.

For items in Block B, the item keys contain common correct responses. Score a response correct if the examinee segments the word reasonably and it contains the correct number of parts, even if the examinee does not pronounce all the parts perfectly. For example, on Item 9 (*master*), accept *mas-ter* or *mast-er* or *ma-ster*.

For items in Block C, the examinee must say each letter sound in the word. When there are two letters between slashes (e.g., /sh/), the examinee must pronounce the letters as one sound to receive credit.

If you are unsure whether the examinee pronounced the sounds correctly for any item in Blocks C or D, do not ask the examinee to repeat their response. Use your best judgment to assign a score and flag the item for later review. You can review the voice recording on *Riverside Score*® to check your scoring accuracy.

You may repeat an item if the examinee requests it.

Do not penalize the examinee for mispronunciations resulting from articulation errors, dialect variations, or regional speech patterns.

Item scoring. For each item, click the option in the scoring key that matches the examinee's response. If the examinee provides an incorrect response, click Incorrect. The platform assigns 1 point for correct responses and 0 points for incorrect responses. If you click I Don't Know or No Response, the item is scored incorrect (0 points).

Possible administration errors. Possible administration errors include not reading corrective feedback when it is provided, scoring Block B items incorrect if the examinee says the correct number of syllables but does not pronounce the sounds exactly as in the key, and scoring Block C items correct if the examinee does not say *all* the required sounds.

CAUTION

Some evaluators may have difficulty hearing phonemes. If this describes you, enlist the help of a speech-language pathologist or reading specialist to administer and score Segmentation.

RAPID NUMBER NAMING

Rapid Number Naming (Rapid Reference 6.11) is a measure of cognitive processing speed (Gs) and retrieval fluency (Gr). The examinee sees numbers on the screen and says the names of as many numbers as possible in 1 minute. Rapid Number Naming is recommended for ages 4 and older. It contributes to the RAN-Math (Gs, Gr) cluster.

Administration. All examinees start with Sample Item A. Read the Sample A instructions to the examinee, and then click on any numbers the examinee says incorrectly or skips. If an examinee incorrectly names or skips any numbers, use your cursor to point to the number(s) on the Examinee's View and read the corrective feedback before advancing

Rapid Reference 6.11

Key Administration Points for Rapid Number Naming

- Recommended for ages 4 and older.
- This test has a 1-minute time limit.
- Click on any number the examinee skips or says incorrectly to mark it as an error.
- If the examinee pauses for 2 seconds and does not appear to be engaged in the task, say: *Do the next one.*
- Do not ask the examinee to repeat a response.
- Tap N on your keyboard when the examinee says the last number on the screen to *immediately* advance to the next item set.

to the second trial. For examinees who do not correctly name all five numbers in two trials of Sample Item A, the test ends. All other examinees proceed to the test items.

This test contains 8 item sets. Each item set contains 3 rows of 5 numbers (15 total numbers per screen). Read the introduction to the test items and then click Next to display the first set of items on the examinee's iPad and say: *Go ahead.*

As the examinee names the numbers, use your cursor to follow along and roll over the numbers in your scoring interface. If the examinee says an incorrect number or skips a number, click the number to score it incorrect. If the examinee self-corrects, click the number again to score it correct.

If the examinee starts naming the numbers down the screen instead of across the rows, say: *Remember to work across the row.* If the examinee pauses for 2 seconds and does not appear engaged in the task, say: *Do the next one.* However, be careful not to give this prompt if the examinee appears to be focused on the task, to avoid distracting the examinee.

When the examinee reaches the last number on each screen, *immediately* click Next or use the hotkey N on your computer keyboard to advance the screen. The item sets alternate between a light gray and dark gray background color to visually cue the examinee that the screen has changed.

If you are unsure whether the examinee named a number, do not stop the examinee to ask. You can review the voice recording later to check your scoring accuracy, and—if necessary—adjust the score then.

Do not penalize the examinee for mispronunciations resulting from articulation errors, dialect variations, or regional speech patterns.

When the 1-minute timer runs out or when the examinee completes Item Set 8, say: *Stop.* If the examinee is still naming numbers when the timer runs out, the platform will prompt you to click the last number the examinee said. Then, it will prompt you to click on any errors that were not marked before the timer ran out. This is to ensure that the platform can accurately compute the score for a partially completed item set.

Item scoring. Click on any numbers that the examinee names incorrectly or skips. The platform assigns 1 point for each number the examinee names correctly and 0 points for each number the examinee skips or names incorrectly.

Possible administration errors. Possible administration errors include not providing corrective feedback if the examinee makes an error on Sample Item A, not marking errors or skipped numbers incorrect, and not advancing the screen *immediately* when the examinee names the last number.

SENTENCE REPETITION

Sentence Repetition (Rapid Reference 6.12) is a measure of auditory working memory capacity (Gwm). The examinee hears a phrase or sentence from an audio recording and then repeats it verbatim. Sentence Repetition is recommended for ages 4 and older. It contributes to the Auditory Memory Span (Gwm) cluster.

Administration. Examinees in preschool to Kindergarten start with Introduction 1 and Sample Item A and then begin testing with Block A (Items 1–8). Examinees who score at least 5 points on Block A then proceed to Introduction 2, Sample Item B, and Item 9 (Block B). Examinees in Grades 2–12 and all adults start with Introduction 2 and are then routed to an appropriate starting item in Block B (Items 9–37).

Administer Sample Item A and Block A (Items 1–8) orally. Administer Sample Item B and Block B (Items 9–37) from the audio recording. You may opt to administer all items orally if the examinee appears to have difficulty understanding the audio-recorded item prompts. If you administer the item prompts orally, say them exactly as they are presented on the audio recording, at a rate of one word per second. Drop your voice slightly at the end of each series so the examinee knows that the series has ended.

The examinee must repeat the phrase or sentence *verbatim*. If the examinee skips or mispronounces any words, score the item incorrect. If you do not hear the examinee's

Rapid Reference 6.12

Key Administration Points for Sentence Repetition

- Recommended for ages 4 and older.
- Use the Suggested Starting Point or select a different starting point.
- Administer Sample Item A and Block A (Items 1–8) orally and administer Sample Item B and Block B (Items 9–31) from the audio recording.
- You may repeat sample items, but do not replay or repeat any of the test items.
- The examinee must say the phrase or sentence exactly as it is presented.
- Block B uses basal and ceiling rules. Examinees who do not have at least 2 correct on Block B are administered Block A, unless it was already administered.

whole response, do not ask the examinee to repeat their answer; if necessary, you can review the voice recording on *Riverside Score®* later to check your scoring accuracy.

You may repeat the sample items, but do not repeat any of the test items.

Block B (Items 9–37) is administered with basal and ceiling rules. Examinees who are administered Block B must obtain a basal (4 consecutive items correct or Item 9) and a ceiling (4 consecutive items incorrect or Item 37) within Block B. Examinees who are administered Block B but have a score of fewer than 2 points are routed back to Block A, unless it was already administered.

Item scoring. For each item, click to score the item correct or incorrect. The platform assigns 1 point for correct responses and 0 points for incorrect responses.

Possible administration errors. Possible administration errors include playing an item more than one time and scoring an item correct if the examinee does not repeat it verbatim.

SOUND DELETION

Sound Deletion (Rapid Reference 6.13) is a measure of phonological awareness (Ga). The examinee hears a word and must omit a word part or sound to form a different word. Although it will yield norm-referenced scores for the entire WJ V age range, Sound Deletion is recommended for ages 5–11. It contributes to the Phonological Manipulation (Ga) cluster.

Administration. This test is administered in blocks of items. Items 1–4 (Block A) require the examinee to omit the beginning part of a compound word. Items 5–16 (Block B) require the examinee to omit the suffix, beginning sound, or ending sound of a word to form a different word. Items 17–28 (Block C) require the examinee to omit the ending, beginning, or middle sound of a word to form a different word.

Examinees in preschool to Kindergarten start with Sample Item A and Block A. Examinees who score at least 2 points on Block A proceed to Sample Item B and Block B.

Examinees in Grade 1 start with Sample Item B and Block B. Examinees who score 0 points on Block B are routed back to Sample Item A and Block A. Examinees who score 10 or more points on Block B proceed to Block C. Otherwise, the test ends.

Rapid Reference 6.13

Key Administration Points for Sound Substitution

- Recommended for ages 5–11.
- Use the Suggested Starting Point or select a different starting point.
- Present Sample Item A orally, and present Sample Item B and all test items from the audio recording.
- You may repeat an item if the examinee requests it.

Examinees in Grades 2–12 and all adults start with Sample Item B and Block C. Examinees who score fewer than 3 points on Block C are routed back to Block B. Otherwise, the test ends.

Present Sample Item A orally. Present Sample Item B and all test items from the audio recording. You may opt to present all items orally if the examinee appears to have difficulty understanding the audio-recorded item prompts. If you administer the item prompts orally, pronounce the letters between slashes as the sound the letter makes, not the name of the letter. Be careful not to add a schwa sound to the phoneme (e.g., pronounce /m/ as *mm* and not as *muh*). When there are two letters between slashes (e.g., /sh/), pronounce the letters as one sound.

If an examinee responds incorrectly to the first trial of a sample item, read the corrective feedback before advancing to the second trial.

You may repeat an item if the examinee requests it.

Do not penalize the examinee for mispronunciations resulting from articulation errors, dialect variations, or regional speech patterns.

Item scoring. For each item, click the option in the scoring key that matches the examinee's response. If the examinee provides an incorrect response, click Incorrect. The platform assigns 1 point for correct responses and 0 points for incorrect responses. If you click I Don't Know or No Response, the item is scored incorrect (0 points).

Possible administration errors. Possible administration errors include not reading corrective feedback when it is provided and not repeating an item if the examinee requests it.

RAPID QUANTITY NAMING

Rapid Quantity Naming (Rapid Reference 6.14) is a measure of cognitive processing speed (Gs), retrieval fluency (Gr), and visual processing (Gv). The examinee sees quantities of between 1 and 9 dots on the screen and names as many quantities as possible in

Rapid Reference 6.14

Key Administration Points for Rapid Quantity Naming

- Recommended for ages 4 and older.
- This test has a 1-minute time limit.
- Click on any quantity the examinee skips or says incorrectly to mark it as an error.
- If the examinee pauses for 2 seconds and does not appear to be engaged in the task, say: *Do the next one.*
- Do not ask the examinee to repeat a response.
- Tap N on your keyboard when the examinee says the last number on the screen to *immediately* advance to the next item set.

1 minute. Rapid Quantity Naming is recommended for ages 4 and older. It contributes to the RAN-Math (Gs, Gr) cluster.

Administration. All examinees start with Sample Item A. Read the Sample A instructions to the examinee, and then click on any quantities the examinee says incorrectly or skips. If an examinee incorrectly names or skips any quantities, use your cursor to point to the dot set(s) on the Examinee's View and read the corrective feedback before advancing to the second trial. For examinees who do not correctly name all five quantities in two trials of Sample Item A, the test ends. All other examinees proceed to the test items.

This test contains 8 item sets. Each item set contains 2 rows of 5 sets of dots each (10 total sets of dots per screen). Read the introduction to the test items and then click Next to display the first set of items on the examinee's iPad and say: *Go ahead.*

As the examinee names the quantities, use your cursor to follow along and roll over the numbers in your scoring interface. If the examinee says an incorrect quantity or skips a set of dots, click the number to score it incorrect. If the examinee self-corrects, click the number again to score it correct.

If the examinee starts naming the quantities down the screen instead of across the rows, say: *Remember to work across the row.* If the examinee pauses for 2 seconds and does not appear engaged in the task, say: *Do the next one.* However, be careful not to give this prompt if the examinee appears to be focused on the task, to avoid distracting the examinee.

When the examinee reaches the last set of dots on each screen, *immediately* click Next or use the hotkey N on your computer keyboard to advance the screen. The item sets alternate between a light gray and dark gray background color to visually cue the examinee that the screen has changed.

If you are unsure whether the examinee named a quantity, do not stop the examinee to ask. You can review the voice recording later to check your scoring accuracy, and—if necessary—you can adjust the score then.

Do not penalize the examinee for mispronunciations resulting from articulation errors, dialect variations, or regional speech patterns.

When the 1-minute timer runs out or when the examinee completes Item Set 8, say: *Stop.* If the examinee is still naming quantities when the timer runs out, the platform will prompt you to click the last number the examinee said. Then, it will prompt you to click on any errors that were not marked before the timer ran out. This is to ensure that the platform can accurately compute the score for a partially completed item set.

Item scoring. Click on any quantity the examinee says incorrectly or skips. The platform assigns 1 point for each quantity the examinee says correctly and 0 points for each quantity the examinee skips or says incorrectly.

Possible administration errors. Possible administration errors include not providing corrective feedback if the examinee makes an error on Sample Item A, not marking errors or skipped quantities incorrect, and not advancing the screen *immediately* when the examinee says the last quantity.

SOUND SUBSTITUTION

Sound Substitution (Rapid Reference 6.15) is a measure of phonological awareness (Ga). The examinee hears a word and must substitute the beginning, end, or middle sound to form a different word. Although it will yield norm-referenced scores for the entire WJ V age range, Sound Substitution is recommended for ages 6–12. It contributes to the Phonological Manipulation (Ga) cluster.

Administration. This test is administered in blocks of items. Items 1–8 (Block A) require the examinee to substitute the beginning or end part of a word to form a different word. Items 9–16 (Block B) require the examinee to substitute the beginning sound of a word to form a different word. Items 17–28 (Block C) require the examinee to substitute the end or middle sound of a word to form a different word.

Examinees in preschool to Grade 2 start with Sample Items A and B. If an examinee does not respond correctly to at least one trial of Sample Items A and B, the test ends. Otherwise, the examinee begins testing with Block A. Examinees who score at least 4 points on Block A proceed to Sample Items C and D and Block B.

Examinees in Grades 3–12 and all adults start with Sample Items C and D. If an examinee does not respond correctly to at least one trial of Sample Items C and D, the platform routes the examinee back to Sample Item A. Otherwise, the examinee begins testing with Block B. Examinees who score 4 or fewer points on Block B are routed to Sample Items A and B and Block A, while examinees who score at least 6 points on Block B are routed to Block C.

Present Sample Items A and B and Block A items orally. Present Sample Items C and D and all items in Blocks B and C from the audio recording. You may opt to present all items orally if the examinee appears to have difficulty understanding the audio-recorded item prompts. If you administer the item prompts orally, pronounce the letters between slashes as the sound the letter makes, not the name of the letter. Be careful not to add a schwa sound to the phoneme (e.g., pronounce /m/ as *mm* and not as *muh*). When there are two letters between slashes (e.g., /sh/), pronounce the letters as one sound.

If an examinee responds incorrectly to the first trial of any sample item, read the corrective feedback before advancing to the second trial.

Rapid Reference 6.15

Key Administration Points for Sound Substitution

- Recommended for ages 6–12.
- Use the Suggested Starting Point or select a different starting point.
- Present Sample Items A and B and Block A (Items 1–8) orally and administer Sample Items C and D and Blocks B (Items 9–16) and C (Items 17–28) from the audio recording.
- You may repeat an item if the examinee requests it.

You may repeat an item if the examinee requests it.

Do not penalize the examinee for mispronunciations resulting from articulation errors, dialect variations, or regional speech patterns.

Item scoring. For each item, click the option in the scoring key that matches the examinee's response. If the examinee provides an incorrect response, click Incorrect. The platform assigns 1 point for correct responses and 0 points for incorrect responses. If you click I Don't Know or No Response, the item is scored incorrect (0 points).

Possible administration errors. Possible administration errors include not reading corrective feedback when it is provided and not repeating an item if the examinee requests it.

TEST YOURSELF

1. If an examinee has trouble understanding the audio-recorded item prompts on Nonsense Word Repetition, you may read all the words orally, provided you pronounce them exactly as they are pronounced on the audio recording. True or false?

2. In which scenario would it be allowable to stop the test timer on a rapid naming (RAN) test?

(A) If the examinee loses their place on the screen.
(B) If the examinee asks to take a break.
(C) If the examinee asks to go back to the previous screen.
(D) None of the above.

3. On Rapid Phoneme Naming, if the examinee adds a schwa sound to a phoneme (such as saying *tuh* instead of /t/), you should still mark the phoneme correct. True or false?

4. On the rapid automatized naming (RAN) tests, you should click the Next button as fast as possible after the examinee finishes saying the last letter, number, phoneme, quantity, or picture on the screen. True or false?

5. Which of the following is true about the Sound Deletion test? (Select all that apply.)

(A) It will yield norm-referenced scores for any examinee ages 4–80+.
(B) It will only yield norm-referenced scores for examinees ages 5–11.
(C) It is recommended for use with examinees from ages 5–11 only.
(D) It can be given to examinees younger than age 4, but then you must administer all items orally.

6. When you are administering Understanding Directions, the examinee taps and holds their finger on the screen so that the iPad registers multiple taps. You should:

(A) Use the Clear Examinee's Response button and ask the examinee to respond again.
(B) Score the response as though only one tap registered in that location on the screen.
(C) Mark the response incorrect because the examinee is only supposed to tap briefly, not hold their finger down on the iPad.
(D) Replay the item prompt.

ANSWERS

1. **False.** While you may read the item prompts orally for Items 5–14 orally if necessary, do *not* attempt to read the item prompts for Items 15–33, as they are very difficult to pronounce correctly and smoothly.
2. **D.** Never click on the test timer during a RAN test. Doing so will end the test, and it will not be scored. If the examinee completes the last screen before the 1-minute timer runs out, the platform will automatically end the test timer.
3. **True.** Although you should take care to pronounce the phonemes correctly without schwa sounds while you are reading the test instructions, do *not* penalize the examinee for adding a schwa sound to any letter during the test.
4. **False.** While you *should* advance the screen as quickly as possible, use the N key on your keyboard, rather than the Next button on your screen, to advance to the next item set.
5. **A and C.** Although the Sound Deletion test will produce norm-referenced scores for ages 4–80+, the test is *recommended* for use with examinees ages 5–11.
6. **B.** If the examinee's finger lingers on the iPad screen (e.g., "tap-and-hold"), you may see multiple numbered markers on your Examinee's View. As long as the *order* of the examinee's taps was correct, do not penalize the examinee for multiple markers that result from a tap-and-hold.

Seven

UNDERSTANDING AND INTERPRETING WJ V SCORES

The WJ V provides a rich variety of interpretive options and scores. Evaluators must know what scores are available, when to use the various scores, and how to interpret these scores. The purpose of the assessment and the audience for the evaluation report dictate which scores are most appropriate to use. In addition, evaluators need to know what the tests and clusters measure, what skills and abilities are required to perform the tasks, and what implications may be derived from the results of the assessment. Clearly, interpreting the WJ V scores requires a higher level of skill than administering the test.

OVERVIEW OF WJ V INTERPRETIVE INFORMATION

The WJ V provides several levels of information in a hierarchical framework. Information from one level cannot be used interchangeably with information from another. Each level provides unique information about a person's test and cluster performance and builds on information from the previous level. Levels 1 through 4 provide information about an individual's performance on tests or on clusters, whereas Level 5 information makes comparisons among the individual's cluster scores.

Rapid Reference 7.1 provides a brief summary of the five levels of information.

Essentials of WJ V™ Assessment, First Edition. Erica M. LaForte, Nancy Mather, and W. Joel Schneider.

Rapid Reference 7.1

Four Hierarchical Levels of Information Available in the WJ V

Level 1: Qualitative

Includes: Qualitative observations made during and after the test session, analysis of individual item responses

Useful for: Describing an examinee's strategies, understanding the examinee's specific challenges or strengths in classroom settings, developing interventions or instructional recommendations.

Level 2: Development

Includes: *W* score, age equivalent score (AE), grade equivalent score (GE)

Useful for: Describing an examinee's level on a developmental continuum, making recommendations for appropriate instructional-level materials, and determining growth or change over time.

Level 3: Proficiency (criterion-referenced)

Includes: *W* Difference score, Relative Proficiency Index (RPI), Cognitive Academic Language Proficiency (CALP) Level, Instructional or Developmental Zone

Useful for: Describing an examinee's proficiency with age- or grade-level tasks, describing an examinee's language proficiency, determining the age or grade level at which the examinee will find tasks manageable or difficult.

Level 4: Relative Standing (norm-referenced)

Includes: *z*-score, standard score (SS), percentile rank (PR)

Useful for: Describing an examinee's position among age- or grade peers.

Level 5: Score Differences (norm-referenced)

Includes: SS/PR profile analysis, Intra-Ability Comparison procedures, Ability/Achievement Comparison procedures

Useful for: Making comparisons among an examinee's scores, describing an examinee's relative strengths and weaknesses, testing hypotheses about an examinee's level of achievement.

(Adapted from Table 6-1 in the WJ V Examiner's Manual [Mather et al., 2025].)

When reporting results to parents, teachers, and examinees, consider the purpose of the assessment and select the scores that are most relevant and meaningful. Some score metrics are more appropriate for describing an examinee's relative standing in a distribution of an examinee's age or grade peers, whereas others are more appropriate for describing the examinee's unique strengths and weaknesses and for planning interventions or accommodations. As an evaluator, you need to understand the purpose and interpretation of each type of score and be able to describe and discuss each type of score accurately if questions are asked.

SELECTING A NORMATIVE BASIS: AGE OR GRADE

Before administering the WJ V, determine the norm basis you will use to generate scores. The *Riverside Score*® platform allows you to compute Level 3 through 5 scores (i.e., Proficiency, Relative Standing, and Base-Rate Comparison scores) based on either grade norms or age norms. Under grade norms, the examinee's performance is compared to individuals in the norm sample who are within one school-year month of the examinee's grade level and are available for examinees in the first month of Kindergarten (i.e., Grade K.0) through the last month of Grade 12 (i.e., Grade 12.9). Age norms, on the other hand, compare the examinee's performance to the performance of individuals in the norm sample who are the same age, in months, as the examinee. Age-based norms are available for all examinees ages 4 years, 0 months through 100 years, 0 months, except for the Letter Writing Fluency test, which provides norms for ages 4 years, 0 months through 9 years, 11 months only.

Generally, use grade norms when WJ V results will be used to make school-based decisions regarding an examinee's achievement levels. In contrast, age-based norms are more applicable in clinical settings and are the only normative option available when administering the WJ V to preschoolers or to adults who are no longer enrolled in high school. Always use age-based norms when the WJ V results will be compared to scores from another test that only provides age norms. Additionally, some testing agencies require the use of age-based norms rather than grade-based norms when a student is requesting standardized test accommodations.

Grade-based WJ V norms were constructed on the assumption that a linear relationship exists between age and grade among the K-12 students in the norming sample. For most examinees in Kindergarten through Grade 12, scoring with grade and age norms produces very similar, but not identical, results. For an examinee who is younger than their same-grade peers in the norming sample (e.g., an examinee with a late school-year birthday or an examinee who skipped a grade), age norms will yield slightly *higher* norm-referenced scores than grade norms. Conversely, when an examinee is older than their same-grade peers in the norming sample (e.g., an examinee with an early school-year birthday or an examinee who is repeating a grade), age norms will yield slightly *lower* norm-referenced scores than grade norms. In Chapter 9, the evaluation report for Noah (Case Study # 1) includes an example of when it might be appropriate to select grade norms over age norms. Noah is currently repeating first grade and is slightly older than many of his grade peers; however, the evaluator believes that it is appropriate to compare Noah to other students who are also in first grade rather than to his age peers, most of whom are now one year ahead of Noah in school. Be sure to clearly indicate in your evaluation report, as Noah's evaluator did, which norm group was used for scoring the tests.

DON'T FORGET

Always include the norm basis (age or grade) that was used to generate the WJ V scores in your evaluation report. When combining results from the WJ V with results from other test batteries in your report, use the same norm basis for both batteries.

MEASUREMENT ERROR

All test scores contain error. The WJ V Technical Manual (LaForte et al., 2025) states that "... measurements of an individual's capabilities are subject to fluctuations in the individual's mental, emotional, and physical state, environmental conditions, and limitations, all of which are fluid" (p. 189). Examinees are human beings with different circumstances, tolerances, and motivations, which can change from day to day or even hour to hour. For example, a student who had a good night's sleep, a healthy lunch, and attended recess prior to the testing session may perform at their optimum level on the tests; however, if the same student was up with a cough in the night, forgot their lunch, and got into trouble at recess just prior to the test session, it is likely that those factors will negatively impact their focus, motivation, and effort on the tests.

Further, although standardized administration procedures serve the purpose of ensuring that all examinees receive the same opportunity to perform the test tasks, *examiner* characteristics and behaviors may introduce error into the test scores. For example:

- An examiner with poor oral reading skills may not read test instructions clearly or fluently or may make pronunciation errors when reading test items;
- An examiner may speak with a different dialect than that of the examinee, making it more difficult for the examinee to understand the test instructions; or
- An examiner who has minimal experience using technology may pause more often during administration or may not administer the tests smoothly and briskly, causing the examinee to lose focus on the test tasks.

You should be aware of potential sources of examiner and examinee score error and take steps to minimize these. For example, if you know that a student often feels sleepy after lunch, then avoid scheduling that student's test session in the afternoon hours. Make sure that you are proficient in test administration on the *Riverside Score*® platform, that you know the pronunciation of all words on the tests, and that you are adequately prepared for the test session to avoid confusing or frustrating the examinee. Always establish rapport before starting the test session and use that opportunity to ask the examinee how their day is going and how they are feeling, ruling out any physical or emotional factors that might preclude them from doing their best work.

CAUTION

Be sure that you are competent in WJ V test administration and that the examinee is comfortable and ready for testing to avoid introducing unnecessary sources of error into the test scores.

Even in best-case scenarios where you have carefully controlled for environmental, intra-examinee, and intra-examiner sources of error, you should never interpret a test score as representing an *exact* value because no test that measures human abilities or traits is perfectly reliable. Indeed, in discussing the concepts of test reliability and measurement error, the WJ V Technical Manual (LaForte et al., 2025) states:

> "...a latent human trait is abstract; it has no length, weight, or mass, so we must measure something that we cannot define by its physical properties, [and] this

physical intangibility creates dissensus regarding both the object of the measurement and the measurement tools themselves. In some sense, the definition of what we are measuring is subject to the properties of the particular tool we have chosen for making our measurements." (p. 189)

Standard error of measurement is the term used to describe the imprecision of a test score. Theoretically, it is the standard deviation (*SD*) of an individual's distribution of scores from multiple repeated administrations of the same test under identical conditions (AERA et al., 2014). To help elucidate this concept, imagine that an athlete is participating in a broad jump competition and is allowed 10 attempts to jump as far as possible. It is very likely—in fact, almost certain—that the athlete's jumps will each be of a different length, but one can get a good sense of the athlete's overall jumping ability by computing an average length over the 10 jumps. The *SD* of the distribution of the 10 jump lengths, then, is the standard error of measurement (*SEM*). Using the *SEM*, it would be possible to predict, with a specified level of confidence, a range of distances within which the athlete's *next* jump would measure. If the athlete's first 10 jump lengths were all very similar, then the *SEM* would be relatively small and we could have more confidence in our prediction for the eleventh jump. In contrast, if the athlete's first 10 jumps were of all very different lengths, the *SEM* would be relatively large, and we would have less confidence in predicting the exact length of jump eleven.

Confidence Bands

In educational testing, of course, it is not practical or reasonable to administer the same test multiple times to the same examinee; however, the interpretation of the *SEM* for a test score is the same as it is for the hypothetical athlete in the example as it quantifies the reliability of the test score when it is used as an estimate of the examinee's actual ability. The *SEM* of a test score is used to construct a *confidence band* around an examinee's obtained test score. The confidence band describes the score range within which we are reasonably confident that the examinee's *actual ability* lies.

To acknowledge the imprecision of any test's scores, you should always report confidence bands in your evaluation report when they are available. In the WJ V, confidence bands are provided for *W* scores, standard scores, and percentile rank (PR) scores at 68% (±1 *SEM*), 90% (±1.645 *SEM*), and 95% (±1.96 *SEM*) around the examinee's obtained score, with higher levels of confidence yielding larger band widths. You can select your desired level of confidence when generating a score report from *Riverside Score*®. For example, Figure 7.1 contains the General Intellectual Ability (GIA) PR score for Connor, a sixth-grade student, at three different levels of confidence. Note that as the level of confidence increases, the confidence band around Connor's obtained score gets larger. Connor obtained a PR score of 38, and we acknowledge that there is error inherent in that measurement. However, we can be 68% confident that his *true* GIA PR score lies between 32 and 45, and we can be 95% confident that it lies between 26 and 52.

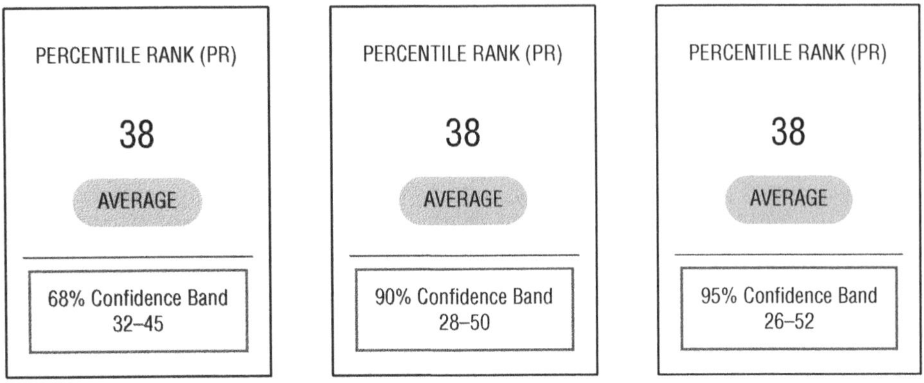

Figure 7.1 Percentile Rank Score and 68%, 90%, and 95% Confidence Bands

DON'T FORGET

Always report confidence bands in your table of scores when they are available. In the WJ V, you can obtain confidence bands around *W* scores, standard scores, and percentile rank scores for 68%, 90%, or 95% confidence levels.

TYPES OF SCORES PROVIDED IN THE WJ V

The following sections contain descriptions and examples of the information and scores available from the WJ V, including examples of how each score might be used in a comprehensive evaluation report.

Level 1: Qualitative Information

Level 1 information is useful in providing context for test scores and for planning appropriate instruction or accommodations. Informal in nature, this information is obtained through behavioral observations and notes taken during the test session and through error analysis of responses to individual items. Watching how the individual performs the task can also provide insights into instructional recommendations. Two ninth-grade students, John and Rebekkah, solved this math problem in different ways, although they both arrived at the correct solution:

> The Roberts have four people in their family. For breakfast they each eat three muffins. If the muffins come in packages of six, how many packages do they need each morning?

John multiplied 4 by 3 and then divided 12 by 6 to get the answer of two packages. Rebekkah drew four people and then put three muffins under each of the people. She then drew a package around two groups of six. Although both students have a conceptual understanding of the problem, Rebekkah's approach was more concrete and suggests that she may not understand how to use multiplication and division to solve a word problem.

Level 1 information might also include comments that the examinee makes (e.g., "I really don't like math"), as well as behavioral observations (e.g., the student was inattentive during timed tests). It can also help with forming hypotheses about the nature of a problem. For example, Phillip, a fourth-grade student, missed several items that involved short vowels on both the Letter-Word Identification and Word Attack tests. One instructional recommendation was that Phillip should be retaught short vowels and practice reading consonant-vowel-consonant (CVC) words with these sounds.

The WJ V provides several features to help you record qualitative observations during the test session. These are described below.

Response Style and Behaviors Statements At the end of each administered test, the WJ V provides an optional set of Response Style and Behavior Statements that can be used to document the examinee's approaches, strategies, and error types during the test. The statements are specific to each test and include possible observations that could be relevant to the skills or abilities measured by the test. If you choose to use these statements to document the examinee's strategies, during the end-of-test review workflow, click Add Response Style and Behavior Statements and then select any statements that apply. Figure 7.2 contains the Response Style and Behaviors Statements for the Math Facts

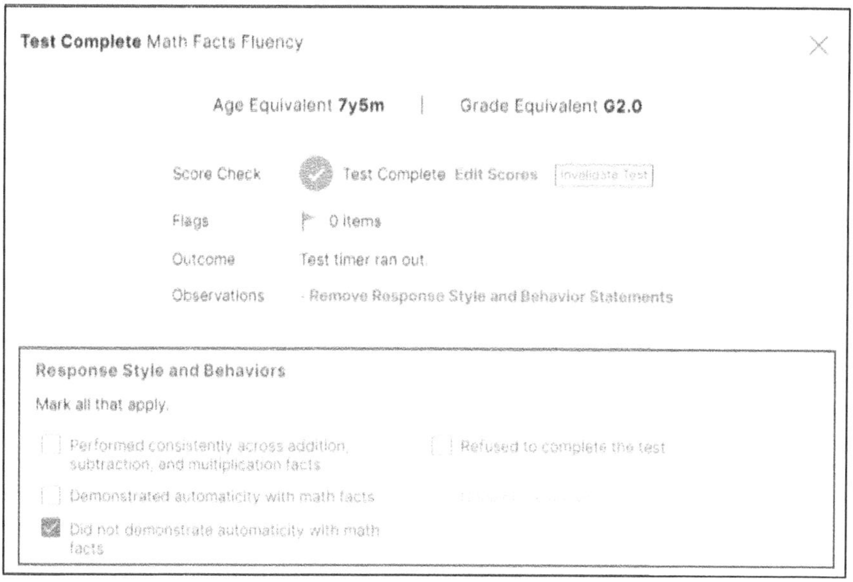

Figure 7.2 Response Style and Behaviors Statements for the WJ V Math Facts Fluency Test for Connor, Age 11

Fluency test for Connor, an 11-year-old student in 6th grade. During the test, the examiner observed that Connor did not demonstrate automaticity with math facts.

Test Session Observations When you have completed administering all assigned tests, Riverside Score provides a Test Sessions Observations checklist to record general observations about the examinee's level of conversational proficiency, cooperation, activity, self-confidence, care in responding, response to difficult items, motivation, and capability with the iPad technology. The Test Session Observations are provided as optional selections during the Test Session Review workflow. There are also questions that allow you to indicate whether you believe that the test session is an accurate reflection of the examinee's abilities and whether you made any modifications to the standardized test procedures. The Test Session Observations can provide useful contextual information to support or explain unusual or unexpected scores from the test session. For example, if you are evaluating a student who presents with attention difficulties in the classroom, then it may be important to note that the student appeared fidgety during testing, was frequently inattentive, and often responded impulsively and carelessly to test items. Figure 7.3 shows the completed

Test Session Observations

Level of Conversational Proficiency

Typical for age/grade

Level of Cooperation

Was cooperative (typical for age/grade)

Level of Activity

Appeared fidgety or restless

Attention and Concentration

Appeared distracted some of the time

Self-Confidence

Appeared hesitant or unsure when providing responses to tasks

Care in Responding

Responded slowly and hesitantly

Response to Difficult Items

Attempted difficult items but gave up easily

Motivation

Was generally engaged with tasks (typical for age/grade)

Use of technology

Was very capable using the tablet

Do you believe that this session represents a fair estimate of the examinee's abilities?

Yes   No (Please explain what happened; include test names and details.)

Did you make any modifications to the standardized administration procedures during this session?

Yes (Please explain; include test names and details.)   No

Figure 7.3 Test Session Observations for Connor, Age 11

Test Session Observations for Connor. See Rapid Reference 3.9 in Chapter 3 for a complete list of the Test Session Observation statements.

Item-, test-, and Test Set-level notes The notetaking features provided on the WJ V platform provide a convenient way to document things the examinee says or does, or unusual or notable responses the examinee provides, during the test session. For example, if you were administering the WJ V Passage Comprehension test to a sixth-grade student who was referred for evaluation because of reading difficulties, and you noticed that the student was mouthing the words to the passages while reading them silently, then you might include a test-level note about this behavior so that you will remember it later when you are reviewing the test scores. See Chapter 3 for more information about how to access the Notes fields on the platform.

Item-level error analysis Examining the types of errors an examinee made during testing can provide important insights into the examinee's particular weaknesses in some areas and help inform targeted interventions. Item-level error analysis can take on different forms. For example, on the Math Facts Fluency test, it might be useful to review the examinee's written responses in the Response Booklet to see if there were specific patterns in the examinee's errors. Perhaps the examinee worked with fairly high accuracy on the first several rows of math problems but then began making errors that suggested they were not watching the signs carefully. Or, perhaps the examinee attempted the addition and subtraction problems but skipped all the multiplication problems. As another example, on the Word Attack test, it might be useful to analyze the types of nonsense words the examinee unexpectedly read incorrectly to determine whether there are certain grapheme patterns that are particularly challenging for the examinee. These types of item-level error analysis are valuable because they can help identify specific skill gaps or misconceptions that may require intervention. By understanding exactly where and why errors occur, you can recommend instructional strategies to address these weaknesses. The *Riverside Score*® platform provides an item-level detail report that facilitates item-level error analysis.

Refer to the case studies in Chapter 9 for examples of how the item-level error analysis can be incorporated into a comprehensive evaluation report. For example, in the evaluation report for William (Case Study #2), the evaluator notes, "He was able to decode a variety of nonsense words, including vowel/consonant (VC), CVC, CVCC, CCVC, VC-e, and words with vowel digraphs (e.g., 'ai'); however, he struggled with nonsense words that included diphthongs (e.g., 'oi') and multisyllabic words." These observations from the item error analysis provide rich information not only for interpreting William's low-average score on the Basic Reading Skills cluster but also for designing targeted interventions to address William's skill deficits in word reading.

DON'T FORGET

You have many opportunities throughout a testing session to observe how an individual approaches tasks. The purpose of testing should not be limited to determining eligibility for services or diagnosing a disability. Through qualitative observations, you can analyze many facets of performance and behavior as well as note the types of strategies an individual uses.

Level 2: Development

Level 2 scores describe an individual's stage of development, and include *W* scores, age equivalents (AEs), and grade equivalents (GEs). These scores are reported for all tests and clusters in the WJ V. All of the Level 2 scores can be derived from the *raw test score.*

Raw test score In the WJ V, the term *raw test score* takes on different meanings across the various tests. For some tests, the raw test score is the sum of the points the examinee earned within a particular set, or block, of items. For Sentence Reading Fluency and Magnitude Comparison, the platform computes the raw score by subtracting the number incorrect from the number correct for each administered item set and then summing across all administered item sets. For tests with basal and ceiling rules, the raw test score is the sum of the item scores (1s and 0s) for all administered items plus one additional point for each unadministered item below the basal. For the rapid automatized naming (RAN) tests, the platform computes a raw score by converting the number of correct responses on each administered set of items into a decile (0–9) score and then summing the decile scores across all administered item sets. For the Visual Working Memory and Symbol Inhibition tests, the platform computes a raw score using a formula that accounts for accuracy as well as omission and commission errors.

> **DON'T FORGET**
>
> Except for some tests that are administered with a Response Booklet, the *Riverside Score®* platform computes all raw test scores. A raw test score on the WJ V is not interpretable until it is converted to a *W* score.

Except for some tests that are administered using a Response Booklet, the *Riverside Score®* platform computes the raw test scores. Unlike in the WJ IV and prior editions, where the examiner was responsible for computing the test raw scores and entering the values into a computerized scoring program, the WJ V does not require you to do the raw-score computations. In fact, the raw score computations are performed "under the hood" by the platform and are not included in the Table of Scores because a raw score, on its own, is not interpretable until it is converted to a *W* score.

***W* score** The *W* score is the foundation of the other Level 2 scores, and all Level 3 and 4 scores. Once a raw test score has been converted to a *W* score, it can be compared to reference values in the WJ V norm tables to derive all other WJ V score metrics. The WJ V platform automatically converts each test raw score to a *W* score. Then, cluster *W* scores are created by averaging the *W* scores from the tests that comprise each cluster.

Through the use of Item Response Theory (IRT) psychometric properties, the *W* score metric has the advantage (over a raw score metric) of being equal interval. Figure 7.4 contains a visual display of this equal-interval scale property. The numbered arrows on the top of the horizontal scale in Figure 7.4 represent test raw scores for a hypothetical 30-item test, while the numbers below the horizontal line represent *W* scores. The *W*-score values are equally spaced along the continuum representing the ability range measured by the test, with lower ability represented by lower *W* scores and higher ability represented by higher *W* scores. Distances between tick marks on the scale

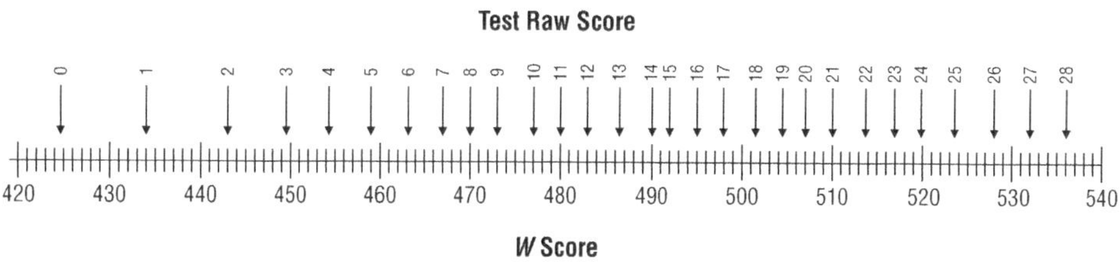

Figure 7.4 Relationship Between Raw Test Score and *W* Score for a Hypothetical 30-Item Test

represent 1 *W*-score unit of score change. The implication of the equal-interval *W*-score spacing is that it takes the same amount of change in ability (i.e., growth) to increase from a *W* score of 440 to a *W* score of 450 as it takes to increase from a *W* score of 500 to a *W* score of 510. In contrast, the test raw scores above the horizontal scale are not equally spaced. It takes a much larger increase in ability to advance from a raw score of 4 to a raw score of 5, for example, than it takes to advance from a raw score of 14 to a raw score of 15. It is useful to think of the *W*-score scale as being similar to a traditional ruler. Like a ruler, the units on the *W*-score scale are equally spaced, with higher numbers corresponding to larger measurements.

The *W* score scale for each test and cluster is designed so that a *W* score of 500 always corresponds to the average ability of a 10-year-old in the norming sample. Other than this property, a single test or cluster *W* score on its own is not especially useful or interpretable in most cases; however, the *W* score is particularly useful for detecting change over time. In fact, some other test batteries that use similar IRT-derived scales call these "change-sensitive scores" or "growth scores" because they are particularly sensitive to change—including growth and decline. For example, if a group of students is tested with the WJ V ACH at the time of entry into an intensive reading intervention program and then tested again one year later, the *W* score would be an appropriate metric for measuring how much the group's average ability grew over the course of the intervention. Norm-referenced scores (such as standard scores and PRs discussed later in this chapter) would not provide this same information because they only describe a student's rank order in a distribution of peers and not the actual level of development.

DON'T FORGET

W scores are the foundation for all other WJ V scores. Raw scores are converted to *W* scores automatically by *Riverside Score*®. *W* scores are not generally interpreted in isolation, but the amount of *W* score change between two time points can be a useful metric for quantifying growth attributed to instruction or interventions.

Age- and grade-equivalent scores. An age-equivalent score, or AE, reflects an examinee's test or cluster performance in terms of the age (in months) in the norming sample at which the median *W* score is the same as the examinee's obtained *W* score. In the WJ V, AEs are expressed in years and months for AEs less than 20 years and in years only for AEs of 20 years and higher (i.e., an AE of 8 years, 2 months is expressed as 8y2m and an AE of 25 years is expressed as 25y). For example, if the median *W* score for 95-month-old examinees in the norming sample is 486, then an examinee who obtains a *W* score of 486 will be assigned an AE of 95 months (7y11m). AEs are useful when testing young children or adults who are seeking accommodations or not attending school.

A grade equivalent score, or GE, reflects an examinee's test or cluster performance in terms of the grade level in the norming sample at which the median *W* score is the same as the examinee's obtained *W* score. In the WJ V, GEs are expressed with the capital letter *G* followed by the grade level in years and months (i.e., a GE representing the fourth month of fifth grade is expressed as G5.4). For example, if the median *W* score for norming sample examinees who are in the seventh month of sixth grade is 506, then an examinee who obtains a *W* score of 506 will be assigned a GE of G6.7. GEs are useful for determining an appropriate level for instructional materials.

At the lower ends of the age and grade scales, less-than signs (<) are used for AEs and GEs that correspond to *W* scores that are lower than the median *W* score of the youngest age or grade group in the WJ V norm tables. For example, an AE of <4y0 means that the examinee obtained a *W* score that is lower than the median *W* score obtained by 48-month-old norming examinees, and a GE of <GK.0 means that the examinee obtained a *W* score that is lower than the median *W* score obtained by norming examinees who are in the first month of Kindergarten. Similarly, greater-than signs (>) are used for AEs that correspond to *W* scores that are higher than the median *W* score at the apex of the norm curve (i.e., >24y if the apex of the norm curve occurs at 24 years of age). Any AE that is higher than 29 years is reported as >29y. Obtained *W* scores that are higher than the median *W* score of students in the 9th month of 12th grade in the norming sample are reported as >12.9.

Unlike *W* scores, AEs and GEs are not equal intervals. Figure 7.5 shows the location of select GEs on the *W* score scale for the WJ V Passage Comprehension test. Note that GEs between GK.0 (first month of Kindergarten) and G4.0 (first month of fourth grade) are fairly spread apart on the *W* scale. This spread reflects the rapid growth of the ability during the early grades. In older grades, the growth is not as rapid, and the GEs are closer together on the scale. Because of this, some cautions are in order for the interpretation of

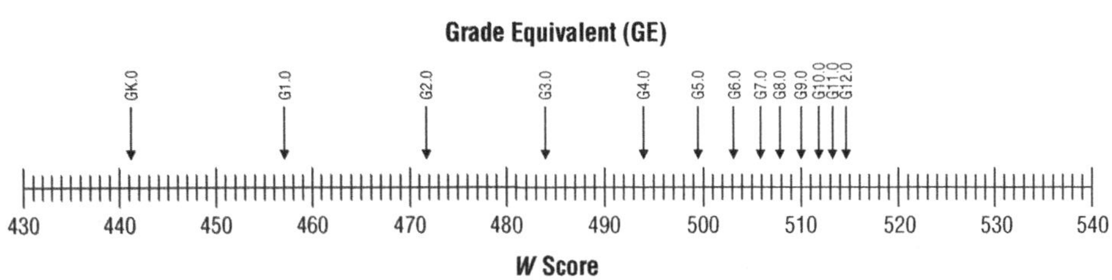

Figure 7.5 Integer-level Grade Equivalent Scores for the WJ V Passage Comprehension Test

AEs and GEs. First, because AEs and GEs are not equal interval, differences in AEs and GEs should not be interpreted as being equal. At older ages and grades where the rapid growth in an ability tapers off, a small change in *W* score can result in a very large increase in an AE or GE. Second, AEs and GEs should not be interpreted as representing mastery of the material at a specific age or grade level. A student who earned a GE of G5.3 on the WJ V Reading Comprehension cluster performed at the same level as the average norming examinee who is in grade 5.3 but is not necessarily showing mastery of fifth-grade reading material. It would not be appropriate to say that this student is "performing at a fifth-grade reading level." Curricular differences across locations and school districts make these types of interpretations impossible using a test like the WJ V.

Because the AE and GE scores are simply transformations of the obtained *W* score, they are not dependent upon the examinee's *actual* age or grade. Additionally, they are independent of which norm basis you select for your score report. This is exemplified in Figure 7.6 for a hypothetical eighth-grade student, Lucy, on the Passage Comprehension test. Lucy's obtained raw test score was 18 points, which corresponds to a *W* score of 501.6 and a GE of G5.7 on Passage Comprehension. Note that the fact that Lucy is *in grade 8* has no bearing on her GE; the GE is simply a transformation of the raw score.

Some examples of appropriate interpretations of AEs and GEs are:

- Jacob's grade equivalent score (GE = G3.1) on the Basic Reading Skills cluster was consistent with students in grade 3.1 from the norming sample.
- Marco, a 10th-grade student, scored similarly to the average student in early 7th grade (GE = G7.2) on the Applied Problems test.
- Diana's knowledge of word meanings as measured by the Vocabulary cluster was comparable to that of an average 8-year-old (AE = 8y3m).
- The number of items that Tom, a 7th-grade student, answered correctly on the Calculation test was comparable to the average 12-year-old examinee in the norming sample (AE = 12y6m).

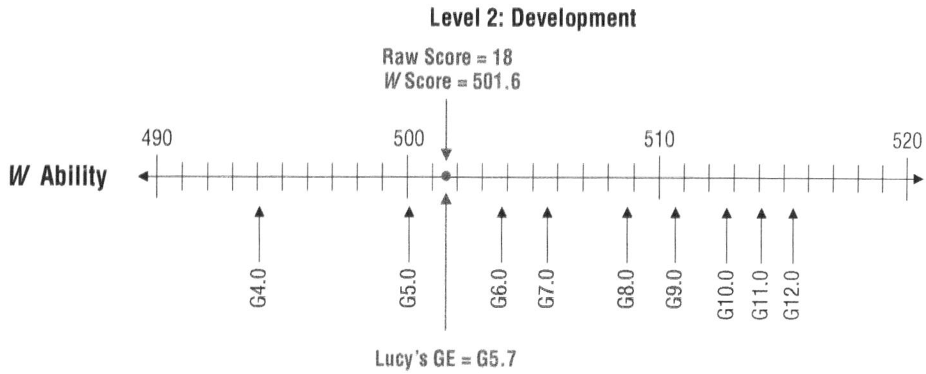

Figure 7.6 Derivation of Lucy's Grade Equivalent (GE) Score on the WJ V Passage Comprehension Test

DON'T FORGET

AEs and GEs describe the age or grade at which the median norming group *W* score is the same as the examinee's obtained *W* score. Use caution when interpreting AEs and GEs. For example, it is not appropriate to say that a student who obtained a GE of 5.3 is "performing at a fifth-grade level" because the GE only describes how the student performed on the WJ V test items compared to norming examinees and does not take into account the local curriculum.

Level 3: Proficiency

Level 3 scores include the Relative Proficiency Index (RPI), Cognitive Academic Language Proficiency (CALP) Level, Instructional Zone, and Developmental Zone. All of the Level 3 scores are derived from the *W* Difference score, and they all describe, in different ways, an examinee's level of proficiency with criterion tasks similar to those measured by the WJ V tests and clusters.

***W* Difference score.** In the same way that the *W* score is the foundation for the Level 2 scores, the *W* Difference score is the foundation for the Level 3 scores. The *W* Difference score is obtained with the equation:

$$W \text{ Difference score} = \text{obtained } W \text{ score} - \text{Reference } W \tag{7.1}$$

where the value of Reference *W* is the median *W* score from the examinee's age- or grade-peer group in the norming sample. The value of Reference *W*, whether for age or grade, is obtained directly from the WJ V norm tables. When the examinee's obtained *W* score is higher than the Reference *W*, the *W* Difference score will be positive. When the examinee's obtained *W* score is lower than the Reference *W*, the *W* Difference score will be negative. Consider the case of Lucy, our hypothetical eighth-grade examinee from Figure 7.6. Lucy obtained a *W* score of 501.6 on the Passage Comprehension test. The Reference *W* value, or the median score from the norming group, for grade 8.2 is 509.1. Plugging the values of Lucy's obtained *W* score and the Reference *W* for her grade-peer group into equation 7.1 yields a *W* Difference score of −7.5:

$$W \text{ Difference score} = 501.6 - 509.1 = -7.5 \tag{7.2}$$

In Figure 7.7, the Reference *W* score for Lucy's grade peers (509.1) is noted with a black dot, and Lucy's obtained *W* score is noted with a gray dot. The *W* Difference score, represented by the length of the double-sided arrow, is the distance in *W* score units from the Reference *W* to Lucy's obtained *W* score. Note that the Reference *W* for Lucy's grade is the origin (i.e., zero point) of the *W* Difference scale. For any age or grade group, the Reference *W* score always serves as the zero point of the *W* Difference scale. Because *W* scores are equal interval, it follows that *W* Difference scores are also equal interval; i.e., a 1-point *W* Difference score has the same meaning, regardless of its location on the *W* scale.

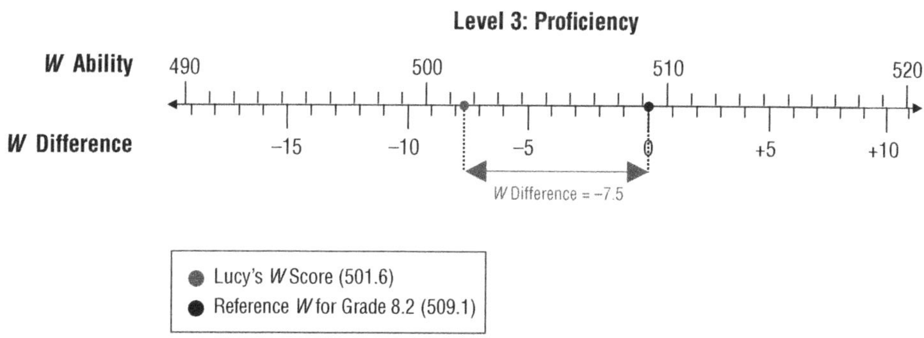

Figure 7.7 Derivation of Lucy's *W* Difference Score on the WJ V Passage Comprehension Test

DON'T FORGET

The *W* Difference score is the distance, in *W*-score points, from the examinee's obtained score to the Reference *W* score for their age or grade. The Reference *W* is always the origin (zero point) of the *W* Difference scale. Like *W* scores, *W* Difference scores are equal-interval metrics.

The *Riverside Score*® platform computes the *W* Difference score automatically using norm tables for WJ V test and clusters that are built into the program.

Relative Proficiency Index The Relative Proficiency Index, or RPI, is a score that predicts how successful an examinee will be on tasks similar to those on the test that the examinee's age or grade peers would find manageable. The RPI is expressed as a fraction (see Figure 7.8). The denominator is always 90, representing the location on the *W* scale where the examinee's typical (i.e., *median*) peer will be 90% successful with tasks similar to the ones on the WJ V tests. The numerator ranges from 0 to 100 and reflects the examinee's *proficiency*, or likelihood of success, on those same tasks. For example, an RPI of 40/90 indicates that an examinee will be only 40% successful with test tasks that their median age or grade peer will be 90% successful with, while an RPI of 96/90 indicates that the examinee will be 96% successful on tasks that a typical peer would be 90% successful with. Note the use of the

$$\text{RPI} = \frac{\text{Examinee's likelihood of success when a typical (i.e., } \textit{median}\text{) peer is 90\% successful}}{90 \text{ (median peer's likelihood of success)}}$$

Figure 7.8 Definition of the WJ V Relative Proficiency Index

word *median* in the definition of the RPI and recall from the earlier section on *W* Difference scores that the location of the examinee's median age or grade peer on the *W* score scale is the Reference *W*. It follows, then, that the denominator of the RPI represents the proficiency of an examinee's age or grade peer whose *W* Difference score is 0.

The RPI is a powerful tool for illustrating an examinee's academic challenges in the classroom setting. For example, if a student has an RPI score of 30/90 on the Letter-Word Identification test, it means that she is likely to succeed with only 30% accuracy at reading words that her average peers can read with 90% success. Describing a student's performance in this way can provide a more meaningful and relatable picture for parents and teachers. To further enhance clarity, the WJ V includes verbal descriptors for various ranges of *W* Difference and RPI scores (see Rapid Reference 7.2). You can include these labels in your WJ V score report using the options available on *Riverside Score®*.

The proficiency labels and descriptive implications in Rapid Reference 7.2 are valuable for illustrating how a specific RPI score may affect an examinee's classroom experience. When combined with RPI scores, they help create a vivid picture of the student's academic strengths and challenges. Examples of sentences that integrate RPI scores with these descriptors include:

- Akeisha's RPI of 30/90 on the Vocabulary cluster indicates that when average sixth-grade students have 90% proficiency, Akeisha will have only 30% proficiency. Her knowledge of vocabulary is limited.

Rapid Reference 7.2

Verbal Labels for RPI Scores

W Difference	RPI	Proficiency Label	Implications (i.e., examinee will find age- or grade-level tasks ...)
+31 and above	100/90	Very advanced	extremely easy
+14 to +30	98/90–100/90	Advanced	very easy
+7 to +13	95/90–98/90	Average to advanced	easy
−6 to +6	82/90–95/90	Average	manageable
−13 to −7	67/90–82/90	Limited to average	difficult
−30 to −14	24/90–67/90	Limited	very difficult
−50 to −31	3/90–24/90	Very limited	extremely difficult
−51 and below	0/90–3/90	Extremely limited	nearly impossible

- Marla's RPI of 99/90 on the Math Problem Solving cluster indicates advanced proficiency in mathematical concepts and reasoning. When average age peers have 90% success on similar tasks, Marla is predicted to have 99% success. Grade-level tasks in mathematics will be easy for Marla.
- Bennett's RPI of 92/90 on the WJ V Academic Knowledge cluster indicates average proficiency in contentarea knowledge compared to peers.
- Kai's RPI of 25/90 on the WJ V COG Story Recall test means that he would be predicted to demonstrate 25% proficiency with similar tasks involving listening comprehension, whereas average individuals in the comparison group (age) would perform with 90% proficiency. His proficiency would be limited, and he would find age-level tasks to be very difficult.

> **DON'T FORGET**
>
> When reporting RPI scores, use the provided proficiency and implications labels to provide a richer description of an examinee's strengths and challenges in the classroom setting.

Note in Rapid Reference 7.2 that the verbal labels are driven by the *W* Difference score rather than the RPI itself. This means that, on occasion, the same RPI may yield two different sets of verbal labels. While there is overlap between the RPI ranges in Rapid Reference 6.1, there is no overlap in the *W* Difference ranges. For example, an RPI of 82/90 appears in both the Average and Average to Advanced proficiency categories; however, when examining the *W* Difference ranges for those two proficiency categories, it is apparent that *W* Difference scores of −6 (in the Average proficiency category) and −7 (in the Average to Advanced proficiency category) both map to an RPI score of 82/90.

Figure 7.9 shows the derivation of the RPI score, as well as the proficiency and implications labels, on the Passage Comprehension test for Lucy, our eighth-grade student. In the figure, the shaded bands represent the verbal labels associated with the various levels of *W* Difference score and the RPIs corresponding to the category bounds shown below the *W* Difference scale. Lucy's *W* Difference score of −7.5 yields an RPI score of 80/90; on other tasks similar to those

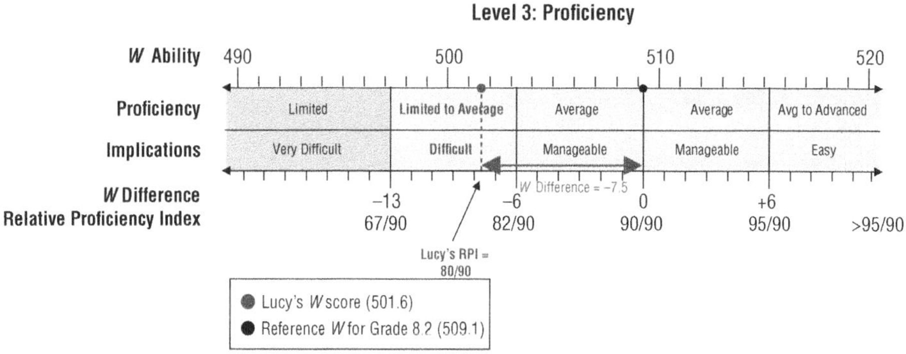

Figure 7.9 Derivation of Level 3 Scores on the WJ V Passage Comprehension Test for Lucy, Grade 8.2

on the WJ V Passage Comprehension test, she will be 80% successful when her average peers will be 90% successful. While the difference between 80% success and 90% success may seem negligible on its surface, note that Lucy's RPI score falls in the limited to average range; she will find similar tasks in the classroom difficult.

Cognitive Academic Language Proficiency (CALP) Cognitive Academic Language Proficiency (CALP) levels, another application of the *W* Difference score, are helpful in determining an individual's language proficiency. CALP is defined as language proficiency in academic situations and includes those aspects of language that are used for instruction in the school setting and emerge with formal schooling. Aspects of language that are acquired naturally, without formal schooling, are referred to as Basic Interpersonal Communication Skills (BICS; Cummins, 1984).

It can be helpful to consider an English learner's (EL) CALP levels to determine language proficiency and language dominance or when planning an appropriate educational program. CALP levels are also helpful when considering the instructional needs of native English speakers with delayed or limited language. Measuring a student's proficiency in the language used in classroom learning may be useful for young students, students with intellectual disabilities, students with specific learning disabilities (SLDs), and/or students with developmental language disorders (Varner, 2023). CALP levels are available for only relevant WJ V clusters (see Rapid Reference 7.3).

The WJ V CALP scores use the same *W* Difference scale that underlies the WJ V proficiency (RPI) metrics. Rapid Reference 7.4 shows how the CALP Levels correspond to the

Rapid Reference 7.3

Clusters that Provide CALP Levels

- Comprehension-Knowledge (Gc; in WJ V COG)
- Oral Language
- Listening Comprehension
- Oral Expression
- Brief Reading
- Basic Reading Skills
- Reading Fluency
- Reading Comprehension
- Brief Writing
- Basic Writing Skills
- Written Expression
- Academic Skills
- Academic Fluency
- Academic Applications
- Academic Knowledge
- Vocabulary

Rapid Reference 7.4

Relationship Between RPI and CALP Levels

W Difference	RPI	CALP Level	CALP Label	Implications (i.e., examinee will find grade-level academic language ...)
+31 and above	100/90	6	Very advanced	extremely easy
+14 to +30	98/90–100/90	5	Advanced	very easy
+7 to +13	95/90–98/90	4–5	Fluent to advanced	easy
−6 to +6	82/90–95/90	4	Fluent	manageable
−13 to −7	67/90–82/90	3–4	Limited to fluent	difficult
−30 to −14	24/90–67/90	3	Limited	very difficult
−50 to −31	3/90–24/90	2	Very limited	extremely difficult
−51 and below	0/90–3/90	1	Extremely limited	nearly impossible

W Difference ranges and includes the verbal labels and implications for each range. For clusters on which CALP scores are provided, you can include these labels in your WJ V score report using the options available on *Riverside Score*®.

Some examples of the appropriate use of CALP level descriptions in reports are:

- Karina met the criteria for fluency on all of the WJ V Oral Language clusters (CALP = 4–5).
- Bashir's performance on the Basic Reading Skills cluster suggests extremely limited functioning in reading English (CALP = 1). It will be nearly impossible for him to read grade-level English books.
- Daniel's CALP level of 6 on the Written Expression cluster suggests that his performance is very advanced and that he will find English writing tasks at the 12th-grade level to be extremely easy.
- Suni's CALP Level of 1 on the Vocabulary cluster suggests that classroom activities involving English vocabulary will be nearly impossible for her.

DON'T FORGET

Use the CALP levels to consider the individual's English language proficiency before interpreting test results or making instructional recommendations. In addition, you can use CALP levels to help determine eligibility for EL or bilingual programs.

Instructional/Developmental Zone The instructional zone and developmental zone, special applications of the RPI, identify the range of an individual's present level of functioning on the WJ V achievement tests and cognitive tests, respectively. The concept of the instructional zone is similar to that found in informal reading inventories, in which instructional reading levels are identified that range from the independent (easy) level to the frustration (difficult) level. Vygotsky's (1978) zone of proximal development is another similar concept, representing the distance between an individual's actual developmental level and the level of potential development when assisted by a more knowledgeable other.

The WJ V instructional zone is expressed as a grade or age band describing the range of *W* Difference corresponding to an RPI of 96/90 to an RPI of 75/90. An examinee will perceive tasks that fall at an RPI of 75/90 (labeled "DIFF" in the score report) to be difficult, whereas tasks that fall at an RPI of 96/90 (labeled "EASY" in the score report) will be easy for the examinee. The examinee's obtained AE or GE represents the midpoint of the zone and provides an estimate of the examinee's current level. For example, Ella, a fourth-grade student, obtained a GE of G2.3 on the WJ V Math Calculation Skills cluster. Her Instructional zone ranges from G1.4 to G3.3, suggesting that she will find math calculation tasks at grade level 1.3 easy but will find math calculation tasks at grade level 3.3 difficult. The concept of instructional ranges is helpful in planning interventions to support growth. Ideally, within a school setting, both homework and seatwork would be at the independent (EASY) level, whereas work that is supported by others (teachers, peers, parents) would be at the instructional (DIFF) level.

The width of the instructional zone represents the rate of growth of an ability in the population at a particular age or grade. A narrow instructional zone suggests that growth of the ability is rapid or "steep" at the examinee's particular location on the scale, whereas a wide instructional zone suggests that growth is slow or "flat" at that location on the scale. For example, the instructional zone on the Word Attack test for a student with a GE of G9.2 is wide because the ability to pronounce phonically regular nonsense words does not change much in the population during the high school years. In contrast, the instructional zone on a test such as Letter-Word Identification for a student with a GE of G2.6 is narrow because the ability to decode increases at a steady rate across the early school years.

Examples of the types of statements used to describe the instructional zone include:

- Arnold's instructional zone on the Phoneme-Grapheme Knowledge cluster indicates that reading and spelling tasks involving speech sounds will be easy at the beginning second-grade level but difficult at the beginning third-grade level.
- Appropriate instructional materials in basic math skills for June would range from beginning fifth-grade level (independent) to end of sixth-grade level (with appropriate supports).
- Jared's instructional zone on the Math Problem Solving cluster indicates that he will find math reasoning tasks at the 9th-grade level to be easy, whereas tasks at the 11th-grade level will be very difficult.

If you choose age norms, then the instructional zone is represented as a range of AEs, and if you choose grade norms, then the zone is represented as a range of GEs.

In the WJ V COG, the EASY to DIFF range is expressed in the same manner but is labeled as "developmental zone" in the score report.

DON'T FORGET

Because they describe an individual's level of functioning from easy (the independent level) to difficult (the frustration level), Instructional Zones can be useful tools for planning targeted interventions.

Level 4: Relative Standing

Level 4 information provides a basis for making peer comparisons. In educational and clinical settings, PRs and standard scores are the most common WJ V Level 4 metrics used to describe an individual's relative standing in a distribution of same-age or same-grade peers. These scores are often used in making placement decisions, such as identifying a need for special education services. The Level 4 scores are derived from the *z* score, and they describe, in different ways, an examinee's location in a standard normal distribution (i.e., "bell curve").

***z* score** A *z* score, or a *standard normal* score, describes an examinee's distance, in *SD* units, from the mean. Figure 7.10 shows the *z*-score distribution. The center of the scale, where $z = 0$, represents the mean of the distribution. The dotted vertical lines represent distances from the mean score in *SD*, or *z*-score, units. Negative *z* scores represent scores that are below the mean, and positive *z* scores represent scores above the mean. The area under the curve represents the proportion of the distribution's scores that fall in the region between any two *z* scores. So, for example, 68% of the scores in the distribution fall into the middle area of the curve between $z = -1$ and $z = 1$, and 95% of the scores in the distribution fall in the wider middle range between $z = -2$ and $z = +2$. These two properties of the standard normal curve (the distance from the mean and the area under the curve) are used to derive a standard score and a PR (described later) from a computed *z* score.

For each WJ V test and cluster, the *Riverside Score*® platform computes a *z* score using the following formula:

$$z = \left(\text{obtained } W \text{ score} - \text{Reference } W\right) / \text{Reference } SD \qquad (7.3)$$

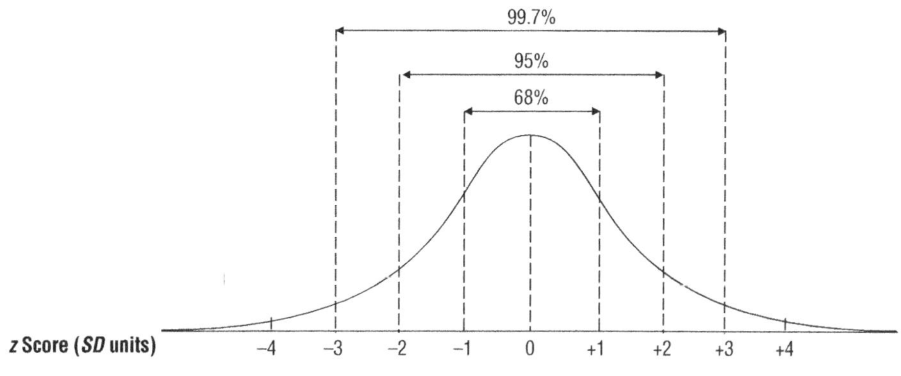

Figure 7.10 The *z*-Score (Standard Normal) Distribution

where Reference *W* and Reference *SD* are the norm-table values for the examinee's actual age or grade. You may recognize the parenthetical term in Equation 7.3 as the value of *W* Difference from Equation 7.1. Substituting *W* Difference into Equation 7.3 yields:

$$z = W \text{ Difference/Reference } SD. \tag{7.4}$$

DON'T FORGET

All other Level 4 scores are computed directly from the derived *z*-score. *Riverside Score*® handles all of these computations for you.

In other words, the *z* score expresses the *W* Difference in a way that relates to the particular width and height of the score distribution for a given age or grade. Note that a *z* score at exactly the mean of the distribution—i.e., when the *W* Difference is 0—is 0; *z* scores below the mean take on negative values.

WJ V half-normal distributions Note that the standard normal distribution in Figure 7.10 is *symmetric*; it has the same shape to the left and right of the center point. In reality, the WJ V models all test and cluster abilities as *half-normal* distributions. Half-normal distributions are a useful way to account for the distinct variations among low- and high-ability examinees. For example, at the early ages, many reading tests tend to exhibit larger score variations among children at the lower end of the score distribution than at the high end. In other words, low-ability examinees tend to have scores that are *more different from each other* than do high-ability examinees. Some other test batteries do not take this variation into account and simply impose a single value of *SD* on each age or grade in the norm tables; however, this practice averages out the score variance across the ability continuum and fails to acknowledge the differences between low- and high-performing populations. In the WJ V, however, each age or grade in the norm tables is assigned two values of *SD*: one value that is used to calculate *z* scores for examinees who fall at or below the mean, and a different value that is used to calculate *z* scores for examinees who fall above the mean. This results in two half-normal distributions. Figure 7.11 contains a graphical display of a pair of half-normal distributions for a hypothetical WJ V test at a specific age or grade. The solid green line (dark gray in figure) represents the model of the ability distribution for examinees below the mean ($SD = 13$), and the solid blue line (light gray in figure) represents the model of the ability distribution for examinees above the mean ($SD = 10$). In this example, to obtain a *z* score of -1.00, an examinee would need a *W* Difference score of -13, but to obtain a *z*-score of $+1.00$, an examinee would need a *W* Difference score of $+10$. Because the *SD* for examinees above the mean is smaller than for those below the mean, *W* Difference scores with smaller absolute magnitudes above the mean yield more extreme *z* scores. In the rare cases where the examinee score variances above and below the mean in the WJ V norming sample are equal, the two half-normal distributions are perfectly symmetric.

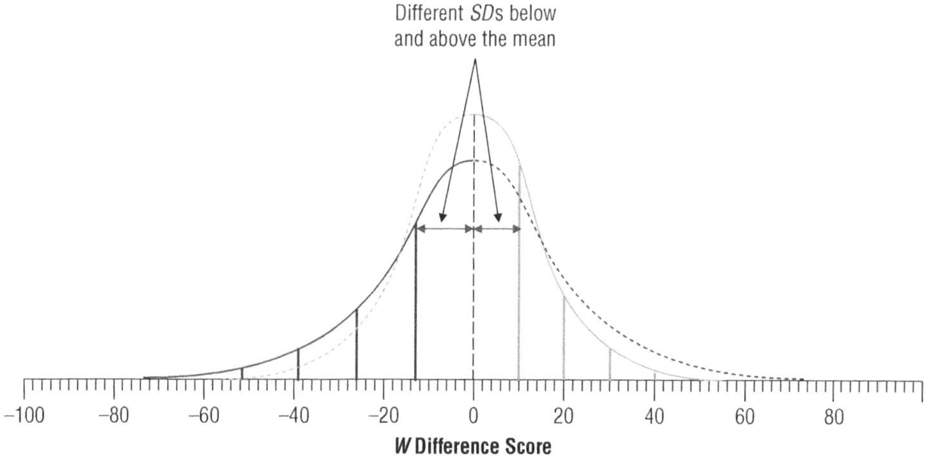

Figure 7.11 A Pair of Half-Normal Distributions for a Hypothetical WJ V Test

Because the *Riverside Score*® platform performs all norm table lookups and score calculations, the use of these half-normal distributions in the WJ V may not be apparent to you as a test user; however, being aware that the WJ V norm tables contain different values of *SD* for scores below and above the mean may help you to better understand patterns of examinees scores that you may observe over many administrations of the WJ V in your testing practice.

DON'T FORGET

The WJ V models the distribution of examinee ability separately below and above the mean. This allows for greater precision in normative scores for very low- and very high-ability examinees. *Riverside Score*® handles all of the normative score derivations for you.

Standard score Although *z*-scores are useful for describing an examinee's location (in *SD* units) in a distribution, they are expressed with decimals and can be negative (i.e., a score that is one *SD* below the mean is expressed as −1.00). These properties of *z* scores make them difficult to explain to parents and examinees. (Imagine explaining to the parents of a student who scored exactly at the median for her peer group that their child had a score of 0 on the test!) The standard score (SS) provides a better alternative for describing an individual's relative standing in a peer group—one that is expressed in integer values and is always positive on the WJ V. The standard score is a transformation of the *z* score and is computed as:

$$SS = \left(z \text{ score} \times 15\right) + 100, \tag{7.5}$$

where the *SS* distribution has a mean of 100 and an *SD* of 15. This is the same as most IQ scales and may be used to relate standard scores from the WJ V to other test scores based on the same mean and *SD*. The WJ V reports standard scores from 40 to 160 (i.e., ±4 *SD*s

CAUTION

Some examiners make the mistake of assuming that the cluster standard scores are computed by averaging the standard scores for the tests included in each cluster. This is not the case. Remember that in the WJ V, the cluster *W* score is first computed as the average of the *W* scores for the tests within the cluster, and then the *W* Difference, *z* score, and standard score are all computed from the cluster *W* score.

DON'T FORGET

In the WJ V, standard scores and PRs are both computed from *z* scores, and, due to rounding, these scores do not have a perfect one-to-one correspondence.

from the mean). Because the level of score precision outside of this range is relatively low, standard scores below 40 are reported as <40, and standard scores above 160 are reported as >160.

Percentile rank Another way to describe an examinee's relative position in a peer group is a percentile rank (PR) score. The PR describes the percentage of examinees in the peer group who have a score *equal to or lower than* the examinee's obtained score. PRs can be useful when communicating test results to parents and teachers, who may not be familiar with standard scores.

Rapid Reference 7.5 shows the relationship between various ranges of SS and PR. You may notice that some values of SS map to multiple values of PR, and likewise, some values of PR map to multiple values of SS. Because the WJ V computes PRs directly from 3-decimal *z* scores, the SS and PR category overlaps are due to integer-level rounding. For this reason, it would not be unusual, for example, for an examinee's PR of 24 on two different tests to yield different standard scores (89 and 90). Likewise, it is possible that an examinee could obtain a standard score of 90 on two different tests that yield different PR scores (24 and 25).

Similar to the proficiency scores described earlier, it is useful to describe standard scores and PRs with verbal labels in addition to numbers when writing reports or communicating test results to parents and others. Rapid Reference 7.6 suggests labels to use when describing WJ V standard scores and PRs. You can include these labels in your score report using the options available on *Riverside Score®*.

Figure 7.12 contains a visual display of the SS and PR scores on the WJ V Passage Comprehension test for Lucy, our eighth-grade student. Lucy's *W* score of 501.6 yields a SS of 91 and a PR of 27, which falls within the average range in a distribution of her same-grade peers.

Using Rapid Reference 7.6 as a guide to describing SS and PR ranges, the following are some examples of appropriate ways to describe these scores to parents and teachers.

- Arnold's low average performance (Percentile Rank = 18) on the Math Problem Solving cluster suggests that he has more difficulty with mathematical concepts and reasoning than do most of his grade-level peers.
- When Mr. Begley's performance is compared to other adults of the same age, his Academic Knowledge cluster score is high average (Standard Score = 120).

Rapid Reference 7.5

Values of Percentile Rank Corresponding to Standard Score Ranges

SS	PR	SS	PR	SS	PR
<62	<1	92–93	31	107–108	69
62–67	1	93	32	108	70
67–71	2	93–94	33	108–109	71
71–73	3	94	34–35	109	72–73
73–75	4	94–95	36	109–110	74
75–76	5	95	37	110	75
76–77	6	95–96	38	110–111	76
77–78	7	96	39–40	111	77
78–79	8	96–97	41	111–112	78
79–80	9	97	42	112	79
80–81	10	97–98	43	112–113	80
81–82	11	98	44–45	113–114	81
82–83	12	98–99	46	114	82–83
83–84	13	99	47–48	115	84
84	14	99–100	49	115–116	85
84–85	15	100	50	116–117	86
85	16	100–101	51	117	87
85–86	17	101	52–53	117–118	88
86–87	18	101–102	54	118–119	89
87	19	102	55–56	119–120	90
87–88	20	102–103	57	120–121	91
88	21	103	58	121–122	92
88–89	22	103–104	59	122–123	93
89	23	104	60–61	123–124	94
89–90	24	104–105	62	124–126	95
90	25	105	63	126–127	96
90–91	26	105–106	64	127–129	97
91	27–28	106	65–66	129–133	98
91–92	29	106–107	67	133–138	99
92	30	107	68	>138	>99

Rapid Reference 7.6

Verbal Labels for Standard Score and Percentile Rank Ranges

Standard Score	Percentile Rank	Verbal Label
131–>140	98–>99	Very superior
121–130	92–97	Superior
111–120	76–91	High average
90–110	25–75	Average
80–89	9–24	Low average
70–79	3–8	Low
<40–69	<1–2	Very low

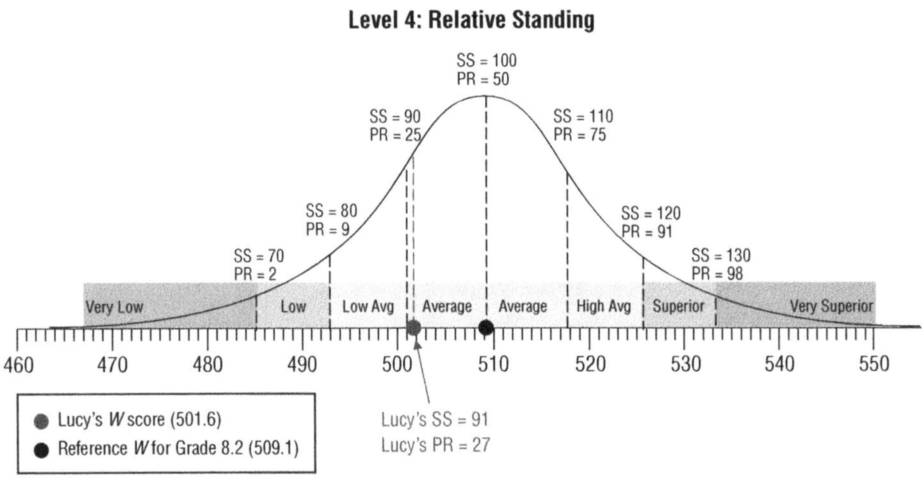

Figure 7.12 Derivation of Level 4 Scores on the WJ V Passage Comprehension Test for Lucy, Grade 8.2

- Rhia's standard score of 125 indicates that her performance on the WJ V COG Fluid Reasoning cluster is in the superior range.
- Martha's percentile rank of 98 on the Basic Math Skills cluster indicates that only 1 out of 100 students of the same age would have a score as high or higher than Martha's.
- Angela's percentile rank of 1 on the Basic Writing Skills cluster indicates that only 1 out of 100 3rd-grade students would obtain a score as low or lower than Angela's score.
- On the Cognitive Efficiency cluster, Dominick's standard score (110) was equal to or higher than 75% of his same-age peers in the WJ V norming sample.

Appropriate use of standard scores and percentile ranks SSs and PRs are *relative-standing* metrics; they describe the examinee's location in a distribution of scores relative to same-age or same-grade peers. They are useful to get a sense of how an examinee performed on the WJ V compared to classmates, but they do *not* describe the quality of the examinee's performance. For example, it would not be appropriate to say, "Samuel's PR of 24 on the WJ V Letter-Word Identification test suggests that he has difficulty with reading grade-level words." The PR of 24 tells us that Samuel's word-reading ability is within the lower quartile of his grade peers, but it does not describe how much difficulty he will encounter when faced with similar grade-level word-reading tasks. In your score report, do not mix relative standing scores with labels or descriptions that imply a level of proficiency. Instead, use relative-standing scores and their associated verbal labels to describe the examinee's relative position in a peer distribution, and use proficiency-based scores (i.e., RPIs, CALP levels, instructional zones) and their associated verbal labels to describe the quality of an examinee's performance or the degree of difficulty the examinee may have with age- or grade-level tasks.

CAUTION

In your evaluation reports, avoid pairing relative-standing scores, such as standard scores or percentile ranks, with language describing the quality of the examinee's performance. While standard scores and PRs indicate an examinee's relative position within a peer group, they do not reflect how easy or difficult a task may be for the individual. To provide insight into how an examinee might perform on grade- or age-appropriate tasks in the classroom, use proficiency scores (e.g., RPI, CALP levels, instructional zones) and their corresponding verbal labels.

When Level 3 and Level 4 Scores Diverge

By this point, you should be familiar with the derivation, meaning, and interpretation of the proficiency (Level 3) and relative standing (Level 4) scores, and you should feel relatively comfortable explaining RPIs, standard scores, and PRs to a teacher or parent. However, in your professional practice, you will inevitably encounter situations where an examinee's proficiency and relative standing scores do not seem to match or are at odds with one another. For example, a student may earn a score in the normative *average* range on the Reading Comprehension cluster but may earn an RPI of only 65/90 on that cluster, suggesting *limited proficiency* with reading comprehension. Conversely, a student may obtain a proficiency score of 84/90 indicating that she should find grade-level classroom tasks *manageable*, but her normative score may be in the *low average* range. When this happens, professionals who are new to using the WJ proficiency metrics may think, *Something must be wrong!* Some might even decide to omit the proficiency metrics from their reports altogether, worrying that it will be difficult to explain the apparent contradiction to parents and teachers or believing that there is, perhaps, an error in the score table.

But if the proficiency and relative standing scores always provided the same insights, then we would not need them both! Remember that the WJ proficiency metrics tell us how *easy* or *difficult* an examinee will find age- or grade-appropriate tasks; they provide information about the quality of the examinee's performance that is beyond what we can learn about an examinee from simply knowing the examinee's relative position in their peer group. From the definitions and derivations of the proficiency and relative standing metrics provided in the prior sections, you may already be able to see why these two scores might not always provide the same interpretations.

A visual representation showing both of these metrics together helps clarify how this phenomenon can occur. First, some reminders about these metrics:

a. Proficiency metrics (RPI, verbal labels, implications) are derived from the examinee's *W* Difference score. The *W* Difference score describes the distance between the examinee's obtained *W* score and the median *W* score for the examinee's peer group (see Figure 7.8).
b. Because the *W* score metric is equal interval, distances on the scale are meaningful and represent differences in the quality of an examinee's performance.
c. Relative standing metrics (SS, PR) are derived from the examinee's *z* score. The *z* score describes an individual's relative position from the mean of the standard normal distribution (i.e., the "bell curve").
d. The variation of an ability in the norming sample at a specific age impacts the shape of the score distribution. When the score variation is small (e.g., retrieval fluency during adolescence and early adulthood), the reference *SD* is small and the model of the score distribution is *tall* and *narrow*. Conversely, when examinee scores vary greatly (e.g., word reading in first grade), the reference *SD* is large and the model of the score distribution is *wide* and *flat*.

Figure 7.13 contains hypothetical *W* score distributions for two WJ V tests at different ages. For purposes of this example, assume that the score distributions are symmetric (i.e., that the *SD* below and above the mean is the same within each distribution). The *W* Difference score underlies each distribution. The center of each scale, where *W* Difference = 0, represents the median *W* ability of the particular age or grade represented by the distribution, where the *W* Difference equals 0. The labels describing the proficiency ranges are shown in the shaded boxes above the scale, from very limited on the left to very advanced on the right.

On Test 1, the range of "average" for both relative standing and proficiency metrics is nearly identical. This will always occur when the *SD* of the *W*-score distribution is approximately 10 points. When this happens, an examinee who scores in the "Average" proficiency range will also score in the "Average" normative range. The interpretations of these scores will align; for examinees near the average range, the metrics will tell a similar story.

On Test 2, where the *SD* of the *W*-score distribution is 13.5 points, note that the shape of the distribution is *flatter* and *wider* than it is for Test 1. This is the result of the larger score spread among examinees on Test 2 at age 6 years. When a distribution's *W*-score *SD* is significantly different than 10, the proficiency score and relative standing score interpretations may be different. For example, a 6-year-old student who obtains a standard score of 92 on Test 2 would be in the "Average" normative range but would have "Limited to Average" proficiency; the student would find age-level tasks *difficult*. Including both of these scores in the report provides a more robust picture of the student's current functioning.

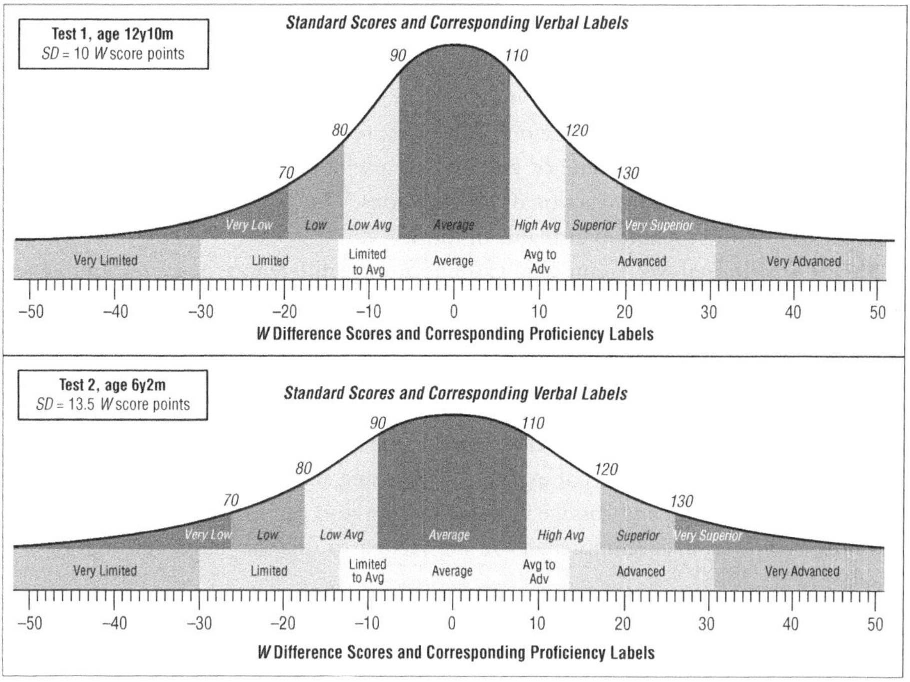

Figure 7.13 ***W* Difference Score Distributions for Two Hypothetical WJ V Tests**

The reference values of *SD* in the WJ V test and cluster norm tables generally range from about 9 *W*-score points to about 30 *W*-score points. Clearly, 30 is very different from 10; for tests with very large *SD*s, proficiency and relative standing score interpretations will be significantly different from each other. For example, consider a test that has a *W*-score *SD* of exactly 30 points. The "Average" range on the standard score scale for this test will span from −20 to +20 on the *W* Difference scale—covering a range from "Limited" to "Advanced" on the proficiency scale! An examinee who obtains a *W* Difference score of, say, −18 points on this test will earn a standard score of 91 ("Average") but an RPI of 55/90—in the "Limited" range. This example underscores the importance of considering *both* relative standing and proficiency metrics in your evaluations. If this examiner had omitted the proficiency scores from their report, then they would have lost the opportunity to obtain valuable insight about this student's challenges in the classroom.

DON'T FORGET

The WJ V Proficiency and Relative Standing metrics sometimes "tell different stories." When this happens, there is often useful information to be gleaned from the Proficiency (Level 3) metrics that is not apparent from the Relative Standing (Level 4) metrics. Look at both types of scores and make appropriate interpretations from each.

Level 5: Score Differences

The Level 2 through 4 scores reviewed in the prior sections describe an individual's performance or ability on *individual* WJ V tests and clusters. In contrast, Level 5 information makes *comparisons* between and among sets of scores to describe patterns of examinee performance. These score-difference patterns are useful for diagnostic decision-making and for planning targeted instruction or interventions. The following sections describe the score difference interpretations available in the WJ V.

SS/PR profile analysis Examining patterns of score differences, or *scatter*, among tests and clusters can be useful for understanding the nature and underlying causes of an examinee's particular strengths and weaknesses. For example, a high degree of scatter among cognitive abilities may be associated with certain clinical populations or may be associated with abnormal cognitive functioning (Oakes et al., 2013). It may also be useful to compare two or more specific scores to understand the nature of an examinee's particular learning difficulties. For example, comparing an examinee's scores from the WJ V Oral Comprehension and Passage Comprehension tests can help determine whether an examinee's weaknesses in comprehension are related to oral language, reading, or both (Mather et al., 2025).

At the time of this book's writing, the *Riverside Score®* platform does not contain an SS/PR Profile among its available report options; however, you can perform this type of analysis manually using information provided in the WJ V Score Report. While it is not possible to simply look at two scores and say that one is statistically higher or lower than the other, you can use the confidence bands around the examinee's obtained SS and PR scores to determine whether a difference between two scores is greater than would be expected simply by chance. As explained earlier in this chapter, a confidence band provides a range within which an examinee's true score is likely to fall. Using confidence bands instead of single obtained values when making comparisons among an examinee's scores minimizes the chance that an observed score difference is due to measurement error rather than a true difference.

The following are some rules of thumb for determining whether an observed difference between two test or cluster scores may represent a true difference in the examinee's abilities, using the 68% confidence bands around the SS or PR scores (Mather & Woodcock, 2001):

- If the 68% confidence bands for any two tests or clusters overlap at all, assume that there is *no difference* between the two scores.
- If a separation exists between the ends of the two 68% confidence bands that is *less* than the width of the wider of the two confidence bands, assume that a *possible difference* exists between the two scores. A score difference of this size would occur on average about 8 times in 100 if a single comparison is made.
- If the separation between the two 68% confidence bands is *greater* than the width of the wider band, assume that a *real difference* exists between the individual's two scores. A difference this size would occur on average about 2 times in 1,000 if a single comparison is being made.

	Relative Standing	
Test Name	**Standard Score** (68% Confidence Band)	
Oral Comprehension	107 (100–114) Average	← Confidence band width = 14 points
Passage Comprehension	91 (84–97) Average	← Confidence band width = 13 points

Figure 7.14 SS Profile Analysis Interpretation for Lucy, Grade 8.2

Note that the significance of observed score differences decreases as the number of score pair comparisons increases.

Figure 7.14 shows the interpretation of a SS profile analysis for Lucy, our eighth-grade student. Recall that Lucy's standard score on the WJ V Passage Comprehension test was 91. When reviewing Lucy's other test and cluster scores, the evaluator notices that Lucy's Oral Comprehension score appears to be fairly high compared to her Passage Comprehension score. Both tests required Lucy to provide a missing word in a short passage. On the Passage Comprehension test, Lucy read the passages to herself; on the Oral Comprehension test, she heard the passages from an audio recording. The examiner wonders if the difference between these two test standard scores is significantly different. Using the rules of thumb above, the examiner compares the distance between the two tests' 68% confidence bands (100 – 97 = 3 points) to the width of the wider of the two confidence bands (14 points) and determines that a possible difference exists between these two test scores. A score difference of this magnitude would be expected to occur fewer than 10 times out of 100 on any comparison between two score pairs. Although Lucy's Passage Comprehension score still falls in the average range relative to her peers, it appears to be significantly lower than her score on the Oral Comprehension test. The examiner makes a note of this for her evaluation report.

You must determine whether a statistically significant score difference has any practical or educational implications. A statistically significant discrepancy may exist between two scores that has little educational relevance. For example, in Lucy's case, her standard scores for both Passage Comprehension and Oral Comprehension are in the average range, making it unlikely that her test results suggest a need for reading interventions based solely on this observation.

Keep in mind that when you are testing very low- or high-ability examinees, score differences should be interpreted in the context of the examinee's location on the ability scale. Often, evaluators will discuss "relative" strengths and weaknesses. For example, a person may obtain a standard score of 80 in Broad Reading and 60 in Broad Mathematics. Although both scores are below average, if the SS profile analysis reveals that the clusters' 68% confidence bands are separated by a width greater than the widest of the two bands, then reading could be described as a "relative" strength for this individual. A "twice exceptional" student (e.g., a gifted student who also has dyslexia) may have a superior score on the Math Problem Solving cluster (e.g., a standard score of 130), but only an average score on the Basic Reading Skills cluster (e.g., a standard score of 95). In this example, reading would be viewed as a relative weakness.

As a general rule, use test scores to generate hypotheses about academic performance. The hypotheses generated need to be compared with other information gathered about the examinee, including relevant background knowledge, additional testing, and interviews with teachers and parents. When the hypotheses are reasonable, you can use them to: (a) clarify the specific nature of an individual's performance, (b) clarify the severity of any problems in development, (c) develop accommodation and intervention recommendations, (d) select appropriate educational programs, or (e) consider an appropriate academic or vocational placement. The comparison score procedures (described later) are appropriate for testing specific hypotheses about an examinee's test performance.

To determine the factors that might account for a certain pattern of scores, consider both the extrinsic (external) factors, as well as the intrinsic (internal) factors. Extrinsic factors include the person's socioeconomic status, education, past services and interventions, special training, social and physical environment, family background, and so forth. Intrinsic factors include the examinee's attention, health, temperament, physical and mental status, motivation, and interest. In some cases, differences among scores may be factors associated with examiner characteristics or factors associated with the assessment situation.

DON'T FORGET

A certain amount of variability is expected in the general population. The significance of observed score differences decreases as the number of comparisons increases. You must determine whether observed score differences have any practical or educational implications.

Comparison scores In contrast to the SS/PR profile analysis described above, the WJ V comparison score procedures use information from the WJ V norming study to make *predictions* about how an examinee will perform. These predictions are then compared to the examinee's *actual* scores, and the differences are expressed as *base rates*. A base rate is similar to a PR and is used to describe how likely a phenomenon is to occur in a population. For example, in the world's population, the base rate for heterochromia (i.e., having two different colored eyes) is less than 1%. In contrast, the base rate for having two brown eyes is around 75%. The lower the base rate, the lower the likelihood that the event will occur.

Figure 7.15 contains the general model describing how the WJ V comparison scores are derived. For each comparison, the examinee's *actual* score (Step 1) is compared to the score that the examinee was *predicted* to obtain (based on the examinee's age or grade and some *predictor* variable; Step 2). The difference (Step 3) between the actual and predicted scores is then compared to a distribution of score differences (Step 4) from the WJ V norming study to determine the base rate—or likelihood—of a score difference of that magnitude and direction occurring in the population. Differences that are negative and large (represented by the left tail of the distribution in Figure 7.15) suggest that the examinee scored

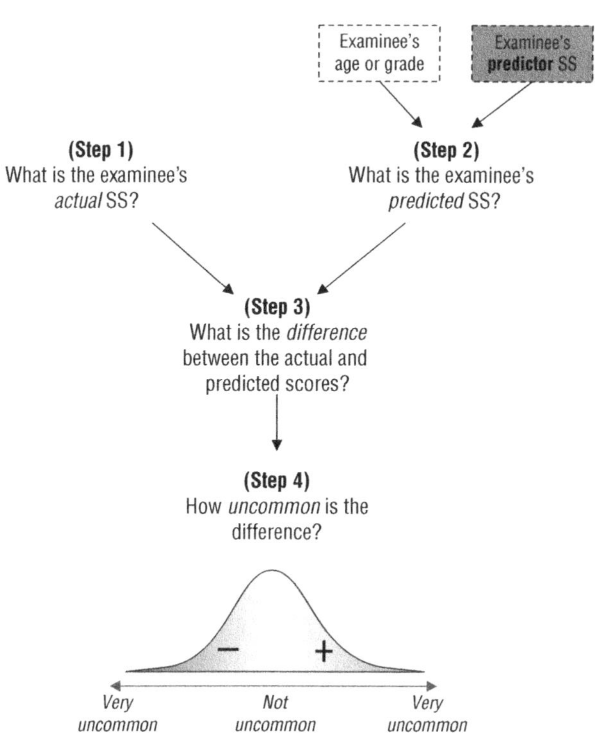

Figure 7.15 General Model for All WJ V Comparison Score Procedures

much lower than expected, while differences that are positive and large (represented by the right tail of the distribution) suggest that the examinee scored much higher than expected.

There are two types of comparison score procedures in the WJ V: Intra-Ability Comparisons and Ability/Achievement Comparisons. Intra-Ability Comparisons are useful for identifying strengths and weaknesses among an individual's cognitive abilities or academic achievement, whereas Ability/Achievement Comparisons are useful for determining if a discrepancy exists between an examinee's overall ability and their academic achievement. The general model in Figure 7.15 applies to both of these comparison types; the difference between them is how the *predictor* standard score (the shaded dashed box in Figure 7.15) is computed. For Intra-Ability Comparisons, the predictor score is the average standard score from a pool of predictor tests. For Ability/Achievement Comparisons, the predictor score is a single cluster standard score. In all procedures, the value of the examinee's actual score (Step 1) is an obtained cluster standard score.

To obtain *any* of the scores within a comparison procedure, you must administer *all* of the predictor tests. Then, depending on which particular cluster score comparisons are of interest, you may administer any additional tests required to obtain those cluster scores. When you generate a report from *Riverside Score®*, you can select the level of significance that the

DON'T FORGET

The comparison score norms in the WJ V are models of how examinees in the norming study performed. When you use the comparison score procedures, the platform uses these norms to make *data-based predictions* about how an examinee is expected to perform, given their age and performance on some criterion predictor. When the examinee's performance is significantly different from what is expected, it should be noted and the possible causes should be explored.

platform will use to determine whether a cluster score is a significant strength or weakness (in the Intra-Ability Comparisons) or whether a cluster score is significantly lower or higher than expected (in the Ability/Achievement Comparisons). The options for significance range from ±1.00 *SD* (i.e., base rates of ≤16% and ≥84% will be flagged as unexpected in the report) to ±2.30 *SD* (i.e., base rates of ≤1% and ≥99% will be flagged as unexpected in the report). The default significance value is ±1.50 *SD*; at this level, cluster score comparison will be flagged as significant or unexpected if they occur in ≤7% of the population at either tail of the difference score distribution.

Intra-Ability Comparison procedures There are three Intra-Ability Comparison procedures available in the WJ V: Intra-Cognitive, Intra-Achievement, and Academic Skills/Fluency/Applications. The Intra-Cognitive comparisons require tests from the COG battery (with optional tests from the VTL). The latter two comparison procedures require only tests from the ACH battery.

Intra-Cognitive Comparison procedure Use the Intra-Cognitive Comparison procedure to determine whether significant differences exist among an examinee's broad CHC cognitive abilities. This procedure can be useful when you have noted weaknesses in one or more academic areas and you are interested in exploring whether the examinee exhibits weaknesses in cognitive processing relevant to those academic areas. It can also be useful to identify cognitive strengths to inform instructional interventions.

In this procedure, the predictor score is the average of the standard scores from the eight tests that comprise the WJ V GIA cluster. Using this procedure, you can obtain comparison scores for any or all of the CHC broad cluster abilities by administering select additional tests in your test session (see Rapid Reference 7.7). Note that if you administer the tests that comprise the GIA cluster in your test session, you will obtain, by default, the Intra-Cognitive Comprehension-Knowledge (Gc) comparison in your score report because the two tests that comprise the Comprehension-Knowledge cluster are already included in the set of required predictor tests.

Table 7.1 contains the Intra-Cognitive Comparisons for Lucy, our eighth-grade student. Based on how Lucy performed on the eight tests that comprise the predictor for the Intra-Cognitive Comparison procedure, she was predicted to obtain standard scores between 94 and 96 on all of the broad CHC ability cognitive clusters. Her obtained standard scores actually range from 77 (for the Auditory Working Memory Capacity cluster) to 107 (for the Long-Term Storage cluster); however, among her cognitive cluster scores, the only one that is significantly different than predicted is Auditory Working Memory Capacity. Compared with other examinees in the norming study who had the same predicted score (SS = 95) as Lucy on this cluster, only 5% had a score as low as, or lower

Rapid Reference 7.7

Required and Optional Tests for Intra-Cognitive Comparison Procedure

Required Predictor Tests (Must Administer All)	Possible Predicted Clusters (Select Those Desired)	Additional Tests That Must Be Administered to Obtain the Desired Comparison
Oral Vocabulary Matrices Spatial Relations Story Recall Semantic Word Retrieval Verbal Attention Number-Pattern Matching Verbal Analogies	Comprehension-Knowledge (Gc)	*No additional tests needed*
	Fluid Reasoning (Gf)	Analysis-Synthesis
	Auditory Working Memory Capacity (Gwm)	Numbers Reversed
	Cognitive Processing Speed (Gs)	Letter-Pattern Matching
	Retrieval Fluency (Gr)	Phonemic Word Retrieval
	Long-Term Storage (Gl)	Story Comprehension
	Visual Processing (Gv)	Block Rotation
	Phonological Processing (Ga)	Sound Blending Segmentation

Table 7.1 Intra-Cognitive Comparisons for Lucy, Grade 8.2

	Earned SS	Predicted SS	Difference	*z* Score	PR (Base Rate)	Interpretation
Comprehension-Knowledge	98	94	4	0.47	68	
Fluid Reasoning	91	95	−4	−0.4	35	
Auditory Working Memory Capacity	77	95	−18	−1.64	5	Weakness
Cognitive Processing Speed	95	95	0	0.01	51	
Retrieval Fluency	106	95	11	0.88	81	
Long-Term Storage	107	95	12	1.2	89	
Visual Processing	94	95	−2	−0.14	45	
Phonological Awareness	93	96	−3	−0.21	42	

Notes: The predictor for each target cluster score is the examinee's average obtained standard scores from the following eight tests: Oral Vocabulary, Matrices, Spatial Relations, Story Recall, Semantic Word Retrieval, Verbal Attention, Number-Pattern Matching, and Verbal Analogies. The difference score significance is based on ±1.50 *SD* (*SEE*).

than, Lucy's obtained standard score of 77. Auditory working memory is a significant weakness for Lucy. She performed better than expected on the Retrieval Fluency (SS = 106) and Long-Term Storage (SS = 107) clusters. While those cognitive abilities appear to be among Lucy's strongest cognitive abilities, they are not statistically significant strengths at the ±1.50 *SD* cutoff level the examiner chose for these comparisons. Nearly 20% of 8th-grade examinees in the norming sample with the same predicted score obtained a Retrieval Fluency cluster score as high or higher than hers, and nearly 11% with the same predicted score obtained a Long-Term Storage cluster standard score as high or higher.

Some additional examples of appropriate interpretive statements for communicating Intra-Cognitive comparison scores in an evaluation report include:

- When compared to his overall cognitive ability, cognitive processing speed presents as a relative weakness for Austin. Among his same-age peers with the same expected score, his Cognitive Processing Speed cluster score is in the bottom 3%.
- Visual processing appears to be a relative strength for Serena. When compared to her age-peers who had the same predicted score on the Visual Processing cluster, Serena obtained a score that is in the upper 2%. This is useful for planning instructional interventions, as Serena may process information more easily if it is presented to her visually.
- Given his overall cognitive ability, Jeremy was expected to obtain a standard score of 77 on the Fluid Reasoning cluster. His actual score (97) is 20 points higher than expected and higher than 96% of his same-age peers with the same overall cognitive ability. Novel thinking and reasoning skills appear to be a significant cognitive strength for Jeremy.

INTRA-ACHIEVEMENT COMPARISON PROCEDURE Use the Intra-Achievement Comparison procedure to determine whether significant differences exist among an examinee's academic achievement cluster scores. This procedure can be useful for identifying relative strengths and weaknesses within and among the examinee's academic skills. Information from this procedure can provide documentation to support the existence of an SLD when the examinee exhibits a significant weakness in one or more of the areas.

In this procedure, the predictor score is the average of the standard scores from the six tests that comprise the WJ V Academic Skills and Academic Applications clusters. Using this procedure, you can obtain comparison scores for any or all of the reading, math, and writing clusters in Rapid Reference 7.8 by administering select additional tests in your test session.

Table 7.2 contains Lucy's Intra-Achievement comparisons. Based on how Lucy performed on the six tests that comprise the predictor for the Intra-Achievement Comparison procedure, she was predicted to obtain a standard score of 98 or 99 for each of the achievement clusters in Table 7.2. Her obtained standard scores actually range from 88 (for Reading Comprehension) to 113 (for Math Calculation Skills). Only her Math Calculation Skills cluster score is significantly different from her predicted score at ±1.50 *SD*. Compared with other examinees in the norming study who had the same predicted score (SS = 98) as Lucy on this cluster, only 5% had a score as high as, or higher than, Lucy's obtained standard score of 113. Math calculation is a significant strength for Lucy. Her score on the Math Problem Solving cluster was also

Rapid Reference 7.8

Required and Optional Tests for Intra-Achievement Comparison Procedure

Required Predictor Tests (Must Administer All)	Possible Predicted Clusters (Select Those Desired)	Additional Tests That Must Be Administered to Obtain the Desired Comparison
Letter-Word Identification Calculation Spelling Passage Comprehension Applied Problems Written Language Samples	Basic Reading Skills	Word Attack
	Reading Fluency	Word Reading FluencySentence Reading Fluency
	Reading Comprehension	Paragraph Reading Comprehension
	Math Calculation Skills	Math Facts Fluency
	Math Problem Solving	Math Problem Identification
	Basic Writing Skills	Sentence Writing Accuracy
	Written Expression	Sentence Writing Fluency

Table 7.2 Intra-Achievement Comparisons for Lucy, Grade 8.2

	Earned SS	Predicted SS	Difference	*z* Score	PR (Base Rate)	Interpretation
Basic Reading Skills	94	98	−4	−0.48	32	
Reading Comprehension	88	98	−10	−1.18	12	
Reading Fluency	95	99	−3	−0.26	40	
Math Calculation Skills	113	98	15	1.63	95	Strength
Math Problem Solving	111	98	13	1.38	92	
Basic Writing Skills	92	98	−7	−0.8	21	
Written Expression	94	98	−4	−0.36	36	

Notes: The predictor for each target cluster score is the average of the examinee's earned standard scores from the following six tests: Letter-Word Identification, Passage Comprehension, Spelling, Written Language Samples, Calculation, and Applied Problems. The difference score significance is based on ±1.50 *SD* (*SEE*).

relatively high (SS = 111). Although it does not surpass the cutoff for significance, only 8% of the grade 8.2 norming sample with the same predicted score of 98 would have a Math Problem Solving cluster score as high or higher than Lucy's score. Looking at Lucy's ACH cluster scores in Table 7.2, it is notable that Lucy's Reading Comprehension score, while not surpassing the level of significance, is relatively low. Among peers with the same predicted score, only 12% would have a score as low or lower than Lucy's. From this table, a picture is emerging about Lucy's academic strengths (math) and weaknesses (reading comprehension).

Some additional examples of appropriate interpretive statements for communicating Intra-Achievement comparison scores in an evaluation report include:

- When compared to her overall academic achievement, Annika displays relative weaknesses in Basic Writing Skills and Basic Reading Skills. Her expected standard scores for both of these clusters were in the high 90s, yet her obtained scores were both in the low 80s—lower than approximately 95% of her peers who had the same expected scores.
- Given Matthew's overall achievement, his score on the Reading Comprehension cluster was unexpectedly low. Among his peers with the same expected standard score (94), his Reading Comprehension cluster standard score (76) was in the bottom 1%.

Academic Skills/Fluency/Applications Comparison procedure Use the Academic Skills/Fluency/Applications Comparison procedure to determine whether significant strengths or weaknesses exist among an examinee's skills, fluency, and applications *across* achievement domains (i.e., reading, math, and writing). When used in conjunction with the Intra-Achievement comparisons, this procedure can provide additional insight about the specific nature of the examinee's strengths and weaknesses. For example, if an examinee had an intra-achievement weakness in math calculation skills and also showed a relative weakness in academic fluency, then it might suggest that the examinee's challenges in math are exacerbated when working under time constraints. In this procedure, the predictor score is the average of the standard scores from the six tests that are *not* represented in the cluster score that is being compared. So, for example, in the comparison for Academic Fluency, the average of the standard scores from the six tests comprising the Academic Skills and Academic Applications clusters is used as the predictor. By administering the nine required tests, you can obtain comparison scores for each of the clusters in Rapid Reference 7.9; no additional tests are required.

Table 7.3 contains Lucy's Academic Skills/Fluency/Applications comparisons. Based on how Lucy performed on the 9 tests that comprise the predictor for this comparison procedure, she was predicted to obtain a standard score between 98 and 100 for each of the clusters in Table 7.3. Her obtained standard scores of 99, 97, and 97 are very similar to her expected scores and are similar to the scores obtained by others in her grade who had the same expected scores. The information in Table 7.3 appears to rule out relative strengths and weaknesses for Lucy across achievement domains on basic skills, working under time pressure, and applying academic concepts.

Some additional examples of appropriate interpretive statements for communicating Academic Skills/Fluency/Applications comparison scores in an evaluation report include:

- When compared to her expected score (89) on the Academic Fluency cluster, Philomena's obtained score was 12 points lower (77). While this is not a significant difference at the −1.50 *SD* cutoff, her Academic Fluency cluster score was in the bottom 10% among her peers with the same expected score. This suggests that doing academic tasks quickly under time constraints is a relative weakness for Philomena, regardless of the academic domain.

Rapid Reference 7.9

Required and Optional Tests for Academic Skills/Fluency/Applications Comparison Procedure

Required Predictor Tests (Must Administer All)	Predicted Clusters	Additional Tests That Must Be Administered to Obtain the Desired Comparison
Letter-Word Identification Calculation Spelling Math Facts Fluency Sentence Reading Fluency Sentence Writing Fluency Passage Comprehension Applied Problems Written Language Samples	Academic Skills/Brief Achievement	*No additional tests needed*
	Academic Fluency	*No additional tests needed*
	Academic Applications	*No additional tests needed*

Table 7.3 Academic Skills/Fluency/Applications Comparisons for Lucy, Grade 8.2

	Earned SS	Predicted SS	Difference	*z* Score	PR (Base Rate)	Interpretation
Academic Skills/Brief Achievement	99	98	1	0.09	54	
Academic Fluency	97	99	−1	−0.1	46	
Academic Applications	97	100	−3	−0.33	37	

Notes: The predictor for each target cluster score is the average of the examinee's earned standard scores from the six tests that are not represented in the target cluster. The difference score significance is based on ±1.50 *SD* (*SEE*). There are no significant strengths or weaknesses among the target clusters.

- Jamal's score on the Academic Applications cluster was significantly lower than expected, given his overall academic achievement. He was predicted to obtain a standard score of 105 on the Academic Applications cluster. His obtained score of 90 was lower than 97% of his peers with the same overall achievement. Although his basic academic skills appear to be intact, applying academic concepts to different types of tasks across reading, math, and writing domains appears to be a relative weakness for Jamal. This may be exacerbated by, or may be the result of, his low oral language abilities.

Ability/Achievement Comparison procedures There are four Ability/Achievement Comparison procedures available in the WJ V: GIA/Achievement, Oral Language/Achievement, Academic Knowledge/Achievement, and Gf-Gc Composite/Other Abilities

Comparisons. These comparison procedures are used to determine if a significant difference exists between an examinee's obtained scores (given their overall ability) and their predicted scores for clusters measuring academic achievement and other abilities. Chapter 8 of this book describes the ability/achievement discrepancy procedure for identifying an SLD; these WJ V comparison procedures provide a *data-based* method for establishing the existence of an ability/achievement discrepancy in a comprehensive SLD evaluation. The Oral Language/Achievement and Academic Knowledge/Achievement Comparison procedures require only tests from the ACH battery, making them accessible to WJ V users who do not have qualifications to access the COG battery. The GIA/Achievement procedure requires the eight COG tests that comprise the GIA. The Gf-Gc/Other Abilities procedure requires the four tests that comprise the Gf-Gc cluster, with options to predict scores from among the ACH and VTL clusters.

GIA/Achievement Comparison procedure Use the GIA/Achievement Comparison procedure to determine whether an individual is performing lower or higher than expected in oral language and/or academic achievement given their overall cognitive abilities. As discussed in Chapter 8, this procedure is a best-practice approach for identifying when an examinee has "unexpected or unexplained" low academic performance, which is one criterion to consider when determining the presence of an SLD. In this procedure, an examinee's GIA cluster score (together with their age or grade) is used to predict their performance on several possible ACH clusters. Refer to Rapid Reference 7.10 for a list of the oral language and achievement cluster scores that can be predicted in this procedure and the tests that must be administered to obtain those comparisons.

Table 7.4 contains Lucy's GIA/Achievement comparisons. Although it is not reported in Table 7.4, Lucy obtained a GIA standard score of 91. Based on this, she was predicted to obtain a standard score between 92 and 95 for each of the clusters in Table 7.4.[1] Her obtained standard scores range from 88 to 115. Her scores for Listening Comprehension (SS = 115), Math Calculation Skills (SS = 113), and Math Problem Solving (SS = 111) are significantly higher than expected given her overall cognitive ability as measured by the GIA cluster. Among other 8th-grade students with the same GIA score, only 3–4% of the students would have scores as high or higher than Lucy on these three clusters. These are unexpected and significant strengths for Lucy.

Although Lucy's Reading Comprehension cluster standard score (SS = 88) is in the low-average range and is lower than its expected value of 94, it does not meet the criteria for significance at the −1.50 *SD* cutoff. Among other 8th-grade examinees with the same GIA score, 30% would have a score as low or lower than Lucy's on the Reading Comprehension cluster.

[1] Readers who are curious about why Lucy's predicted achievement standard scores are all higher than her obtained GIA standard score should refer to the section "Further Information About the WJ V Ability/Achievement Comparisons: Statistical Regression" later in this chapter.

Rapid Reference 7.10

Required and Optional Tests for the GIA/Achievement Comparison Procedure

Required Tests Comprising the Predictor Cluster (Must Administer All)	Possible Predicted Clusters (Select Those Desired)	Additional Tests That Must Be Administered to Obtain the Desired Comparison
Oral Vocabulary Matrices Spatial Relations Story Recall Semantic Word Retrieval Verbal Attention Number-Pattern Matching Verbal Analogies	Listening Comprehension	Oral Comprehension Story Comprehension
	Oral Expression	Picture Vocabulary Oral Language Samples
	Basic Reading Skills	Letter-Word Identification Word Attack
	Reading Fluency	Sentence Reading Fluency Word Reading Fluency
	Reading Comprehension	Passage Comprehension Paragraph Reading Comprehension
	Basic Writing Skills	Spelling Sentence Writing Accuracy
	Spelling Skills	Spelling Spelling of Sounds
	Written Expression	Written Language Samples Sentence Writing Fluency
	Math Calculation Skills	Calculation Math Facts Fluency
	Math Problem Solving	Applied Problems Math Problem Identification
	Academic Skills	Letter-Word Identification Calculation Spelling
	Academic Fluency	Math Facts Fluency Sentence Reading Fluency Sentence Writing Fluency
	Academic Applications	Passage Comprehension Applied Problems Written Language Samples
	Academic Knowledge	Academic Vocabulary Academic Facts
	Phoneme-Grapheme Knowledge	Word Attack Spelling of Sounds

Table 7.4 GIA/Achievement Comparisons for Lucy, Grade 8.2

	Earned SS	Predicted SS	Difference	*z* Score	PR (Base Rate)	Interpretation
Listening Comprehension	115	94	21	1.84	97	Significant (+)
Oral Expression	111	94	17	1.42	92	
Basic Reading Skills	94	95	−1	−0.07	47	
Reading Comprehension	88	94	−6	−0.52	30	
Reading Fluency	95	93	2	0.19	58	
Math Calculation Skills	113	93	20	1.86	97	Significant (+)
Math Problem Solving	111	92	19	1.77	96	Significant (+)
Basic Writing Skills	92	94	−3	−0.24	41	
Spelling Skills	92	94	−2	−0.19	43	
Written Expression	94	94	0	0.03	51	
Academic Skills/ Brief Achievement	99	94	5	0.42	66	
Academic Fluency	97	94	4	0.34	63	
Academic Applications	97	93	3	0.34	63	
Academic Knowledge	109	93	16	1.49	93	
Phoneme-Grapheme Knowledge	95	95	1	0.05	52	

Notes: The predictor for each target cluster score is the examinee's earned standard score on the General Intellectual Ability (GIA) cluster. The difference score significance is based on ±1.50 *SD* (*SEE*).

Some additional examples of appropriate interpretive statements for communicating GIA/Achievement comparison scores in an evaluation report include:

- Given Sara's overall cognitive ability as measured by the GIA cluster, she was expected to score among the top 10% of her grade peers in most achievement areas. While her reading and writing cluster scores are all commensurate with those expectations, her math scores are unexpectedly low. For example, she was expected to score 111 on the Math Calculation cluster but obtained a score of 92. While her score is still in the normative average range, it is unexpectedly low for Sara given her high-average intelligence, and it is among the lowest 1% of scores from her peers with the same GIA score.

- Samuel's GIA cluster score, which measures his overall cognitive ability, is in the average normative range (SS = 103, PR = 57). Based on this, his expected scores for the achievement domain clusters are also in the average (100–104) range. Compared to those expectations, Samuel scored unusually high in math areas and unusually low on several reading clusters. For example, given Samuel's overall cognitive ability, he was expected to obtain a standard score of 101 on the Math Calculation Skills cluster, which measures his computational skill and automaticity with math facts. Instead, Samuel obtained a score of 119, 18 points higher than expected. Among his peers with the same GIA score, Samuel's Math Calculation Skills cluster score is in the top 3%; however, his obtained standard score on the Reading Comprehension cluster was 90, which is lower than 75% of his same-grade peers with the same cognitive ability. Further testing is needed to determine the nature and causes of Samuel's unexpectedly high and low domain-level achievement scores.

Oral Language/Achievement Comparison procedure Use the Oral Language/Achievement Comparison procedure to determine whether an individual is performing lower or higher than expected in academic achievement given their overall oral language ability. This procedure can be helpful in validating the presence of academic difficulties, even in the absence of oral language deficits. The predictor for the Oral Language/Achievement Comparison procedure is the Oral Language cluster score. Refer to Rapid Reference 7.11 for a list of the achievement cluster scores that can be predicted in this procedure and the tests that must be administered to obtain those comparisons.

Table 7.5 contains Lucy's Oral Language/Achievement comparisons. Although it is not reported in Table 7.5, Lucy obtained an Oral Language Cluster standard score of 115, which is in the high average normative range. Given this, her examiner can rule out low overall oral language skills as a cause for Lucy's relative difficulty with reading comprehension. Given her Oral Language cluster score, in fact, she was predicted to obtain achievement standard scores in the range of 106–109 for the clusters in Table 7.5. Instead, most of her achievement cluster standard scores are in the 90s—slightly lower than expected but not statistically significantly different than expected, with the exception of Reading Comprehension (SS = 88). Lucy's Reading Comprehension score is lower than all but 3% of 8th graders who have the same Oral Language ability as her. This provides additional evidence to support that Lucy's achievement in reading comprehension is lower than expected.

Some additional examples of appropriate interpretive statements for communicating Oral Language/Achievement comparison scores in an evaluation report include:

- Given that Maria's oral language skills are in the high-average normative range, her achievement in reading comprehension is unexpectedly low. Her predicted Reading Comprehension cluster score was 108, but her obtained score was 82. Her score is lower than 99% of her grade peers who had the same oral language ability as Maria. This provides additional support for Maria's earlier diagnosis of an SLD in the area of reading comprehension.

Rapid Reference 7.11

Required and Optional Tests for the Oral Language/Achievement Comparison Procedure

Required Tests Comprising the Predictor Cluster (Must Administer All)	Possible Predicted Clusters (Select Those Desired)	Additional Tests That Must Be Administered to Obtain the Desired Comparison
Picture Vocabulary Oral Comprehension Oral Language Samples Story Comprehension	Basic Reading Skills	Letter-Word Identification Word Attack
	Reading Comprehension	Passage Comprehension Paragraph Reading Comprehension
	Reading Fluency	Sentence Reading Fluency Word Reading Fluency
	Math Calculation Skills	Calculation Math Facts Fluency
	Math Problem Solving	Applied Problems Math Problem Identification
	Basic Writing Skills	Spelling Sentence Writing Accuracy
	Spelling Skills	Spelling Spelling of Sounds
	Written Expression	Written Language Samples Sentence Writing Fluency
	Academic Skills	Letter-Word Identification Calculation Spelling
	Academic Fluency	Math Facts Fluency Sentence Reading Fluency Sentence Writing Fluency
	Academic Applications	Passage Comprehension Applied Problems Written Language Samples
	Phoneme-Grapheme Knowledge	Word Attack Spelling of Sounds

Table 7.5 Oral Language/Achievement Comparisons for Lucy, Grade 8.2

	Earned SS	Predicted SS	Difference	*z* Score	PR (Base Rate)	Interpretation
Basic Reading Skills	94	107	−13	−0.94	17	
Reading Comprehension	88	109	−21	−1.88	3	Significant (−)
Reading Fluency	95	107	−12	−0.91	18	
Math Calculation Skills	113	106	7	0.54	71	
Math Problem Solving	111	109	2	0.2	58	
Basic Writing Skills	92	107	−16	−1.24	11	
Spelling Skills	92	108	−15	−1.19	12	
Written Expression	94	106	−12	−0.92	18	
Academic Skills/ Brief Achievement	99	107	−8	−0.66	26	
Academic Fluency	97	107	−10	−0.77	22	
Academic Applications	97	109	−12	−1.14	13	
Phoneme-Grapheme Knowledge	95	107	−12	−0.87	19	

Notes: The predictor for each target cluster score is the examinee's earned standard score on the Oral Language cluster. The difference score significance is based on ±1.50 *SD* (*SEE*).

- Emilio's overall oral language skills in English are in the low-average normative range (SS = 88, PR = 21). Given this, his expected scores on the academic achievement clusters were all in the range of 86–89; however, he has several unexpectedly high academic cluster scores. For example, his score on the Written Expression cluster (SS = 104) is in the average range (PR = 60) compared to all of his age peers but is in the top 5% of his age peers who had the same oral language ability.

Academic Knowledge/Achievement Comparison procedure. Use the Academic Knowledge/Achievement Comparison procedure to determine whether an individual is performing lower or higher than expected in skills, applications, and/or fluency across the academic domains of reading, math, and writing, given their overall academic knowledge. See Rapid Reference 7.12 for a list of required and optional tests for this comparison procedure. The Academic Knowledge/Achievement procedure is useful for predicting

Rapid Reference 7.12

Required and Optional Tests for the Academic Knowledge/Achievement Comparison Procedure

Required Tests Comprising the Predictor Cluster (Must Administer All)	Possible Predicted Clusters (Select Those Desired)	Additional Tests That Must Be Administered to Obtain the Desired Comparison
Academic Facts Academic Vocabulary	Academic Skills	Letter-Word Identification Calculation Spelling
	Academic Fluency	Math Facts Fluency Sentence Reading Fluency Sentence Writing Fluency
	Academic Applications	Passage Comprehension Applied Problems Written Language Samples

academic achievement from a cluster that does not require reading, writing, or math. In essence, the Academic Knowledge cluster in this procedure serves as a "proxy" for ability (LaForte et al., 2025). It also serves as a comparison procedure that is fully accessible to test users who do not have qualifications to use the WJ V COG, because all required and optional tests are included in the ACH battery. Given that the Academic Knowledge cluster contains only two tests, however, this procedure should not be used for diagnosis or decision-making. Instead, it should be used only as a "screener" or to provide additional support for findings from a more comprehensive evaluation.

Table 7.6 contains Lucy's Academic Knowledge/Achievement comparisons. Although it is not reported in Table 7.6, Lucy obtained an Academic Knowledge cluster standard score of 109, which is at the top of the average normative range. Her expected standard scores on the Academic Skills, Academic Fluency, and Academic Applications clusters are between 105 and 106. Her obtained standard scores on those clusters are slightly lower than expected (99, 97, and 97, respectively); however, none of these scores is significantly lower than expected at ±1.50 *SD*. Compared to other eighth-grade students with the same Academic Knowledge cluster score as Lucy, her scores on the achievement clusters in Table 7.6 are not unusual or unexpected.

Some additional examples of appropriate interpretive statements for communicating Academic Knowledge/Achievement comparison scores in an evaluation report include:

- This evaluator was interested in determining whether any of Malik's cross-domain achievement scores (i.e., basic skills, fluency, and/or applications) were lower than expected. He was administered the tests from the Academic Knowledge cluster as a

Table 7.6 Academic Knowledge/Achievement Comparisons for Lucy, Grade 8.2

	Earned SS	Predicted SS	Difference	*z* Score	PR (Base Rate)	Interpretation
Academic Skills/ Brief Achievement	99	106	−7	−0.62	27	
Academic Fluency	97	105	−8	−0.63	27	
Academic Applications	97	106	−10	−0.98	16	

Notes: The predictor for each target cluster score is the examinee's earned standard score on the Academic Knowledge cluster. The difference score significance is based on ±1.50 *SD* (*SEE*). No cluster scores are significantly higher or lower than predicted.

proxy for overall ability that does not require any reading, writing, or math. Given Malik's score on the Academic Knowledge cluster (SS = 105), his score on the Academic Fluency cluster was predicted to be 104. He obtained a score of 94, which represents a difference of −10 points from expectations. Among his grade peers with the same expected Academic Fluency score, his score was in the bottom 15%. While not low enough to meet the threshold for significance at ±1.50 *SD*, it does suggest that across academic domains, completing tasks under timed conditions presents as a challenge for Malik.

- Using Emily's Academic Knowledge cluster score (SS = 87, PR = 20) to predict her achievement, her expected scores on the cross-domain achievement clusters were in the range of 85–88. Her obtained scores all fell in the range between 82 and 90. None of these achievement scores were unexpected given her Academic Knowledge score.

Gf-Gc Composite/Other Abilities Comparison procedure Although it is included as an Ability/Achievement Comparison procedure in the WJ V test documentation, the Gf-Gc Composite/Other Abilities Comparison procedure is actually a hybrid comparison procedure. It is similar to the other Ability/Achievement Comparison procedures in that the predictor is a single cluster score, the Gf-Gc Composite, that can be used to predict an examinee's performance on various achievement clusters However, similar to the Intra-Cognitive Comparison procedure, it also provides comparisons between obtained and expected scores for the broad CHC ability clusters (excluding Gc and Gf, because they are contained in the predictor cluster) and narrow CHC ability and clinical clusters. Users who want to include this comparison procedure in their report will need access to the WJ V COG battery; optional predictions rely on tests from the WJ V COG, ACH, and VTL. See Rapid Reference 7.13 for a complete list of the tests required for the predictor cluster and the optional comparisons.

The Gf-Gc Composite/Other Abilities Comparison procedure can be useful when (a) you have reason to believe that the GIA score is not an adequate representation of the examinee's abilities due to deficits in working memory capacity, processing speed, long-term storage, or retrieval fluency; (b) you wish to document relative cognitive strengths and weaknesses using a more theoretically "pure" measure of overall cognitive ability that

Rapid Reference 7.13

Required and Optional Tests for the Gf-Gc Composite/Other Abilities Comparison Procedure

Required Tests Comprising the Predictor Cluster (Must Administer All)	Possible Predicted Clusters (Select Those Desired)	Additional Tests That Must Be Administered to Obtain the Desired Comparison
Oral Vocabulary Matrices Verbal Analogies Analysis-Synthesis	Auditory Working Memory Capacity	Verbal Attention Numbers Reversed
	Cognitive Processing Speed	Number-Pattern Matching Letter-Pattern Matching
	Retrieval Fluency	Semantic Word Retrieval Phonemic Word Retrieval
	Long-Term Storage	Story Recall Story Comprehension
	Visual Processing	Spatial Relations Block Rotation
	Phonological Awareness	Sound Blending Segmentation
	Phonological Manipulation	Sound Deletion Sound Substitution
	Auditory Memory Span	Memory for Words Sentence Repetition
	Cognitive Efficiency	Verbal Attention Number-Pattern Matching
	Phonemic Retrieval Fluency	Rapid Phoneme Naming Phonemic Word Retrieval
	RAN–Reading	Rapid Picture Naming Rapid Letter Naming Rapid Phoneme Naming
	RAN–Math	Rapid Number Naming Rapid Quantity Naming
	Basic Reading Skills	Letter-Word Identification Word Attack
	Reading Fluency	Sentence Reading Fluency Word Reading Fluency

Required Tests Comprising the Predictor Cluster (Must Administer All)	Possible Predicted Clusters (Select Those Desired)	Additional Tests That Must Be Administered to Obtain the Desired Comparison
	Reading Comprehension	Passage Comprehension Paragraph Reading Comprehension
	Basic Writing Skills	Spelling Sentence Writing Accuracy
	Spelling Skills	Spelling Spelling of Sounds
	Written Expression	Written Language Samples Sentence Writing Fluency
	Math Calculation Skills	Calculation Math Facts Fluency
	Math Problem Solving	Applied Problems Math Problem Identification
	Academic Skills	Letter-Word Identification Calculation Spelling
	Academic Fluency	Math Facts Fluency Sentence Reading Fluency Sentence Writing Fluency
	Academic Applications	Passage Comprehension Applied Problems Written Language Samples
	Phoneme-Grapheme Knowledge	Word Attack Spelling of Sounds

does not contain content overlap with the predicted clusters; or (c) you want to develop and test hypotheses to document the presence of an SLD.

Table 7.7 contains Lucy's Gf-Gc/Other Abilities comparisons. Although it is not reported in Table 7.4, Lucy obtained a Gf-Gc Composite standard score of 93. Based on that overall ability estimate, she was predicted to obtain standard scores in the 95–98 range on all predicted clusters. Her obtained standard scores range from 84 for Auditory Memory Span to 113 for Math Calculation Skills. Interestingly, neither of these cluster scores is statistically different from expected at ±1.50 *SD*. Her standard score for Math Problem Solving (111), however, *is* higher than expected. Among other 8th-grade students with the same Gf-Gc Composite score as Lucy's, only 6% would have a Math Problem Solving score as high or higher than hers.

Note in Table 7.7 that the comparison *z* score for the Auditory Working Memory Capacity cluster, one of several COG clusters available with this procedure, is just shy of the threshold for significance at ±1.50 *SD*. Among Lucy's peers with the same overall cognitive ability as measured by the Gf-Gc cluster, only 7% had a score as low or lower than Lucy's score (SS = 77). Recall that this cluster showed up as a significant weakness in the Intra-Cognitive comparisons in Table 7.1.

Some additional examples of appropriate interpretive statements for communicating Gf-Gc Composite/Other Abilities comparison scores in an evaluation report include:

- Because Tong was diagnosed with Attention Deficit/Hyperactivity Disorder (ADHD) and has documented deficits in the cognitive areas of working memory and processing speed, her GIA score (SS = 86) may not provide the best representation of her overall cognitive ability. The Gf-Gc Composite cluster, in comparison, includes four tests measuring only the areas of comprehension-knowledge and fluid reasoning and may provide a better estimate of Tong's potential. Her Gf-Gc Composite score was 96. Compared to other 4th-grade students with the same Gf-Gc Composite score as Tong, her scores on the Basic Reading Skills, Reading Comprehension, and Reading Fluency clusters were in the bottom 5–6%. This provides support for the hypothesis that Tong may have an SLD in the areas of basic reading skills, reading comprehension, and reading fluency.
- Given that Jessamyn's Intra-Cognitive profile suggested relative weaknesses in working memory capacity and long-term storage, this evaluator's hypothesis was that these cognitive processing deficits contribute to Jessamyn's difficulties remembering what she has read. Because the Intra-Cognitive Comparison procedure predictor score contains one test in common with each of the Auditory Working Memory Capacity and Long-Term Storage cluster scores, a purer way to assess Jessamyn's abilities in these areas is to use a nonoverlapping cluster score as the predictor. Because the Gf-Gc Composite cluster score contains only fluid reasoning and comprehension-knowledge tests, it will not be spuriously deflated by Jessamyn's known difficulties with working memory and long-term storage. When compared to her overall cognitive abilities as measured by the Gf-Gc Composite (SS = 97), her Auditory Working Memory (SS = 78) and Long-Term Storage (SS = 83) cluster scores were unexpectedly low. In fact, they were among the bottom 2% of scores from her peers with the same Gf-Gc Composite cluster score. This provides further evidence to confirm that Jessamyn is experiencing difficulties with the cognitive processes underlying reading comprehension.

Further information about the WJ V ability/achievement comparisons: statistical regression

As discussed in the prior sections, in the WJ V Ability/Achievement comparison calculations, the examinee's obtained achievement scores are compared to the scores that the student was

Table 7.7 Gf-Gc Composite/Other Abilities Comparisons for Lucy, Grade 8.2

	Earned SS	Predicted SS	Difference	*z* Score	PR (Base Rate)	Interpretation
Auditory Working Mem1ory Capacity	77	96	−19	−1.49	7	
Cognitive Processing Speed	95	97	−2	−0.13	45	
Retrieval Fluency	106	97	9	0.63	74	
Long-Term Storage	107	97	10	0.91	82	
Visual Processing	94	97	−3	−0.23	41	
Phonological Awareness	93	97	−4	−0.3	38	
Phonological Manipulation	91	97	−6	−0.48	32	
Auditory Memory Span	84	97	−13	−1.06	15	
Cognitive Efficiency (CE)	86	97	−10	−0.79	22	
Phonemic Retrieval Fluency	96	98	−2	−0.11	46	
RAN–Reading	96	98	−2	−0.12	45	
RAN–Math	105	98	7	0.49	69	
Basic Reading Skills	94	97	−3	−0.21	42	
Reading Comprehension	88	96	−8	−0.67	25	
Reading Fluency	95	97	−1	−0.11	46	
Math Calculation Skills	113	96	17	1.4	92	
Math Problem Solving	111	95	16	1.55	94	Significant (+)
Basic Writing Skills	92	97	−5	−0.4	35	
Spelling Skills	92	97	−4	−0.34	37	
Written Expression	94	97	−2	−0.17	43	
Academic Skills/Brief Achievement	99	96	2	0.2	58	
Academic Fluency	97	97	1	0.07	53	
Academic Applications	97	95	1	0.13	55	
Phoneme-Grapheme Knowledge	95	97	−2	−0.12	45	

Notes: The predictor for each target cluster score is the examinee's earned standard score on the Gf-Gc Composite cluster. The difference score significance is based on ±1.50 *SD* (*SEE*).

predicted to obtain given their overall ability score (i.e., GIA, Oral Language, Academic Knowledge, or Gf-Gc Composite), not to the ability score itself. For example, consider a student with an overall cognitive ability (GIA) standard score of 70 who obtains a WJ V Broad Reading score of 60. If we were to compare this student's achievement score directly to their GIA score, it would result in only a 10-point difference (60 − 70 = −10), which may not be large enough to interpret as an ability/achievement discrepancy. However, given this student's cognitive ability score, they might be *expected* to obtain a Broad Reading score of 79. Comparing their actual Broad Reading score to their expected Broad Reading score yields a more significant discrepancy (60 − 79 = −19). By comparing a student's obtained achievement scores to their predicted achievement scores and not directly to the obtained cognitive ability score, the WJ V comparison procedure norms correct for the effects of *statistical regression*; without these corrections, high-performing individuals would be overidentified as having a discrepancy and low-performing individuals would be under-identified.

Statistical regression is a phenomenon that occurs when a predictor variable is used to forecast a criterion variable, such as when a general ability score from an intelligence battery predicts an achievement test score. Because the scores are not perfectly correlated, two people with the same general ability score will not necessarily have the same achievement score. Among all people with a particular general ability score, their average score on the achievement test will be closer to the achievement test mean than the general ability score is to the general ability mean.

While the WJ V performs these regression calculations automatically, it is useful to understand how they work. To illustrate, in Figure 7.16, both general ability and achievement have a mean of 100 and an *SD* of 15 in the reference group. Both variables are normal and correlated at 0.60. The gray ellipse in the middle contains 95% of the data points. The upward-sloping line is the regression line. At regular intervals on the *X*-axis, selected IQ predictor scores are paired with predicted achievement values on the *Y*-axis, along with 95% confidence intervals.

Note that for each value of general ability, the predicted achievement score (the number in the white box) is closer to the mean than the general ability score. For example, when general ability = 70, the predicted achievement score is 82. When general ability = 115, the predicted achievement is 109.

The predicted value of Y (i.e., $\hat{Y}$) depends on the correlation between X and Y (i.e., r_{XY}), the means of X and Y (μ_X and μ_Y), and the *SD*s of X and Y (σ_X and σ_Y):

$$\hat{Y} = r_{XY}\left(X - \mu_X\right)\frac{\sigma_Y}{\sigma_X} + \mu_Y. \tag{7.6}$$

If the correlation between the intelligence test and the achievement test is 0.60, then an IQ of 70 would be associated with a predicted achievement score of 82.

$$\hat{Y} = 0.60(70 - 100)\frac{15}{15} + 100 = 82. \tag{7.7}$$

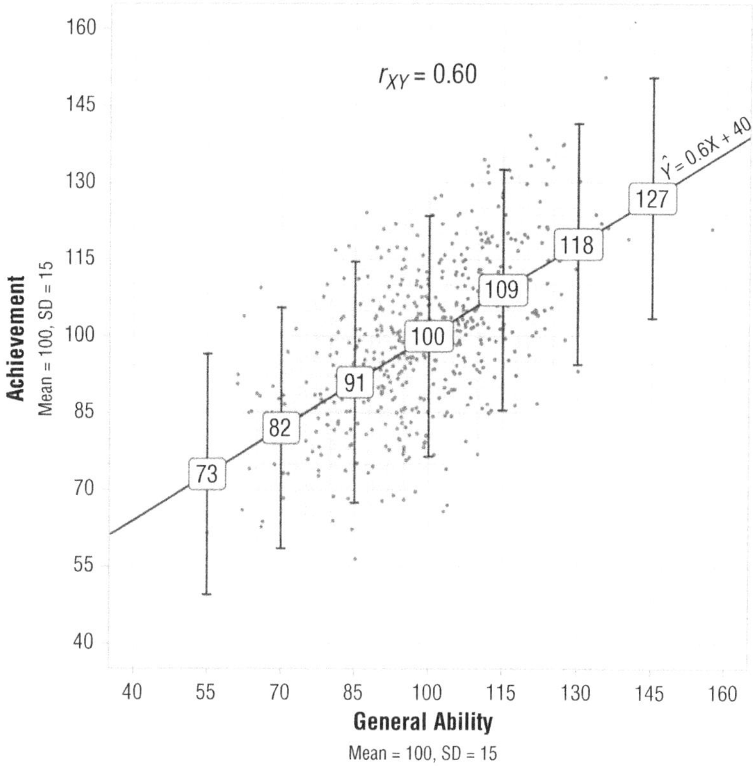

Figure 7.16 IQ Predicting Achievement, with the Regression Line and 95% Confidence Intervals Around Predicted Values

On the other hand, if the intelligence score is 130, then one may expect the achievement score to be that high as well, and if the individual obtains an achievement score of 118, then one may conclude this individual is underachieving. In fact, this person is performing exactly as predicted.

$$\hat{Y} = 0.60(130 - 100)\frac{15}{15} + 100 = 118. \quad (7.8)$$

When the general ability and achievement variables have higher correlations, the effect of regression is reduced. For example, if the correlation is 0.70, then an IQ of 70 would yield an expected achievement score of 79. If the two variables were perfectly correlated (1.0), then there would be no expected difference in scores. In addition, when the predictor score is at or very close to the mean (e.g., in this example, a general ability score of 100), the effect of regression is minimal.

The best practice for comparisons is to use co-normed tests that provide actual difference score norms, like the WJ V. If the tests being used are not co-normed, then the prevalence of large differences needs to be estimated with smaller samples and may rely on

DON'T FORGET

Without a correction for statistical regression, high-performing individuals are overidentified as having a discrepancy, and low-performing individuals are underidentified. There is no need to correct for regression on the WJ V because the tests were co-normed and so the comparison norms on the *Riverside Score*® platform already account for regression.

statistical assumptions that may not hold in a larger representative sample (e.g., that the predictive relationship is linear and the same for every age group and at every ability level).

CONFIGURING A SCORE REPORT IN *RIVERSIDE SCORE*®

The *Riverside Score*® platform provides several options for configuring your score report. When you are ready to generate a report, you can use these options to:

- select the type of report you want to produce (e.g., Score Report, Item Detail Report);
- select the format for your report (HTML display or MS Word);
- select from among Development, Proficiency, and Relative Standing metrics to include in the report;
- select whether you want the scores to be based on age norms or K-12 grade norms;
- select the level for the reported confidence intervals (68%, 90%, or 95%);
- select the significance level for comparison scores (between ±1.00 *SD* and ±2.30 *SD*); and
- select from among the options to include qualitative information (e.g., Test Session Observations, Response Style, and Behavior statements).

As of this writing, *Riverside Score*® provides a Score Report and an Item Detail Report. More report options will become available in the future.

CAUTIONS ABOUT INTERPRETING VERY LOW TEST SCORES

In cases in which an examinee obtains a test raw score of 0, you must decide whether that score represents a true assessment of low ability or whether it simply reflects an inability to perform the test task. If an examinee has not been exposed to the type of task in question, then it may be more appropriate to not interpret the score rather than to interpret a zero raw score. For example, Josie, a kindergarten student, obtained a raw score of 0 on the Word Attack test. This score may indicate that she has not yet been exposed to letters and sounds and, therefore, the Word Attack test is not developmentally appropriate for her. Max, a fifth-grade student, also obtained

CAUTION

Use your professional judgment to determine whether a raw test score of zero reflects a true low ability or whether the test was not developmentally appropriate for the examinee.

a raw score of 0 on the Word Attack test. In Max's case, the score may be an accurate reflection of his very limited reading ability and should, therefore, be interpreted.

The *Riverside Score*® platform contains some features to help prevent misinterpretation of tests and clusters with very low or zero raw scores. First, the recommended age ranges for the tests and clusters provide guidance for the minimum age at which a test's tasks are considered "developmentally appropriate" (see Rapid References 1.7 and 1.8). For instance, the minimum recommended age for administering the Paragraph Reading Comprehension test is 6 years. *Most* typical 4- and 5-year-old examinees will not be able to complete the task of reading a passage and answering comprehension questions. Administering this test to a typical child who is 4 or 5 may lead to frustration for the child and may be a waste of valuable testing time because most children this age will obtain a raw test score of 0; however, if you are testing a high-ability 4- or 5-year-old child who is a proficient reader, then it could be appropriate to administer Paragraph Reading Comprehension, and normative scores are available for *all* WJ V tests as low as age 48 months. Although the recommended age ranges for the tests and clusters provide some guidance, you need to consider the individual child to determine which tests and clusters are appropriate to administer and interpret.

Second, the platform includes a feature to allow you to remove a test from your test set if you determine (during or after administration) that the examinee was younger than the minimum recommended administration age for the test and, therefore, the test was not developmentally appropriate for the examinee. For example, if you attempted to administer the Oral Reading test to a 4-year-old examinee who could not read. Removing the test from the test set ensures that the 0 raw test score will not be misinterpreted as "low ability" in these scenarios.

Third, the *Riverside Score*® platform has built-in features to guard against the misinterpretation of zero raw test and cluster scores for children. In some cases, very low or 0 raw test or cluster scores can yield derived scores that are spuriously high due to a lack of score variance at very young ages in the norming sample. For example, if a 4-year, 2-month-old child was administered the Sentence Writing Accuracy test and received a raw score of 0, then the child's standard score would be 108 (70th percentile). Clearly, the "average" score on this test should not be interpreted as meaningful, because he was unable to write any correct sentences. The average-looking standard score simply indicates that *most* 4-year-old children in the norming sample also obtained raw scores of 0 on this test. In cases where an examinee obtains a very low *W* score on a test or cluster (usually, the *W* score associated with a raw score of 0), the platform will omit the test or cluster's proficiency, relative standing, and comparison scores from the report. In other cases, the scores will be reported, but the report will contain a footnote warning the examiner to interpret the test or cluster score with caution. Rapid Reference 7.14 contains the rules for how the *Riverside Score*® platform handles very low or 0 test and cluster scores.

Rapid Reference 7.14

When Are Very Low or Zero Scores Test and Cluster Scores Omitted from WJ V Reports?

- **For WJ V tests:**
  - If a very low or zero *W* score yields a standard score greater than 85, test scaled scores are omitted from the report, and the following footnote appears: *The examinee earned 0 points on this test. To avoid misinterpretation, derived scores have been omitted.*
  - If a very low or zero *W* score yields a standard score of 85 or lower, test scaled scores are included in the report with the following footnote: *The examinee earned 0 points on this test; interpret these scores with caution.*
- **For WJ V clusters:**
  - If the examinee's age is within the recommended age range for the cluster, cluster-scaled scores are *always* reported. For an examinee whose age is within the recommended range and who obtains very low or zero raw scores on all tests that contribute to a cluster, the following footnote appears on the report: *The examinee earned 0 points on all contributing tests; interpret this cluster's scores with caution.*
  - If the examinee's age is within the recommended age range for the cluster, and they obtain very low or zero scores on all tests that contribute to the cluster *but* the obtained *W* score yields a standard score that is 85 or lower, cluster scaled scores are included in the report with the following footnote: *The examinee earned 0 points on all contributing tests; interpret this cluster's scores with caution.*
  - If the examinee's age is below the recommended age range for the cluster, and if the examinee obtains very low or zero raw scores on all tests that contribute to the cluster, and if the obtained *W* score yields a standard score greater than 85, cluster scaled scores are included in the report with the following footnote: *The examinee earned 0 points on all contributing tests. To avoid misinterpretation, derived scores have been omitted for this cluster.*

TEST YOURSELF

1. Selecting grade-based norms does not affect:

(A) Age equivalents
(B) RPIs
(C) Percentile ranks
(D) Standard scores

2. The cluster scores on the WJ V are derived from the average of the _____ from the contributing tests.

(A) RPIs
(B) *W* scores
(C) Percentile ranks
(D) Standard Scores

3. **Which of the following scores provides the best insight into how manageable the examinee finds academic tasks in the classroom:**
   (A) Standard score
   (B) Percentile rank
   (C) RPI
   (D) Age equivalent
4. **When administering a standardized test such as the WJ V, it is acceptable to make notes about your observations during testing but you should *not* include these in your evaluation report. True or false?**
5. **An examinee earned an age equivalent (AE) of >24 on the WJ V Calculation test. This means (select all that apply):**
   (A) The examinee's obtained *W* score is above the median *W* score for 24-year-olds in the norming sample.
   (B) The examinee is 24 years old.
   (C) The highest median *W* score for the Calculation test in the WJ V norming sample was at age 24 years.
   (D) The examinees scored higher than *all* of the 24-year-olds in the WJ V norming sample.
6. **Which of the following is an appropriate way to describe Huan's RPI score of 41/90 on the WJ V Passage Comprehension test to his parents?**
   (A) Huan obtained an RPI score of 41/90. This means that he answered 41 out of 90 comprehension questions correctly.
   (B) Huan's obtained RPI score of 41/90 means that he is expected to be only 41% successful with typical reading comprehension tasks that his average peers will be 90% successful with.
   (C) Huan obtained an RPI score of 41/90. When Huan's peers are expected to get 41 questions correct on a reading test, Huan would get 90 questions correct.
   (D) Huan's RPI score of 41/90 means that 41 out of 90 students would have a score as low or lower than Huan's score on the Passage Comprehension test.
7. **What does the instructional zone illustrate?**
8. **Why is it important to interpret test scores with confidence bands?**
9. **What does it mean if two tests have overlapping confidence bands on the SS/PR Profile?**
10. **Write a statement describing a significant GIA/Achievement comparison for Basic Reading Skills (base-rate PR = 4) for Jamal, a fifth-grade student.**

ANSWERS

1. **A.**
2. **B.**
3. **C.**
4. **False.** Qualitative observations provide a rich source of information that can be useful for understanding and describing an individual's strengths and weaknesses. Where relevant, these observations should be included in the evaluation report to add context to the test scores.

5. **A *and* C.**
6. **B.**
7. The range of instructional level from where the examinee will find tasks to be *easy* to where the examinee will find tasks to be *difficult*.
8. Because test scores are not exact measurements, confidence bands help us understand the level of precision in the test scores. A test score with a wide confidence band should be interpreted with caution; it may not be reliable for high-stakes decision-making.
9. There is no statistically significant difference between the two test scores.
10. Given his overall cognitive ability, Jamal's Basic Reading Skills cluster score was unexpectedly low. Among his fifth-grade peers who had the same overall GIA score as Jamal, only 4% had a Basic Reading Skills cluster score as low or lower than Jamal's.

REFERENCES

American Educational Research Association [AERA], American Psychological Association [APA], & National Council on Measurement in Education [NCME]. (2014). *Standards for educational and psychological testing.* American Educational Research Association.

Cummins, J. (1984). *Bilingualism and special education: Issues in assessment and pedagogy.* PRO-ED.

LaForte, E. M., Dailey, D., & McGrew, K. S. (2025). *Technical manual. Woodcock-Johnson V.* Riverside Assessments, LLC.

Mather, N., Wendling, B. J., Snader, E. H., (Contributor), Jeantete, G. T., & (Contributor). (2025). *Examiner's manual. Woodcock-Johnson V.* Riverside Assessments, LLC.

Mather, N., & Woodcock, R. W. (2001). *Examiner's manual. Woodcock-Johnson III Tests of Achievement.* Riverside Assessments, LLC.

Oakes, H., Lovejoy, D., Tartar, S., & Holdnack, J. A. (2013). Understanding index and subtest scatter in healthy adults. In J. Holdnack, L. W. Drozdick, L. G. Weiss, & G. L. Iverson (Eds.), *WAIS-IV, WMS-IV, and ACS: Advanced clinical interpretation* (pp. 103–169). Academic Press. https://doi.org/10.1016/B978-0-12-386934-0.00003-1

Varner, B. (2023, August 30). *Cognitive-academic language proficiency & the WJ IV. Riverside Insights Blog.* https://blog.riversideinsights.com/cognitive-academic-language-proficiency-wjiv

Vygotsky, L. S. (1978). *Mind in society: The development of higher psychological processes.* Harvard University Press.

Eight

CLINICAL APPLICATIONS FOR SLD

Diagnosis must take second place to instruction, and must be made a tool of instruction, not an end in itself.

(Cruickshank, 1977, p. 193)

The purposes of psychological and educational evaluations vary. In some cases, the purpose is to help determine the existence of a specific disability. In other cases, the intent is to determine eligibility for a certain program or service. In most cases, evaluations are designed to identify an individual's strengths and weaknesses and then design an educational or vocational plan to meet their needs. This plan may include specific accommodations, such as oral testing and extended time on tests; a recommendation for specific services, such as counseling or speech and language services; and/or specific recommendations for interventions, such as descriptions of instructional strategies and materials.

The focus of this chapter is on clinical applications of the WJ V for SLD identification. The most common clinical use of the WJ V is for the diagnosis of specific learning disabilities (SLD), particularly in the areas of reading, writing, and mathematics. The WJ V is also used to help identify individuals with developmental language disorders (DLD), as well as those who have exceptionally high or low cognitive and academic performance. In addition, an analysis of comparisons can help the evaluator determine specific strengths and weaknesses and whether intelligence and oral language are commensurate with the person's other areas of performance.

Essentials of WJ V™ Assessment, First Edition. Erica M. LaForte, Nancy Mather, and W. Joel Schneider.

SPECIFIC LEARNING DISABILITIES

The WJ V can provide helpful information for documenting SLD. SLD forms the largest category of special education students who are identified in the United States (National Center for Education Statistics, 2022). A *learning disability* is defined in the Individuals with Disabilities Education Improvement Act (IDEA, 2004) as "a disorder in one or more of the basic psychological processes." Under IDEA 2004, for a student to be identified as having a learning disability, one of eight achievement areas must be significantly affected. These eight areas include: oral expression, listening comprehension, basic reading skills, reading fluency, reading comprehension, written expression, mathematics calculation, and mathematics reasoning. Rapid Reference 8.1 lists the WJ V ACH clusters that measure the eight IDEA SLD areas.

The category of SLD consists of a heterogeneous group of disorders with different etiologies, so identification requires an evaluation of multiple data sources (Alfonso & Flanagan, 2018). These disabilities are often characterized as "unexpected" or "unexplained" poor performance based on observations of the person's other capabilities and their general intellectual or oral language competence.

DON'T FORGET

Even though basic writing skills and academic knowledge are not included under the IDEA 2004 categories for SLD, you will still want to consider these abilities in an evaluation. Many students with SLD in reading and writing have adequate oral language abilities and relative strengths in reasoning and knowledge with relative weaknesses in basic writing skills, particularly spelling.

Ability/Achievement Discrepancy

Prior to IDEA 2004, the primary criterion used to operationalize the construct of unexpected underachievement was a discrepancy between intelligence, which was used to predict potential for school success, and achievement, or the present levels of academic performance. With the reauthorization, however, an ability/achievement discrepancy was

Rapid Reference 8.1

IDEA SLD Areas

The Eight SLD Areas (IDEA, 2004) Measured by the WJ V ACH

- Oral expression
- Listening comprehension
- Basic reading skills
- Reading fluency
- Reading comprehension
- Math calculation
- Math reasoning
- Written expression

no longer required. School districts may, however, still use a discrepancy procedure if they wish, but they cannot be required to do so.

Over the past several decades, considerable controversy has existed regarding the use and implementation of this criterion for SLD identification. Historically, many have objected to the sole use of this criterion for SLD identification. For example, Stanovich (1994) stated: "None of the critics of discrepancy definitions are denying the existence of severe reading disability per se or the importance of remedial help. Instead, they are questioning the rationale of differential treatment and resources being allocated on the basis of IQ-achievement discrepancy" (p. 355).

More recently, Fletcher et al. (2019) recommended evaluating domain-specific achievement skills, or the intra-individual differences across achievement domains, and the abilities related to these skills as a more appropriate approach to SLD identification than the use of an ability/achievement discrepancy. They also recommended that students should not be identified as having SLD "...until a systematic attempt at instruction has been made" (p. 86) and that intervention should begin as soon as a weakness in achievement has been noted.

If an ability/achievement discrepancy is part of the evaluation process, the WJ V offers a best-practice approach via the Ability/Achievement Comparison Procedures. Because the tests in the WJ V ACH are co-normed with the tests in the WJ V COG and the WJ V VTL, scores from the same group of individuals were used to develop the comparison norms, eliminating the inherent error introduced when comparing results from tests with different norm groups. In addition, both age and grade norms are provided for all clusters and tests, allowing you to choose the most relevant norm comparison group. Finally, the WJ V provides actual difference, or *comparison*, score norms that reflect developmental differences, correlations, and regression to the mean. Chapter 7 provides details regarding the derivation and interpretation of the WJ V comparison procedures.

Scores from the WJ V ACH may also be compared to scores from other intelligence tests when determining whether an ability/achievement discrepancy exists. However, when using another test to make comparisons for an ability–achievement discrepancy, use age norms because most other intelligence tests only provide age norms.

CAUTION

If comparing scores from the WJ V ACH to cognitive ability scores from a test other than the WJ V COG, score the WJ V ACH tests with age norms because most other intelligence tests only provide age norms. In addition, you must use a procedure to correct for statistical regression.

DON'T FORGET

Use of the WJ V ACH in Ability/Achievement Discrepancies

Although IDEA 2004 does not *require* the existence of an ability/achievement discrepancy for SLD identification, districts may still use this criterion as part of the process. The WJ V ACH and the WJ V VTL can be used in conjunction with the WJ IV COG or any other intelligence test to determine whether a discrepancy exists between overall cognitive ability and any of the eight IDEA achievement areas.

Identification of a Processing Disorder

Before diagnosing a student as having SLD, some states require the identification of a processing disorder. Determining the presence of a processing disorder generally involves using cognitive and linguistic tests (e.g., tests of memory, oral language, phonological processing, rapid automatized naming [RAN], or processing speed) that measure the abilities believed to underlie and affect academic learning. When the co-normed WJ V COG, WJ V ACH, and WJ V VTL are used in conjunction with each other, you can obtain comprehensive information about cognitive and linguistic processing, academic performance, and variations using the comparison norms. Fletcher et al. (2007) noted: "Generally, the more information that is brought to bear on any eligibility or diagnostic decision, the more reliable the decision" (p. 53). The WJ V comparison procedures (see Chapter 7) are designed to help document the individual's strengths and weaknesses among both cognitive abilities and achievement.

READING

The WJ V ACH has eight reading tests: Letter-Word Identification, Passage Comprehension, Word Attack, Oral Reading, Sentence Reading Fluency, Reading Recall, Word Reading Fluency, and Paragraph Reading Comprehension. These tests provide important measures of various aspects of reading achievement. Rapid Reference 8.2 shows the abilities measured

Rapid Reference 8.2

Abilities Measured by the WJ V ACH Reading Tests

Test	Ability Measured	Required SLD Area
Letter-Word Identification (Grw)	Letter and word reading	Basic reading skills
Passage Comprehension (Grw, Gc)	Use of syntactic and semantic cues	Reading comprehension
Word Attack (Grw, Ga)	Nonsense word reading	Basic reading skills
Oral Reading (Grw)	Word reading accuracy and prosody	Reading fluency
Sentence Reading Fluency (Gs, Grw)	Automaticity and rate	Reading fluency
Reading Recall (Grw, Gl)	Meaningful memory	Reading comprehension
Word Reading Fluency (Gs, Grw)	Reading rate	Reading fluency
Paragraph Reading Comprehension (Grw, Gc)	Comprehension of text	Reading comprehension

Rapid Reference 8.3

Factors That Can Affect Reading Performance

Possible Reasons for Low Performance in Basic Reading Skills:

- Poor phonological awareness
- Poor orthographic processing (knowledge and recall of English spelling patterns)
- Slow processing speed
- Limited alphabetic knowledge
- Difficulty pronouncing multisyllabic words

Possible Reasons for Low Performance in Reading Rate and Fluency:

- Poor attention
- Slow rapid automatized naming (RAN)
- Slow processing speed
- Poor basic reading skills

Possible Reasons for Low Performance in Reading Comprehension:

- Poor basic reading skills
- Limited oral language
- Low vocabulary
- Low reasoning ability
- Limited use of strategies
- Lack of experience and exposure
- Low motivation and interest

by the WJ V ACH reading tests as well as which SLD areas are assessed. Rapid Reference 8.3 lists possible reasons an individual may have low performance in basic reading skills, reading rate and fluency, or reading comprehension. Any of these areas can be low based on limited instruction or limited time spent reading.

Early Identification of Children at Risk for Reading Failure

Considerable research on the early identification of reading difficulties has focused on identifying measures to predict future reading achievement in preschool or kindergarten children. Three abilities appear to be good predictors of risk for reading failure: letter/sound knowledge, phonological awareness (sensitivity to the sounds in spoken words), and rapid automatized naming (RAN), which is the capacity to name arrays of letters, digits, colors, or pictured objects rapidly (Georgiou & Parrila, 2014; Wolf et al., 2000; see Rapid Reference 8.4). The WJ V ACH has several measures of letter-sound knowledge, phonological awareness, and phoneme–grapheme knowledge, and the WJ V VTL includes several measures of RAN.

Rapid Reference 8.4

Best Predictors of Beginning Reading Achievement

Phonological awareness

- **WJ V TL tests**: Nonsense Word Repetition, Sound Reversal, Sound Blending, Segmentation, Sound Deletion, and Sound Substitution

Phoneme–grapheme knowledge

- **WJ V ACH tests**: Word Attack and Spelling of Sounds

Letter-sound and sound-letter identification

- **WJ V ACH tests**: Letter-Word Identification, Word Attack, Spelling, and Spelling of Sounds

Rapid naming

- **WJ V VTL tests**: Rapid Picture Naming, Rapid Letter Naming, and Rapid Phoneme Naming

Dyslexia

The most common type of SLD is dyslexia. Students with dyslexia have trouble blending and segmenting phonemes, learning letter–sound correspondences, memorizing letter sequences for sight word reading and spelling, and rapidly recognizing words. Multiple neurological, behavioral, and environmental factors interact to cause difficulty in learning to read (Catts & Petscher, 2022). Therefore, it is important to consider a constellation of indicators when diagnosing or determining the risk for dyslexia (Erbeli et al., 2023; Pennington et al., 2019).

The International Dyslexia Association (2025) has updated their 2002 definition of dyslexia as follows (IDA Board of Directors, 2025):

> Dyslexia is a specific learning disability characterized by difficulties in word reading and/or spelling that involve accuracy, speed, or both and vary depending on the orthography. These difficulties occur along a continuum of severity and persist even with instruction that is effective for the individual's peers. The causes of dyslexia are complex and involve combinations of genetic, neurobiological, and environmental influences that interact throughout development. Underlying difficulties with phonological and morphological processing are common but not universal, and early oral language weaknesses often foreshadow literacy challenges. Secondary consequences include reading comprehension problems and reduced reading and writing experience that can impede growth in language, knowledge, written expression, and overall academic achievement. Psychological well-being and employment opportunities may also be affected. Although identification and targeted instruction are important at any age, language and literacy support before and during the early years of education is particularly effective.

Dyslexia is often comorbid with other disorders. In fact, approximately 40% of individuals with dyslexia have another disorder, such as ADHD, dyscalculia, or DLD (Moll et al., 2019, 2020). In addition, dyslexia is highly heritable (Pennington et al., 2019). As part of an evaluation, always ask parents if anyone in the family has had difficulty learning to read or spell. Rapid Reference 8.5 reviews some of the most common symptoms of dyslexia.

DON'T FORGET

Family history is a key risk indicator for dyslexia. As part of an evaluation, always ask: "Has anyone in the family had difficulty learning to read and spell?"

Decoding (pronouncing words) and encoding (spelling words) involve similar processes, including knowledge of phoneme–grapheme relationships as well as the ability to recall letter strings and words. To pronounce a word, an individual needs to know how to break apart the sounds and then how to blend the sounds back together to make a word; to spell a word, an individual needs to be able to break the pronunciations into the component sounds (segmentation). Impaired phonological and phonemic awareness is often described as the predominant core linguistic risk factor for dyslexia (Fletcher et al., 2019; Shaywitz & Shaywitz, 2020; Snowling et al., 2019).

DON'T FORGET

Blending is necessary for acquiring phonics and segmentation is necessary for spelling.

Another core deficit in dyslexia appears to affect automaticity or rapid symbol processing, often referred to as RAN (McWeeny et al., 2022; Norton & Wolf, 2012; Wolf et al., 2000). Slow RAN speed is most related to the rapid processing of words or reading fluency and rate rather than to phonological abilities and phonics skills (Fletcher et al., 2019). Students with slow symbol processing speeds do not recognize words easily and rapidly. Their lack of automaticity then affects their comprehension. The ability to recognize words rapidly by sight is the most important variable in predicting reading comprehension for individuals with SLD (Meltzer, 1994).

Rapid Reference 8.5

Common Symptoms of Dyslexia

- Poor phonological awareness
- Poor orthographic processing
- Slow processing speed and/or RAN
- Letter reversals and transpositions (e.g., *was* for *saw*) that persist past the age of 7
- Spelling words the way they sound rather than the way they look
- Trouble pronouncing multisyllabic words
- Trouble sequencing sounds in spelling
- Slow reading rate

When identifying individuals with dyslexia, consider the following to be the most relevant information from the WJ V ACH: (a) word identification (e.g., out-of-context word decoding of both real words and nonsense words); (b) measures of spelling (e.g., real word and nonsense word spelling); and (c) measures of speed (e.g., reading fluency). Students with dyslexia who have not received systematic instruction will have low phoneme–grapheme knowledge and will also perform slowly on measures of reading rate and fluency.

WJ V Dyslexia Test Set. The *Riverside Score*® platform provides a preconfigured Dyslexia Test Set that includes the most relevant WJ V tests for assessing dyslexia. It is designed to be used both for screening and when a more comprehensive evaluation is needed. Because states have different requirements regarding dyslexia screening, you can select specific tests within this Test Set that satisfy your state's requirements. Table 8.1 lists the clusters that are obtained from administering the tests in the preconfigured WJ V Dyslexia Test Set as well as the minimum recommended age for each cluster and test.

Table 8.1 Dyslexia Test Set

	Cluster	Test Name	ACH-Std	ACH-Ext	VTL	Minimum Recommended Age: Tests	Minimum Recommended Age: Clusters
Basic Reading Skills and Reading Fluency	Basic Reading Skills	Letter-Word Identification (Grw)	X			4	5
		Word Attack (Grw, Ga)*	X			5	
	Reading Fluency	Sentence Reading Fluency (Gs, Grw)	X			5	6
		Word Reading Fluency (Gs, Grw)	X			6	
Phonics Knowledge and Spelling	Phoneme–Grapheme Knowledge	Word Attack (Grw, Ga)*	X			5	6
		Spelling of Sounds (Ga, Grw)*		X		6	
	Spelling Skills	Spelling (Grw)	X			5	6
		Spelling of Sounds (Ga, Grw)*		X		6	

Table 8.1 (*Continued*)

	Cluster	Test Name	ACH-Std	ACH-Ext	VTL	Minimum Recom-mended Age: Tests	Minimum Recom-mended Age: Clusters
Linguistic Risk Factors	Phonological Awareness	Sound Blending (Ga)			X	4	4
		Segmentation (Ga)			X	4	
	Phonological Manipulation	Sound Deletion (Ga)**			X	5	6
		Sound Substitution (Ga)**			X	6	
	RAN–Reading	Rapid Picture Naming (Gs, Gr)			X	4	6
		Rapid Letter Naming (Gs, Gr)			X	4	
		Rapid Phoneme Naming (Gr, Ga)			X	6	
	Auditory Memory Span	Memory for Words (Gwm)			X	4	4
		Sentence Repetition (Gwm)			X	4	
Vocabulary	Vocabulary	Picture Vocabulary (Gc)	X			4	5
		Academic Vocabulary (Gc)		X		5	
	Single Tests	Oral Reading (Grw)		X		6	
		Nonsense Word Repetition (Ga, Gwm)			X	4	

* Word Attack and Spelling of Sounds each contribute to two clusters.

** Sound Deletion is recommended for examinees age 5–11, and Sound Substitution is recommended for examinees age 6–12. The platform will, however, allow the user to administer these two tests to examinees outside the recommended age ranges. From the *Woodcock-Johnson® V.*

Typically, the first step of a reading evaluation is to answer this question: Is the student struggling with one or more aspects of reading? To answer that question, administer four reading tests—Letter-Word Identification, Word Attack, Sentence Reading Fluency, and Word Reading Fluency—which together take between 10 and 15 minutes, depending on the examinee's age or grade. For younger students in Kindergarten to Grade 1, in most cases, the only two tests to administer are Letter-Word Identification and Word Attack. These two tests combine to form the Basic Reading Skills (Grw) cluster. For students in Grade 2 and above, also administer Sentence Reading Fluency and Word Reading Fluency. These timed tests combine to form the additional Reading Fluency (Grw) cluster. For older students who are accurate but slow readers, administer only Sentence Reading Fluency and Word Reading Fluency (i.e., the timed tests). If a student has low scores on one or more of the reading tests, consider administering additional tests. Two additional clusters of reading and spelling skills—Phoneme–Grapheme Knowledge (Grw, Ga) and Spelling Skills (Grw, Ga)—are provided because individuals with dyslexia often continue to struggle with both phonics and spelling into adulthood.

The Dyslexia Test Set also includes measures of specific linguistic risk factors that are often associated with or predictive of poor reading and spelling. The clusters obtained include: Phonological Awareness (Ga), Phonological Manipulation (Ga), RAN–Reading (Gs, Gr), and Auditory Memory Span (Gwm). The WJ V COG includes Auditory Working Memory Capacity and Retrieval Fluency clusters which may also be of interest.

Results from the Vocabulary (Gc) cluster can be compared to reading and writing skills to indicate if an examinee's reading and writing scores are "unexpected" or significantly lower than would be predicted by oral vocabulary. Students with dyslexia tend to have relatively strong performance on measures of vocabulary knowledge (Adlof et al., 2021). Two single tests, Oral Reading and Nonsense Word Repetition, can provide additional diagnostic information.

Depending on the reason for referral and the examinee's age or grade, you may wish to administer additional tests from the WJ V COG, WJ V ACH, and/or the WJ V VTL. For example, if the referral question indicated concerns with both reading and math, you would want to administer tests that measure specific linguistic risk factors associated with dyscalculia, such as working memory and processing speed, along with the VTL RAN–Math tests, Rapid Number Naming, and Rapid Quantity Naming. Or, if the referral question indicated concerns regarding both reading and oral language, you would want to administer additional measures of oral language as well as measures of academic knowledge. When combined with additional qualitative information (e.g., family history, prior interventions, teacher reports), WJ V results can help confirm or negate a diagnosis of dyslexia.

When analyzing the reading tests, an individual with dyslexia is likely to have higher scores on tests involving context and language comprehension and lower scores on measures of phoneme–grapheme knowledge and reading rate. For example, the person's performance will likely be higher on Passage Comprehension and Reading Recall than on Letter-Word Identification, Word Attack, Sentence Reading Fluency, and Word Reading Fluency.

In contrast, an individual with poor reading comprehension will likely have higher scores on measures of basic reading skills and rate. When decoding skills and fluency are intact, most problems in reading comprehension arise from weaknesses in a range of oral language abilities, including poor vocabulary, background knowledge, grammar, and listening comprehension rather than reading skills, per se (Snowling & Hulme, 2012; Spencer et al., 2014). Individuals who struggle with reading comprehension that does not stem from poor decoding have weaknesses that are general to language comprehension rather than specific to reading (Adolf & Hogan, 2019; Spencer et al., 2014).

DON'T FORGET

Most difficulties with reading comprehension arise from weaknesses in oral language (Adlof & Hogan, 2019).

Because individuals with dyslexia have a specific impairment that affects reading and spelling development, they require explicit instruction and practice in reading and spelling single words. They often require more repetition, more practice, and more review to acquire basic reading skills. Instruction needs to be more systematic and more carefully designed, aimed at improving the overall level of skill as well as the efficiency of the learner. Effective strategies focus on phonemic awareness instruction coupled with direct reading instruction and a structured phonics approach followed by fluency training (Pennington et al., 2019). In addition, teachers need to adapt instruction to the level of reading development and provide appropriate accommodations, such as extended time on tests and the use of a spell checker.

CAUTION

Consider the Effects of Reading Intervention on Test Performance

Many children with dyslexia, particularly if they have received effective intervention, can obtain average scores on some reading tests, such as untimed measures of single-word reading (Pennington et al., 2019). This does not mean that they no longer have dyslexia; it means that the interventions have improved their word-reading skills. Their performance is often lower, however, when they are asked to read text rapidly and fluently because their speed of word perception and reading rate are still compromised.

CAUTION

Not Everyone with Reading Difficulties has Dyslexia

To identify dyslexia, look for specific impairments in basic reading skills, reading rate, and spelling. In addition, the individual will often show some areas of relative strength (e.g., oral language, reasoning, knowledge, or math). Do not forget to consider additional factors, such as family history and early speech and/or language weaknesses.

DON'T FORGET

When doing an evaluation, always document the specific strengths of an individual. These findings can often provide helpful information for accommodations and instruction as well as provide ideas for vocational and career planning.

CAUTION

When assessing individuals for disabilities, never use test scores as the sole indicators of an individual's functioning. Use multiple sources of information (AERA et al., 2014).

Individuals with dyslexia often have strengths in other areas, including oral language, mathematics, or academic knowledge. Because the impairment does not affect all domains of functioning, they may have specific variations within and among their abilities. Thus, an evaluation should document specific areas of strength in addition to any areas of weakness, and intervention should target the individual's strengths and weaknesses, regardless of diagnostic labels (Adlof & Hogan, 2018). In addition to the Dyslexia Test Set, the Appendix of this chapter includes a WJ V Dyslexia Profile that may be used in a more comprehensive assessment of dyslexia that includes tests from the WJ V COG (Proctor & Mather, 2025).

No single test or score can accurately diagnose SLD, including dyslexia. In addition to test scores, you should consider family history, educational history, parent and teacher reports, behavioral observations, informal work samples, and the results of other tests to make an accurate diagnosis. Pennington et al. (2009) stated:

> If a child has dyslexia, then certain things ought to be true and not true across heterogeneous domains of data, including presenting symptoms, the early developmental history, the school history, the behavior during testing (including kinds of errors), and the test results. A particular diagnosis is supported by a converging pattern of results across these different domains of data and by a diverging pattern of results for competing diagnoses (p. 32).

CAUTION

The consequences of having one or more cognitive processing difficulties associated with dyslexia are not inevitable. They are risk factors, meaning that they raise the risk of reading problems, but do not guarantee them (Flanagan & Schneider, 2016). Thankfully, many people with cognitive processing deficits associated with dyslexia find ways—often with help—to work around the obstacles before them and come to read well. When you encounter someone who reads well despite having cognitive processing deficits associated with reading difficulty, the story of how they beat the odds can be quite instructive. A success in one uphill struggle often serves as a template for how other difficulties can be overcome.

WRITTEN LANGUAGE

The WJ V ACH contains six writing tests that measure different aspects of writing ability: Spelling, Written Language Samples, Sentence Writing Fluency, Sentence Writing Accuracy, Spelling of Sounds, and Letter Writing Fluency. Rapid Reference 8.6 reviews the writing abilities measured by the WJ V ACH. Under IDEA 2004, all of these measures fall under the broad category of written expression. Only two tests, Written Language Samples and Sentence Writing Fluency, are needed to obtain the WJ V Written Expression cluster. The other writing tests, however, can be useful in documenting a specific problem in writing, such as poor basic writing skills. In fact, difficulty with basic skills is often the reason for limited written expression. It is important to consider how these basic skills are affecting an individual's written expression.

Individuals who struggle with basic reading skills typically also struggle with spelling. Similarly, individuals who have poor reading comprehension are likely to struggle with written expression. A few individuals, however, have adequate or even advanced reading skills but struggle with one or more aspects of written language development. Some individuals have adequate written expression but struggle primarily with basic writing skills; other individuals write with ease but have trouble coming up with ideas.

Comparing performance on the WJ V ACH Basic Writing Skills and Written Expression clusters can help determine which aspects of writing are the most difficult

Rapid Reference 8.6

Abilities Measured by WJ V ACH Writing Tests

Test	Ability Measured	Required SLD Area
Spelling (Grw)	Spelling real words	
Written Language Samples (Grw)	Expressing ideas in writing	Written expression
Sentence Writing Fluency (Gs, Grw)	Automaticity with writing	Written expression
Sentence Writing Accuracy (Grw)	Writing dictated sentences that are scored for dictation accuracy, spelling, capitalization, and punctuation.	
Spelling of Sounds (Ga, Grw)	Spelling phonically regular nonsense words	
Letter Writing Fluency (Gs)	Producing and copying letters quickly	

for an individual and help pinpoint the individual's specific writing difficulties. For example, the Spelling test measures the ability to spell real words, whereas the Spelling of Sounds test measures the ability to use phonological and orthographic information to spell nonsense words. The Sentence Writing Fluency test measures the ability to compose sentences quickly, whereas the Written Language Samples test looks at sentence construction and ideation. The Sentence Writing Accuracy test looks at the person's ability to apply spelling, capitalization, and punctuation rules when writing. It also requires accurate writing of the dictated sentence.

The Letter Writing Fluency test includes two 30-second tasks: printing the letters of the alphabet from memory in any order and then copying a model of the alphabet in order. Several early research studies documented the importance of automatic letter writing for writing development, both with typically developing writers and individuals with dysgraphia (Abbott & Berninger, 1993; Graham et al., 1997). More recent reviews have continued to support the impact of slow letter writing fluency and handwriting speed on the quality of written composition (Berninger, 2020; Kent & Wanzek, 2016; Ray et al., 2022).

Dysgraphia

Researchers have used the term *dysgraphia* to describe both impairments in spelling and/or weaknesses in the motor planning or production processes required for handwriting (McCloskey & Rapp, 2017). Individuals with dysgraphia have difficulty copying or writing letters, words, or numbers. Others have suggested a broader definition of dysgraphia that includes all aspects of writing. For example, Chung et al. (2020) state: "Dysgraphia is a disorder of writing ability at any stage, including problems with letter formation/legibility, letter spacing, spelling, fine motor coordination, rate of writing, grammar, and composition" (p. S46). The International Dyslexia Association (2020) provides a broader definition: "Dysgraphia is a specific learning disability that affects how easily children acquire written language and how well they use written language to express their thoughts" (International Dyslexia Association, 2020). As with dyslexia, dysgraphia often coexists with other conditions. For example, Mayes et al. (2018) found that dysgraphia (described as impaired handwriting) was present in children with ADHD (56%), autism spectrum disorder (56%), and an SLD in reading (71%) or math (72%).

Some individuals with writing difficulties may be able to copy words but have trouble producing words from memory; they recognize words when they see them and can copy and read them, but they have trouble writing spontaneously or from dictation. Others have difficulties formulating their thoughts or expressing their ideas in writing; they can communicate orally, copy words, and spell correctly, but they have trouble with written expression and make errors in writing that they do not necessarily make when speaking. Rapid Reference 8.7 suggests possible reasons for low performance in basic writing skills and written expression.

Rapid Reference 8.7

Factors That Can Affect Written Language Performance

Possible Reasons for Low Performance in Basic Writing Skills:

- Poor phonological awareness
- Poor orthographic awareness
- Weak fine-motor skills
- Physical disabilities
- Limited phoneme–grapheme knowledge
- Limited instruction

Possible Reasons for Low Performance in Written Expression:

- Weak fine-motor skills
- Limited basic writing skills
- Limited oral language
- Lack of experience and exposure
- Low motivation and interest
- Low reasoning ability
- Limited instruction

Even older students can continue to struggle with basic writing skills. Figure 8.1 illustrates the responses of Evan, a high school junior with dysgraphia, on items 21–24 from the WJ V Written Language Samples test. In his case, he has difficulties with handwriting and spelling. Although his handwriting is difficult to read, note how sophisticated his responses are. Fortunately, Evan has developed strong keyboarding skills and can compose with relative ease on his laptop.

Transcription of Responses to Items 21–24:

21. The exquisite aromas emanating from the kitchen were a delectable surprise.
22. The level of apathy that had settled in.
23. If you are considering a gift for a significant other, you might consider a bouquet of flowers.
24. The findings provide an invaluable insight into the daily life of the Iceman's culture and the depths of knowledge contained within.

MATHEMATICS

Although difficulties with mathematics have not been studied as extensively as difficulties with reading, attempts have also been made to identify specific disorders of mathematics. Most studies have focused on basic numeracy skills. In a large birth cohort, the prevalence of a math learning disability ranged from 6% to 13% depending on the definition of

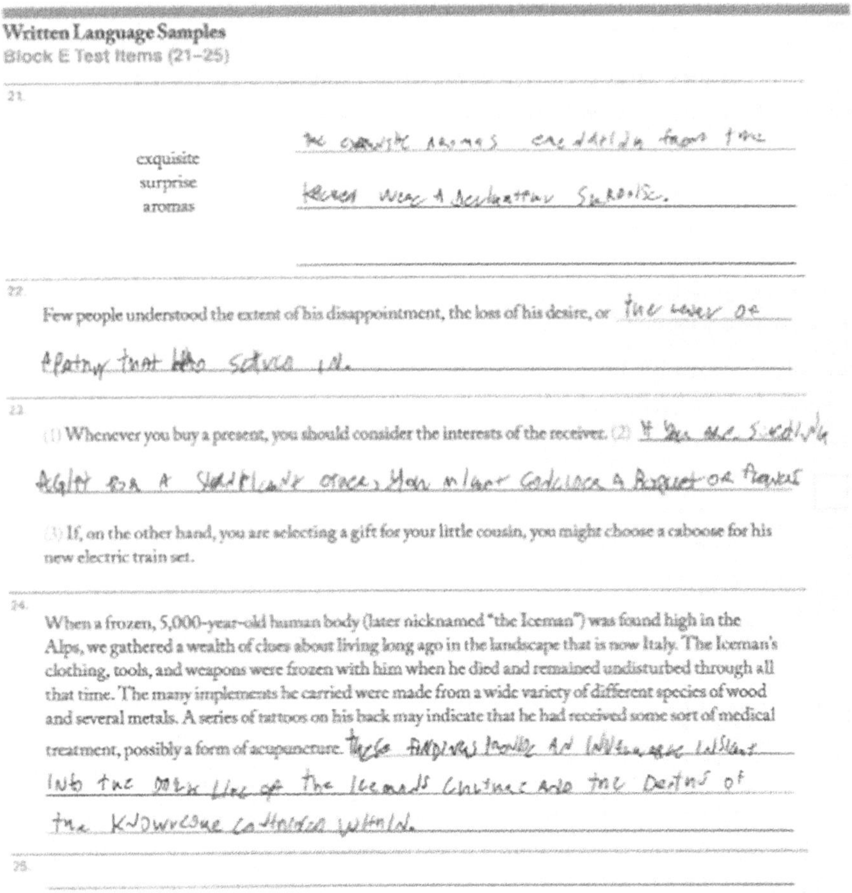
Written Language Samples
Block E Test Items (21–25)

21.

exquisite
surprise
aromas

22.

Few people understood the extent of his disappointment, the loss of his desire, or

23.

(1) Whenever you buy a present, you should consider the interests of the receiver. (2)

(3) If, on the other hand, you are selecting a gift for your little cousin, you might choose a caboose for his new electric train set.

24.

When a frozen, 5,000-year-old human body (later nicknamed "the Iceman") was found high in the Alps, we gathered a wealth of clues about living long ago in the landscape that is now Italy. The Iceman's clothing, tools, and weapons were frozen with him when he died and remained undisturbed through all that time. The many implements he carried were made from a wide variety of different species of wood and several metals. A series of tattoos on his back may indicate that he had received some sort of medical treatment, possibly a form of acupuncture.

25.

Figure 8.1 Evan's Responses on Written Language Samples, Items 21–24

disability that was used (regression-based IQ/achievement discrepancy, unadjusted discrepancy of IQ and math achievement, and low math achievement) (Barbaresi et al., 2005). Others have estimated prevalence rates of between 3% and 6% (Price & Ansari, 2013) or between 4% and 10% (Dowker, 2024). Although other areas of mathematics need to be studied, acquisition of mathematical concepts, more than any other content area, is tied closely to the teacher's knowledge of mathematics and the manner in which these concepts are taught. Teachers who do not understand mathematical principles or know how to teach them are likely to create additional learning difficulties for their students (Campbell et al., 2014; Hill et al., 2005).

Rapid Reference 8.8

Abilities Measured by WJ V ACH Math Tests

Test	Ability Measured	Required SLD Area
Calculation (Gq)	Math computation	Math calculation
Math Facts Fluency (Gs, Gq)	Automaticity with math facts	Math calculation
Applied Problems (Gq)	Problem-solving and reasoning	Math reasoning
Math Problem Identification (Gq, Gf)	Quantitative reasoning	Math reasoning
Number Sense (Gq)	Mathematical knowledge	
Magnitude Comparison (Gs, Gq)	Knowledge of number value	

The complexity and diversity of mathematical skills and knowledge increase the difficulty of documenting specific disorders. Some students have trouble primarily with the mastery of computational skills such as adding, subtracting, multiplying, and dividing. These individuals have deficits in fundamental arithmetic operations, even though they may have adequate reasoning, language, and visual-spatial skills. Other students have adequate computational skills but experience trouble with the conceptual component, such as the abilities involved in learning mathematical concepts and solving story problems. Thus, computational skills and problem-solving ability are two separate aspects of mathematics to assess when diagnosing and planning instruction for students (Fuchs et al., 2014).

The WJ V contains six tests that measure different aspects of mathematics ability: Calculation, Math Facts Fluency, Applied Problems, Math Problem Identification, Number Sense, and Magnitude Comparison. Rapid Reference 8.8 reviews the abilities measured by the WJ V ACH math tests, as well as which SLD areas are assessed.

Dyscalculia

Dyscalculia, a neurologically based math learning disability, is often defined as significant difficulties in learning mathematics that cannot be attributed to other factors, such as low intelligence, sensory impairments, or limited educational opportunities (Dowker, 2024). The most universal behavioral characteristics of dyscalculia are: (a) poor learning and retrieval of arithmetic facts from memory, (b) immature counting and problem-solving strategies, (c) slow number naming and calculation fluency, and (d) difficulty comparing the magnitudes of numbers (Price & Ansari, 2013). The most documented research finding regarding students with dyscalculia is persistent difficulties memorizing and then retrieving basic arithmetic facts once they have been committed to memory (Geary, 2013). Children with dyscalculia also appear to have significantly lower spatial skills compared to children without dyscalculia (Peters et al., 2020).

DON'T FORGET

Students with dyscalculia have difficulty memorizing and retrieving math facts.

Although reading and math problems have unique cognitive correlates, shared linguistic risk factors include weaknesses in processing speed, working memory, and verbal ability (Fletcher et al., 2019; Pennington et al., 2019).

As with reading comprehension and written expression, multiple factors can affect an individual's ability to effectively solve math problems. Oral language abilities play a key role, as does the ability to shift back and forth between verbal and visual representations. Difficulty with the language aspects of math may result in confusion about terminology, difficulty following verbal explanations, and weak verbal skills for monitoring the steps of complex calculations. Weaknesses in spatial abilities may contribute to weak understanding of concepts, poor number sense, difficulty with pictorial representations, confused arrangements of numbers and signs on the page, and poor handwriting. Individuals with weaknesses in working memory will likely have difficulty learning math facts. Similar to success in reading comprehension and written language, success in mathematics depends largely upon background knowledge, automaticity with math facts, and the use of strategic behaviors. Rapid Reference 8.9 lists several factors that can affect math performance. Rapid Reference 8.10 lists examples of difficulties in basic math skills and math reasoning.

On the WJ V ACH, you can compare a person's performance in math calculation skills and math problem-solving to help determine if the problem lies in knowledge of how to perform calculations, automaticity with basic math facts, or application of math concepts and knowledge to tasks involving reasoning and problem-solving.

Careful observation of the examinee during the administration of the math tests may also reveal characteristics typical of individuals with math disabilities. One of the most common characteristics is the use of immature problem-solving procedures even when solving simple arithmetic problems. For example, Randy, a fifth-grade student, still counts on his fingers when performing basic calculations. Evan, a junior in high school with dysgraphia, also has dyscalculia. Figure 8.2 illustrates his responses on the Calculation test. When he got to item 28, he looked at the rest of the problems and said, "I have no idea how to solve them."

As discussed, another common characteristic of individuals with dyscalculia is difficulty memorizing and recalling math facts. They have persistent trouble memorizing basic number facts in all four operations, despite great effort and an adequate understanding of the concepts. Analyzing an examinee's performance on the Math Facts Fluency test can help validate these difficulties. The WJ V VTL also contains a RAN–Math cluster. As with measures of RAN–reading, RAN–math measures can be early predictors of math difficulties and are most related to arithmetic fluency (Koponen et al., 2017). Just as with dyslexia and dysgraphia, from an instructional point of view, it is not enough to label someone as having dyscalculia or an SLD in math. Instead, you should describe the specific areas that are problematic for that individual and then design a specific intervention plan.

Rapid Reference 8.9

Factors That Can Affect Math Performance

Possible Reasons for Low Basic Math Skills:

- Limited attention
- Slow processing speed
- Poor working memory
- Slow rapid automatized number naming
- Inadequate number sense
- Weak fine-motor skills
- Poor spatial abilities
- Limited knowledge of procedures
- Limited instruction

Possible Reasons for Low Math Reasoning:

- Low basic math skills
- Low oral language
- Limited background knowledge
- Poor working memory
- Poor spatial abilities
- Poor reasoning abilities
- Limited instruction

Rapid Reference 8.10

Examples of Behaviors Associated with Math Difficulties

Basic Math Skills:

- Using ineffective counting strategies
- Difficulty identifying the meanings of signs (e.g., ×, <, %)
- Difficulty recalling basic math facts (e.g., 8 × 6)
- Difficulty solving multidigit problems that involve regrouping
- Difficulty solving computations with fractions and decimal points

Math Reasoning:

- Difficulty understanding what the problem is asking
- Difficulty identifying and eliminating any extraneous information
- Difficulty following multiple steps involving different calculations
- Not selecting the correct calculation(s) to solve the problem

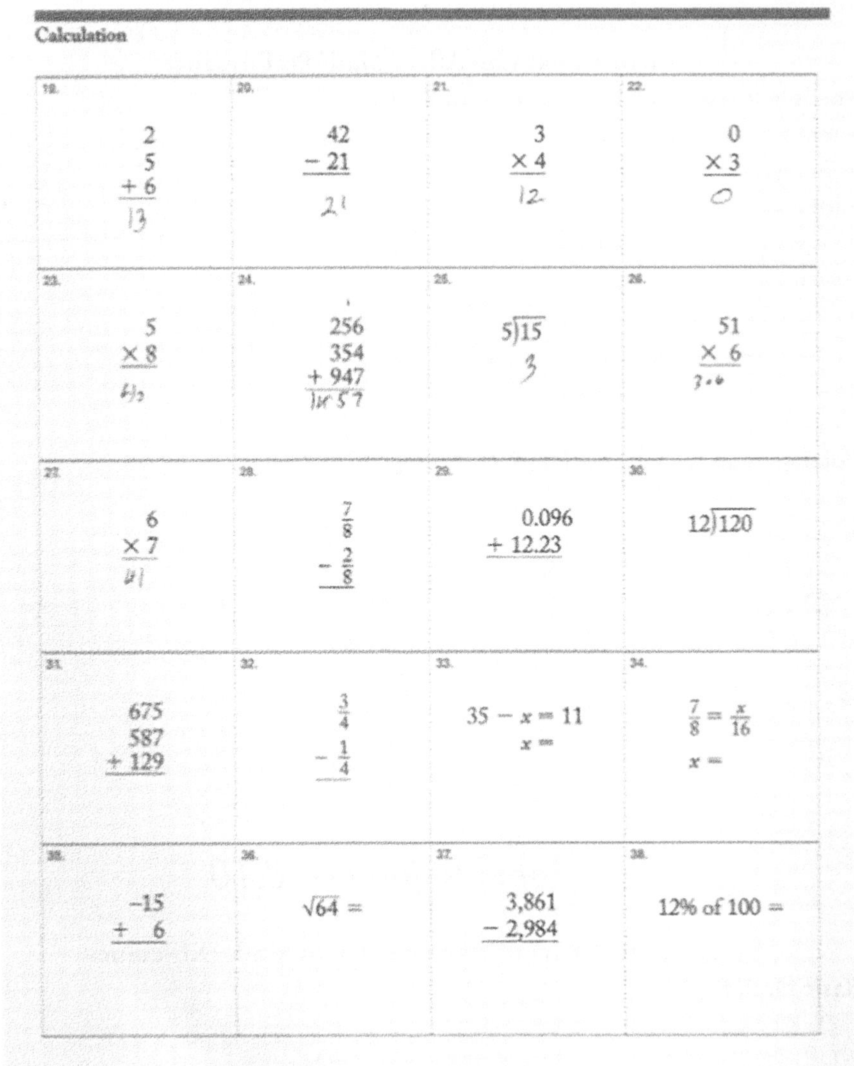

Calculation

19. 2 + 5 + 6 = 13	20. 42 − 21 = 21	21. 3 × 4 = 12	22. 0 × 3 = 0
23. 5 × 8 = [illegible]	24. 256 + 354 + 947 = [illegible]	25. 5)15 = 3	26. 51 × 6 = [illegible]
27. 6 × 7 = [illegible]	28. $\frac{7}{8} - \frac{2}{8}$	29. 0.096 + 12.23	30. 12)120
31. 675 + 587 + 129	32. $\frac{3}{4} - \frac{1}{4}$	33. 35 − x = 11, x =	34. $\frac{7}{8} = \frac{x}{16}$, x =
35. −15 + 6	36. $\sqrt{64}$ =	37. 3,861 − 2,984	38. 12% of 100 =

Figure 8.2 Evan's Responses on the WJ V Calculation Test

ORAL LANGUAGE

Oral language abilities are not only the foundation for success in most academic areas but also the primary avenue through which learning occurs; they predict future achievement, as well as life outcomes (Adlof & Hogan, 2019). For this reason, consideration of an individual's oral language abilities is an essential component of a comprehensive evaluation. The WJ V helps explore the role of oral language in an individual's performance by providing measures of both receptive and expressive oral language abilities. Four WJ V ACH tests combine to form the Oral Language cluster: Picture Vocabulary, Oral Comprehension, Oral Language Samples, and Story Comprehension. Other tests that measure aspects of oral language are found in the WJ V COG, the WJ V ACH, and the WJ V VTL. Rapid Reference 8.11 reviews the abilities measured by the WJ V oral language tests, as well as which SLD areas are assessed.

DON'T FORGET

The WJ IV oral language tests have been moved into the WJ V COG, WJ V ACH, or WJ V VTL.

Rapid Reference 8.11

Abilities Measured by the WJ V Oral Language Tests

WJ V COG Tests	Ability Measured
Oral Vocabulary (Gc)	Knowledge of synonyms and antonyms
Story Recall (Gl)	Listening to and retelling short stories
Semantic Word Retrieval (Gr)	Saying as many words as possible in 1 minute in a semantic category
Verbal Attention (Gwm)	Answering questions about a series of animals and digits
Verbal Analogies (Gwm)	Saying a word to complete an analogy
Story Comprehension (Gl)	Listening to and answering questions about a story
Phonemic Word Retrieval (Gr)	Saying as many words as possible in 1 minute that begin with a specific sound
General Information (Gc)	Answering general knowledge questions

WJ V ACH Tests	Ability Measured	Required SLD Area
Picture Vocabulary (Gc)	Naming pictured objects	Oral Expression
Oral Comprehension (Gc)	Listening to a short passage and supplying the missing word	Listening Comprehension
Oral Language Samples (Gl, Gc)	Providing words and sentences to prompts	Oral Expression
Story Comprehension (Gl)	Listening to and answering questions about a story	Listening Comprehension
Academic Vocabulary (Gc, Gkn)	Answering vocabulary questions	
Academic Facts (Gc, Gkn)	Answering factual questions about academic topics	

WJ V VTL Tests	Ability Measured
Nonsense Word Repetition	Repeating nonsense words
Rapid Picture Naming	Naming pictures for one minute
Animal-Number Sequencing (Gwm)	Listening to a list of animals and digits and then naming the animals followed by the digits
Sound Reversal (Ga)	Hearing a word and then saying the sounds in the word backward
Understanding Directions (Gwm, Gf)	Tapping elements in a picture in a specific order
Sound Blending (Ga)	Blending sounds together to form words
Rapid Phoneme Naming (Gr, Ga)	Naming phonemes for 1 minute
Memory for Words (Gwm)	Repeating a list of unrelated words
Segmentation (Ga)	Breaking apart the sounds in words
Sentence Repetition (Gwm)	Repeating words, phrases, and sentences
Sound Deletion (Ga)	Deleting a sound from a word
Sound Substitution (Ga)	Substituting a sound in a word

Receptive language refers to an individual's ability to understand or comprehend language, including gestures and both spoken and written words. Listening ability is the major skill needed for success in the area of receptive language; listening requires individuals to receive and correctly interpret the message that is being conveyed. Individuals with poor receptive language experience difficulty in both understanding what has been said and following directions. They frequently become confused while listening to lectures and experience difficulty understanding what they read. Although they may decode and spell words accurately, they may also have limited knowledge of word meanings in addition to limited experiential knowledge. When children are in school, teachers expect them to be able to follow verbal instructions, lectures, and guidelines. For students who have difficulties in listening comprehension, the ability to follow through on a given verbal task can be a barrier. Poor receptive language often results in lower grades, gaps in a knowledge base, and difficulty working effectively with others. It can also affect social interactions due to difficulties listening to and understanding conversations. As individuals reach adulthood and become employed, poor receptive language abilities can hinder opportunities and/or job performance.

Some students have adequate receptive language abilities but poor expressive language skills. These students understand what is being said to them but have difficulty producing responses orally, through gestures, or through written language. *Expressive oral language* relates to our ability to retrieve ideas and vocabulary and further express these thoughts in an appropriate manner through speaking. Speaking requires developing an intention to speak and formulating thoughts into words and sentences. This requires developing an intention to produce language through speech, a motor process, and formulating thoughts into words and sentences. Deficiencies in the use of expressive language in preschool children have been found to predict subsequent academic difficulties. Often, individuals with weaknesses in expressive language have difficulty organizing their thoughts, choosing the "right" words, and expressing their ideas in a clear and concise manner. These individuals may understand what they hear, but they may not be able to express what they know. Further, these individuals may have trouble expressing their ideas in writing. Deficits in RAN have been associated with individuals with speech and/or language and reading disorders (Georgiou & Parrila, 2014), so rapid naming tests may also provide valuable insights.

DON'T FORGET

Developmental language disorder (DLD) is the preferred term for impairments in language development.

If the language difficulties are severe enough, the student may be classified as having a speech or language impairment (SLI) or a DLD. Although both SLI and DLD refer to neurodevelopmental conditions that impair spoken language, use of the term DLD is recommended because it links advocacy efforts in the United States with those in other English-speaking countries (McGregor et al., 2020). Within schools, however, under IDEA 2004, students under the age of 9 with DLD are often classified as having a specific language impairment (SLI), whereas older students tend to be identified under the SLD category (Georgan et al., 2023).

A student with weaknesses in oral language will primarily have difficulty on tasks involving the use and comprehension of language, including reading comprehension, written expression, and math problem-solving. Students with DLD may also have relative weaknesses in spelling that persist across the life span (Tucci & Choi, 2023). Tests such as Understanding Directions and Animal-Number Sequencing require language and memory skills, both of which are frequently problematic for individuals with DLD. A developmental trend exists on tests involving oral language, where oral language difficulties tend to increase with age. This may be due in large part to the increased demands on language and memory as students progress through school.

An individual who has low performance on several of the WJ V oral language tests will likely require a more comprehensive evaluation from a speech-language pathologist. This evaluation will help reveal the intrinsic and extrinsic factors affecting language development. In addition, a speech-language pathologist will develop a treatment plan. Rapid Reference 8.12 indicates possible reasons for low performance on receptive or expressive language tasks.

Rapid Reference 8.12

Factors That Can Affect Oral Language Performance

Possible Reasons for Low Performance in Receptive Language:

- Phonological processing deficits
- Attention problems
- Lack of experience and opportunity
- Reduced vocabulary
- Poor understanding of sentence structure
- Difficulty with oral comprehension
- Weaknesses in memory
- Cultural differences

Possible Reasons for Low Performance in Expressive Language:

- Poor receptive language
- Lack of experience and opportunity
- Difficulty with articulation
- Cultural differences
- Poor word retrieval (inability to recall known words with ease)
- Difficulty formulating ideas or organizing thoughts
- Weaknesses in memory

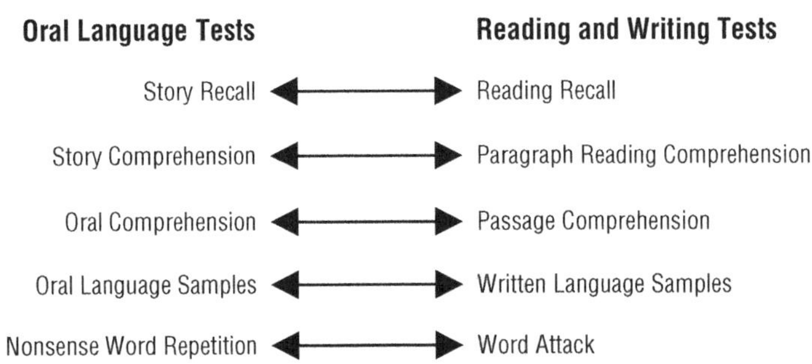

Figure 8.3 Comparing WJ V Oral Language Tests to WJ V Reading and Writing Tests

Several of the WJ V oral language tests were designed to be compared to reading and writing measures with similar formats. For example, you might compare a student's performance on Oral Language Samples to their performance on Written Language Samples. These tests share a similar item format; however, the mode of examinee responding is different (in this case, oral versus written). Many students with SLD have higher scores on oral language tests than on written language tests. In contrast, individuals with DLD tend to have similar scores on oral and written language tests (Figure 8.3).

INTRA-ABILITY COMPARISONS

In addition to the Ability/Achievement Comparison procedures described earlier in this chapter, the WJ V provides Intra-Ability Comparison procedures that can aid in differentiating among SLD (e.g., dyslexia, dysgraphia, dyscalculia, and DLD) and differentiating between SLD and generalized low academic performance.

Patterns of Strengths and Weaknesses

The WJ V Intra-Ability Comparison procedures can also help you determine and document both strengths and weaknesses in an individual's performance. This type of analysis is often referred to as a *pattern of strengths and weaknesses* (PSW) approach. Although various methods are used by different districts in a PSW approach, the essential elements involve: (a) identifying an academic weakness in one of the eight IDEA 2004 areas; (b) determining if there are cognitive or linguistic risk factors that have an established link to the academic area (e.g., phonological awareness and basic reading skills, RAN and reading fluency, working memory and math computation); (c) identifying intact abilities; and (d) determining whether or not the pattern seems related to SLD (Schultz et al., 2012). The PSW approach is not tantamount to merely listing an individual's unique strengths and weaknesses to determine the existence of SLD but rather determining whether the particular PSW is indicative of SLD, such as a child with dyslexia who has weaknesses in orthographic processing but strengths in listening comprehension and reasoning, or a child who has dyscalculia with weaknesses in reasoning or working memory but a strength in oral language.

DON'T FORGET

A PSW approach requires the identification of both strengths and weaknesses.

Often, a student's strengths can be used to inform the selection of accommodations. For example, a student with advanced oral language but lower reading and writing skills would benefit from oral examinations in content-area classes as well as the use of assistive technology. In addition, identification of an individual's overall pattern of cognitive strengths and weaknesses can increase self-understanding and is, in itself, therapeutic as it provides an explanation of why the person is struggling and what can be done about it (Pennington et al., 2019; Suhr, 2008). A diagnosis of an SLD using a PSW approach results in the identification of the specific type of SLD that can have implications for both instruction and prognosis. The ultimate goal is to document a student's unique PSW to provide better services and more targeted interventions (National Joint Committee on Learning Disabilities, 2011; Norton & Wolf, 2012).

Useful information regarding strengths and weaknesses can be gained by analyzing the WJ V Intra-Cognitive and Intra-Achievement Comparison procedures. For example, Sarah, a fourth-grade student, has significant Intra-Achievement weaknesses in basic reading skills and basic writing skills. In contrast, she has significant strengths in math problem-solving and academic knowledge. Although more information is needed, these findings are suggestive of SLD in reading and writing (significant weaknesses in domain-specific areas such as reading and writing skills with strengths in other domains such as math problem-solving and academic knowledge). Her Intra-Cognitive comparisons indicate that she has significant strengths in vocabulary and fluid reasoning, but a significant weakness in phonological awareness. Additionally, her RAN–Reading cluster score is significantly lower than expected, given her overall cognitive ability as measured with the Gf-Gc Composite. Unexpected low scores on phonological awareness and RAN are both linguistic risk factors for dyslexia. Coupled with information from family history (her father has dyslexia), as well as reports from her teacher (she struggles with reading aloud), the results support a diagnosis of dyslexia.

DON'T FORGET

Look at the comparisons among cognitive and achievement scores using the WJ V Intra-Ability Comparison procedures to help determine significant strengths and weaknesses.

After reviewing the comparison scores, you can analyze the cluster and test scores to reveal possible factors influencing performance. Richer clinical information can be obtained when using tests from the WJ V COG, WJ ACH, and WJ V VTL together.

One important aspect of an SLD evaluation is to determine whether an individual's difficulties are specific to one or more risk factors or whether they result from a more pervasive impairment in language skills that may be more appropriately classified as a DLD (Snowling & Hulme, 2012). Children who struggle in most aspects of language, as well as in many nonverbal domains, may be more appropriately classified as having some degree of intellectual disability (e.g., mild to severe).

Rapid Reference 8.13 provides information on the trends noted when using cognitive abilities to predict achievement for various reading and mathematics tests and clusters from the WJ V (LaForte et al., 2025). Table 8.2 describes common characteristics of SLD in reading, writing, and math.

Rapid Reference 8.13

Trends in Predicting Reading and Mathematics Performance from Cognitive Abilities

Reading

- While the influence of retrieval fluency (Gr) increases after basic reading skills are acquired, the influence of processing speed (Gs) lessens.
- Among the broad cognitive abilities, comprehension-knowledge (Gc), working memory (Gwm), and long-term storage (Gl) are among the most important for reading comprehension across the age range.
- Perceptual speed (Gs-P), an intermediate-stratum processing speed ability, has a significant relationship with both basic reading skills and reading comprehension across ages.
- Phonetic coding (Ga-PC), a narrow auditory processing ability, has a significant relationship with basic reading skills at the early ages but becomes less significant at older ages.

Mathematics

- Comprehension-knowledge (Gc) plays a significant role in math reasoning across all ages, which may be due to the linguistic demands of math reasoning tasks.
- Fluid reasoning (Gf) and working memory (Gwm) are strong predictors of basic math skills and math reasoning across ages.
- Processing speed (Gs) is important to both basic math skills and math reasoning.
- Phonetic coding, a narrow auditory processing ability, and several narrow long-term retrieval abilities are important to basic math skills, especially in the early school years.

Table 8.2 WJ V Diagnostic Indicators of a Specific Learning Disability

Reading Disability Dyslexia	Writing Disability Dysgraphia	Math Disability Dyscalculia
Low performance on one or more of the following clusters: Reading, Broad Reading, Basic Reading Skills, Reading Fluency, Reading Comprehension, or Reading Rate	Low performance on one or more of the following clusters: Written Language, Broad Written Language, Basic Writing Skills, or Written Expression	Low performance on one or more of the following clusters: Mathematics, Broad Mathematics, Math Calculation Skills, or Math Problem-Solving
Adequate oral language	Adequate oral language	Adequate oral language
Poor phonological or orthographic awareness resulting in poor decoding and spelling	Poor motor skills, phonological, or orthographic awareness resulting in poor spelling	Difficulty memorizing and recalling basic math facts
Low phoneme–grapheme knowledge	Low reading skills and/or comprehension	Strong concepts and weak basic skills
Slow reading rate	Poor handwriting and slow writing rate	Limited fluency with math
Slow processing speed	Difficulty copying	Low spatial abilities
Higher scores in oral language and math than in reading	Organizational difficulties and difficulties formulating ideas in writing	Low working memory and reasoning ability
Intra-ability comparison procedures indicate significant weaknesses in reading	Intra-ability comparison procedures indicate significant weaknesses in writing	Intra-ability comparison procedures indicate significant weaknesses in mathematics

GENERALIZED PERFORMANCE

Some students do not show discrepancies among achievement areas or variations among abilities and may have generally low or high performance. This is important information to consider when evaluating an individual for SLD. Typically, if the individual has generalized low or high performance, evaluators would usually rule out SLD diagnosis because one or more domain-specific difficulties, when coupled with one or more relative strengths, are important indicators of SLD.

Generalized Low Performance

Students with overall low performance may be several years below grade level in all academic subjects as well as in oral language and acquired knowledge. These students require adaptations and adjustments in the curriculum. The difficulty level of the instructional materials must be adapted to both the present performance levels and the level of knowledge.

When a student has low academic performance and acquired knowledge, be sure to consider extrinsic factors as well. Because of their environment, some students come to school with very limited background knowledge. For other students, their primary language is not English. Often, the reasons that these students struggle in school are more related to a lack of educational opportunity or limited knowledge of English than to a disability. Because vocabulary knowledge is needed for most academic tasks, the breadth and depth of an individual's vocabulary can also affect school success. Although these students need help and modifications in the classroom, many do not have disabilities. Rather than special instructional methods, these students often require a developmental curriculum that will provide language enrichment within the general education setting. Rapid Reference 8.14 lists possible reasons for why a student might show generalized low cognitive or academic performance.

In addition to low scores on the WJ V COG GIA and Gf-Gc composites, students with generalized low academic performance will usually obtain low scores on oral language tests, as well as the WJ V ACH Academic Knowledge cluster. Rapid Reference 8.15 presents several reasons why an individual might have low scores on the WJ V Oral Language and Academic Knowledge clusters.

Rapid Reference 8.14

Possible Reasons for Generalized Low Cognitive or Academic Performance

- Limited educational opportunity
- English-language learner
- Developmental language disorder
- Cultural differences
- Poor reasoning abilities
- Intellectual disability
- Linguistic differences or delays
- Developmental delays
- Traumatic brain injury

Rapid Reference 8.15

Possible Reasons for Low Oral Language and Academic Knowledge Scores

- Attention problems
- Developmental delays
- Lack of educational experiences and opportunities
- Low listening comprehension
- Cultural differences
- Poor word retrieval (difficulty recalling words that are known)
- Difficulty formulating ideas or organizing thoughts

Generalized High Performance

Other students have advanced academic knowledge and are above grade level in most academic subjects. Students with well-established oral language and rich vocabularies tend to speak, read, and write more effectively than other students. Because they learn easily, these students often require an accelerated curriculum. They may take advanced courses, use higher-level textbooks, or complete special projects. In some cases, students with advanced academic performance participate in gifted and talented programs. The WJ V COG Gf-Gc composite can be particularly useful for gifted identification as it measures both reasoning and verbal knowledge.

TEST YOURSELF

1. **What two types of comparison procedures on the WJ V may be helpful in documenting the presence of an SLD?**
2. **List the eight SLD areas from IDEA 2004 that are measured by WJ V ACH clusters.**
3. **One advantage of using the Gf-Gc composite for SLD identification is that it does not include limitations in abilities such as working memory capacity or processing speed. True or false?**
4. **Which three WJ V TL RAN tests are most predictive of reading fluency?**
5. **If the WJ V ACH scores are being compared to the scores from the WISC-V, score the WJ V ACH using age norms. True or False?**
6. **The Phoneme–Grapheme Knowledge cluster score is usually average or above average for individuals with dyslexia. True or False?**

7. **Typically, a domain-specific deficit is present for the identification of an SLD. True or False?**
8. **Which of these findings is most inconsistent with a dyslexia profile?**
   (A) Low oral language
   (B) Low basic reading skills
   (C) Low phoneme–grapheme knowledge
   (D) Low basic writing skills
9. **WHICH statement is true?**
   (A) If the IQ score is high, the achievement score should be as high or higher.
   (B) If the IQ score is high or low, the achievement score should be closer to the mean.
   (C) If the IQ score is low, the achievement score should be as low or lower.
   (D) None of the above. The IQ score should be similar to the achievement score.
10. **Dyslexia and DLD are often comorbid with other disorders. True or False?**

ANSWERS

1. Intra-ability and Ability/Achievement Comparisons
2. Oral expression, listening comprehension, basic reading skills, reading fluency, reading comprehension, math calculation, math reasoning, and written expression
3. **True.**
4. Rapid Picture Naming, Rapid Letter Naming, Rapid Phoneme Naming
5. **True.**
6. **False.**
7. **True.**
8. **A.**
9. **B.**
10. **True.**

APPENDIX

DYSLEXIA PROFILE FOR THE WJ V

Name______________________________ Date of Birth __________ ID______________

School ______________________________ Grade________ Date______________

The [name of state or country] Education Code [§ statute number] defines dyslexia in the following way:

International Dyslexia Association Definition (2025)

Dyslexia is a specific learning disability characterized by difficulties in word reading and/or spelling that involve accuracy, speed, or both and vary depending on the orthography. These difficulties occur along a continuum of severity and persist even with instruction that is effective for the individual's peers. The causes of dyslexia are complex and involve combinations of genetic, neurobiological, and environmental influences that interact throughout development. Underlying difficulties with phonological and morphological processing are common but not universal, and early oral language weaknesses often foreshadow literacy challenges. Secondary consequences include reading comprehension problems and reduced reading and writing experience that can impede growth in language, knowledge, written expression, and overall academic achievement. Psychological well-being and employment opportunities may also be affected. Although identification and targeted instruction are important at any age, language and literacy support before and during the early years of education is particularly effective.

Authors' note: Dyslexia affects reading at the single word level, reading fluency and rate, and spelling. In turn, these weaknesses cause difficulties with reading comprehension and written expression. According to research, the major linguistic risk factors of dyslexia include weaknesses in one or more of the following abilities: phonological awareness, orthographic awareness, memory, rapid automatized naming, and processing speed. Other abilities, such as general intelligence, reasoning, oral language, mathematics, and knowledge, that do not require reading, are often intact. In other words, the reading and spelling difficulties are often unexpected in relation to the student's other abilities.

Section I: Summary (For use with the WJ V[1])

A. Primary and Secondary Reading, Spelling, and Writing Difficulties Check the areas of concern.

Primary Reading and Spelling Difficulties		Secondary Reading and Writing Difficulties

☐ ***Letter-Sound Knowledge***[2]
  ☐ *Letter names*[2]
  ☐ *Letter sounds*[2]
☐ **Basic Reading Skills**[3]
  ☐ Letter-Word Identification[3]
  ☐ Word Attack[3]
☐ **Phoneme-Grapheme Knowledge**[4]
  ☐ Word Attack[4]
  ☐ Spelling of Sounds[4]
☐ **Reading Fluency**
  ☐ Word Reading Fluency
  ☐ Sentence Reading Fluency
☐ Oral Reading*
	Spelling[2,3,4]
	☐ **Spelling Skills**[3,4]
	  ☐ Spelling[3]
	  ☐ Spelling of Sounds[3,4]
	☐ **Phoneme-Grapheme Knowledge**[4]
	  ☐ Word Attack[4]
	  ☐ Spelling of Sounds[4]
	☐ ***Spelling in Context***[2]
	  ☐ *Class Work Samples*[2]
	  ☐ *Written Language Samples*[2]
	  ☐ Sentence Writing Accuracy[2]
		Reading Comprehension
		☐ **Reading Comprehension**
		  ☐ Passage Comprehension
		  ☐ Paragraph Reading Comprehension
		☐ **Written Expression**[5]
		  ☐ Sentence Writing Fluency
		  ☐ Written Language Samples[5]

B. Cognitive and Linguistic Abilities: Possible Contributing Factors Check the areas that are possible contributing factors.

Phonological Processing[3]	*Orthographic Awareness*[6]	Memory	Rapid Automatized Naming (RAN)	Processing Speed

☐ **Phonological Awareness**[3]
  ☐ Sound Blending[3]
  ☐ Segmentation[3]
☐ **Phonological Manipulation**[3]
  ☐ Sound Deletion[3]
  ☐ Sound Substitution[3]
☐ **Phonemic Retrieval Fluency**[3]
  ☐ Phonemic Word Retrieval[3]
  ☐ Rapid Phoneme Naming[3]
☐ Sound Reversal[3]*
☐ Nonsense Word Repetition[3]*
	☐ Number-Pattern Matching[6]
	☐ Letter-Pattern Matching[6]
	☐ Letter-Word Identification[6]
	☐ Word Attack[6]
	☐ Spelling[6]
	☐ Spelling of Sounds[6]
		☐ **Auditory Working Memory Capacity**
		  ☐ Verbal Attention
		  ☐ Numbers Reversed
		☐ Visual Working Memory
		☐ **Auditory Memory Span**
		  ☐ Memory For Words
		  ☐ Sentence Repetition
		☐ **Long-Term Storage**
		  ☐ Story Recall
		  ☐ Story Comprehension
		☐ Animal-Number Sequencing*
		☐ Understanding Directions*
			☐ **RAN Reading**
			  ☐ Rapid Number Naming
			  ☐ Rapid Letter Naming
			  ☐ Rapid Phoneme Naming
				☐ **Cognitive Processing Speed**
				  ☐ Number-Pattern Matching
				  ☐ Letter-Pattern Matching

C. Ability to Learn When Reading is Not Required Check the areas that are significantly higher than the individual's basic reading and spelling skills.

Cognitive Abilities	Oral Language[5]	Mathematics	Knowledge
☐ **General Intellectual Ability** ☐ **Gf-Gc Composite** ☐ **Fluid Reasoning**	☐ **Oral Expression**[5] ☐ **Listening Comprehension**[5] ☐ **Vocabulary**[5]	☐ **Math Calculation Skills** ☐ **Number Concepts** ☐ **Math Problem Solving**	☐ **Comprehension Knowledge**[5] ☐ **Academic Applications**[5] ☐ **Academic Knowledge**[5]

D. At-Risk Indicators: Check the areas below that are additional at-risk factors.

☐ Family history ☐ Early speech-language issues

Committee Consideration

☐ Data demonstrate characteristics of dyslexia.

☐ Data do not demonstrate characteristics of dyslexia.

☐ Data demonstrate characteristics of dyslexia; however, these characteristics would not be consistent with [State] guidelines for the identification of dyslexia.

Evaluator(s) ______________________________ ______________________________ **Date:** ____________

Section II: Scores

Area Tested		Battery	Test Date	Cluster/Test/CHC Broad Ability	Low/Below Average SS <40-89 PR <1-24	Average SS 90-110 PR 25-75	High/Above Average SS 111> PR 76>	RPI[7]
Primary Reading and Spelling Difficulties	Letter-Sound Knowledge	Informal Assessment		***Letter-Sound Knowledge*[2]**				
				Letter Names[2]** ☐ Limited ☐ Typical ☐ Advanced				
				Case: Lower ____/26 Upper ____/26				
				Letter Sounds[2]** ☐ Limited ☐ Typical ☐ Advanced				
				Consonants ___ Vowels ___				
	Basic Reading Skills	WJ V ACH		**Basic Reading Skills[3]**				___/90
				Letter-Word Identification (Grw)[3]				___/90
				Word Attack (Grw, Ga)[3]				___/90
	Reading Fluency	WJ V ACH		**Reading Fluency**				___/90
				Word Reading Fluency (Gs, Grw)				___/90
				Sentence Reading Fluency (Gs, Grw)				___/90
				Oral Reading (Grw)*				___/90
	Spelling	WJ V ACH		**Spelling Skills[3,4]**				___/90
				Spelling (Grw)[3]				___/90
				Spelling of Sounds (Ga, Grw)[3,4]				___/90
				***Spelling in Context*[2]**				
				Class Work Samples[2]** ☐ Limited ☐ Typical ☐ Advanced				
				Written Language Samples[2]** ☐ Limited ☐ Typical ☐ Advanced				
				Sentence Writing Accuracy (Grw)[2] ☐ Limited ☐ Typical ☐ Advanced				
	Phoneme - Grapheme Knowledge	WJ V ACH		**Phoneme-Grapheme Knowledge[4]**				___/90
				Word Attack (Grw, Ga)[4]				___/90
				Spelling of Sounds (Ga, Grw)[4]				___/90
Secondary Reading & Writing Difficulties	Reading Comprehension	WJ V ACH		**Reading Comprehension**				___/90
				Passage Comprehension (Grw, Gc)				___/90
				Paragraph Reading Comprehension (Grw, Gc)[6]				___/90
	Written Expression	WJ V ACH		**Written Expression[5]**				___/90
				Sentence Writing Fluency (Gs, Grw)				___/90
				Written Language Samples (Grw)[5]				___/90

Primary and Secondary Reading and Writing Difficulties/Comments

Area Tested		Battery	Test Date	Cluster/Test/CHC Broad Ability	Low/Below Average SS <40-89 PR <1-24	Average SS 90-110 PR 25-75	High/Above Average SS 111> PR 76>	RPI[7]
Cognitive and Linguistic Abilities: Possible Contributing Factors	Phonological Processing[2]	WJ V VTL		**Phonological Awareness[3]**				___/90
				Sound Blending (Ga)[3]				___/90
				Segmentation (Ga)[3]				___/90
				Phonological Manipulation[3]				___/90
				Sound Deletion (Ga)[3]				___/90
				Sound Substitution (Ga)[3]				___/90
				Sound Reversal (Ga)[3]*				___/90
		WJ V COG		**Phonemic Retrieval Fluency** (Ga)[3]				___/90
		WJ V VTL		Rapid Phoneme Naming (Gs, Gr)[3]				___/90
		WJ V COG		Phonemic Word Retrieval (Gr)[3]				___/90
		W V VTL		Nonsense Word Repetition (Ga, Gwm)[3]*				___/90
	Orthographic Awareness[3,4]			***Orthographic Awareness[6]***				
		WJ V COG		Number-Pattern Matching (Gs)[6]				___/90
				Letter-Pattern Matching (Gs)[6]				___/90
		WJ V ACH		Letter-Word Identification (Grw)[6]				___/90
				Word Attack (Grw, Ga)[6]				___/90
				Spelling (Grw)[6]				___/90
				Spelling of Sounds (Grw)[6]				___/90
	Memory	WJ V COG		**Auditory Working Memory Capacity**				___/90
				Verbal Attention (Gwm)				___/90
				Numbers Reversed (Gwm)				___/90
				Auditory Memory Span				___/90
				Memory for Words (Gwm)				___/90
				Sentence Repetition (Gwm)				___/90
				Long-Term Storage				___/90
				Story Recall (Gl)				___/90
				Story Comprehension (Gl)				___/90
		W V VTL		Animal-Number Sequencing (Gwm)*				___/90
				Understanding Directions (Gwm, Gf)*				___/90
	Rapid Automatized Naming	WJ V VTL		**RAN-Reading**				___/90
				Rapid Number Naming (Gs, Gr)				___/90
				Rapid Letter Naming (Gs, Gr)				___/90
				Rapid Phoneme Naming (Gr, Ga)				___/90
	Processing Speed	WJ V COG		**Cognitive Processing Speed**				___/90
				Number-Pattern Matching (Gs)				___/90
				Letter-Pattern Matching (Gs)				___/90

Cognitive and Linguistic Abilities: Possible Contributing Factors/Comments

Area Tested		Battery	Test Date	Cluster/Test/CHC Broad Ability	Low/Below Average SS <40-89 PR <1-24	Average SS 90-110 PR 25-75	High/Above Average SS 111> PR 76>	RPI[7]
Ability to Learn When Reading is Not Required	Cognitive Abilities	WJ V COG		**General Intellectual Ability (GIA)**				/90
				Oral Vocabulary (Gc)[5]				___/90
				Matrices (Gf)				___/90
				Spatial Relations (Gv)				___/90
				Story Recall (Gl)				___/90
				Semantic Word Retrieval (Gr)				___/90
				Verbal Attention (Gwm)				___/90
				Number-Pattern Matching (Gs)				___/90
				Verbal Analogies (Gc,Gf)[5]				___/90
		WJ V COG		**Gf-Gc Composite**				___/90
				Oral Vocabulary (Gc)[5]				___/90
				Matrices (Gf)				___/90
				Verbal Analogies (Gc, Gf)[5]				___/90
				Analysis-Synthesis (Gf)				___/90
		WJ V COG		**Fluid Reasoning (Gf)**				___/90
				Matrices (Gf)				___/90
				Analysis-Synthesis (Gf)				___/90
				Concept Formation (Gf)*				___/90
	Oral Language	WJ V ACH		**Oral Expression[5]**				___/90
				Picture Vocabulary (Gc)[5]				___/90
				Oral Language Samples (Gl, Gc)[5]				___/90
				Listening Comprehension[5]				___/90
				Oral Comprehension (Gc)[5]				___/90
				Story Comprehension (Gl)[5]				___/90
				Vocabulary[5]				___/90
				Picture Vocabulary (Gc)[5]				___/90
				Academic Vocabulary (Gc)[5]				___/90
	Mathematics	WJ V ACH		**Math Calculation Skills**				___/90
				Calculation (Gq)				___/90
				Math Facts Fluency (Gs, Gq)				___/90
				Math Problem Solving				___/90
				Applied Problems (Gq)				___/90
				Math Problem Identification (Gq, Gf)				___/90
	Knowledge	WJ V COG		**Comprehension Knowledge (Gc)[5]**				___/90
				Oral Vocabulary (Gc)[5]				___/90
				Verbal Analogies (Gc, Gf)[5]				___/90
		WJ V ACH		**Academic Applications[5]**				___/90
				Passage Comprehension (Grw, Gc)[5]				___/90
				Applied Problems (Gq)[5]				___/90
				Written Language Samples (Grw)[5]				___/90
				Academic Knowledge[5]				___/90
				Academic Vocabulary(Gc)[5]				___/90
				Academic Facts (Gc)				___/90

Ability to Learn When Reading is Not Required/Comments

Determination of Characteristics of Dyslexia for Committee Consideration/Additional Comments

*** Single Tests**
**** Qualitative Observation Ratings[5]**
Italicized clusters and tests indicate informal measures

1. The WJ V Dyslexia Profile (Proctor & Mather, 2025) was adapted from the WJ IV Dyslexia Profile by C. Proctor, N. Mather, T. Stephens-Pisecco, and L. E. Jaffe (May, 2017).
2. Qualitative observation ratings of "limited," "typical," and "advanced" as they pertain to letter names, letter sounds, and spelling in context are subjective assessments of a student's letter knowledge in isolation and spelling abilities when they are writing within sentences, paragraphs, or longer pieces of text. The ratings in regard to spelling abilities go beyond simply identifying correctly or incorrectly spelled words in isolation and consider how spelling impacts the overall clarity and fluency of the writing.
3. If the student exhibits reading and spelling difficulties and currently has average phonological/phonemic awareness, review the student's history to determine if there is evidence of previous interventions Addressing phonological/phonemic awareness. Prior effective instruction in phonological/phonemic awareness may remediate these skills in isolation. Thus, average phonological awareness scores alone do not rule out the existence of dyslexia. Ongoing phonological awareness deficits can also be exhibited in word reading and/or spelling.
4. Word Attack and Spelling of Sounds are measures of phonic decoding and encoding skills (sounding out or spelling unfamiliar or pseudowords using blending and letter-sound correspondences). They are not pure phonological awareness tasks because they involve letters so both phonological and orthographic awareness are required.
5. Consider that as an individual grows older, limited reading affects the development of vocabulary and knowledge.
6. A weakness in orthographic awareness can be a significant contributing factor to dyslexia. Orthographic awareness is often assessed through tests of irregular word reading and spelling. A person's recognition and retrieval of orthographic patterns may be ascertained by analysis of the patterns of responses, as well as the scores, on measures of exception word reading and spelling. Students with a weakness in orthographic awareness are more successful in reading and spelling phonically regular words than irregular words and tend to spell irregular words the way they sound, rather than the way they look.
7. The Relative Proficiency Index (RPI) is derived from a mathematical prediction based on the normative data. It predicts a person's expected percentage of proficiency for tasks that the comparison group (age or grade) would perform with 90 percent proficiency. The RPI is recorded as two numbers separated by a slash (/). The first number is the person's expected level of proficiency; the second number is always 90, the criterion of mastery. For example, Jeremy's Word Attack score of 47/90 indicates that when reading unfamiliar words at grade level, his proficiency is likely to be 47% when his average age- or grade-peer's proficiency would be 90%. The following table presents the level of proficiency and the instructional implications of some possible RPI ranges when the individual is doing grade- or age-level work.

RPI	Proficiency	Instructional Implications
100/90	Very Advanced	extremely easy
98/90 to 100/90	Advanced	very easy
95/90 to 98/90	Average to Advanced	easy
82/90 to 95/90	Average	manageable
67/90 to 82/90	Limited to Average	difficult
24/90 to 67/90	Limited	very difficult
3/90 to 24/90	Very Limited	extremely difficult
0/90 to 3/90	Extremely Limited	nearly impossible

REFERENCES

Abbott, R., & Berninger, V. W. (1993). Structural equation modeling of relationships among developmental skills and writing skills in primary- and intermediate-grade writers. *Journal of Educational Psychology, 85*(3), 478–508. https://doi.org/10.1037/0022-0663.85.3.478

Adlof, S. M., & Hogan, T. P. (2018). Understanding dyslexia in the context of developmental language disorders. *Language Speech and Hearing Services in Schools, 49*, 762–773. https://doi.org/10.1044/2018_LSHSS-DYSLC-18-0049

Adlof, S. M., & Hogan, T. P. (2019). If we don't look, we won't see: Measuring language development to inform literacy instruction. *Policy Insights from the Behavioral and Brain Sciences, 6*(2), 210–217. https://doi.org/10.1177/2372732219839075

Adlof, S. M., Baron, L. S., Bell, B. A., & Scoggins, J. (2021). Spoken word learning in children with developmental language disorder or dyslexia. *Journal of Speech, Language, and Hearing Research: JSLHR, 64*(7), 2734–2749. https://doi.org/10.1044/2021_JSLHR-20-00217

Alfonso, V. C., & Flanagan, D. P. (2018). *Essentials of specific learning disability identification* (2nd ed.). Wiley.

American Educational Research Association, American Psychological Association, & National Council on Measurement in Education (AERA). (2014). *Standards for educational and psychological testing*. American Educational Research Association.

Barbaresi, W. J., Katusic, S. K., Colligan, R. C., Weaver, A. L., & Jacobsen, S. J. (2005). Math learning disorder: Incidence in a population-based birth cohort, 1976–82, Rochester, MN. *Ambulatory Pediatrics, 5*, 281–289.

Berninger, V. (2020). *Revised user guide for process assessment of the learner II for reading and writing (PAL II RW)*. Pearson.

Campbell, P. F., Nishio, M., Smith, T. M., Clark, L. M., Conant, D. L., Rust, A. H., DePiper, J. N., Frank, T. J., Griffin, M. J., & Choi, Y. (2014). The relationship between teachers' mathematical content and pedagogical knowledge, teachers' perceptions, and student achievement. *Journal for Research in Mathematics Education, 45*(4), 419–459. https://doi.org/10.5951/jresematheduc.45.4.0419

Catts, H. W., & Petscher, Y. A. (2022). Cumulative risk and resilience model of dyslexia. *Journal of Learning Disabilities, 55*(3), 171–184. https://doi.org/10.1177/00222194211037062

Chung, P. J., Patel, D. R., & Nizami, I. (2020). Disorder of written expression and dysgraphia: Definition, diagnosis, and management. *Translational Pediatrics, 9*(Suppl 1), S46–S54. https://doi.org/10.21037/tp.2019.11.01

Cruickshank, W. M. (1977). Least-restrictive placement: Administrative wishful thinking. *Journal of Learning Disabilities, 10*, 193–194.

Dowker, A. (2024). Developmental dyscalculia in relation to individual differences in mathematical abilities. *Children, 11*, 623. https://doi.org/10.3390/children11060623

Erbeli, F., He, K., Cheek, C., Rice, M., & Qian, X. (2023). Exploring the machine learning paradigm in determining risk for reading disability. *Scientific Studies of Reading, 27*(1), 5–20. https://doi.org/10.1080/10888438.2022.2115914

Flanagan, D. P., & Schneider, W. J. (2016). Cross-Battery Assessment? XBA PSW? A case of mistaken identity: A commentary on Kranzler and colleagues' "Classification agreement analysis of Cross-Battery Assessment in the identification of specific learning disorders in children and youth.". *International Journal of School & Educational Psychology, 4*(3), 137–145. https://doi.org/10.1080/21683603.2016.1192852

Fletcher, J. M., Lyon, G. R., Fuchs, L. S., & Barnes, M. A. (2007). *Learning disabilities: From identification to intervention.* Guilford Press.

Fletcher, J. M., Lyon, G. R., Fuchs, L. S., & Barnes, M. A. (2019). *Learning disabilities: From identification to intervention* (2nd ed.). Guilford Press.

Fuchs, L. S., Fuchs, D., Schumacher, R. F., & Seethaler, P. M. (2014). Instructional intervention for students with mathematics learning difficulties. In H. L. Swanson, K. R. Harris, & S. E. Graham (Eds.), *Handbook on learning disabilities* (2nd ed., pp. 388–404). Guilford Press.

Geary, D. C. (2013). Early foundations for mathematics learning and their relations to learning disabilities. *Current Directions in Psychological Science, 22*, 23–27.

Georgan, W. C., Archibald, L. M. D., & Hogan, T. P. (2023). Speech/language impairment or specific learning disability? Examining the usage of educational categories. *Journal of Speech, Language, and Hearing Research: JSLHR, 66*(2), 656–667. https://doi.org/10.1044/2022_JSLHR-21-00636

Georgiou, G. K., & Parrila, R. (2014). Rapid automatized naming and reading. In H. L. Swanson, K. R. Harris, & S. Graham (Eds.), *Handbook of learning disabilities* (2nd ed., pp. 169–185). Guilford Press.

Graham, S., Berninger, V. W., Abbott, R. D., Abbott, S. P., & Whitaker, D. (1997). Role of mechanics in composing of elementary school students: A new methodological approach. *Journal of Educational Psychology, 89*, 170–182. https://doi.org/10.1037/0022-0663.89.1.170

Hill, H. C., Rowan, B., & Ball, D. L. (2005). Effects of teachers' mathematical knowledge for teaching on student achievement. *American Educational Research Journal, 42*(2), 371–406. https://doi.org/10.3102/00028312042002371

Individuals with Disabilities Education Improvement Act (IDEA). (2004). *Individuals with disabilities education improvement act Pub. L. No. 108–446, 20 USC 1400.*

International Dyslexia Association. (2020). *Understanding dysgraphia. Just Facts Sheet.* Retrieved from https://dyslexiaida.org/understanding-dysgraphia/

IDA Board of Directors. (2025, October 22). *Defintion of Dyslexia.*

Kent, S. C., & Wanzek, J. (2016). The relationship between component skills and writing quality and production across developmental levels. *Review of Educational Research, 86*(2), 570–601. https://doi.org/10.3102/0034654315619491

Koponen, T., Georgiou, G., Salmi, P., Leskinen, M., & Aro, M. (2017). A meta-analysis of the relation between RAN and mathematics. *Journal of Educational Psychology, 109*(7), 977–992. https://doi.org/10.1037/edu0000182

LaForte, E. M., Dailey, D., & McGrew, K. S. (2025). *Woodcock-Johnson V technical manual.* Riverside Insights.

Mayes, S. D., Frye, S. S., Breaux, R. P., & Calhoun, S. L. (2018). Diagnostic, demographic, and neurocognitive correlates of dysgraphia in students with ADHD, autism, learning disabilities, and neurotypical development. *Journal of Developmental and Physical Disabilities, 30*(4), 489–507. https://doi.org/10.1007/s10882-018-9598-9

McCloskey, M., & Rapp, B. (2017). Developmental dysgraphia: An overview and framework for research. *Cognitive Neuropsychology, 34*(3-4), 65–82. https://doi.org/10.1080/02643294.2017.136901

McGregor, K. K., Goffman, L., Horne, A. O. V., Hogan, T. P., & Finestack, L. H. (2020). Developmental language disorder: Applications for advocacy, research, and clinical service. *Perspectives of the ASHA Special Interest Groups, 5*(1), 38–46. https://doi.org/10.1044/2019_PERSP-19-00083

McWeeny, S., Choi, S., Choe, J., LaTourrette, A., Roberts, M. Y., & Norton, E. S. (2022). Rapid Automatized Naming (RAN) as a kindergarten predictor of future reading in English: A systematic review and meta-analysis. *Reading Research Quarterly, 57*(4), 1187–1211. https://doi.org/10.1002/rrq.467

Meltzer, L. J. (1994). Assessment of learning disabilities: The challenge of evaluating cognitive strategies and processes underlying learning. In G. R. Lyon (Ed.), *Frames of reference for the assessment of learning disabilities: New views on measurement issues* (pp. 571–606). Brookes.

Moll, K., Landerl, K., Snowling, M. J., & Schulte-Körne, G. (2019). Understanding comorbidity of learning disorders: Task-dependent estimates of prevalence. *Journal of Child Psychology and Psychiatry, and Allied Disciplines, 60*(3), 286–294. https://doi.org/10.1111/jcpp.12965

Moll, K., Snowling, M. J., & Hulme, C. (2020). Introduction to the special issue "Comorbidities between reading disorders and other developmental disorders". *Scientific Studies of Reading, 24*(1), 1–6. https://doi.org/10.1080/10888438.2019.1702045

National Center for Education Statistics. (2022). *Students with disabilities. Annual reports and information staff.* https://nces.ed.gov/programs/coe/indicator/cgg/students-with-disabilities#:~:text=In_2020%E2%80%9321%2C_the_number,of_all_public_school_students

National Joint Committee on Learning Disabilities. (2011). Learning disabilities: Implications for policy regarding research and practice: A report by the National Joint Committee on Learning Disabilities March 2011. *Learning Disability Quarterly, 34,* 237–241.

Norton, E., & Wolf, M. (2012). Rapid automatized naming (RAN) and reading fluency: Implications for understanding and treatment of reading disabilities. *Annual Review of Psychology, 63,* 427–452.

Pennington, B. F., Peterson, R. L., & McGrath, L. M. (2009). Dyslexia. In B. F. Pennington (Ed.), *Diagnosing learning disorders* (2nd ed., pp. 45–82). Guilford.

Pennington, B. F., McGrath, L. M., & Peterson, R. L. (2019). *Diagnosing learning disorders: From science to practice* (3rd ed.). Guilford.

Peters, L., Op de Beeck, H., & De Smedt, B. (2020). Cognitive correlates of dyslexia, dyscalculia and comorbid dyslexia/dyscalculia: Effects of numerical magnitude processing and phonological processing. *Research in Developmental Disabilities, 107*, 103806. https://doi.org/10.1016/j.ridd.2020.103806

Price, G. R., & Ansari, D. (2013). Dyscalculia: Characteristics, causes and treatments. *Numeracy, 6*(1), Article 2. Retrieved from http://scholarcommons.usf.edu/numeracy/vol6/iss1/art2

Proctor, C., & Mather, N. (2025). *WJ V dyslexia profile*. Authors.

Ray, K., Dally, K., Rowlandson, L., Tam, K. L., & Lane, A. E. (2022). The relationship of handwriting ability and literacy in kindergarten: A systematic review. *Reading and Writing, 35*, 1119–1155. https://doi.org/10.1007/s11145-021-10224-8

Schultz, E. K., Simpson, C. G., & Lynch, S. (2012). Specific learning disability identification: What constitutes a pattern of strengths and weaknesses? *Learning Disabilities, 18*, 87–97.

Shaywitz, S., & Shaywitz, J. (2020). *Overcoming dyslexia* (2nd ed.). Alfred A. Knopf.

Snowling, M. J., & Hulme, C. (2012). The nature and classification of reading disorders: A commentary on proposals for DSM-5. *Journal of Child Psychology and Psychiatry, 53*, 593–607.

Snowling, M. J., Nash, H. M., Gooch, D. C., Hayiou-Thomas, M. E., Hulme, C., & Wellcome Language and Reading Project Team. (2019). Developmental outcomes for children at high risk of dyslexia and children with developmental language disorder. *Child Development, 90*(5), e548–e564. https://doi.org/10.1111/cdev.13216

Spencer, M., Quinn, J. M., & Wagner, R. K. (2014). Specific reading comprehension disability: Major problem, myth, or misnomer? *Learning Disabilities Research & Practice, 29*, 3–9.

Stanovich, K. E. (1994). Are discrepancy-based definitions of dyslexia empirically defensible? In K. P. Bos, L. S. Siegel, D. J. Bakker, & D. L. Share (Eds.), *Current directions in dyslexia research* (pp. 15–30). Swets & Zeitlinger.

Suhr, J. A. (2008). Assessment versus testing and its importance in learning disability diagnosis. In E. Fletcher-Janzen & C. R. Reynolds (Eds.), *Neuropsychological perspectives on learning disabilities in the era of RTI: Recommendations for diagnosis and intervention* (pp. 99–114). Wiley.

Tucci, A., & Choi, E. (2023). Developmental language disorder and writing: A scoping review from childhood to adulthood. *Journal of Speech, Language, and Hearing Research: JSLHR, 66*(8), 2900–2920. https://doi.org/10.1044/2023_JSLHR-22-00583

Wolf, M., Bowers, P. G., & Biddle, K. (2000). Naming-speed processes, timing, and reading: A conceptual review. *Journal of Learning Disabilities, 33*, 387–407.

Nine

ILLUSTRATIVE CASE REPORTS

The purpose of this chapter is to illustrate the use of the WJ V in evaluations. In most instances additional data—such as the results from group administered tests, standardized tests, and informal measures—would be collected as part of a comprehensive evaluation, additional standardized tests. The intent of this chapter is however, to demonstrate the type of information that can be derived from the WJ V. Knowledge of the test content, administration, and scoring and interpretive options (presented in Chapters 1 through 7 of this book) is required to fully understand the information presented here.

This chapter includes the following illustrative case reports:

- **Noah**, a student who is currently repeating first grade. Noah has specific weaknesses in phonological awareness, basic reading and spelling, and handwriting. His math skills are grade-appropriate.
- **William**, a fifth-grade student with particular weaknesses in oral language comprehension, reading comprehension, and math problem-solving.
- **Victoria**, a seventh-grade student who was diagnosed with dyslexia in second grade and received special education programming until fifth grade but is now struggling with the reading demands in middle school.
- **Sophia**, an eighth-grade student with weaknesses in reading fluency, some isolated weaknesses in word recognition and spelling, and significant processing deficits indicated by the WJ V Phonemic Retrieval Fluency and RAN Reading clusters.

Essentials of WJ V™ Assessment, First Edition. Erica M. LaForte, Nancy Mather, and W. Joel Schneider.

- **Evan**, an 11th-grade student who was referred for a re-evaluation because of continued difficulties with both handwriting and mathematics.
- **Veronica**, a recent college graduate who has been accepted to graduate school. She is seeking information about whether she has a learning disability and what she should do about her slow reading rate.

Although in all cases further documentation may be required to justify eligibility decisions, the reports illustrate the type of information that can be obtained from the WJ V. A common theme across all of the case reports is that the focus is on the characteristics and educational needs of the person rather than on an in-depth description of the scores. Although these were actual cases and the background information is real, the examinee names, ages, birthdates, school names, and locations have been changed to protect confidentiality.

The reports in this chapter provide some examples of how WJ V results can be organized and displayed. The reports include a variety of score metrics, including relative-standing metrics such as standard scores and percentile ranks, and proficiency metrics such as Relative Proficiency Indexes (RPIs). Some evaluators include verbal labels for these scores to aid in interpretation. While each report includes some common elements (see Rapid Reference 9.1), the report sections are organized and presented in a slightly different way by each evaluator. Your district or organization may have a standard report format, or you may develop your own using the reports in this chapter as examples.

As you attempt to address referral questions and make appropriate recommendations in your own professional practice, always consider and integrate findings from behavioral observations, error analysis, and test scores. The basic score report generated by *Riverside Score®* provides the test and cluster scores and the comparison base-rate scores in a table format and may include any notes or observations you made during testing. While the basic score report can serve as a starting point for a case report, it does not provide score interpretations. As an assessment professional, you are responsible for interpreting scores, integrating information from various other sources, drawing conclusions, and making specific recommendations to address the referral concern(s).

CAUTION

A computer-generated table of scores is only a starting point for your case report. You are responsible for interpreting the information and developing specific, individualized recommendations.

Rapid Reference 9.1

Key Information to Include in an Evaluation Report

- Identifying information
- Reason for referral
- Background information

- Tests administered
- Behavioral observations
- Test results that provide specific examples of both strengths and weaknesses
- Conclusions and recommendations

CASE STUDY #1: NOAH

Psychoeducational Evaluation

Student: Noah Vega	School: Wayne Academy
Birthdate: September 7	Grade: 1.7
Age: 7 years, 6 months	Test dates: February 15–19
Parents: Sophia and Anthony Vega	Evaluator: Lynne E. Jaffe, Ph.D.

Reason for referral Noah was referred by his mother due to his extreme difficulty learning basic reading, spelling, and writing skills. She wanted information regarding the reasons for his difficulties, his pattern of strengths and weaknesses, and recommendations for effective instructional methods.

Developmental and family history Noah was born at 38 weeks gestation, weighing 6 lb. 0 oz. His mother stated that he met all of his childhood developmental milestones, including language milestones, on time. He's a physically active child, small for his age, and looks younger than his same-age peers. Noah attends a taekwondo class twice a week and recently received a stripe on his belt for attention and effort. Sophia and Anthony also have a 2-year-old son, Leo. English is the only language spoken in the home. Neither parent is aware of any diagnosed disabilities in their families.

Educational history Noah attended preschool at Casa de Los Niños daycare and entered kindergarten at Wayne Academy, a charter school, on his fifth birthday. As the youngest child in his class, Noah had some difficulty participating in group activities for as long as expected and tended to wander off. By mid-year, however, his participation was age-appropriate, but the teacher noted that he was having difficulty with some of the academic coursework such as learning the alphabet song and the names of letters. When the class focused on skills related to academic coursework rather than engaging in playtime, Noah became frustrated, refused to participate, and, sometimes cried.

Ms. Travers, Noah's first-grade teacher, observed that as class time increasingly focused on basic reading and writing skills, Noah's behavior became more problematic. For example, when the class focused on learning and working with letter sounds, Noah refused to participate; he might put his head down on the desk or get up and walk to the back of the room. In contrast, he enjoyed learning about numbers, their values, and basic addition and subtraction. He had an aptitude for solving basic arithmetic problems with manipulatives or counting on his fingers.

Because Noah was so young when he started school, seemed socially immature, and had significantly more difficulty learning reading and writing skills than his classmates, his parents chose to have him repeat first grade. This year, his first-grade teacher, Ms. Martin, described Noah as "wicked smart with a gigantic vocabulary and a vivid imagination"; however, Noah's extensive vocabulary is mostly focused on topics of particular interest, such as the Harry Potter stories that his mother reads to him nightly and Pokémon cards.

As a class-wide reading program, Ms. Martin has just started using Wilson Fundations® and explained that the children recite each letter, keyword, and sound every morning. She stated that Noah can write all of the letters but has to be reminded to do so legibly. She said that he also knows the sounds of all of the letters and some digraphs, although that was not evident in this current assessment.

Behavioral observations Noah said that he likes school; his favorite part is recess and playing games with his friends. He likes his teacher and described Ms. Martin as being "super easy-going." Noah was tested over three sessions for approximately two hours each, in a quiet room, with frequent breaks. As an incentive for focused attention and effort, he earned play money with which he could buy Pokémon cards during breaks. Although Noah was motivated by the prospect of earning Pokémon cards and was appropriately engaged most of the time, he was not thrilled with the prospect of spending his weekend mornings doing "schoolwork."

Tests administered

- *Woodcock-Johnson V Tests of Cognitive Abilities* (WJ V COG)
- *Woodcock-Johnson V Tests of Achievement* (WJ V ACH)
- *Woodcock-Johnson V Virtual Test Library* (WJ V VTL)

Although other tests were administered in this evaluation, the purpose of the sample report is to illustrate findings from the WJ V.

Explanation of scores and score ranges Noah's scores on the tests administered are reported as standard score ranges (SSs), percentile ranks (PRs), and Relative Proficiency Indexes (RPIs). The RPI is a score unique to the Woodcock-Johnson test batteries. Whereas the SS and PR indicate the *position* of Noah's score within the range of scores in his grade-peer group, the RPI is a prediction of his *success* on a task similar to the one used in the test and on which typical grade-peers would be 90% successful. The RPI is shown as a fraction, with Noah's predicted success as the numerator and 90 as the denominator, representing 90% success as mastery . RPIs are particularly useful in showing a weakness in performance that may not be evident from standard scores. For example, Noah's standard score on the Word Attack test was 83 (low average); however, his RPI of 38/90 indicates that when typical grade-peers read nonsense words with 90% success, Noah's success is likely to be about 38%.

The appendix of this report contains a score table for all of the tests and clusters administered. This evaluator chose to use first-grade norms for several reasons. Noah barely made the age cut-off to start kindergarten and did not benefit from much of the reading and writing instruction offered in his first time in first grade. As he is repeating first grade, it seems appropriate to monitor his progress against the children with whom he is being educated rather than those a grade ahead of him.

Note: Some of the examples of test items in this report are similar to the actual items but are fabricated to maintain the security of the test items.

Descriptors for standard scores, PRs, and RPI ranges are shown in the table below:

Standard Score	Percentile Rank	Descriptor	RPI	Descriptor	Instructional Implications
131 and above	98 and above	Very superior	100/90	Very advanced	extremely easy
121–130	92–97	Superior	98/90–100/90	Advanced	very easy
111–120	77–91	High average	95/90–98/90	Average to advanced	easy
90–110	25–76	Average	82/90–95/90	Average	manageable
80–89	9–24	Low average	67/90–82/90	Limited to average	difficult
70–79	3–8	Low	24/90–67/90	Limited	very difficult
69 or below	2 and below	Very low	3/90–24/90	Very limited	extremely difficult

Cognitive abilities Although provided in the Appendix, this evaluator did not include in the discussion the scores for either General Intellectual Ability (GIA) or the Gf-Gc cluster (a combination of nonverbal and verbal problem-solving). As Noah's GIA and Gf-Gc composites are comprised of scores that differ by over two standard deviations, their validity is, at best, questionable. Consequently, this report focuses on the abilities that make up Noah's cognitive, oral language, and academic skills.

Visual-spatial processing and nonverbal reasoning Noah exhibited average to high abilities in fluid reasoning, visualization, and perceptual speed in addition to some types of auditory memory. These abilities likely contribute to his artistic abilities on which his teacher has commented.

Fluid Reasoning is the ability to use inductive and deductive reasoning to solve visual, nonverbal problems that often involve unfamiliar information or procedures. Academically, these abilities are strongly related to math reasoning, understanding scientific concepts and procedures, and, eventually, higher-level reading comprehension. This area was Noah's strongest cognitive ability (SS = 113, PR = 81). His RPI of 96/90 indicates that when typical children in mid-first grade would be 90% successful on solving reasoning problems, Noah would be 96% successful.

Visual Processing is the ability to use mental imagery for a variety of purposes. Among the many aspects of visual processing are visualization, i.e., the ability to grasp the spatial relationships among objects and to imagine what an object or design would look like from a different perspective or if the components were rearranged. Noah demonstrated average visual processing for his grade level (SS = 101, PR = 52, RPI = 90/90).

Cognitive Processing Speed, as measured by the WJ V, is the rate at which one can scan visual stimuli, compare for similarities and differences, and recognize patterns. It allows us to develop automaticity in recognizing visual symbols so that cognitive attention and energy are available to focus on the more complex and higher-level aspects of tasks, such as reading, writing, and math. Noah's cognitive processing speed is in the high end of the average range. Although in the average range, Noah's score on the Number-Pattern Matching test, a test of both accuracy and speed, is comparatively low. Noah talked to himself through the first minute or so (e.g., "and now, it's gonna be . . ."), named each number as he tapped it, and had to be reminded to click on "Next" at the bottom of the screen to advance to the next screen. His responses were accurate, but his approach slowed him down, lowering his score.

Memory Noah's auditory memory span was average for his grade, but he had considerably more difficulty with short-term working memory. Consequently, tasks requiring Noah to hold information in mind for immediate use should be manageable, but holding that information in mind while working with it may prove difficult. This difference increases the importance of Noah learning basic skills to an automatic level so that working memory is available for more complex processes.

On many of the tests that required Noah to listen and then retell information, such as memory tests or story recall, he seemed to get stuck on a piece of information given in an early item and insert it into later responses. For example, an early story included a girl's name; Noah then used her name instead of the boy's name in the next story. Some of the errors Noah made in early items of a few tests seemed to be more due to a lack of focus than to task-related difficulty.

Auditory Memory Span is the amount of auditory (and, in this case, verbal) information one can hold in immediate awareness before using it. Thus, the information is available to be used for verbal rehearsal (i.e., repeating it until the task is completed) or to work with to solve a problem or transfer it to long-term memory. Noah's memory for short pieces of verbal information, such as sentences or a string of unrelated words, was average for his grade level. On the Sentence Repetition test, Noah often retained the meaning of the sentences but made odd syntactical errors or omitted syllables from words (SS = 97, PR = 42, RPI = 86/90).

Auditory Working Memory Capacity is called the "scratch pad of the mind." It describes a person's ability to direct attention to the information held in short-term memory and maintain it while other cognitive abilities work with it, transform it, and/or transfer it to long-term memory. Working memory is a dynamic process or operation performed on information rather than a stable ability. Some tasks at Noah's level that depend on working memory include:

- Working the steps of a subtraction problem requiring regrouping while simultaneously retrieving the needed math facts from long-term memory.

- Retrieving the individual sounds of the letters in a word and holding them in short-term memory while trying to blend them into a word.

Numbers Reversed is a test that required Noah to repeat a string of numbers in reverse order. Although his performance was average for his grade level, he was successful in reversing only items of two digits (SS = 98, PR = 46, RPI = 87/90).

Verbal Attention is a test in which Noah was told a short series of numbers and animals and was then asked to name a specific one. He had significant difficulty with this test; he needed several reminders to wait for the two beeps that signaled the end of the string of items and the request for the target item, rather than just repeating everything. There was no particular pattern to his errors. When other first-grade children would be expected to be 90% proficient on similar tasks, Noah's would be only 51% successful (SS = 81, PR = 10, RPI = 51/90).

Oral language

Vocabulary Noah had difficulty when tested on the meaning of individual words, especially when he had to retrieve a specific word from memory, such as a synonym for a given word. Surprisingly, he could not name a common musical instrument or everyday objects from pictures but answered higher-level questions that were science oriented, such as the functions of bodily organs, geographic features of the Earth, and astronomy. During a break, he explained how an animal on his Pokémon card "evolved." In general, based on his RPI scores, his on-demand vocabulary is limited to average but is more sophisticated regarding science and topics of particular interest to him (Academic Vocabulary: SS = 98, PR = 45, RPI = 88/90; Picture Vocabulary: SS = 87, PR = 20, RPI = 73/90; Oral Vocabulary: SS = 90, PR = 24, RPI = 74/90).

The **General Information** test measures familiarity with real-world information usually acquired through life experiences; however, it is also strongly dependent on vocabulary knowledge. The test asks the function of specific objects and where one would find other specific objects; accordingly, the examinee must know the names of the objects to which the items refer. Like his assessed vocabulary (see below), Noah's general knowledge was limited; however, even his errors reflected his interest in science. When asked where he would find a faucet, Noah said, "In the sand." Then, seeing that this evaluator made a note of it, he said, "I thought you said fossil." (SS = 83, PR = 13, RPI = 64/90). He did not know where one would find a faucet.

Language comprehension Noah's ability to understand spoken language, including vocabulary in context, is *at least* average for his grade level. He followed instructions incorporating complex syntax, filled in the missing word in sentences of increasing length and complexity, and retold elements of recorded stories. All of these tests require not only comprehension but also working memory and expression of the target information. When retelling stories, however, despite his average score, Noah did not seem to recognize the expectation to tell *as much as* he remembered. When asked specific questions about other stories, his responses lacked specificity, or he did not make an expected inference. It is likely that Noah's scores are an underrepresentation of his language comprehension

(Oral Comprehension: SS = 101, PR = 52, RPI = 90/90; Understanding Directions: SS = 96, PR = 40, RPI = 87/90; Story Recall: SS = 100, PR = 50, RPI = 90/90; Story Comprehension: SS = 85, PR = 16, RPI = 73/90).

Expressive language Overall, Noah's expressive language varies greatly depending on the task and the specificity of the instructions given. His descriptions of pictures were detailed, if not always syntactically correct. For example, on the Oral Language Samples test, his description of a picture incorporating a crossing monitor was: "The person is safe stop so the cars won't run over the people." Still, his performance was in the superior range. Errors in syntax and articulation were not penalized (Oral Language Samples: SS = 125, PR = 95, RPI = 98/90).

Prerequisites of reading and spelling skills

Phonological/phonemic awareness Phonological awareness is the understanding that a stream of speech can be broken down into smaller units, such as words, syllables, and sounds. Abilities that demonstrate phonological awareness include rhyming, repeating nonsense words, blending sounds into words, segmenting words into sounds, and phonological manipulation (i.e., substituting or deleting a sound in a word to make a different word). The highest level of phonological awareness is called phonemic awareness, and it involves manipulating individual sounds (phonemes). These skills are critical for learning to sound out words for reading and spelling and, thus, create the foundation for developing phonics and the large bank of sight words necessary for fluent reading and comprehension.

Nonsense Word Repetition. Noah performed in the low average range on repeating nonsense words verbatim. He missed or substituted sounds and added a schwa sound to the end of 1-syllable words (e.g., slindle for splinder, braduh for brad). Noah may not be discriminating the individual sounds in words; alternatively, when he repeats a word to himself, he may misarticulate it, giving him the wrong feedback regarding its sound (SS = 89, PR = 23, RPI = 77/90).

Phonological Awareness. Noah performed in the low average range for mid-year first graders on blending and segmenting; however, his RPI of 45/90 indicates that tasks requiring these skills will be very difficult for him. He was able to blend two syllables into a word but not two sounds; nor could he segment two-sound words into phonemes. In informal testing, Noah was able to blend a vowel sound followed by a consonant into a word (e.g., in, at) but could not then add an initial consonant sound (e.g., adding /m/ to *an* to make *man*). Noah could usually recognize a picture based on its first sound (e.g., "Which picture starts with /n/?") but not based on its last sound (Phonological Awareness: SS = 84, PR = 14, RPI = 45/90).

Phonological Manipulation Compared with his grade-peers, Noah demonstrated significant difficulty manipulating the individual sounds in words, a skill that serves as a foundation for using phonics for reading. Phonological manipulation includes substituting or deleting a syllable or sound in a word to make a new word (e.g., Change the /t/ in "top" to /h/; say "spin" without saying /s/). Noah's RPI of 56/90 indicates that similar tasks that are already mastered by his grade-peers are expected to be very challenging for him (SS = 80, PR = 9, RPI = 56/90).

Retrieval fluency and rapid automatized naming Noah demonstrated no difficulty when asked to rapidly retrieve words based on their meanings. He demonstrated clear difficulty when the task focused on letter names and phonemes.

Retrieval Fluency. Retrieval fluency is the ability to rapidly retrieve verbal information from long-term memory. The ability to retrieve words based on their meaning enables one to comfortably and efficiently express one's thoughts. Noah performed in the high average range when asked to rapidly name categories of words, such as articles of clothing (Semantic Word Retrieval: SS = 112, PR = 78, RPI = 93/90).

Noah demonstrated considerable more difficulty thinking of words in terms of their sounds. For example, given 1 minute, he was asked to list as many words as possible beginning with a specific sound. Within this time frame, he could only come up with four words that started with the /n/ sound; he could only think of one for each of the other two sounds. Throughout the task, Noah appeared frustrated, touching his head repeatedly and saying "think, think" (Phonemic Word Retrieval: SS = 88, PR = 20, RPI = 81/90).

Rapid automatized naming (RAN). RAN assesses the ability to rapidly recognize and name a visual symbol. The tests requiring rapid retrieval of letter names and letter sounds use only six letters repeatedly (different letters appear on each test). Noah's scores demonstrated both his reduced rate and inaccuracy in naming the letters and providing their corresponding sounds; however, he likely does not have all of the names or sounds of letters memorized to an automatic level, so his low score is most likely due to limited letter and sound knowledge. In contrast, Noah's ability to rapidly name pictures and numbers was in the middle of the average range. His RPIs indicate that his proficiency in tasks requiring rapid retrieval of letter names and sounds would be 56% and 48% respectively, compared with 90% proficiency for his grade-peers.

Orthographic processing Phonics knowledge and the ability to blend and segment letter sounds serve as the foundation for orthographic processing. After sounding out a word several times, a letter pattern is, typically, embedded into memory, forming an orthographic image. Subsequently, the word is recognized "on sight" and triggers its sound. Orthographic processing is also necessary for the recognition of irregular words, i.e., words that do not follow the phonics patterns of one's specific language and cannot be easily sounded out.

Noah has not developed sufficient phonics skills on which to layer orthographic processing and did not demonstrate automatic recognition of any words during the reading tests. He did attempt to sound out words but was generally unsuccessful. Noah's fast visual processing will support orthographic processing, but he must first have the sounds of letters embedded in memory and available for automatic retrieval, along with the ability to blend and segment sounds.

Academic achievement

Reading Basic reading skills incorporate letter-sound associations, word attack (the ability to sound out unfamiliar words), and word identification (the ability to identify whole words on sight).

Sound-symbol associations. During informal testing, Noah was unable to recite the alphabet in order but named random letters, sometimes repeating. Later, when asked to sing the alphabet song, he did so up to the letter "G," but then could not go any further. Given lowercase letter tiles, Noah named all letters except b, d, g, j, l, q, u, v, and z. He confused b with d (and vice versa) and misnamed j, g, p, z, l, and v. Noah gave the correct primary sounds of most of the letters except for e, f, g, j, u, v, and w. During the evaluation, he frequently said "E" for upper- and lowercase C, even after receiving a reminder. He did not accurately pronounce any consonant digraphs or blends. When asked to read phonically regular nonsense words, Noah was only able to provide the sounds of individual letters.

Basic Reading Skills. Overall, Noah's RPI on the WJ V Basic Reading Skills cluster indicates that when grade peers are 90% proficient on sounding out and recognizing individual words, Noah will be 14% proficient, rendering this task "extremely difficult." His grade equivalent was "first month of kindergarten."

Whether attempting to read real words or phonically regular nonsense words, Noah consistently appeared motivated to make serious attempts. Over several days of testing, his attempts at sounding out familiar, phonically regular words proved occasionally successful. At times, he was able to sound out two- and three-letter words (e.g., it, mat). Other times, he provided the sounds of the letters and then blended them out of order. On words with less familiar letter sounds, he provided the sounds of each letter multiple times, often incorrectly, and then provided a completely unrelated word (e.g., "like"—/i/ /l/ /i/ /k/ "bit").

Basic Writing Skills Noah's handwriting does not evidence formal writing instruction, and his parents do not remember Noah previously engaging in handwriting practice. His pencil grasp looks functional, but when he is writing, most of the movement originates from his wrist. Noah was unable to tap each finger to his thumb in sequence indicating difficulty with fine-motor planning and integration.

Noah demonstrated extreme difficulty on the Letter Writing Fluency test. When trying to write letters quickly and from memory, some of his letters were barely recognizable. Noah's writing was slow, and he often repeated and reversed letters; Noah did not appear to have any strategy to help him decide what letters to write. When asked to write the letters in alphabetical order with a model on the top of the page, he worked carefully but appeared to draw the letters rather than write them fluidly from memory (SS = 69, PR = 2, RPI = 3/90).

Later, informally and with no time limit, this evaluator asked Noah to write the alphabet. When given a choice of papers with a variety of guidelines, he chose regular, lined notebook paper. A graphic of Noah's alphabet is below. When asked to name each letter, he called the Y "V" and did not know the name of the uppercase E. Noah writes some of his letters and numbers from the bottom up, usually (not always) facing the correct direction. We did not attempt the spelling of any words.

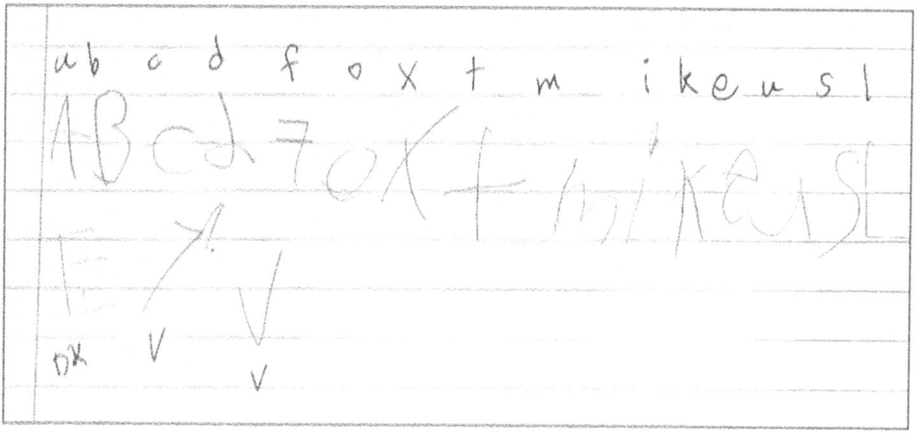

Sample of Noah's Alphabet Writing

Math Calculation Skills Math calculation is a clear strength for Noah. He does not know addition and subtraction facts automatically but is very quick at counting on his fingers. In a timed test of math facts (1-digit addition and subtraction), Noah scored in the high average range. He talked himself through solving each problem and responded to 34 facts with only one error (he misread the sign) (Math Facts Fluency: SS = 115, PR = 84, RPI = 96/90).

On the Calculation test, Noah scored in the upper limit of the average range. Again, he counted on his fingers but responded correctly to all single-digit addition and subtraction problems and one double-digit plus single-digit problem. Of note, he did not recognize the provided multiplication sign ("What's the X for?") (Calculation: SS = 105, PR = 63, RPI = 95/90).

Math Problem Solving Noah's overall performance on the Math Problem-Solving cluster was in the low average range (SS = 87, PR = 19, RPI = 71/90). Compared with his grade-peers, he would be expected to be 71% proficient when solving practical problems requiring math when they are 90% proficient.

Applied Problems. Noah's ability to solve practical problems using math was in the low average range. He answered all addition and subtraction problems presented with pictures correctly; however, he answered calculation problems without pictures by counting on his fingers. Notably, he used his fingers after counting the four dollars he held in his hand to deduce that he needed one more dollar (totaling five dollars) to trade for a Pokémon card. When presented with a problem that asked how many items were "around" a table, Noah could not provide the correct answer to the problem because he did not understand the meaning of the word "around." For problems including two-digit numbers, he drew circles on his scratch sheet to represent the numbers but not accurately. Noah demonstrated unfamiliarity with the names and/or value of coins and could not accurately read the time on a digital watch. Also, he did not recognize that problems including the phrase, "how many more" often require subtraction.

Math Problem Identification. This test requires an understanding of math algorithms and reasoning. Given a variety of problems, with and without pictures, Noah was asked to identify what information was wrong or missing. In both illustrated problems and simple written addition and subtraction problems, he recognized a wrong answer. Noah demonstrated most difficulty recognizing what information was missing from a problem, thereby making it impossible to solve. In word problems in which one must know a starting quantity from which to add or subtract, Noah seemed to recognize what was missing but could not express it. For example, when asked how much a person has after spending $3, he said, "We don't know much—'cause we don't know how much he had any more. . .now."

Summary

Noah demonstrates average or above average abilities in fluid reasoning, spatial relations, visual processing speed, and oral language, with some limitations in general vocabulary knowledge. His short-term auditory memory is average, but he demonstrates some difficulty with holding verbal information in mind while working with it. He demonstrates significant weaknesses in phonological awareness. These weaknesses are the major contributing factors to Noah's difficulties in learning basic phonics skills for reading and spelling. His handwriting is slow and labored, with poor representation of most letters. In contrast, although he has not memorized basic math facts, his conceptual understanding of math is at least grade-appropriate.

Diagnostic impressions The current test results strongly indicate that Noah has dyslexia. Dyslexia is a learning disability that impairs the acquisition of basic reading and spelling skills. In turn, these deficits cause difficulties with reading fluency, reading comprehension, and written expression. According to research, the major cognitive correlates of dyslexia include weaknesses in one or more of the following abilities: phonological awareness, orthographic awareness, memory, RAN, and processing speed. Other abilities, such as general intelligence, reasoning, oral language, mathematics, and knowledge, that do not require reading, are often unimpaired, as is true in Noah's case.

Diagnostic and Statistical Manual of Mental Disorders, Fifth Edition, Text Revision uses the following code for dyslexia (DSM-5-TR):

315.00 Specific Learning Disorder with Impairment in Reading

Recommendations The school has chosen to use the Wilson Fundations® program, a multisensory structured language program, to teach beginning reading and spelling skills. This is an appropriate program for Noah's needs. To this end, his teacher should follow the scope and sequence of the Fundations® program, using the Fundations® materials and reinforcing with classroom materials, especially manipulatives. It is critical that Noah does not move on to the next skill until he has consistently demonstrated mastery of the current skill. As the skills progress, make sure that Noah is developing automaticity in, and regularly practicing, the skills previously taught.

Activities to be used simultaneously or as reinforcement of Fundations® The following activities may prove useful in the classroom and/or at home.

ALPHABET AND LETTER NAMES.

1. To help Noah learn the alphabet and the names of the letters, teach him to sing the alphabet song, incorporating letter tiles. Break up the song into the melodic parts so that he only has to memorize one part at a time (e.g., a b c d e f g—h i j k l m n o p—q r s—t u v—w x y (and) z). Practice each part multiple times pointing to the letter as he sings its name. Be careful that the letters "l m n o" do not become one word "elemenno," which is common for young children. Do this separately with both upper- and lowercase letters.
2. After practicing each part of the alphabet, mix up letter tiles for only those letters practiced. Then, have Noah put them in order, name them, mix them up again, and repeat. Practice each set as it is learned and then incorporate previously learned letters until he can name every letter, on command, out of order.
3. As Noah demonstrates confusion as to the difference between upper- and lowercase letters, providing matching and sorting activities focused on upper- and lowercase letters will likely prove beneficial. First, provide upper- and lowercase alphabet strips to use as a reference. Then have Noah work from memory. Some potential activities include:
   a. Using letter tiles, mix up upper- and lowercase letters and have Noah practice matching upper- to lowercase letters. At this point, the letters need not be in alphabetical order.
   b. Have Noah sort the letters into two piles—uppercase and lowercase—and put them into alphabetical order.
   c. Move to more advanced activities, such as having Noah circle and name all of the uppercase letters on a page of text. On another sheet, have him circle and name only the lowercase letters.

BLENDING AND SEGMENTING

1. Noah understands the concept of blending and segmenting sounds but needs practice and reinforcement. A helpful activity uses interlocking cubes that represent speech sounds. First, interlock the cubes and tell Noah the word that they represent (e.g., sun). Then, break the cubes apart and explain that you are breaking the word into its sounds. Space the cubes a few inches apart and point to each cube, saying its sound, with a pause in between each sound.

Gradually move the cubes closer together, saying the sounds with shorter pauses. Continue until you have pushed together and locked the cubes, say the whole word, and lift the interlocked cubes as a unit to show that you now have a whole word.

2. When teaching segmentation of words into individual sounds, start with two-phoneme words composed of a consonant and a long vowel sound, such as ape, eat, knee, and toe. Long vowel sounds are easier to perceive than short vowel sounds. For words with initial consonants, use those with "stretchy sounds," such as /m/ and /s/, as these are easier to articulate in isolation. Progress to 3-sound words with a "consonant-vowel team-consonant" pattern, such as soap and rain. Be careful not to use final consonant sounds, such as /l/ or /r/, that change the sound of the preceding long vowel.

Basic reading skills reinforcement activities

1. When Noah has learned to sound out phonically regular words, alter simple board games to include a reading or spelling step. For example, make small cards with one word (or later, a sentence) on each and pile them face down on the board. Player 1 reads the word/sentence, then takes his turn. Provide whatever reading support Noah needs so that the game remains fun. Consistent difficulty indicates the need for more instruction; the skill level required by the game is too advanced. Games that lend themselves to this type of activity include Chutes and Ladders and Uncle Wiggly. Consider incorporating the following skills into these games:
   a. Phoneme–Grapheme relationships: use individual letters and ask for the sounds.
   b. Phonics study: use nonsense words that are structured like real words.
   c. Irregular word recognition: use irregular words.
2. Once Noah has learned to sound out 3-sound words and knows some basic sight words (e.g., the, is, says), he will be ready to engage with various decodable texts. A good source of decodable books, in addition to Fundations® and Wilson Reading®, is *DOG ON A LOG Books* by Pamela Brookes. The words in the stories of these books progress in accordance with the Wilson Reading System.

Handwriting

1. Teach Noah handwriting using the Fundations® handwriting style and program. For most lowercase letters, once a student has put his pencil down on the paper, he can complete the letter without picking it up again. The Fundations® paper uses names for the lines (plane, grass, worm) so that the teacher can use a verbal cue as to how to draw the letter. Do not use a stick-and-ball handwriting style, as it increases the burden on visual-fine motor coordination.

2. As Noah frequently confuses b and d, use a strategy to help him remember which is which. Several strategies are included in the Strategy section of this report.
3. To increase interest in practicing letter formation, provide different surfaces (e.g., shaving cream, white board, wet sand, chocolate pudding on a cookie sheet) and different writing implements (e.g., colored markers, glitter pens).
4. If Noah continues to have significant difficulty with letter formation after focused intervention using the Fundations® handwriting instruction, seek the consultation of an occupational therapist to help him develop the dexterity needed specifically for handwriting.

MATHEMATICS Noah understands the concepts of addition and subtraction but has not memorized the facts. He must learn the facts using 0–12 automatically so that working memory is available for more advanced calculations (e.g., regrouping) and applied problems. It is important that Noah memorize the math facts so that retrieval becomes automatic; automatic retrieval is necessary for more complicated calculations. For example, once retrieval becomes automatic for Noah, he may focus on the steps of an algorithm or the concepts in a word problem without being interrupted by his need to calculate basic facts; interrupted focus hijacks the working memory that is needed for more complex aspects of mathematical equations.

1. Use an organizational structure when teaching math facts. Mental organization of math facts reduces memory demands and facilitates retrieval. The organizational structure attached to this report presents a sequence in which each new set of facts is related to facts or processes Noah already knows.
2. Once Noah has initially learned certain math facts, provide practice sessions with flash cards until his responses become automatic. Additionally, have him practice on his own for several minutes daily using flash cards with the answer on the reverse side. Provide frequent review of newly mastered facts.
3. As a supplement, use computer programs to motivate drill and practice, but do not let them replace regular monitoring of fact knowledge through oral response to flashcards and written timed tests.
4. To increase motivation and avoid Noah feeling overwhelmed by the perceived number of facts to memorize, have him monitor his progress in developing automaticity of math facts by using a grid chart with one math fact in each square. As he learns each fact to an automatic level, have him highlight the square. Make sure he understands the commutative property, so he may fill in 2 squares for each fact learned.
5. Teach Noah how to add and subtract two-digit numbers without regrouping. Noah has a good conceptual understanding of addition and subtraction. When he has mastered these concepts, teach regrouping using manipulatives and a "place value" mat.

Appendix: *Woodcock-Johnson V* Table of Scores

CLUSTERS/Tests	Standard Score	SS Band (68%)	SS Classif.	PR	RPI	RPI Proficiency	RPI Implication	AE	GE
GENERAL INTELLECTUAL ABILITY (GIA)	94	91–97	Avg.	35	86/90	Avg.	Manageable	6y8m	G1.2
Matrices	120	110–129	High avg.	91	97/90	Avg./Adv.	Easy	10y6m	G5.1
Semantic Word Retrieval	112	105–118	High avg.	78	93/90	Avg.	Manageable	8y4m	G2.9
Spatial Relations	106	101–112	Avg.	67	94/90	Avg.	Manageable	8y0m	G2.5
Verbal Analogies	96	90–102	Avg.	40	86/90	Avg.	Manageable	—6y7m	1.2
Story Recall	100	95–104	Avg.	49	90/90	Avg.	Manageable	6y4m	K.9
Number Pattern Matching	93	90–95	Avg.	31	73/90	Lmtd./Avg.	Difficult	6y3m	K.8
Oral Vocabulary	90	85–95	Low avg.	24	74/90	Lmtd./Avg.	Difficult	6y1m	K.7
Verbal Attention	81	75–86	Low avg.	10	51/90	Lmtd.	Very difficult	5y3m	<K.0
GF-GC COMPOSITE	102	98–106	Avg.	56	91/90	Avg.	Manageable	7y3m	1.8
Matrices	120	110–129	High avg.	91	97/90	Avg./Adv.	Easy	10y6m	5.1
Analysis-Synthesis	106	100–111	Avg.	65	95/90	Avg./Adv.	Easy	7y9m	2.3
Oral Vocabulary	90	85–95	Low avg.	24	74/90	Lmtd./Avg.	Difficult	6y1m	K.7
Verbal Analogies	96	90–102	Avg.	40	86/90	Avg.	Manageable	6y7m	1.2
COMPREHENSION-KNOWLEDGE	**92**	**88–96**	**Avg.**	**30**	**81/90**	**Lmtd./Avg.**	**Difficult**	**6y4m**	**K.9**
Verbal Analogies	96	90–102	Avg.	40	86/90	Avg.	Manageable	6y7m	1.2
Oral Vocabulary	90	85–95	Low avg.	24	74/90	Lmtd./Avg.	Difficult	6y1m	K.7

[General Information]	83	71–95	Low avg.	13	64/90	Lmtd.	Very difficult	5y2m	<K.0
FLUID REASONING	**113**	**107–119**	**High avg.**	**81**	**96/90**	**Avg./Adv.**	**Easy**	**8y8m**	**3.0**
Matrices	120	110–129	High avg.	91	97/90	Avg./Adv.	Easy	10y6m	5.1
Analysis-Synthesis	106	100–111	Avg.	65	95/90	Avg./Adv.	Easy	7y9m	2.3
COGNITIVE PROCESSING SPEED	99	97–101	Avg.	47	89/90	Avg.	Manageable	6y11m	1.5
Letter-Pattern Matching	106	103–109	Avg.	65	96/90	Avg./Adv.	Easy	7y9m	2.3
Number-Pattern Matching	93	90–95	Avg.	31	73/90	Lmtd./Avg.	Difficult	6y3m	K.8
COGNITIVE EFFICIENCY	86	82–89	Low avg.	17	62/90	Lmtd.	Very difficult	5y10m	K.4
Number-Pattern Matching	93	90–95	Avg.	31	73/90	Lmtd./Avg.	Difficult	6y3m	K.8
Verbal Attention	81	75–86	Low avg.	10	51/90	Lmtd.	Very difficult	5y3m	<K.0
ORAL LANGUAGE	97	93–102	Avg.	43	88/90	Avg.	Manageable	6y9m	1.4
Oral Language Samples	125	112–138	Superior	95	98/90	Avg./Adv.	Easy/very easy	10y10m	5.5
Oral Comprehension	101	94–108	Avg.	52	90/90	Avg.	Manageable	7y1m	1.7
Picture Vocabulary	87	80–94	Low avg.	20	73/90	Lmtd./Avg.	Difficult	5y7m	K.2
Story Comprehension	85	77–92	Low avg.	16	73/90	Lmtd./Avg.	Difficult	4y11m	<K.0
[Understanding Directions]	96	90–102	Avg.	40	87/90	Avg.	Manageable	6y8m	1.2
VOCABULARY	**92**	**86–98**	**Avg.**	**30**	**82/90**	**Avg.**	**Manageable**	**6y4m**	**K.9**
Academic Vocabulary	98	84–112	Avg.	45	88/90	Avg.	Manageable	6y10m	1-4
Picture Vocabulary	87	80–94	Low avg.	20	73/90	Lmtd./Avg.	Difficult	5y7m	K.2

(*Continued*)

CLUSTERS/Tests	Standard Score	SS Band (68%)	SS Classif.	PR	RPI	RPI Proficiency	RPI Implication	AE	GE
LISTENING COMPREHENSION	92	87–98	Avg.	30	84/90	Avg.	Manageable	6y3m	K.8
Oral Comprehension	101	94–108	Avg.	52	90/90	Avg.	Manageable	7y1m	1.7
Story Comprehension	85	77–92	Low avg.	16	73/90	Lmtd./Avg.	Difficult	4y11m	<K.0
[Understanding Directions]	96	90–102	Avg.	40	87/90	Avg.	Manageable	6y8m	1.3
ORAL EXPRESSION	93	97–110	Avg.	59	92/90	Avg.	Manageable	7y4m	1.9
Oral Language Samples	125	112–138	Superior	95	98/90	Avg./Adv.	Easy/very easy	10y10m	5-5
Picture Vocabulary	87	80–94	Low avg.		73/90	Lmtd./Avg.	Difficult	5y7m	K.2
AUDITORY MEMORY SPAN	**97**	**93–101**	**Avg.**	**42**	**86/90**	**Avg.**	**Manageable**	**6y8m**	**1.2**
Memory for Words	101	95–106	Avg.	52	91/90	Avg.	Manageable	6y8m	1.2
Sentence Repetition	94	84–103	Avg.	34	80/90	Lmtd./Avg.	Difficult	6y2m	K.7
AUDITORY WORKING MEMORY CAPACITY	91	87–95	Avg.	27	73/90	Lmtd./Avg.	Difficult	6y2m	K.8
Numbers Reversed	98	92–104	Avg.	46	87/90	Avg.	Manageable	6y10m	1.4
Verbal Attention	81	75–86	Low avg.	10	51/90	Lmtd.	Very difficult	5y3m	<K.0
LONG-TERM STORAGE	91	87–96	Low avg/ avg.	29	83/90	Lmtd./Avg.	Difficult	5y9m	K.3
Story Recall	100	95-104	Avg.	49	90/90	Avg.	Manageable	6y4m	K.9
Story Comprehension	85	77–92	Low avg.	16	73/90	Lmtd./Avg.	Difficult	4y11m	<K.0

RETRIEVAL FLUENCY	94	88–101	Avg.	35	88/90	Avg.	Manageable	6y5m	1.0
Semantic Word Retrieval	112	105–118	High avg.	78	93/90	Avg.	Manageable	8y4m	2.9
Phonemic Word Retrieval	88	73–102	Low avg.	20	81/90	Lmtd./Avg.	Difficult	5y7m	K.1
VISUAL PROCESSING	**101**	**95–106**	**Avg.**	**52**	**90/90**	**Avg.**	**Manageable**	**7y1m**	**1.7**
Spatial Relations	106	101–112	Avg.	67	94/90	Avg.	Manageable	8y0m	2.5
Block Rotation	93	85–101	Avg.	32	84/90	Avg.	Manageable	6y4m	K.9
PHONOLOGICAL AWARENESS	**84**	**80–88**	**Low avg.**	**14**	**45/90**	**Lmtd.**	**Very difficult**	**5y3m**	**<K.0**
Segmentation	83	77–89	Low avg.	13	51/90	Lmtd.	Very difficult	4y10m	<K.0
Sound Blending	87	83–91	Low avg.	19	39/90	Lmtd.	Very difficult	5y6m	K.1
[Nonsense Word Repetition]	89	77–101	Low avg.	23	77/90	Lmtd./Avg.	Difficult	5y5m	K.0
PHONOLOGICAL MANIPULATION.	**80**	**74–85**	**Low avg.**	**9**	**56/90**	**Lmtd.**	**Very difficult**	**5y2m**	**<K.0**
Sound Substitution	83	69–98	Low avg.	13	58/90	Lmtd.	Very difficult	5y2m	<K.0
Sound Deletion	81	69–93	Low avg.	10	54/90	Lmtd.	Very difficult	5y3m	<K.0
RAN–READING	72	61–84	Low	3	69/90	Lmtd./Avg.	Difficult	<4y0m	<K.0
Rapid Picture Naming	100	95–105	Avg.	51	90/90	Avg.	Manageable	7y1m	1.7
Rapid Letter Naming	70	51–89	Very low	2	56/90	Lmtd.	Very difficult	<4y0m	<K.0
Rapid Phoneme Naming	72	57–86	Low	3	48/90	Lmtd.	Very difficult	<4y0m	<K.0
[Rapid Number Naming]	100	98–102	Average	50	90/90	Avg.	Manageable	7y1m	1.7

(*Continued*)

CLUSTERS/Tests	Standard Score	SS Band (68%)	SS Classif.	PR	RPI	RPI Proficiency	RPI Implication	AE	GE
BASIC READING SKILLS	**81**	**78–84**	**Low avg.**	**10**	**14/90**	**Very Lmtd.**	**Ext. difficult**	**5y6m**	**K.1**
Word Attack	83	76–90	Low avg.	13	38/90	Lmtd.	Very difficult	5y7m	K.2
Letter-Word Identification	80	78–82	Low avg.	9	4/90	Very Lmtd.	Ext. difficult	5y6m	K.0
[Letter Writing Fluency]	69	66–73	Very low	2	3/90	Ext. Lmtd.	Virtually impossible	4y6m	<K.0
MATH CALCULATION	**110**	**107–113**	**Avg.**	**75**	**96/90**	**Avg./Adv.**	**Easy**	**7y9m**	**2.3**
Math Facts Fluency	115	112–119	High avg.	84	96/90	Avg./Adv.	Easy	8y3m	2.9
Calculation	105	101–109	Avg.	63	95/90	Avg./Adv.	Easy	7y6m	2.0
MATH PROBLEM-SOLVING	**87**	**82–91**	**Low avg.**	**19**	**71/90**	**Lmtd./Avg.**	**Difficult**	**6y1m**	**K.7**
Math Problem Identification	91	86–97	Avg.	28	79/90	Lmtd./Avg.	Difficult	6y4m	K.9
Applied Problems	85	79–91	Low avg.	16	60/90	Lmtd.	Very difficult	5y10m	K.4

Notes: Cluster names are in all capital letters. Bolded cluster names indicate that the standard score bands for the tests within the cluster overlap or are close enough to make the cluster score representative of the tests. Brackets indicate tests that are not part of the cluster but are related to the ability the cluster represents.

CASE STUDY #2: WILLIAM

Name: William Jones
Age: 11 years, 5 months
Grade: 5th
School: Wayside Elementary
Evaluator: John Garruto, D.Ed., NCSP

Psychoeducational Evaluation Report

This case report describes the current performance levels of William Jones, an 11-year-old student in fifth grade. William has been making gains in the areas of reading fluency, although he often becomes confused about what is happening in class. He experiences difficulty with math word problems but is a bit more successful with math operations. His writing skills are described by his teacher as "satisfactory."

Background

William is an outgoing and engaging 11-year-old. He lives with his parents, older brother, Brian (15), and younger sister, Susan (8). William is in fifth grade at Wayside Elementary School. The social history was conducted through an interview with William's mother, Mrs. Shirley Jones. According to Mrs. Jones, her pregnancy with William was unremarkable. No complications accompanied delivery, though William was delivered by cesarean section. Family history is positive for learning concerns on the maternal side and ADHD on the paternal side.

William produced basic words such as "mama" and "dada" at 4 months old and words like "no" at 8–9 months. William spoke in complete sentences at 2 years of age. He crawled at 6 months and walked at 11 months. William does not have a history of illnesses or injuries and is not on any medications. Mrs. Jones notes that William excels in art, works hard, and builds and maintains strong relationships; he makes friends easily and is well-liked by peers. Mrs. Jones did note that William sometimes struggles to complete tasks. She further noted that William seems to be able to read the words in his books but often does not understand what he reads. His progress is slow in math computation, but he has the most difficulty with math word problems. Ms. Jones remarked that she often has to clarify information that he does not understand.

A record review indicates that William entered kindergarten during the COVID-19 pandemic. He only attended school two days a week that fall and engaged in virtual learning for the other three days until December, when in-person classes resumed full-time. William has been noted to struggle in school. Although he does not have an IEP, he has been receiving academic intervention support in both reading and math for the last two years. Reading interventions have primarily targeted basic reading skills and reading fluency, while math interventions have targeted mastery of basic operations. Growth has been slow for William. He has recently been receiving more individualized interventions, including having word math problems read aloud, using place-value charts, and having information clarified. William has been increasing his reading fluency and is now reading 98 words per minute on grade-level material, up from 65 at the beginning of the school year. He passed both his vision and hearing screenings and has had seven absences or less each year.

An interview with William's teacher, Ms. Smith, notes that William can appear "with it." He might try to speak more knowingly about a topic that he truly understands. He often repeats things other students have said and sometimes says things that are off topic. When engaged in comprehension-like tasks, William will often relate his own experiences rather than respond to what was asked.

Observations

William was observed on March 15 during a math lesson on decimals. During the lesson, William appeared to be closely attending to the board and was writing down information. He was able to read the number 15.6 properly. The teacher then gave a math problem related to money. William did not understand what he was supposed to do, although he wrote down what the teacher said to write.

William readily joined the examiner for this evaluation. He was cooperative and smiled easily. He always answered the examiner's questions, although he rarely engaged in spontaneous conversation. William showed good attention. He sometimes misunderstood things that were asked by the examiner. Sometimes, when limits were tested and information was clarified, William performed more satisfactorily. It will be important to consider William's misunderstandings when interpreting the results.

Test Scores

William was administered several tests and clusters from the *Woodcock-Johnson V* (WJ V). The table below presents a summary of the obtained SSs and PRs. These scores describe William's standing in a distribution of peers who are the same age. The cluster names are in bold, and the tests that contribute to each cluster are listed below the cluster name in regular font. A full WJ V table of scores that includes grade equivalents, RPIs, and confidence intervals for the SSs and PRs is attached as an appendix to this report.

Cognitive abilities William's score on the GIA cluster, which measures his overall cognitive ability, fell in the below average range (SS = 84, PR = 15); however, it's important to interpret this information cautiously. First, William presents with a variety of strengths and weaknesses. Second, on many of the cognitive tests that are not included in the GIA cluster, William scored in the average range or higher. A more accurate picture of William's present performance levels can be obtained by looking at his various strengths and weaknesses.

Cluster/Test	SS	PR
General Intellectual Ability (GIA)	**84**	**15**
Oral Vocabulary	83	13
Matrices	92	30
Spatial Relations	91	28
Story Recall	75	5
Semantic Word Retrieval	100	49
Verbal Attention	86	17
Number-Pattern Matching	96	40
Verbal Analogies	84	15

Comprehension-Knowledge (Gc) William's overall Comprehension-Knowledge cluster score was also within the below average range (SS = 83, PR = 13). He showed below average ability in identifying synonyms and antonyms of various words. He also showed some word-finding difficulties. For example, on some of the words, he exclaimed, "I know what that is, but I can't think of another word for it!" William also performed below average when asked to complete verbal analogies. He performed better when the first two words were directly related. For example, if given an item such as: on is to off as in is to_____, he was more successful. However, if the first two were dependent on the second two, he struggled. For example, when given an item such as "boy is to girl, as son is to_____," he became confused. William demonstrated difficulty understanding what some questions were asking. This is discussed further in the math (particularly math problem-solving), language (particularly listening comprehension), and reading (particularly reading comprehension) sections of this report.

Cluster/Test	SS	PR
Comprehension-Knowledge (Gc)	**83**	**13**
Oral Vocabulary	83	13
Verbal Analogies	84	15

Fluid Reasoning (Gf) William's overall fluid reasoning, or nonverbal reasoning skills, were within the average range (SS = 98, PR = 44). William showed average inductive reasoning skills when he was shown a grid and asked to identify the pictures that logically fit within the grid. Similarly, William's general-sequential reasoning skills were average. Here, William was required to draw conclusions from given information. Overall, William showed relatively strong nonverbal reasoning abilities.

Cluster/Test	SS	PR
Fluid Reasoning (Gf)	**98**	**44**
Matrices	92	30
Analysis-Synthesis	101	52

Visual Processing (Gv) The visual processing tests measure the ability to visualize objects in space. William's score on the Visual Processing cluster fell in the average range (SS = 90, PR = 25). William showed age-appropriate skills when asked to identify the component pieces that comprised a figural puzzle. He also showed age-appropriate mental rotation skills when asked to identify which configurations of blocks looked identical when they were turned or rotated. Overall, William's average visual processing scores suggest he is able to visualize objects in space.

Cluster/Test	SS	PR
Visual Processing (Gv)	**90**	**25**
Spatial Relations	91	28
Block Rotation	91	28

Auditory Working Memory Capacity (Gwm) Auditory working memory represents one's ability to hold and manipulate information in short-term memory. One task required William to listen to a series of numbers and animals and then answer a question about the list (e.g., "What was the second animal in the list?"). William performed below average on this task. William seemed to misunderstand the directions that were given. He showed slightly stronger skills, within the average range, when given a series of digits and asked to recite them in reverse order. His stronger ability on the latter task may be related to the lower demand on auditory comprehension. Overall, this suggests that while William may be able to hold information in short-term memory, he may misunderstand when the directions and content become more complex. Taken together, his overall performance in the area of auditory working memory capacity was in the average range (SS = 90, PR = 25).

Cluster/Test	SS	PR
Auditory Working Memory Capacity (Gwm)	94	35
Numbers Reversed	101	52
Verbal Attention	86	17

Cognitive Processing Speed (Gs) Cognitive processing speed measures the ability to quickly process information, often involving quick visual-motor response tasks. William's slightly low average score on the Cognitive Processing Speed cluster (SS = 88, PR = 22) is suggestive of mild difficulty. When required to tap identical numbers as quickly as possible, William performed within the average range; however, he showed much more difficulty when asked to tap similar letters or letter pairs. William displayed high accuracy on this task, but it took him somewhat longer to scan the information and correctly determine the matching pairs; his score on the letter-matching task was in the low range.

Cluster/Test	SS	PR
Cognitive Processing Speed (Gs)	**88**	**22**
Letter-Pattern Matching	78	7
Number-Pattern Matching	96	40

Phonological Awareness (Ga) This cluster measures the ability to analyze phonological information within spoken words. On one task, William was given a word (such as "chocolate") and then asked to segment the sounds in the word (i.e., /ch/, /o/, /k/, /oa/, /l/, /i/, /t/). William's average ability is suggestive of appropriate skill in this area. This is an important precursor for spelling skills. William's blending skills were also within the average range. Here, William was presented with the various sounds of a word (e.g., /k/, /ow/, /n/, /t/) and then asked to blend the sounds together to form the word (e.g., "count"). Overall, William performed within the average range on the Phonological Awareness cluster (SS = 97, PR = 43), indicative of sufficient skill in blending and segmenting phonemes, important skills for decoding and encoding (spelling).

Cluster/Test	SS	PR
Phonological Awareness (Ga)	97	43
Sound Blending	101	53
Segmentation	95	37

Long-Term Storage (Gl) This area measures the ability to store new information in long-term memory. William performed well below average on the Long-Term Storage cluster (SS = 70, PR = 2); his score fell within the low range. He was administered two tests that comprised this cluster. The first required him to listen to a story and tell it back. The second required him to listen to a story and answer orally administered questions about the story. Both tasks required William to remember the information so that he could retell a story or answer comprehension questions. William's difficulty on these tests appeared less to do with memory and more to do with comprehension. On the story recall task, William seemed to misunderstand elements of the story; he remembered details about the story but was unable to contextualize the details appropriately. Similarly, William seemed able to remember the stories he heard on the story comprehension task, but he struggled to answer the associated comprehension questions. Again, he seemed to misunderstand either the point of the story or what the question was asking. Both of these test scores were well below average.

To get a better idea of William's long-term memory storage capacity, an ancillary test called Visual-Auditory Learning was administered. On this task, William was required to remember the names of various symbols that he learned throughout the test. William performed within the average range on this task (SS = 100, PR = 50). His score profile in this area suggests that he may be able to store new information in long-term memory but may misunderstand the information as the language becomes more complex.

Cluster/Test	SS	PR
Long-Term Storage (Gl)	**70**	**2**
Story Recall	75	5
Story Comprehension	71	3
Additional Test		
Visual-Auditory Learning	100	50

Retrieval Fluency (Gr) Retrieval fluency assesses how efficiently and quickly one can retrieve information from long-term memory. William performed within the average range on the Retrieval Fluency cluster (SS = 100, PR = 50). Here, William was required to name as many objects related to a category (e.g., clothing items) as he could within a minute. He was also asked to identify as many words as he could that begin with the same sound within a minute. The former task relates to his ability to fluently recall semantic information, while the latter relates to his ability to fluently recall phonemically based information. William's average ability is suggestive of age-appropriate skill in both areas. William was also administered a set of RAN tests, which require quick retrieval of information from long-term memory. William generally performed in the average range on these tests.

Cluster/Test	SS	PR
Retrieval Fluency (Gr)	100	50
Semantic Word Retrieval	100	49
Phonemic Word Retrieval	100	50

Academic achievement This section reviews William's overall academic achievement. The areas assessed were basic reading skills, reading fluency, reading comprehension, math calculation, math problem-solving, written expression, and listening comprehension.

Reading The reading tests that were administered assessed William's ability to read words, read fluently, and understand what he reads. William's overall basic reading skills were below average (SS = 85, PR = 16). He showed below average ability with word recognition. He was able to read various words, usually up to three syllables, but irregular words, such as "colonel," were more difficult for him. William's ability to decode nonsense words was slightly below average. He was able to decode a variety of nonsense words, including vowel/consonant (VC), CVC, CVCC, CCVC, VC-e, and words with vowel digraphs (e.g., "ai"); however, he struggled with nonsense words that included diphthongs (e.g., "oi") and multisyllabic words. While basic reading skills present with some challenges, he has been making steady progress in this area as indicated by his classroom progress monitoring.

Reading fluency describes both reading accuracy and rate. William's overall Reading Fluency cluster score was well below average (SS = 76, PR = 6). On one task, William was required to read relatively easy sentences and identify whether the sentences were true or not. The second task required William to quickly scan words and identify the two that go together. William made errors on both tasks, indicating difficulty with the comprehension components of the reading fluency tasks. Indeed, another fluency task, oral reading, focused primarily on accuracy. He performed significantly higher (SS = 88, PR = 22) on this task. Furthermore, William's weekly classroom progress monitoring reports note that he has been improving with the number of words per minute he is able to read. Thus, the relatively low Reading Fluency cluster score partially reflects his difficulty with comprehension rather than rate. For this reason, his Reading Fluency score should be interpreted cautiously.

Reading comprehension describes the ability to understand what is read. William was given two comprehension tests; he performed well below average on both. The first test required him to read a passage and provide a missing word, also known as a cloze task. He struggled to understand the passages and to identify words that logically belonged. The latter test required William to read a passage and then answer comprehension questions about the passage. When reading the longer passages, the subsequent questions often confused William. Overall, his Reading Comprehension cluster score was in the low range (SS = 72, PR = 3).

Cluster/Test	SS	PR
Brief Reading (Grw)	**79**	**8**
Letter-Word Identification	84	14
Passage Comprehension	73	4
Basic Reading Skills (Grw)	**85**	**16**
Letter-Word Identification	84	14
Word Attack	88	20
Reading Fluency (Grw)	**76**	**6**
Sentence Reading Fluency	75	5
Word Reading Fluency	81	10
Reading Comprehension (Grw)	**72**	**3**
Passage Comprehension	73	4
Paragraph Reading Comprehension	70	2
Additional Test		
Oral Reading	88	22

Mathematics The WJ V math tests measure the areas of math calculation skills (including computation and fluency) and problem-solving skills (i.e., setting up and solving word problems). William's Math Calculation Skills cluster score was in the low-average range (SS = 81, PR = 10). On an untimed test of math computation skills, William was able to add and subtract and could regroup when adding but struggled to regroup when subtracting. He often took the smaller number from the larger, regardless of the presentation format of the math problem. William was able to multiply a few single-digit numbers, although he could not multiply when the problems included more than one digit. William was not yet able to divide numbers. William's math fluency was also assessed via a timed test of simple math problems. He performed in the low-average range on this test. He was generally accurate, although he moved more slowly through the problems. Overall, math calculation is an area that presents some difficulty for him.

Math problem solving is an area of more significant impairment. His score on the Math Problem-Solving cluster was in the low range (SS = 72, PR = 3). When asked to solve various word problems, William performed well below average. He did not understand what some of the problems were asking him to do. He often would take the numbers that were in the problem and simply add them. William also struggled on a test where he was asked to identify what was missing or what was wrong with math problems that caused them to be unsolvable; he was not able to identify what information was wrong or was missing. His misunderstanding of the math problems seemed to stem from weaknesses in both math knowledge and language comprehension.

Cluster/Test	SS	PR
Brief Math (Gq)	**75**	**5**
Calculation	80	9
Applied Problems	71	3
Math Calculation Skills (Gq)	**81**	**10**
Math Facts Fluency	85	16
Calculation	80	9
Math Problem Solving (Gq)	**72**	**3**
Math Problem Identification	74	4
Applied Problems	71	3

Writing William was administered several tests to assess his overall basic writing skills as well as his ability to express ideas in writing. William's score on the Basic Writing Skills cluster was slightly below average (SS = 88, PR = 21). His spelling skills were slightly below average. His errors tended to be phonetically correct, which is consistent with his auditory segmentation skills, but revealed limits in his orthographic knowledge. An example would be William spelling "national" as "nashonul." William also performed slightly below average with regard to his ability to write dictated sentences. He showed minor errors with capitalization and punctuation, though he was usually accurate with transcribing the sentence provided by the examiner. Overall, basic writing skills, while slightly below average, are developing.

William showed proficiency with writing sentences, as reflected in his average score (SS = 98, PR = 46) on the Written Expression cluster. He performed in the average range on a sentence writing fluency task where he was required to take three words and put them together to form simple sentences within 5 minutes. He also showed average ability to write sentences in response to examiner-provided prompts. William did ask the examiner to repeat or explain a few of the prompts; the examiner reminded William that he could not further explain the prompts. Overall, writing presents as an area of relative strength for William.

Cluster/Test	SS	PR
Brief Writing (Grw)	**96**	**40**
Sentence Writing Accuracy	89	24
Written Language Samples	102	57
Written Expression (Grw)	**98**	**46**
Written Language Samples	102	57
Sentence Writing Fluency	96	40

Listening Comprehension William's overall listening comprehension skills as reflected by his score on the Listening Comprehension cluster (SS = 74, PR = 4) were well below average. When engaged in a cloze listening task, where William was required to identify a missing word from a sentence, William performed below average. Again, he seemed to misunderstand the main idea of some of the sentences. This performance is consistent with William's below average performance on the Story Comprehension test described earlier. Although not included in the composite, William was also administered a test that assessed his ability to follow multistep directions. William performed well below average on this test (SS = 72, PR = 3). When the information was concrete, William was able to follow up to three-step directions (e.g., "point to the dog, the cat, and then the mouse."). However, as the language became more complex, William struggled to understand the directions (e.g., "Point to the cat before you point to the mouse, but after you point to the dog"). Overall, tasks involving listening comprehension were a significant weakness for William.

Cluster/Test	SS	PR
Listening Comprehension (Gc)	74	4
Oral Comprehension	80	9
Story Comprehension	71	3
Additional Test		
Understanding Directions	72	3

Comparison procedures

Intra-Cognitive Comparisons The WJ V Intra-Cognitive comparison procedures compare how William performed in each cognitive area against how he was *predicted* to perform given his age and overall cognitive abilities. Within his cognitive abilities, William shows a relative weakness in the area of long-term storage (Gl). Given William's overall cognitive abilities, he was predicted to obtain an SS of 89. His actual SS was 70. Among his same-age peers with the same overall cognitive ability, only 4% of students would be expected to have a lower Long-Term Storage cluster score than William.

Target Cluster	Predicted SS	Obtained SS	Difference	*z* Score	PR	Interpretation at ±1.50 *SD*
Comprehension-Knowledge (Gc)	86	83	−3	−0.35	37	
Fluid Reasoning (Gf)	88	98	9	0.85	80	
Auditory Working Memory Capacity (Gwm)	89	94	6	0.56	71	
Cognitive Processing Speed (Gs)	90	88	−2	−0.16	44	
Retrieval Fluency (Gr)	89	100	11	0.91	82	
Long-Term Storage (Gl)	89	70	−18	−1.8	4	Weakness
Visual Processing (Gv)	88	90	2	0.28	61	
Phonological Awareness (Ga)	89	97	8	0.66	75	

Intra-Achievement Comparisons The Intra-Achievement Comparison procedures compare how William performed in each achievement area against how he was *predicted* to perform given his age and overall achievement. William's Reading Comprehension score was lower than expected, just barely missing the cutoff for significance at −1 *SD*. Among William's same-grade peers with similar overall achievement, 7% or fewer of the students would be expected to have a Reading Comprehension score as low as William's. This suggests that Reading Comprehension is a relative weakness for William.

Target Cluster	Predicted SS	Obtained SS	Difference	*z* Score	PR	Interpretation at ±1.50 *SD*
Basic Reading Skills	84	85	1	0.18	57	
Reading Comprehension	83	72	−11	−1.49	7	
Reading Fluency	89	76	−12	−1	16	

Target Cluster	Predicted SS	Obtained SS	Difference	*z* Score	PR	Interpretation at ±1.50 *SD*
Math Calculation Skills	84	81	−3	−0.34	37	
Math Problem Solving	84	72	−11	−1.33	9	
Basic Writing Skills	82	88	5	0.72	77	
Written Expression	84	98	14	1.32	91	

GIA/Achievement Comparisons The GIA/Achievement Comparison procedures assess whether any of William's achievement cluster scores are lower than expected, given his overall cognitive ability (measured by the GIA cluster score). Compared to his expected scores, William performed significantly lower in the areas of reading comprehension and math problem-solving. In both areas, only 6% of the population with the same overall cognitive ability would be expected to have reading comprehension and math problem-solving as low or lower than William's. While not significant, William's Listening Comprehension cluster score was also lower than expected.

Target Cluster	Predicted SS	Obtained SS	Difference	*z* Score	PR	Interpretation at ±1.50 *SD*
Listening Comprehension	90	74	−16	−1.38	8	
Basic Reading Skills	90	85	−5	−0.45	33	
Reading Comprehension	89	72	−17	−1.59	6	Significant (−)
Reading Fluency	89	76	−13	−1.17	12	
Math Calculation Skills	88	81	−7	−0.68	25	
Math Problem Solving	88	72	−15	−1.59	6	Significant (−)
Basic Writing Skills	89	88	−1	−0.12	45	
Written Expression	89	98	9	0.79	79	
Academic Skills	88	82	−6	−0.55	29	
Academic Fluency	88	82	−7	−0.61	27	
Academic Applications	87	82	−5	−0.54	30	

Overall Impressions

William is a student with various strengths and weaknesses. Cognitively, he shows good nonverbal reasoning, auditory working memory, retrieval fluency, and phonological awareness skills. He demonstrates some difficulty with background knowledge. While significant difficulty was noted with long-term memory storage, during testing this seemed more related to misunderstanding the stories he needed to remember rather than a failure to remember. He demonstrates difficulty with language comprehension. His relatively strong fluid reasoning skills may seem counterintuitive given his difficulty with comprehension; however, the visual processing tests required William to visually analyze information, and these skills appear to be intact.

Academically, William is performing at an age-appropriate level for overall writing skills. Math computation skills present as an area of some weakness. William demonstrates significant struggle with math problem solving, seemingly more due to the language of the math problems than to the operations themselves. Similarly, William is making progress with basic reading skills, though he is still performing below average in this area. His low reading fluency scores on the WJ V are likely an underestimate of his ability given the comprehension elements of those tasks as well as William's progress monitoring results in school. Finally, his listening comprehension skills are significantly below average. William often misunderstands what is asked of him. A review of this information is suggestive of significant language comprehension deficits, which manifest most significantly for William in the areas of listening comprehension, math problem-solving, and reading comprehension. Given the pattern of strengths (visual processing, retrieval fluency, phonological processing, fluid reasoning) and weaknesses (comprehension-knowledge and language comprehension), William's profile is consistent with that of a student with specific learning disabilities (SLDs) impacting the areas of listening comprehension, math problem solving, and reading comprehension.

Recommendations

1. Given a pattern of strengths (fluid reasoning, auditory working memory, retrieval fluency, phonological awareness) and weaknesses (comprehension-knowledge, long-term storage when it relates to comprehension) in tandem with related academic weaknesses in listening comprehension, math problem-solving, and reading comprehension, despite ongoing intervention, the IEP team may wish to consider William as a student with an SLD impacting the areas of listening comprehension, reading comprehension, and math problem solving.
2. Given his difficulties with language comprehension, a comprehensive speech/language evaluation is recommended.
3. As William may misunderstand information that is presented, checking for understanding will be important. After the provision of both verbal and written directions, ask William to tell you what he is supposed to do.
4. Given William's difficulty with comprehending lengthy instructions, keep directions short and repeat/clarify the directions as needed.
5. Given difficulties with math problem solving, make the abstract more concrete. Using manipulatives and representational drawings may help William to conceptualize the information.

6. Given difficulties with math problem solving, consider highlighting the important information and discussing with William what the problem is asking. It may help William to draw pictures or make diagrams.
7. Consider various strategies to help William with reading comprehension. One such strategy is "click or clunk," where a student self-monitors their understanding of reading and identifies those elements that are understood (click) and those that are not (clunk).
8. Incorporate activities in the classroom that will use William's strengths in nonverbal reasoning and visual processing, such as illustrating stories, solving mazes, and constructing objects with LEGO® sets or blocks.

Appendix: *Woodcock-Johnson V* Table of Scores

Cluster/Test	SS	SS 95% Confidence Band	PR	PR 95% Confidence Band	GE	RPI
General Intellectual Ability (GIA)	**84**	**80–88**	**15**	**10–22**	**G3.5**	**75/90**
Oral Vocabulary	83	74–92	13	4–30	G3.1	63/90
Matrices	92	83–101	30	13–54	G3.7	83/90
Spatial Relations	91	84–98	28	14–45	G3.0	78/90
Story Recall	75	63–87	5	1–19	G1.2	59/90
Semantic Word Retrieval	100	77–123	49	6–93	G5.8	90/90
Verbal Attention	86	79–93	17	8–32	G3.1	67/90
Number-Pattern Matching	96	94–99	40	34–47	G5.1	81/90
Verbal Analogies	84	73–95	15	4–38	G3.0	69/90
Gf-Gc Composite	**89**	**84–94**	**24**	**14–35**	**G3.9**	**79/90**
Matrices	92	83–101	30	13–54	G3.7	83/90
Analysis-Synthesis	101	95–106	52	39–66	G6.1	91/90
Oral Vocabulary	83	74–92	13	4–30	G3.1	63/90
Verbal Analogies	84	73–95	15	4–38	G3.0	69/90
Comprehension-Knowledge (Gc)	**83**	**76–91**	**13**	**6–27**	**G3.1**	**66/90**
Oral Vocabulary	83	74–92	13	4–30	G3.1	63/90
Verbal Analogies	84	73–95	15	4–38	G3.0	69/90
Fluid Reasoning (Gf)	**98**	**92–103**	**44**	**31–59**	**G5.2**	**88/90**

(Continued)

Cluster/Test	SS	SS 95% Confidence Band	PR	PR 95% Confidence Band	GE	RPI
Matrices	92	83–101	30	13–54	G3.7	83/90
Analysis-Synthesis	101	95–106	52	39–66	G6.1	91/90
Visual Processing (Gv)	**90**	**85–95**	**25**	**16–31**	**G2.9**	**/90**
Spatial Relations	91	84–98	28	14–45	G3.0	78/90
Block Rotation	91	77–104	28	22–34	G3.0	84/90
Cognitive Processing Speed (Gs)	**88**	**86–90**	**22**	**18–26**	**G3.7**	**49/90**
Letter-Pattern Matching	78	75–81	7	5–11	G2.1	18/90
Number-Pattern Matching	96	94–99	40	34–47	G5.1	81/90
Long-Term Storage (Gl)	**70**	**62–79**	**2**	**1–8**	**GK.9**	**54/90**
Story Recall	75	63–87	5	1–19	G1.2	59/90
Story Comprehension	71	61–81	3	<1–10	GK.6	49/90
Retrieval Fluency (Gr)	100	**85–115**	**50**	**16–85**	**G5.8**	**90/90**
Semantic Word Retrieval	100	77–123	49	6–93	G5.8	90/90
Phonemic Word Retrieval	100	82–118	50	14–89	G5.8	90/90
Auditory Working Memory Capacity (Gwm)	94	**88–100**	**35**	**30–40**	**G4.2**	**85/90**
Numbers Reversed	101	92–109	52	32–73	G6.1	91/90
Verbal Attention	86	79–93	17	8–32	G3.1	67/90
Phonological Awareness (Ga)	97	**92–103**	**43**	**29–58**	**G5.1**	**87/90**
Sound Blending	101	93–108	53	33–71	G6.1	91/90
Segmentation	95	88–102	37	22–55	G4.4	81/90
Cognitive Efficiency (CE)	**92**	**89–95**	**30**	**23–38**	**G4.4**	**75/90**
Verbal Attention	86	79–93	17	8–32	G3.1	67/90
Number-Pattern Matching	96	94–99	40	34–47	G5.1	81/90

Cluster/Test	SS	SS 95% Confidence Band	PR	PR 95% Confidence Band	GE	RPI
RAN–Math (Gs; Gr)	**92**	**86–98**	**30**	**17–45**	**G4.2**	**83/90**
Rapid Number Naming	99	94–103	46	34–58	G5.5	88/90
Rapid Quantity Naming	85	74–96	16	4–40	G2.5	75/90
Listening Comprehension (Gc)	74	**65–82**	**4**	**1–12**	**G1.7**	**55/90**
Oral Comprehension	80	68–91	9	2–28	G2.4	61/90
Story Comprehension	71	61–81	3	<1–10	GK.6	49/90
Brief Reading (Grw)	**79**	**74–85**	**8**	**4–15**	**G3.1**	**34/90**
Letter-Word Identification	84	78–89	14	7–23	G3.4	27/90
Passage Comprehension	73	63–84	4	1–15	G2.6	42/90
Basic Reading Skills (Grw)	**85**	**80–90**	**16**	**9–25**	**G3.4**	**46/90**
Letter-Word Identification	84	78–89	14	7–23	G3.4	27/90
Word Attack	88	79–96	20	8–41	G3.5	66/90
Reading Fluency (Grw)	**76**	**74–79**	**6**	**4–8**	**G2.1**	**12/90**
Sentence Reading Fluency	75	72–79	5	3–8	G1.4	5/90
Word Reading Fluency	81	77–85	10	6–16	G2.8	24/90
Reading Comprehension (Grw)	**72**	**66–78**	**3**	**1–7**	**G2.3**	**30/90**
Passage Comprehension	73	63–84	4	1–15	G2.6	42/90
Paragraph Reading Comprehension	70	64–76	2	1–6	G2.0	20/90
Brief Math (Gq)	**75**	**69–80**	**5**	**2–9**	**G2.7**	**31/90**
Calculation	80	73–87	9	4–20	G3.1	36/90
Applied Problems	71	64–78	3	1–7	G2.2	27/90
Math Calculation Skills (Gq)	**81**	**75–87**	**10**	**5–19**	**G3.2**	**55/90**

(*Continued*)

Cluster/Test	SS	SS 95% Confidence Band	PR	PR 95% Confidence Band	GE	RPI
Math Facts Fluency	85	76–94	16	6–35	G3.2	73/90
Calculation	80	73–87	9	4–20	G3.1	36/90
Math Problem Solving (Gq)	**72**	**67–78**	**3**	**1–7**	**G2.3**	**32/90**
Math Problem Identification	74	64–83	4	1–13	G2.3	37/90
Applied Problems	71	64–78	3	1–7	G2.2	27/90
Brief Writing (Grw)	**96**	**92–101**	**40**	**29–53**	**G5.1**	**86/90**
Sentence Writing Accuracy	89	84–95	24	15–37	G4.1	75/90
Written Language Samples	102	95–110	57	38–76	G6.5	92/90
Written Expression (Grw)	**98**	**93–104**	**46**	**33–60**	**G5.5**	**88/90**
Written Language Samples	102	95–110	57	38–76	G6.5	92/90
Sentence Writing Fluency	96	90–102	40	26–55	G5.1	82/90
Academic Skills/Brief Achievement (Grw; Gq)	**82**	**79–86**	**12**	**8–17**	**G3.6**	**37/90**
Letter-Word Identification	84	78–89	14	7–23	G3.4	27/90
Calculation	80	73–87	9	4–20	G3.1	36/90
Spelling	87	83–91	20	13–28	G4.1	51/90
Academic Fluency (Gs)	**82**	**78–86**	**11**	**7–17**	**G3.1**	**46/90**
Math Facts Fluency	85	76–94	16	6–35	G3.2	73/90
Sentence Reading Fluency	75	72–79	5	3–8	G1.4	5/90
Sentence Writing Fluency	96	90–102	40	26–55	G5.1	82/90
Academic Applications (Grw; Gq)	**82**	**77–87**	**12**	**6–20**	**G3.4**	**59/90**
Passage Comprehension	73	63–84	4	1–15	G2.6	42/90

Cluster/Test	SS	SS 95% Confidence Band	PR	PR 95% Confidence Band	GE	RPI
Applied Problems	71	64–78	3	1–7	G2.2	27/90
Written Language Samples	102	95–110	57	38–76	G6.5	92/90
Single Tests						
Visual-Auditory Learning	100	99–102	50	46–54	G5.8	90/90
Oral Reading	88	79–97	22	8–42	G3.7	64/90
Rapid Picture Naming	102	92–112	55	25–78	G6.7	92/90
Rapid Letter Naming	107	102–112	68	57–78	G7.9	95/90
Understanding Directions	72	60–84	3	<1–14	G1.4	43/90

CASE STUDY #3: VICTORIA

Psychoeducational Report

Name: Victoria Jennings
Age: 13
Grade: 7
Date of testing: March 14
Evaluator: Ed Schultz, Ph.D.

Reason for referral Victoria is a seventh-grade student attending Bluebonnet Middle School. Her teachers and parents are concerned about her performance in her English Language Arts (ELA) class, as she struggles with reading despite additional support. She is currently being served in the school's MTSS program. She was referred for testing to help determine the nature of her reading difficulties and whether or not special education services were warranted.

Sources of information

- Review of educational records and documentation from the MTSS team
- Parent Information Form (March12)
- School & Teacher Information Form (March12)
- Classroom observation (March13)
- *Woodcock-Johnson V Tests of Cognitive Abilities* (WJ V COG)
- *Woodcock-Johnson V Tests of Achievement* (WJ ACH)
- Selected tests from the *Woodcock-Johnson V Virtual Test Library* (WJ V VTL)

Educational history and current status Victoria was diagnosed with dyslexia, an SLD, in the spring semester of second grade. At this time, she was provided with an intensive phonics intervention that continued until the spring of her fifth-grade year. Upon completing the program, she was dismissed from special education and referred for Section 504 accommodations, including extra time, checks for understanding, and a seat near the teacher. See the Full and Individual Evaluation (FIE) in her school records for details. After dismissal from special education, she was able to meet standards in her ELA classroom and was approaching standards on her state tests in fifth and sixth grade.

Victoria is passing all classes this school year but requires support. She did not meet standards on the most recent state assessment in seventh grade and has failed two district benchmark assessments this school year. Victoria demonstrates strengths in both math and science and is described by her teacher as "hard-working and persistent," even with challenging tasks. Victoria uses her classroom accommodations and is provided general education support via the school's MTSS. She receives supplemental reading instruction three times a week for 30 minutes. The interventionist says that Victoria has "hit a wall" and seems to struggle as the reading demands increase.

Parent information Victoria lives with her mother, father, and two younger siblings. Her parents state that she is a well-behaved, responsible child. Victoria will occasionally complain and roll her eyes when asked to do her chores or stop watching videos, but she is compliant. They say she enjoys school but that reading "makes her tired." Victoria was proud that she "defeated" dyslexia in fifth grade and has never let her reading struggles get her down. Consistent with feedback from her teachers, her parents report that she is a motivated and hard-working student. Victoria met all of her developmental milestones at the appropriate ages. There is no family history of dyslexia.

Emotional and behavioral According to her parents and teachers, Victoria is a well-behaved, well-adjusted child. All of her teachers report that she is respectful to adults, gets along well with her peers in the classroom, and that she rarely, if ever, needs to be reminded to follow the classroom rules. During testing, Victoria was friendly and cooperative. She had good conversational skills, seemed to give her best effort, and persisted with items as they increased in difficulty.

Adaptive behavior Victoria has strong adaptive behavior skills. There are no concerns in this area.

Class observation This examiner observed Victoria in her ELA class for 30 minutes. The class was doing mini-presentations over a brief two-page essay they had written on "Tom Sawyer Today vs. 1840." Victoria's presentation was 5 minutes long and well-structured. She described a situation in which Tom Sawyer would explore abandoned buildings instead of caves. The teacher provided a copy of the essay for the examiner to analyze. She was also observed during her Tier 2 instruction for 20 minutes. She was working on "homework completion." Her Tier 2 instruction can be described as more focused on work completion and test preparation than targeted instruction.

School achievement data Victoria has passed all of her classes this instructional year with all A's except in ELA, where her grade is a C. She excels in math and science and does well in history and her electives. This year's NWEA Measures of Academic Progress (MAP) indicate well-developed math skills with the following scores: Fall 234 (69th percentile) and Spring 236 (69th percentile), indicating high achievement and average growth. Her reading MAP scores are considered "at-risk," as she obtained a 201 in the Fall (9th percentile) and the same score in the spring administration (201).

Her district-created benchmark testing, administered in the fall and spring semesters, yielded similar results. Her math was well-developed, but her reading was considered "at-risk." These benchmarks are designed to predict performance on the end-of-the-year state test. Since Victoria did not meet the minimum passing standard on the seventh-grade state test last year, the state requires 30 hours of accelerated instruction. The type of instruction is a local decision. This instruction is provided in her district as part of the MTSS program and through the tutoring center (before and after school). At this time, there is no structured data collection process. Victoria has, however, completed her 30 hours and continues to access these programs.

Victoria's teacher provided work samples from ELA from the most recent grading period. Several writing samples were analyzed. Overall, her written expression can be described as average. Her grammar was appropriate as well. Her writing did contain numerous spelling errors (e.g., busy, exercising, people), most likely related to her dyslexia. Her spelling may distract the reader (e.g., her teacher) from the well-developed themes, organization, and word choice. When her writing samples were compared to those of her peers and the state standards, she met or exceeded them. She also performed satisfactorily on the state test in this area. She is not exhibiting an SLD in written expression at this time based on the preponderance of data.

Work samples and state test data related to reading were also assessed. She struggles with inferencing, paraphrasing, summarizing, and getting the main idea. She is not making adequate progress toward state standards in this area.

Present levels of development Victoria's present levels of development were assessed by administering norm-referenced tests that measure cognitive abilities, oral language, and academic skills. During this assessment, she was administered the *Woodcock-Johnson V Tests of Cognitive Abilities* (WJ V COG) and the *Woodcock-Johnson V Tests of Achievement* (WJ V ACH), along with selected tests from the WJ V Virtual Test Library (WJ V VTL). These results were integrated with all the other collected data. One indicator of SLD is the presence of abilities and skills with significant variability, referred to as a pattern of strengths and weaknesses approach. These data are considered part of the preponderance of evidence when determining if a child meets the state criteria for an SLD.

The Core-Selective Evaluation Process (CSEP) was used for this evaluation. CSEP testing principles include starting with a well-defined core set of tests (WJ V COG, Tests 1–8) and then making further testing decisions selectively based on an analysis of the core set of tests. All tests were administered and scored according to the publisher's instructions. The table below contains her scores for the WJ V clusters, or groups of tests, as well as for the individual tests. The RPI provides an estimate of Victoria's likelihood of success with similar material that a typical same-age peer would be 90% successful on. The standard score and

PR scores describe Victoria's relative standing in a group of her same-age peers. The test scores were analyzed and integrated with other data, and a task demand analysis was performed to gain insight and understanding into Victoria's reading struggles.

WJ V test results

WJ V Cognitive Clusters and Tests	Relative Proficiency Index	Standard Score (95% Confidence Band)	Standard Score Description	Percentile Rank (95% Confidence Band)
General Intellectual Ability (GIA)	87/90	96 (91–101)	Average	40 (28–54)
Oral Vocabulary	83/90	94 (84–104)	Average	34 (14–61)
Matrices	84/90	93 (79–108)	Average	32 (8–74)
Spatial Relations	66/90	85 (75–96)	Low average	16 (5–39)
Story Recall	83/90	92 (83–100)	Average	29 (12–51)
Semantic Word Retrieval	94/90	120 (110–130)	High average	91 (76–98)
Verbal Attention	71/90	88 (75–100)	Low average	20 (5–50)
Number-Pattern Matching	98/90	107 (101–112)	Average	67 (53–78)
Verbal Analogies	90/90	100 (88–112)	Average	50 (21–81)
Comprehension-Knowledge (Gc)	87/90	96 (88–104)	Average	41 (22–63)
Oral Vocabulary	83/90	94 (84–104)	Average	34 (14–61)
Verbal Analogies	90/90	100 (88–112)	Average	50 (21–81)
Long-Term Storage (Gl)	72/90	82 (74–90)	Low average	12 (4–26)
Story Recall	83/90	92 (83–100)	Average	29 (12–51)
Story Comprehension	58/90	76 (64–88)	Low	6 (1–22)

WJ V Achievement Clusters and Tests	Relative Proficiency Index	Standard Score (95% Confidence Band)	Standard Score Description	Percentile Rank (95% Confidence Band)
Listening Comprehension (Gc)	59/90	76 (66–85)	Low	5 (1–16)
Oral Comprehension	60/90	79 (66–91)	Low	8 (1–28)
Story Comprehension	58/90	76 (64–88)	Low	6 (1–22)

WJ V Cognitive Clusters and Tests	Relative Proficiency Index	Standard Score (95% Confidence Band)	Standard Score Description	Percentile Rank (95% Confidence Band)
Oral Expression (Gc; Gl)	88/90	98 (88–108)	Average	44 (22–71)
Picture Vocabulary	81/90	92(81–104)	Average	30 (10–60)
Oral Language Sample	93/90	106 (92–120)	Average	66 (31–91)
Vocabulary (Gc)	82/90	93 (84–101)	Average	31 (15–52)
Picture Vocabulary	81/90	92(81–104)	Average	30 (10–60)
Academic Vocabulary	83/90	93 (82–104)	Average	32 (11–62)
Basic Reading Skills (Grw)	64/90	89 (84–94)	Low average	23 (15–34)
Letter-Word Identification	62/90	91 (85–97)	Average	27 (15–42)
Word Attack	65/90	86 (79–83)	Average	17 (8–31)
Reading Fluency (Grw)	57/90	91 (87–94)	Average	27 (20–34)
Sentence Reading Fluency	68/90	94 (90–97)	Average	34 (26–43)
Word Reading Fluency	46/90	88 (83–93)	Low average	21 (13–31)
Reading Comprehension (Grw)	39/90	74 (67–82)	Low	4 (1–11)
Passage Compre-hension	56/90	78 (66–91)	Low	7 (1–27)
Paragraph Reading Comp.	24/90	70 (61–79)	Low	2 (<1–8)

WJ V Virtual Test Library Clusters and Tests	Relative Proficiency Index	Standard Score(95% Confidence Band)	Standard Score Description	Percentile Rank(95% Confidence Band)
Auditory Memory Span	34/90	74 (66–83)	Low	4 (1–13)
Memory for Words	18/90	70 (58–82)	Low	2 (<1–11)
Sentence Repetition	56/90	83 (72–95)	Low average	13 (3–37)

Summary of test results Victoria's GIA score of 96 is in the average range and is considered a fair estimate of her cognitive abilities. This is supported by Victoria's ability to think, reason, and learn in academic areas such as math and science. Some aspects of her intellectual development are considered weaknesses and inhibit her reading comprehension.

Reading According to the test data, Victoria struggles with several aspects of reading. To be a skilled reader and meet grade-level expectations, a student must be able to recognize words, read words fluently, and comprehend what they read. Overall, her results indicate a pattern of strengths and weaknesses in areas related to reading. Basic reading skills include phonological awareness, recognizing sight words, and decoding. Victoria's basic reading skills are low to low average. Her test scores related to basic reading indicate that she has some difficulties decoding words. The Letter-Word Identification (SS = 91; RPI = 64/90) and Word Attack (SS = 86; RPI = 65/90) tests yielded a composite standard score of 89 (84–94; RPI = 64/90). These standard scores are in the low to low average range, and her RPI scores suggest that she struggles with pronouncing words when compared to her typical peers, which may contribute to her reading fluency and comprehension difficulties.

Reading fluency is defined as the ability to read words with automaticity, accuracy, and prosody. Victoria's reading fluency skills range from low to low average. Reading fluently depends on proficiency in word decoding and recognition of sight words. Tests measuring reading fluency include Sentence Reading Fluency (SS = 94; RPI = 68/90) and Word Reading Fluency (SS = 88; RPI = 46/90). Despite achieving average standard scores on these assessments, the RPI score for the Reading Fluency composite (57/90) indicates that she will find grade-level reading tasks quite challenging. This finding is supported by parent reports indicating that Victoria becomes fatigued while reading. Victoria's history of dyslexia and the increasing complexity of text demands require her to expend significant mental energy to decode words, retain them in her working memory, read at a sufficient rate to hold information in her auditory memory, and derive meaning. Underlying cognitive abilities (Gr; Semantic Word Retrieval; SS = 120) and (Gs; Number-Pattern Matching; SS = 107) related to reading fluency fall within the high average to average range, suggesting her fluency difficulties are primarily linked to decoding rather than these specific cognitive processes.

Reading comprehension is the ability to understand and interpret what is read and is facilitated by basic reading skills, fluency, and oral language skills. Victoria's reading comprehension skills were below average, as evidenced by her low scores on both the Passage Comprehension (SS = 78; RPI = 56/90) and Paragraph Reading Comprehension (SS = 70; RPI = 24/90) tests. These findings align with multiple other sources of achievement data for Victoria, including MAP scores, local benchmarks, classroom data, and state assessments.

Cognitive processes The underlying cognitive processes and linguistic skills related to reading comprehension were assessed to help understand and explain Victoria's reading difficulties. Oral language skills contribute to written language skills. Overall, her expressive language skills were more developed than her listening comprehension skills. She obtained a standard score of 98 (RPI = 88/98) on Oral Expression and a standard score of 76 (RPI = 59/90) on Listening Comprehension. Both reading comprehension and listening comprehension require Victoria to understand the syntactical and semantic features of language, make inferences and predictions, and reason with words. Listening comprehension also requires auditory working memory and learning efficiency. Since Victoria's vocabulary skills are average, as evidenced by the Oral Vocabulary (SS = 94) and Picture Vocabulary (SS = 92) test scores, her comprehension problems are most likely related to weaknesses in specific cognitive processes, described next.

Two key cognitive processing areas essential for reading comprehension are learning efficiency, or long-term storage (Gl), and auditory memory span (Gwm). Both processes were evaluated with below average standard scores of 82 and 74, respectively. Victoria's deficits in these cognitive processes and her listening comprehension challenges are evident in both the test environment and the classroom. While Victoria exhibited listening comprehension weaknesses during her testing, these issues do not appear to manifest in the school environment, as she understands and follows all instructions in classes except ELA. She also received a low score on a visual-spatial task (Spatial Relations), but this does not seem to present as a weakness in the classroom. These scores, combined with the academic achievement data, are consistent with a student who has an SLD in reading comprehension. In addition, Victoria does have dyslexia, but years of instructional intervention have improved her basic reading skills.

Ability/Achievement Comparisons When compared to her expected scores in listening comprehension and reading comprehension, given her overall GIA score, her actual scores were significantly lower. Only 3 out of 100 students with the same GIA score would have a Listening Comprehension cluster score as low as Victoria's, and only 1 out of 100 students would have a Reading Comprehension cluster score as low as Victoria's.

General Intellectual Ability (GIA)/ Achievement	Earned SS	Predicted SS	Difference	*z* Score	PR (Base Rate)	Interpretation
Listening Comprehension	76	98	−22	−1.85	3	SIGNIFICANT (−)
Oral Expression	98	98	0	0.02	51	
Basic Reading Skills	89	98	−9	−0.79	22	
Reading Comprehension	74	98	−24	−2.18	1	SIGNIFICANT (−)
Reading Fluency	91	98	−7	−0.65	26	

When compared to her expected score in Reading Comprehension given her overall Oral Language ability, her actual score is also lower. Only 10 out of 100 students with the same Oral Language score would have a Reading Comprehension score as low as Victoria's.

Oral Language/ Achievement	Earned SS	Predicted SS	Difference	z Score	PR (Base Rate)	Interpretation
Basic Reading Skills	89	91	−2	−0.20	42	
Reading Comprehension	74	88	−14	−1.30	10	SIGNIFICANT (–)
Reading Fluency	91	92	−2	−0.12	45	

Exclusionary factors Victoria does not have visual, hearing, or motor disabilities, nor is there evidence of an intellectual disability or emotional disturbance. Victoria enjoys a supportive environment with no socioeconomic disadvantages. Her English language skills are well-developed, and she has received appropriate instruction in both reading and math. Overall, these factors do not interfere with her academic success.

Assistive technology Victoria can access general education without the use of assistive technology.

Conclusions In this state, to meet the criteria for an SLD, four conditions must be met:

1. **The student must be provided with learning experiences and instructions appropriate for the student's age, or state-approved standards are not achieved adequately.**
   Victoria has been provided appropriate instruction this school year and in prior school years, has received specially designed instruction in the past, and has been constantly monitored. Comparison data also indicated that the rest of the class, on multiple measures, performed at much higher rates, suggesting she was in an environment conducive to learning.
2. **The student received appropriate instruction in reading and math, evidenced by data and data-based documentation of repeated assessments at regular intervals, reflecting formal evaluation during instruction.**
   Victoria's progress has been monitored throughout the school year as evidenced by progress reports, grade averages over time, MAP data, and district benchmarks.
3. **Exclusionary factors were considered and ruled out as the primary cause of the learning difficulty.**
   All exclusionary factors were considered and ruled out as the primary cause of her learning difficulties.
4. **The student exhibits a pattern of strengths and weaknesses in performance, achievement, or both, relative to age, state-approved grade-level standards, or intellectual development, that the group determines to be relevant to the identification of an SLD, using appropriate assessments, consistent with §§ 300.304 and 300.305.**
   Victoria exhibits a pattern of strengths and weaknesses in both performance and achievement. She has achievement strengths in math, science, and oral expression and weaknesses in reading and spelling. Her performance data indicate strengths

in her quantitative reasoning, perceptual reasoning, processing speed, and ability to rapidly retrieve previously learned information. Her weaknesses in auditory working memory, listening comprehension, and learning efficiency contribute to her difficulty in reading comprehension, as well as her failure to meet grade-level reading standards. These findings, along with all other collected data, suggest that Victoria has an SLD in Reading Comprehension.

Recommendations

1. The IEP team should consider changing Victoria from a 504 Plan to an IEP. She needs to receive specially designed instruction to improve her basic reading skills and reading comprehension.
2. Victoria should be taught specific reading comprehension strategies, such as:
   a. Monitoring comprehension
   b. Using graphic and semantic organizers
   c. Question–answer relationship strategy
   d. Generating questions
   e. Summarizing and paraphrasing

   Victoria will benefit from learning and practicing these types of strategies.
3. Encourage Victoria to read texts at her instructional level to build fluency.
4. Provide Victoria with instruction in both decoding and spelling irregular and multisyllabic words.
5. Continue providing Victoria with her accommodations (e.g., extra time, checking for understanding).

CASE STUDY #4: SOPHIA

Psychoeducational Evaluation

Student Name: Sophia Perez	**Parent/Guardian:** Stephanie and George Perez
Date of Birth: September 8	**Parent Preferred Language:** English
Age at time of testing: 14 years, 6 months	**Primary Language:** English
Grade Level: 8	**Language of Instruction:** English
School: Rosa Parks School	**Examiner:** Martha Youman, Ph.D.

Date of Report: March 8
Assessment Type: Triennial Psychoeducational Evaluation
Examination Dates: February 3, 6, and 19

Reason for referral Sophia was referred for this assessment as part of the triennial review of her Individualized Education Plan (IEP). The Individuals with Disabilities Education Act (IDEA) requires that students receiving special education services be re-evaluated every three years to determine continued eligibility for placement, services, accommodations, and interventions.

The objectives of this evaluation are to:

1. Determine Sophia's learning and processing abilities;
2. Identify her academic strengths and weaknesses;
3. Review her continued eligibility for special education services; and
4. Provide assessment information for the Individualized Education Program (IEP) Team.

The information will be presented to the IEP team to plan how to best support Sophia in school.

Evaluation methods

Background information

- Family information provided by Sophia
- Early development and health history provided by S. Perez
- Cultural and linguistic factors
- Review of school records
- Review of previous evaluations

Interviews and observations

- Parent interviews/questionnaires
- Teacher interview/questionnaires
- Student interview
- Behavioral observations

Cognitive and processing measures

- *Woodcock-Johnson V Tests of Cognitive Abilities* (WJ V COG)
- *Woodcock-Johnson V Virtual Test Library* (WJ V VTL)

Academic achievement assessment

Woodcock-Johnson V Tests of Achievement (WJ V ACH)

Background information Sophia is a 14-year-old, eighth-grade student currently attending the Rosa Parks School. She lives with her parents and her brother, Luca (21). For fun, Sophia enjoys swimming and currently practices three days per week with her team. At school, Sophia enjoys the social aspects the most, so recess and lunch are her favorite periods. Writing is the most difficult subject for Sophia. Short-term goals for Sophia include starting to save money to buy a car and finishing reading three books by the summer. Long-term goals for Sophia include attending college and having a career working with children. Those who know Sophia well describe her as caring and interested in others. She is organized, creative, responsible, and a good friend and leader.

Medical and developmental background Sophia's mother reports that she had a healthy, full-term pregnancy and an uncomplicated birth. Sophia's developmental milestones were met at the expected rate. She was diagnosed with vision tracking difficulties at the age of 6 and requires corrective glasses for reading. No hearing issues were reported.

Linguistic background Sophia was born in the United States and has lived in an English-speaking environment her entire life. All academic instruction has been provided in English. For this evaluation, Sophia demonstrated knowledge and understanding of English, and this was the only language used for this assessment.

Educational history Sophia attended daycare and preschool prior to enrolling in Havens Elementary School for Transitional Kindergarten at age 5. She attended Beach Elementary School in the Sun Valley Unified School District from Kindergarten through the fifth grade, followed by sixth grade at Sun Valley Middle School. In the seventh grade, Sophia transferred to Rosa Parks School in San Rafael, where she is currently in the eighth grade.

Sophia has consistently experienced difficulties with reading and writing throughout her time in school. An initial psychoeducational evaluation completed in the second grade revealed below average phonological processing skills and well below average RAN abilities. It was determined at that time that Sophia met eligibility criteria under the category of SLD and that her learning profile was consistent with dyslexia. During her triennial evaluation (January 2022), Sophia continued to meet SLD eligibility criteria due to well below average RAN performance and her slow reading rate.

Behavioral observations Classroom observation–science Sophia was observed during her eighth-grade science period at the Rosa Parks School. Overall, she followed along with the lesson, participating in all activities completed. Sophia appeared comfortable and at ease in the classroom and remained focused and engaged, although she appeared to be more passively listening than actively participating.

Behavioral observations during assessment Sophia was evaluated at her school in a quiet and nondistracting environment. Rapport was easily established by engaging Sophia in conversation about her hobbies, favorite subjects at school, and her family. Sophia had a positive attitude and seemed to try very hard to complete all portions of the assessment. She indicated that she enjoyed most of the activities completed for the assessment and that she felt she tried her hardest. Sophia's behavior during the assessment was typical for her age and developmental level.

Assessment results Cognitive test results In order to determine current cognitive functioning as well as processing skills in areas that relate to learning, Sophia was administered several tests from the *Woodcock-Johnson V Test of Cognitive Abilities* (WJ V COG) and the *Woodcock-Johnson V Virtual Test Library* (WJ V VTL). The WJ V was used for the purpose of: (a) establishing present cognitive levels, (b) determining strengths and weaknesses among abilities, (c) comparing performance to age or grade peers, (d) exploring eligibility for special programs, (e) monitoring educational progress across the school years, (f) investigating the effectiveness of curricula, and (g) assisting with rationales for recommendations that propose specific curricular adaptations and modifications. The tests within the WJ V COG and WJ V VTL are organized into groups of two or more, called *clusters*, for interpretive purposes. Cluster scores are generally more reliable than individual test scores and are useful for interpreting both within-ability strengths and weaknesses and between-ability discrepancies. A cluster standard score (SS) can range from 40 to 160, with scores from 90 to 110 considered average. These test scores provide a snapshot of Sophia's current level of intellectual development. When these scores are used as part of a comprehensive evaluation, they contribute to an understanding of her current strengths and any needs that can be addressed. Below is a table that describes how the WJ V scores are interpreted.

Woodcock-Johnson V Score Interpretation

Standard Score	Percentile Rank	Verbal Label
131 and above	98–>99	Very superior
121–130	92–97	Superior
111–120	76–91	High average
90–110	25–75	Average
80–89	9–24	Low average
70–79	3–8	Low
69 and below	<1–2	Very low

Sophia completed testing in several areas of cognitive processing. These tests measure how well an individual understands, reasons with, and uses different types of information. Below is a summary of testing completed with Sophia, beginning with an estimate of her overall cognitive abilities, followed by a more in-depth analysis of specific areas that relate to her learning and history of challenges.

Test	Broad Ability	ClusterScore	Percentile Rank	Verbal Label
General Intellectual Ability	**GIA**	**99 (95–103)**	**47**	**Average**
Oral Vocabulary	Gc	105 (100–110)	63	Average
Matrices	Gf	112 (104–120)	79	High average
Spatial Relations	Gv	106 (98–114)	66	Average
Story Recall	Gl	94 (86–102)	46	Average
Semantic Word Retrieval	Gr	100 (93–107)	50	Average
Verbal Attention	Gwm	102 (95–109)	55	Average
Number-Pattern Matching	Gf	101 (91–111)	53	Average
Verbal Analogies	Gc, Gf	100 (92–108)	50	Average

Based on information from the WJ V, Sophia's overall cognitive abilities are in the average range (GIA; SS = 99) and the same as or above 47% of her peers. Generally speaking, Sophia demonstrates the ability to perform at the level of individuals her age in activities that involve cognitive demands. Below is a more in-depth analysis of Sophia's processing abilities.

Comprehension-Knowledge (Gc). Comprehension knowledge refers to the depth and breadth of knowledge and skills that are valued by one's culture. This area includes vocabulary, general knowledge on a variety of topics, verbal reasoning, and the ability to use language effectively. Low comprehension knowledge impacts academic achievement primarily in reading comprehension and written expression and becomes increasingly important with age. Sophia's Comprehension-Knowledge score was within the average range.

Comprehension Knowledge (Gc)			
Test	Task Demands	Score	Verbal Label
Oral Vocabulary	Measures oral vocabulary. The test consists of two subtests: Synonyms and Antonyms. Requires providing a synonym or antonym for a word presented orally and on the tablet screen.	105 (100–110)	Average
Verbal Analogies	Measures oral vocabulary and syllogistic (i.e., inductive and deductive) reasoning. Requires orally reading an incomplete verbal analogy (e.g., *A* is to *B* as *C* is to . . .) and then saying a word to complete the verbal analogy.	100 (92–108)	Average
Comprehension-Knowledge cluster score: SS = 103 (97–108); 58th percentile			

Fluid Reasoning (Gf). Fluid reasoning refers to one's ability to solve novel or unfamiliar problems using logic skills such as induction and sequential reasoning. This area includes forming and recognizing concepts, identifying relationships, and reorganizing information. Fluid reasoning often impacts academic achievement in the areas of reading comprehension, math reasoning, and writing. Sophia obtained scores within the average and high average ranges on tests that measure fluid reasoning.

Fluid Reasoning (Gf)			
Test	Task Demands	Score	Verbal Label
Matrices	Measures inductive reasoning. Requires inducing a rule and deducing which among four options best completes the rule-based pattern in a figural matrix. Early items contain 2 × 2 matrices; later items contain 3 × 3 matrices.	112 (104–120)	High average

Fluid Reasoning (Gf)			
Test	Task Demands	Score	Verbal Label
Analysis-Synthesis	Measures deductive reasoning. Requires learning to use a key containing colored squares to solve puzzles and then using deductive reasoning to solve each puzzle and name the missing color(s). With the exception of the last several items, immediate feedback is provided for both correct and incorrect answers.	100 (92–108)	Average
Fluid Reasoning cluster score: SS = 107 (102–112); 68th percentile			

Auditory Working Memory Capacity (Gwm). Working memory capacity refers to the ability to maintain information in memory and manipulate the information. It includes remembering information in the exact sequence presented as well as reordering or manipulating it. Working Memory Capacity often impacts many areas of academic achievement, such as following directions, understanding long passages, decoding, and solving math problems. Sophia's short-term working memory is currently within the average range.

Auditory Working Memory Capacity (Gwm)			
Test	Task Demands	Score	Verbal Label
Verbal Attention	Measures attentional control and auditory working memory. Requires hearing a series of intermingled digits and animals presented from an audio recording and then answering a specific question about the sequence, such as, "Tell me the animal that came before five."	102 (95–109)	Average
Numbers Reversed	Measures attentional control and auditory working memory. Requires hearing a sequence of numbers from an audio recording and then saying the numbers in reverse order.	105 (95–115)	Average
Auditory Working Memory Capacity cluster score: SS = 104 (99–109); 61st percentile			

Long-Term Storage (Gl). Long-term storage refers to the ability to learn and store new information over time. It can impact almost all areas of academic achievement, as this deficit will lead to a tendency to lose information soon after it is taught. On tests of long-term storage, Sophia obtained scores within the average range.

Long-Term Storage (Gl)			
Test	Task Demands	Score	Verbal Label
Story Recall	Measures meaningful (i.e., narrative) memory and retrieval. Requires listening to short stories from an audio recording and then retelling the stories with as much detail as possible.	94 (86–102)	Average
Story Comprehension	Measures meaningful (i.e., narrative) memory and retrieval. Requires listening to short stories from an audio recording and then answering story-specific comprehension questions read orally by the examiner.	102 (95–109)	Average
Long-Term Storage cluster score: SS = 100 (95–105); 50th percentile			

Phonological Awareness (Ga). Phonological awareness refers to the abilities to hear phonemes, blend sounds into words, and segment words into parts. Phonological awareness is particularly important for the acquisition of basic reading skills and spelling. Sophia obtained scores within the average range on tests of phonological awareness.

WJ V VTL Phonological Awareness (Ga)			
Test	Task Demands	Score	Verbal Label
Segmentation	Requires listening to whole words and then breaking them into parts, including syllables and phonemes.	90 (82–98)	Average
Sound Blending	Measures phonological processing. Requires listening to a series of phonemes or syllables presented and blending them together to form a whole word.	103 (95–111)	Average
Phonological Awareness cluster score: SS = 96 (90–102); 39th percentile			

Visual Processing (Gv). Visual processing refers to one's ability to use mental imagery to solve problems often involving nonlinguistic images, such as shapes and patterns. Visual processing may impact many areas of learning, such as certain areas of math (e.g., geometry, trigonometry, or interpreting a graph). In tests that measure visual processing, Sophia obtained scores within normal limits.

Visual Processing (Gv)			
Test	Task Demands	Score	Verbal Label
Block Rotation	Measures visual-mental rotation processes. Requires determining which two, from among five options, 3-dimensional block figures match the figure shown in the key.	111 (104–118)	High average
Spatial Relations	Measures visualization and mental rotation processes. Requires determining which two or three 2-dimensional puzzle pieces, from among six options, fit together to form the shape shown in the key.	106 (98–114)	Average
Visual Processing cluster score: SS = 110 (105–115); 75th percentile			

Cognitive Processing Speed (Gs). Processing speed refers to one's ability to perform simple and repetitive cognitive tasks quickly and efficiently. It likely impacts academic achievement in many areas, as individuals with deficits in this area may take longer to complete tasks and/or to process information. Sophia's processing speed scores were within the average range.

Cognitive Processing Speed (Gs)			
Test	Task Demands	Score	Verbal Label
Number-Pattern Matching	Measures processing speed (timed 3 minutes). Requires tapping pairs of identical 1- to 3-digit numbers among rows of six numbers	101 (91–111)	Average
Letter-Pattern Matching	Measures processing speed (timed 3 minutes). Requires tapping pairs of identical letters and letter patterns among rows of six	109 (102–116)	Average
Symbol Inhibition (single test; does not contribute to Cognitive Processing Speed cluster score)	Measures processing speed (timed 3 minutes). Requires tapping successive colored shapes in a row of shapes, avoiding the shape(s) that are identical to the shape(s) shown in the key at the top of the screen. The task becomes more complex as additional shapes are added to the key.	110 (105–115)	Average
Cognitive Processing Speed cluster score: SS = 107 (102–112); 68th percentile			

Retrieval Fluency (Gr). Retrieval Fluency refers to the rate and fluency at which an individual can access known information in memory. It can impact almost all areas of academic achievement, as this deficit will lead to a tendency to take longer to access well-known information. Often, individuals with deficits in Retrieval Fluency have lower reading fluency and math facts fluency. Historically, Sophia has demonstrated a significant deficit on tests of Retrieval Fluency. To obtain an estimate of her present skills in this area, Sophia completed two retrieval fluency tests from the WJ V COG, as well as an additional test from the WJ V VTL, in order to gain a more in-depth understanding of her retrieval fluency challenges. Sophia scored in the average range when asked to provide words to fit into a category. In contrast, her score was in the very low range when she was asked to provide words that began with a specific phoneme. Her cluster score for Retrieval Fluency (SS = 78) should be interpreted with caution due to the large difference between the two test scores that comprise the cluster.

Retrieval Fluency (Gr)—WJ V COG

Test	Task Demands	Score	Verbal Label
Semantic Word Retrieval	Measures the rate and fluency of accessing information stored in long-term memory (four different trials of 1 minute). Requires saying as many words as possible that fit into the respective category (things to eat or drink, names of people, animals, and things to wear).	100 (93–107)	Average
Phonemic Word Retrieval	Measures the rate and fluency of accessing information stored in long-term memory (four different trials of 1 minute). Requires saying as many words as possible that begin with a different initial sound.	67 (57–77)	Low
Composite score: SS = 78 (72–84); 7th percentile			

On the Phonemic Retrieval Fluency cluster, Sophia's scores were very low and low, suggesting her difficulty is primarily with tasks requiring the retrieval of phonemes rather than the retrieval of words to fit semantic categories.

Phonemic Retrieval Fluency (Gr)—WJ V COG and WJ V VTL

Test	Task Demands	Score	Verbal Label
Phonemic Word Retrieval	Measures the rate and fluency of accessing information stored in long-term memory (four different trials of 1 minute). Requires saying as many words as possible that begin with a different initial sound.	67 (57–77)	Very low

Phonemic Retrieval Fluency (Gr)—WJ V COG and WJ V VTL			
Test	Task Demands	Score	Verbal Label
Rapid Phoneme Naming	Measures processing speed and speed of picture naming, a narrow ability of processing speed. Requires naming single pictures presented in successive rows. There is a 1-minute time limit.	75 (65–85)	Low
Composite Score: SS = 69 (63–75); 1st percentile			

WJ V VTL RAN–Reading			
Test	Task Demands	Score	Verbal Label
Rapid Picture Naming	Measures processing speed and speed of picture naming, a narrow ability of processing speed. Requires naming single pictures presented in successive rows. There is a 1-minute time limit.	75 (70–80)	Low
Rapid Letter Naming	Measures processing speed and speed of letter retrieval, a narrow ability of processing speed. Requires naming single letters presented in successive rows. There is a 1-minute time limit.	70 (63–77)	Low
Rapid Phoneme Naming	Measures processing speed, naming facility, and auditory processing (timed for 1 minute). Requires pronouncing phonemes (e.g., /m/) for single letters (graphemes) presented in successive rows.	75 (65–85)	Low
Composite score: SS = 67 (61–73); 1st percentile			

Summary of cognitive abilities Sophia demonstrates average overall cognitive abilities as indicated by her GIA score (SS = 99; 47th percentile). A more in-depth analysis of her processing profile provides evidence of average skills in most areas of processing with a relative strength in visual-spatial thinking (Gv; SS = 110; 75th percentile). While most areas of processing for Sophia are in the average range, she demonstrated significant relative weaknesses in naming words that begin with a specific letter (i.e., Phonemic Word Retrieval; SS = 67) and naming phonemes rapidly (Rapid Phoneme Naming; SS = 75). Her scores were also consistently low on two other measures of RAN: Rapid Picture Naming (SS = 75) and Rapid Letter Naming (SS = 70). Rapid retrieval of symbolic information, including pictures, letters, and letter sounds, is difficult for Sophia.

Academic achievement test results The WJ V ACH was administered to assess Sophia's academic achievement. The WJ V ACH is composed of individually administered tests measuring the academic areas of reading, oral language, mathematics, and written language.

Test/Cluster	Standard Score	Descriptor
Oral Expression*	**97 (91–103)**	**Average**
Picture Vocabulary	100 (92–108)	Average
Oral Language Samples	96 (88–104)	Average
Listening Comprehension*	**97** (92–102)**	**Average**
Oral Comprehension	98 (91–106)	Average
Story Comprehension	111 (104–118)	Average
Basic Reading Skills*	**80** (75–85)**	**Low average**
Letter-Word Identification	73 (65–81)	Low
Word Attack	92 (85–99)	Average
Reading Fluency*	**72 (67–77)**	**Low**
Sentence Reading Fluency	68 (61–75)	Very low
Word Reading Fluency	78 (70–86)	Low
Reading Comprehension*	**96 (92–100)**	**Average**
Passage Comprehension	90 (84–96)	Average
Paragraph Reading Comprehension	107 (100–114)	Average
Written Expression*	**94 (90–98)**	**Average**
Written Language Samples	99 (92–106)	Average
Sentence Writing Fluency	88 (80–96)	Low average
Math Calculation Skills*	**95 (90–100)**	**Average**
Calculation	97 (90–104)	Average
Math Facts Fluency	95 (89–101)	Average
Math Problem Solving*	**102 (97–107)**	**Average**
Applied Problems	108 (101–115)	Average
Math Problem Identification	95 (88–102)	Average
Spelling Skills	**80 (74–86)**	**Low average**
Spelling	76 (69–83)	Low
Spelling of Sounds	96 (87–105)	Average
Phoneme–Grapheme Knowledge	**93 (87–99)**	**Average**
Word Attack	92 (85–99)	Average
Spelling of Sounds	96 (88–104)	Average

* These cluster scores measure areas of specific learning disability (SLD) identified by IDEA.

** Interpret cluster score with caution due to significant variability between tests comprising the cluster score.

Oral Expression. This cluster is a combination of Picture Vocabulary (measures oral language development and word knowledge) and Oral Language Samples (measures the ability to produce words and sentences). Sophia scored in the average range.

Listening Comprehension. This cluster is a combination of Oral Comprehension (measures the ability to comprehend short passages and supply the missing word), and Story Comprehension (measures oral language skills and meaningful memory). Sophia scored in the average range.

Basic Reading Skills. This cluster is a combination of Letter-Word Identification (reading a list of words aloud) and Word Attack (reading nonsense letter combinations that are phonetically consistent or regular patterns in orthography). These tests measure sight word vocabulary, the application of phonics, and structural analysis skills. Sophia scored in the low-average range.

Reading Fluency. This cluster measures aspects of reading fluency (i.e., prosody, automaticity, and accuracy) and comprises the Sentence Reading Fluency (reading simple sentences quickly, decide if the statement is true, and select either yes or no) and Word Reading Fluency (requires marking pairs of words that go together among rows of six words) tests. Sophia scored in the very low and low ranges on these tests, respectively.

Reading Comprehension. This cluster is a combination of Passage Comprehension (using syntactic and semantic cues to identify the missing words in a text) and Paragraph Reading Comprehension (reading a short story silently and then answering comprehension questions). It is a measure of comprehension and reasoning. Sophia scored in the average range.

Written Expression. This cluster is a measure of meaningful written expression and fluency, and is a combination of Written Language Samples, which is evaluated with respect to the quality of expression, and Sentence Writing Fluency (formulation of simple sentences when presented with a picture and three stimulus words in a five-minute time limit). Sophia scored in the average range.

Math Calculation Skills. This cluster is a measure of computational skills and automaticity and is composed of Calculation (completing math computations on a worksheet) and Math Facts Fluency (completing simple addition, subtraction, and multiplication facts within a three-minute time limit). Sophia scored in the average range.

Math Problem Solving. This cluster is a combination of Applied Problems (analyzing and solving word problems) and Math Problem Identification (requires listening to an unsolvable math problem and describing what is wrong with, or missing from, the problem). It is a measure of mathematical knowledge and reasoning. Sophia scored in the average range.

Spelling Skills. Although not an area of IDEA eligibility, the two tests in this cluster measure the ability to spell orally presented real words and nonsense words correctly. Sophia scored in the low-average range.

Phoneme–Grapheme Knowledge. Although not an area of IDEA eligibility, this cluster measures the reader's established connections between phonemes (speech sounds) and graphemes (printed letters that represent these speech sounds), which is often the initial impediment for most individuals with dyslexia. Sophia scored in the average range.

Summary of findings Sophia is a 14-year-old, eighth-grade student who is enrolled in Rosa Parks School. She was referred for this assessment as a part of her triennial review. She is currently eligible for special education services under the category of SLD.

Sophia's performance on the cognitive processing tests administered indicates that she has average processing abilities in most cognitive areas, with her overall cognitive ability as measured by the GIA cluster score falling within the average range (SS = 99). Processing deficits were identified on both the Phonemic Retrieval Fluency cluster (SS = 78; Low) and the RAN–Reading cluster (SS = 69; Very low).

Generally, results of the cognitive tests suggest that Sophia should be able to meet the demands of grade-level tasks in all academic areas; however, her Reading Fluency cluster score (SS = 72; Low) indicates that she will take much longer than her peers to read information. She also demonstrates challenges with some aspects of basic reading and writing skills, such as poor word recognition (i.e., Letter-Word Identification; SS = 73; Low) and Spelling Skills (SS = 80; Low average). Sophia's scores in these academic areas are in contrast to her overall cognitive abilities.

Given the factors that led to this evaluation, Sophia's educational, medical, and behavioral history, as well as Sophia's current functioning at school, the areas of eligibility considered for this assessment were: SLD in Reading Fluency.

Eligibility review

Specific learning disability This assessment used the Patterns of Strengths and Weaknesses (PSW) model for determining eligibility under the SLD category. The criteria for a student to qualify for Special Education in this district under the category of SLD within the PSW model include five main points:

1. Identification of a normative weakness in an area of academic achievement. Areas of academic achievement include: oral expression, listening comprehension, basic reading skills, reading fluency, reading comprehension, math calculation, math reasoning, and written expression.
2. Identification of a deficit in an area of cognitive processing.
3. Cognitive functioning is otherwise within normal limits.
4. Exclusionary factors are not the primary cause of either the academic or cognitive deficits. Exclusionary factors include: visual, hearing, or motor disabilities, intellectual disability, emotional disturbance, cultural factors, environmental or economic disadvantage, limited English proficiency, limited school experience, poor school attendance, or lack of appropriate instruction.
5. There is a research-based consistency between the cognitive and academic weaknesses.

Based on data from this evaluation, Sophia demonstrated consistent, normative weaknesses in reading fluency, with some isolated weaknesses in word recognition and spelling that are consistent with her past diagnosis of dyslexia. Sophia demonstrated many cognitive strengths but demonstrated significant processing deficits on the Phonemic Retrieval Fluency and RAN–Reading clusters. A direct research-based comparison can be made between Sophia's weaknesses and her slower reading fluency as depicted below:

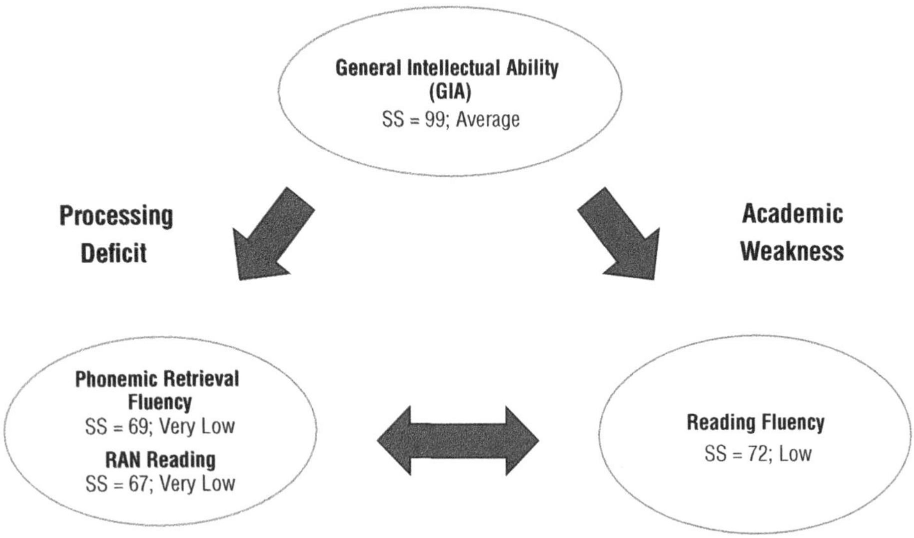

Consistency between the processing deficit and the academic weakness

Phonemic Retrieval Fluency and RAN–Reading relating to Reading Fluency

Recommendations Given the results of this assessment and Sophia's history of academic difficulties, the following recommendations will be made to Sophia's IEP team:

- Sophia should continue to be eligible for an IEP under IDEA in the category of SLD in Reading Fluency
- To improve reading fluency, have Sophia use the Great Leaps digital program, 15 minutes per day, 3–5 days per week (www.greatleaps.com). During each session, Sophia should work with an instructor on phonics, sight phrases, and stories with comprehension questions. The instructor should provide immediate correction of errors. The program provides automatic charting, which ensures that student data are kept accurately.
- Provide Sophia with text-to-speech and speech-to-text technology (e.g., scribe, ReadWrite, etc.) to support her weaknesses in word reading and spelling.
- To help increase her reading fluency, provide audiobooks and have Sophia follow along as she listens with a print copy.
- Provide Sophia with opportunities to complete tasks orally or using technology in order to increase success and foster self-esteem.
- Allow for 50% extended time on high-stakes time-limited tests. Sophia will also need extra time to complete classroom tasks and tests that involve extended reading.

The information in this report will be presented during Sophia's IEP meeting to determine eligibility, along with further recommendations to assist Sophia in her learning.

CASE STUDY #5: EVAN

Educational Evaluation Report

Student: Evan Feeney
Parents: Gil and Jeanette Feeney
Date of Birth: July 7
Grade: 11.9
Age: 17 years, 11 months
School: Walnut Cove High
Dates of Testing: 6/7, 6/10

Reason for referral Evan was referred for his three-year review of special education services. He has been receiving special education services under the category of SLD since third grade. For the past 3 years, he has been receiving learning disability services in a resource setting at Walnut Cove High School in Peoria, Wisconsin. The school team recommended an evaluation to help determine transition goals for postsecondary education. In addition, his parents expressed concerns to Ms. Elkins, the school psychologist, about Evan's continued difficulties in mathematics, his poor handwriting, and his general apathy about school and educational goals.

Background information Evan is the adopted son of Gil and Jeanette Feeney. He currently lives with his parents and an older brother, Jeremy, who is also adopted. The Feeneys adopted Evan at birth. His biological mother was 14 years old and smoked during the pregnancy. Although little is known about prenatal care, concerns were also raised about his biological mother's possible drug and/or alcohol abuse during pregnancy. Although little is known about his biological father, information from a court interview indicated that Evan's biological father struggled throughout school with mathematics.

Evan attended preschool for 2 years and then entered Walnut Cove Elementary for kindergarten. Based upon parental and teacher concerns regarding motor development, Evan was referred for an occupational therapy evaluation in first grade. Results from the Peabody Developmental Motor Scale indicated delays of up to 17 months in fine-motor development and up to 26 months in gross-motor development. He demonstrated weakness in his flexor muscles, particularly abdominals and hip flexors, toe walking, and weaknesses in visual-motor planning. Evan was unable to hop on one foot without losing his balance. On the Gardner Test of Visual-Perceptual Skills (nonmotor), Evan obtained average scores on measures of visual discrimination and visual-spatial relations and a below average score in visual memory. Recommendations were made for occupational therapy with the goals of improving fine- and gross-motor skills, visual-perceptual motor planning, and muscle weaknesses. In addition, Evan began to receive resource support for reading, writing, and math.

The Feeneys reported that although Evan was encouraged to participate in team sports throughout elementary school (baseball, soccer, swimming, and karate), the experiences were not positive. During baseball games, Evan would often sit down in the outfield. On the soccer field, Evan tried to stay away from the ball. His mother reported that on several occasions when she picked Evan up from practice, he would be crying. In swimming, he was also 20 strokes behind the other children, and in karate he could not keep his balance.

Delays were also noted in gross-motor development. At the age of 9, Evan was unable to ride a bike or tie his shoes with ease. He walked with an unstable gait and often tripped. Because of continued toe walking, Evan had casts put on both legs to stretch his heel cords and position his feet flat on the ground. Results from a brain magnetic resonance imaging (MRI) indicated subtle cortical dysplasia involving the cerebellar hemispheres (the areas of the brain involved in motor development and balance).

Evan is currently in the 11th grade. He has received special education services in a resource setting under the category of SLD since the third grade. Currently, he is also receiving occupational therapy services for 30 minutes, 1 day per week, with the goal of teaching him how to use technology to compensate for his handwriting difficulties. He currently uses a laptop in all of his classes to assist with lengthy writing assignments. Presently, in high school, Evan is not involved in any extracurricular activities. He notes that he likes to play video games and spends most of his free time in this way. Evan's parents note that he is creative and has a good vocabulary and sense of humor. On the WJ V Written Language Samples test, when asked to write about three things he likes to do in his free time, Evan wrote: "Watch TV, play video games, and fall down the stairs."

Classroom observation Evan was observed for the first 20 minutes of his algebra class. He was sitting in the back of the room. He looked at the floor and his shoes, glancing up only occasionally. He appeared to be listening. Fifteen minutes into the discussion, Evan began digging into the tread of his shoe with a pencil. He then removed his shoe and continued to run the tip of his pencil through the shoe treads, until a nearby student, then a teacher's aide, prompted him to put his shoe back on and listen. When independent seatwork began, Evan did not understand what he was supposed to do. The classroom aide came over and re-explained the assignment to Evan. Evan then began to work but after 5 minutes had only attempted one problem.

Tests administered Evan was administered the *Woodcock-Johnson V Tests of Achievement* (WJ V ACH) and several tests from the *Woodcock-Johnson V Virtual Test Library* (WJ V VTL). In addition, a writing sample was collected.

Behavior during testing Evan was tested over three sessions. In the first session, Evan complained of being tired, yawned, and kept his head down on the desk. He said that he did not get much sleep, then became teary-eyed and asked if he could please finish tomorrow. He completed two tests before he was dismissed to go back to class. Evan returned for testing the next morning and was once again mildly to moderately resistant. He complained that the examiner, while trying to get him engaged in the testing, was "annoying" him. When reminded that he agreed to come back to finish the test after being allowed to stop the day before, he became more cooperative. Nonetheless, he did not seem to have much stamina and struggled to maintain an adequate energy level. In contrast, during tests that measure oral language abilities, he showed persistence and enthusiasm.

By the third session, Evan was cooperative. He was informed that he could earn coupons for "homework passes" by complying with requests and trying his hardest. He appeared at ease, comfortable, and attentive. He responded promptly but carefully to test questions and generally persisted with difficult tasks.

Test results The WJ V ACH and VTL were scored according to age norms. Evan's performance is compared to his age peers using PR and PR ranges:

PR Range	Verbal Label
<1–2	Very low
3–8	Low
9–24	Low average
25–75	Average
76–91	High average
92–97	Superior
98–>99	Very superior

Note: Percentile ranks (PR) are scores that indicate rank order within the norm group and range from <1 to >99. They indicate the percentage of the population that scored the same or lower.

His academic proficiency on specific tasks is described by the RPI levels:

RPI Levels	Proficiency	Implications for Age-Level Tasks
0/90–3/90	Negligible	Impossible
4/90–24/90	Very limited	Extremely difficult
25/90–67/90	Limited	Very difficult
68/90–82/90	Limited to average	Difficult
83/90–94/90	Average	Manageable
95/90–97/90	Average to advanced	Easy
98/90–99/90	Advanced	Very easy
100/90	Very advanced	Extremely easy

Note: An RPI is expressed as a fraction with the bottom number (denominator) fixed at 90. The 90 represents the 90% proficiency level of average peers. The top number (numerator) ranges from 0 to 100 and reflects the student's proficiency on the task.

Achievement Evan was administered WJ V ACH tests in the areas of reading, writing, math, and oral language. His proficiency ranged from limited to very advanced on various measures of achievement. In general, his proficiency in reading and written language was average, but his proficiency in mathematics was limited.

Oral language Evan's proficiency on measures of oral language ranged from average to advanced.

Oral Language Cluster/ Tests	RPI	Proficiency	PR (±1 *SEM*)
Oral Language	97/90	Average to advanced	91 (85–95)
Picture Vocabulary	99/90	Advanced	94 (87–98)
Oral Comprehension	96/90	Average to advanced	81 (66–92)
Oral Language Samples	94/90	Average	70 (48–87)
Story Comprehension	97/90	Average to advanced	86 (75–93)

Reading Evan's proficiency with reading was mostly average to advanced. He was able to pronounce both real words and nonsense words with ease. He had average to advanced proficiency on measures of reading rate and fluency. His lowest score was on the Passage Comprehension test. This was somewhat surprising given his high score on the Oral Comprehension test, a test of listening comprehension in the same format.

WJ V Reading Clusters/ Tests	RPI	Proficiency	PR (±1 SEM)
Basic Reading Skills	98/90	Advanced	87 (79–92)
Letter-Word Identification	99/90	Advanced	84 (76-91)
Word Attack	98/90	Advanced	83 (67–93)
Reading Fluency	99/90	Advanced	74 (72–77)
Sentence Reading Fluency	93/90	Average	54 (51–57)
Word Reading Fluency	100/90	Very advanced	86 (83–88)
Reading Comprehension	82/90	Average	32 (24–40)
Passage Comprehension	82/90	Average	31 (20–44)
Paragraph Reading Comprehension	81/90	Limited to average	33 (24–43)
Phoneme–Grapheme Knowledge	97/90	Average to advanced	84 (74–91)

Written language Evan's responses on the Written Language Samples test were sophisticated both in terms of writing style and use of vocabulary (see Figure 8.2 in Chapter 8). He wrote responses quickly and easily. In contrast, his responses on the Sentence Writing Accuracy test were difficult to score because of his handwriting. He used uppercase letters within sentences and so received a 0 on all items for Capitalization. The sample below illustrates a few of his responses.

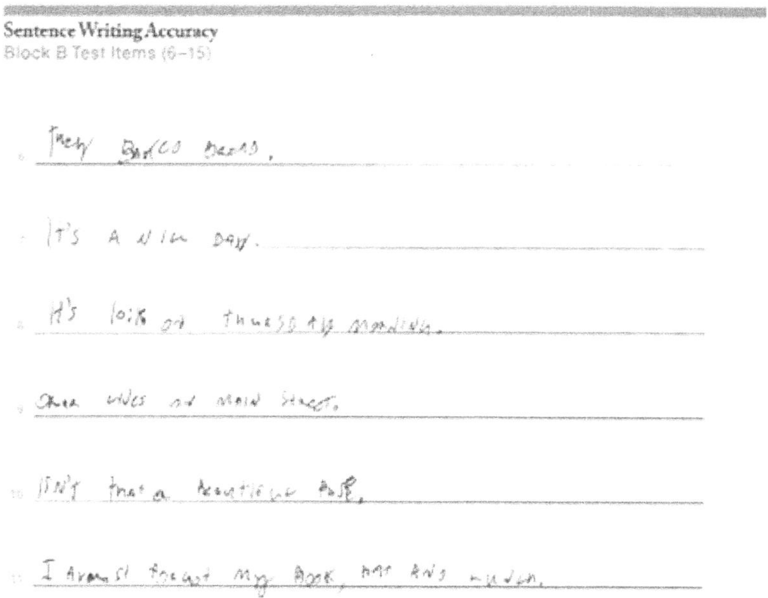

Evan's Sentence Writing Accuracy Responses

WJ V Written Language Cluster/Tests	RPI	Proficiency	PR (±1 SEM)
Basic Writing Skills	74/90	Limited to average	27 (21–33)
Spelling	79/90	Limited to average	36 (28–45)
Sentence Writing Accuracy	69/90	Limited to average	14 (10–21)
Written Expression	99/90	Advanced	92 (90–93)
Written Language Samples	100/90	Very advanced	>99 (>99–>99)
Sentence Writing Fluency	98/90	Advanced	68 (64–72)

Evan also provided the first page of his first draft of a short story he was writing for his English class. Several aspects about his writing can be gleaned from this sample: He has an excellent vocabulary; his story is cohesive; he uses both simple and complex sentence structures; and his handwriting is difficult but not impossible to read.

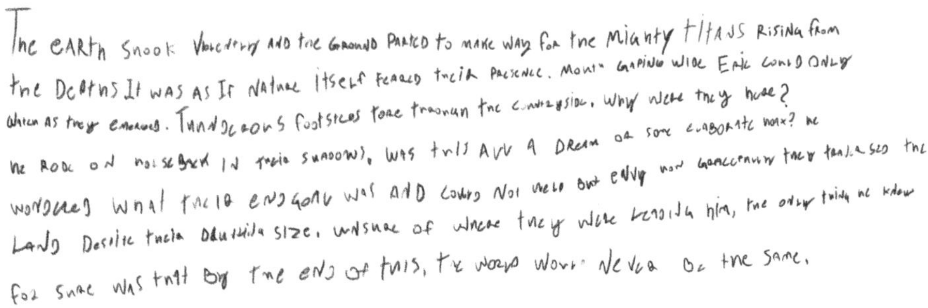

Translation:

The earth shook violently and the ground parted to make way for the mighty titans rising from the depths. It was as if nature itself feared their presence. Mouth gaping wide Eric could only watch as they emerged. Thunderous footsteps tore through the countryside. Why were they here? He rode on horseback in their shadows. Was this all a dream or some elaborate hoax? He wondered what their end goal was and could not help but envy how gracefully they traversed the land despite their daunting size. Unsure of where they were leading him, the one thing he knew for sure was that by the end of all this, the world would never be the same.

Evan's First Page of a Short Story for English Class

MATHEMATICS Evan's proficiency was limited in most aspects of math performance. His performance on the Calculation test, a measure of computational skills, exceeded only 6% of his age peers. On this test, he was able to solve simple addition, subtraction, and multiplication problems but was unable to solve problems that involved division, addition, and subtraction of fractions, or simple algebraic equations. Figure 8.2 in Chapter 8 illustrates his responses on the Calculation test.

WJ V Mathematics Cluster/Tests	RPI	Proficiency	PR (±1 SEM)
Math Calculation Skills	51/90	Limited	8 (6–12)
Calculation	26/90	Limited	6 (4–9)
Math Facts Fluency	76/90	Limited to average	20 (12–31)
Number Concepts	57/90	Limited	17 (13–21)
Magnitude Comparison	43/90	Limited	20 (16–26)
Number Sense	69/90	Limited to average	14 (9–20)

WJ V Mathematics Cluster/Tests	RPI	Proficiency	PR (±1 SEM)
Math Problem Solving	67/90	Limited	17 (12–24)
Applied Problems	80/90	Limited to average	31 (20–43)
Math Problem Identification	50/90	Limited	8 (5–13)

ACADEMIC KNOWLEDGE Evan's proficiency was average regarding content area knowledge. This is somewhat surprising given his more advanced oral language and vocabulary knowledge; however, Evan did demonstrate limited to average proficiency on the Paragraph Reading Comprehension test, even though his proficiency on other reading tasks was average to advanced. Because the majority of content area knowledge is acquired by reading texts, Evan's limits in comprehension of connected text may be related to the differences noted between his academic knowledge and his oral language. Another possible explanation may be that Evan was pulled out of the general education classroom to receive special education services during content area instruction in both elementary and middle school.

WJ V Academic Knowledge Cluster/Tests	RPI	Proficiency	PR (±1 SEM)
Academic Knowledge	87/90	Average	41 (32–50)
Academic Vocabulary	90/90	Average	49 (36–63)
Academic Facts	83/90	Average	32 (21–44)

Virtual Test Library Evan was administered several additional tests from the WJ V Virtual Test Library (VTL) to gather more information about his working memory, phonological awareness, and rapid naming abilities. Evan's proficiency was average to very advanced on all measures administered. His ability to repeat back orally presented words and sentences and his ability to blend speech sounds together and push them apart (segmentation) were all advanced to very advanced. His proficiency was also average to advance on measures of RAN. Evan has a solid foundation in the skills that could otherwise impede reading and spelling development.

WJ V VTL Cluster/Tests	RPI	Proficiency	PR (±1 SEM)
Auditory Memory Span	99/90	Advanced	92 (88–95)
Memory for Words	98/90	Advanced	83 (77–88)
Sentence Repetition	100/90	Advanced	94 (89–97)

WJ V VTL Cluster/Tests	RPI	Proficiency	PR (±1 SEM)
Phonological Awareness	100/90	Advanced	96 (94–98)
Sound Blending	100/90	Very advanced	98 (96–99)
Segmentation	99/90	Advanced	88 (83–93)
RAN–Reading	98/90	Advanced	89 (83–93)
Rapid Picture Naming	99/90	Advanced	94 (90–97)
Rapid Letter Naming	98/90	Advanced	81 (72–88)
Rapid Phoneme Naming	96/90	Average to advanced	70 (53–84)

Comparisons The WJ V ACH includes comparison procedures that can be used to identify significant strengths and weaknesses that may be present among a student's academic skills. On the Intra-achievement Comparison procedure, Evan had significant relative strengths on the Basic Reading Skills and Written Expression clusters. When compared to Evan's same-age peers with the same overall achievement score, only 3% of the students would have a Basic Reading Skills cluster score as high as Evan's, and only 5% of the students would have a Written Expression score as high as his. In contrast, Evan exhibited significant weaknesses in mathematics. Only 1% and 3%, respectively, of Evan's same-age peers with the same overall achievement would have scores as low or lower than his scores on the Math Calculation and Math Problem-Solving clusters, respectively.

The WJ V ACH also includes procedures to compare a student's academic achievement to their predicted achievement, given their overall oral language ability. Because Evan's oral language abilities are generally above average, his achievement scores should be commensurately high; however, Evan showed unexpectedly low performance in several achievement areas. For example, his scores on the Math Calculation and Math Problem Solving clusters were in the bottom 2% and 1%, respectively, of scores from his same-age peers with the same oral language ability. He also showed significantly lower than expected scores on Reading Comprehension and Basic Writing Skills; his scores on these clusters were in the bottom 3% and 6%, respectively, of peers with the same oral language ability.

The fact that Evan's Reading Comprehension is significantly lower than predicted by his oral language ability should be noted. His strong oral language predicts equally strong reading skills, which is not the case, especially for comprehension of connected text as is measured by the Paragraph Reading Comprehension test. There may be other factors, such as attention/concentration, working memory, or processing speed, that are impacting Evan's ability to comprehend what he reads at a level that is commensurate with his oral language abilities. Limits in these types of cognitive abilities may also explain Evan's ongoing difficulties in mathematics.

Conclusions Evan is a student with both dysgraphia and dyscalculia who has advanced oral language and superior writing skills in terms of content. He uses a laptop in most of his classes. Evan has received services as a student with SLD in handwriting and mathematics since third grade, but he continues to struggle with handwriting and most areas of mathematics. The multidisciplinary team will determine Evan's continued eligibility for special education services as well as further develop a postsecondary transition plan.

Recommendations

Further assessment and educational programming Conduct further intellectual/cognitive assessment to help determine the specific factors that are inhibiting math development and performance. Administer measures of fluid reasoning, working memory, rapid naming, visual-spatial thinking, and processing speed to determine if any of these abilities are affecting Evan's mathematical performance. Integrate these findings with the results from the present evaluation.

- Schedule a multidisciplinary conference in the fall to consider Evan's continued eligibility for special education services, his need for math instruction, and his need for accommodations and support during his senior year.
- Administer the KeyMath3 or do informal testing to determine additional relevant instructional goals for mathematics.
- Based on the findings of the more comprehensive report, Evan and his parents should explore modified entrance requirements to the state university as well as procedures for applying to the program for students with SLD.
- If possible in a postsecondary setting, consider waiving any credit requirements in mathematics due to his extreme difficulty with mathematical skills and concepts and provide an acceptable substitution.
- For the first semester of college, consider a reduced course load so that Evan has enough time and energy to devote to his courses.
- Provide Evan with ongoing assistance in vocational planning.

Mathematics Evan needs to continue receiving instruction in basic math skills.

1. As part of math instruction, reteach and review procedures involved in computations with fractions, percentages, and decimals. Use manipulatives to demonstrate the meaning of fractions. Also, review the concept of place value so that Evan can understand the meaning of a decimal point.
2. Specifically teach strategies for translating word problems into computations. Help Evan learn to visualize what is happening in the problem.
3. Encourage Evan to take his school's class in functional mathematics. This course will review math skills that are needed for independent living, such as balancing a checkbook, figuring interest on a car loan, determining the amount of tip to leave at a restaurant, measuring for cooking, adjusting a recipe, and using map skills.

CASE STUDY #6: VERONICA

Educational Evaluation

Name: Veronica Peters
Dateof Birth: April 16
Age: 22 years
Grade: 16.9
School: University of Hampshire
Evaluation Dates: July 27, July 28

Reason for referral Veronica, a recent graduate from the University of Hampshire with a BS in biomedical engineering, referred herself for an evaluation because of difficulties with reading rate, test-taking, and studying. Although she reports that she does very well on projects, she has trouble recalling information that is delivered in a lecture format as well as difficulty on exams that require a great deal of memorization or a considerable amount of reading. Veronica wanted to gain a deeper understanding of her strengths and weaknesses and explore whether she has a learning disability and if she will need specific accommodations in graduate school to help her compensate for her reading difficulties.

Background information Veronica is currently living at her parents' home with a roommate. For the next few years, both of her parents will reside in France. Her father is an electrical engineer, and her mother is a research technician who does database/computer work from home. Veronica's younger brother Manuel, age 17, who is also in France, was recently diagnosed with both dyslexia and ADHD.

Veronica attended elementary and middle school at Fountain Hills Academy, a private school. In first through third grade, Veronica was in the school's Gifted and Talented Education Program (GATE). In third grade, Veronica told her parents that she could not keep up with the other kids and it was too hard for her. Her parents then requested that she not participate in the program anymore. From third to sixth grade, Veronica received private tutoring to help her build her reading skills. She completed all 12 steps of the Wilson Reading System® with a Level II certified Wilson instructor.

Veronica attended Redfield High School, a private charter school, and achieved high grades in all of her classes. Although she has never been evaluated for learning disabilities, she has received additional support at school throughout her educational career. Veronica noted that she has always been a slow reader and has needed more time to complete work in her English and history classes. She felt that she did not do well on the SATs because she did not have enough time to complete all of the items. Throughout her school years, she has taken advantage of the extra help provided by teachers during their office hours or after school. Her teachers have always granted her additional time on tests when needed. Veronica commented that she comprehends lectures much better when she has a copy of the notes or a study guide to take notes as she listens.

As a student at the University of Hampshire, Veronica completed 13 credit hours per semester. In the fall, she had difficulty with Economics 214, a course that depended heavily on lecture notes and the textbook. She then applied for tutoring support and help with time management from the school's Alternative Learning Techniques (ALT) Center. In the spring, she started receiving tutorial help at the ALT Center and was then able to pass the class. Veronica graduated this summer and has been accepted for graduate school at Gateway State to earn a master's degree in sustainability science, a program that focuses on ways to create a cleaner Earth and a healthier environment. Presently, Veronica's main interests lie in mathematics, science, and art, particularly oil painting. She is a hard-working student who is willing to put in a great deal of effort to accomplish her goals. She is excited to start a graduate degree but concerned that she will struggle with the reading requirements.

Tests administered

- *Woodcock-Johnson V Tests of Cognitive Abilities* (WJ COG)
- *Woodcock-Johnson V Tests of Achievement* (WJ V ACH)
- *Woodcock-Johnson V Virtual Test Library* (WJ V VTL)

Although additional tests from the WJ V and a few other tests were administered as part of this evaluation, the purpose of this shortened report is to illustrate the use of the WJ V Dyslexia Test Set. The WJ V tests were scored using age norms (22y).

Test behavior Veronica was extremely cooperative during the two 1.5-hour-long testing sessions. In both sessions, she was attentive and maintained interest and effort.

Results from the WJ V Dyslexia Test Set The WJ V Dyslexia Test Set consists of several tests from the WJ V ACH and the WJ V VTL. The table below presents Veronica's WJ V results.

	Cluster	SS	PR	RPI	Test	SS	PR	RPI
Basic Reading Skills and Reading Fluency	Basic Reading Skills	83 (78–88)	13	47/90	Letter-Word Identification (Grw)	83 (76–90)	13	33/90
					Word Attack (Grw, Ga)	83 (74–92)	13	62/90
	Reading Fluency	88 (80–96)	21	36/90	Sentence Reading Fluency (Gs, Grw)	92 (82–102)	29	50/90
					Word Reading Fluency (Gs, Grw)	85 (76–94)	16	24/90
Phonics Knowledge and Spelling	Phoneme–Grapheme Knowledge	82 (77–87)	11	64/90	Word Attack (Grw, Ga)	83 (72–94)	13	62/90
					Spelling of Sounds (Ga, Grw)	83 (74–93)	13	65/90
	Spelling Skills	83 (76–90)	13	55/90	Spelling (Grw)	85 (75–95)	16	46/90
					Spelling of Sounds (Ga, Grw)	83 (75–91)	84	65/90
Linguistic Risk Factors	Phonological Awareness	110 (104–116)	75	97/90	Sound Blending (Ga)	108 (100–116)	70	96/90
					Segmentation (Ga)	110 (103–117)	74	97/90
	Phonological Manipulation	91 (84–98)	28	79/90	Sound Deletion (Ga)[b]	90 (80–100)	25	76/90
					Sound Substitution (Ga)[b]	92	31	81/90
	RAN–Reading	60 (52–68)	<1	25/90	Rapid Picture Naming (Gs, Gr)	75 (66–84)	5	45/90
					Rapid Letter Naming (Gs, Gr)	62 (50–74)	<1	12/90
					Rapid Phoneme Naming (Gr, Ga)	68 (60–76)	2	26/90

	Auditory Memory Span	84 (80–88)	14	59/90	Memory for Words (Gwm)	82 (72–92)	12	49/90
					Sentence Repetition (Gwm)	88 (79–97)	21	68/90
Vocabulary	Vocabulary	114 (108–120)	82	97/90	Picture Vocabulary (Gc)	115 (107–123)	84	97/90
					Academic Vocabulary (Gc)	112 (104–120)	79	96/90
	Single Tests				Oral Reading (Grw)	95 (90–100)	37	82/90
					Nonsense Word Repetition (Ga, Gwm)	82 (74–90)	12	67/90

Reading On the Letter-Word Identification test, Veronica's ability to read real words exceeded only 13% of her age peers; on the Word Attack test, a measure of her ability to use phonics skills to read nonsense words, Veronica also scored higher than only 13% of her age peers. Her RPI on the Basic Reading Skills cluster indicated that when typical age peers have 90% success in reading words, she will have only 47% success.

Veronica's scores were average and low average on the timed reading tests. On the Sentence Reading Fluency test, which required her to read simple sentences quickly and determine if the sentence is true or false (e.g., A cat has nine legs: *yes* or *no*), her performance exceeded only 29% of her age peers. On the timed Word Reading Fluency test, which required her to read rows of four words and identify the two that go together (e.g., apple can tree orange), her performance exceeded only 16% of her peers. Her RPI on the Reading Fluency cluster indicated that when typical age peers have 90% success in reading quickly, she will have only 36% success.

Spelling Veronica's spelling skills were low-average compared to her age peers; her score on the Spelling test exceeded only 16% of her age peers. A few of her misspellings were unusual for a college graduate, as the sounds in the word were out of order, such as spelling the word *garden* as *graden*. Although a longer sample, such as an essay, was not analyzed, Veronica commented that she has some difficulties with spelling, grammar, and organization when she writes longer papers.

Linguistic risk factors Veronica demonstrated well-developed phonological awareness skills, particularly in tasks involving the blending and segmenting of speech sounds (PR = 75). This relative strength can likely be attributed to the 3 years of systematic reading intervention she received. Her performance was somewhat weaker on the Phonological Manipulation cluster (PR = 28), which places additional demands on verbal working memory. Consistent with this pattern, Veronica showed relative weaknesses on the Auditory Memory Span cluster (PR = 14), confirming that she has difficulty maintaining verbal information in conscious awareness. Veronica's most profound difficulties were observed on the RAN–Reading cluster (PR < 1), reflecting severe deficits in RAN, a measure of the accuracy and fluency of retrieval of common items from memory. In contrast, Veronica's Vocabulary cluster score fell in the high average range (PR = 82). Her RPI of 97/90 on the Vocabulary cluster indicated that when typical age peers have 90% success in understanding oral vocabulary, she will have 97% success.

WJ V COG summary Veronica was also administered the WJ V COG as part of a more complete evaluation. Many of her scores fell within the average range, but a significant pattern of strengths and weaknesses was noted across the different types of abilities. Veronica excelled on tasks that required visual-spatial thinking, such as those involved in perceiving and recalling visual details and designs. She was able to quickly discern spatial relationships and visual patterns. Her score on the Visual Processing cluster exceeded 93% of her age peers. She also excelled on measures of reasoning ability. On the Fluid Reasoning cluster, her performance exceeded 83% of her age peers. These findings suggest that Veronica is well suited for a career that involves visual-spatial thinking and reasoning abilities. In contrast, Veronica had several significant weaknesses on timed measures. Similar to the findings on the RAN–Reading tests, her main area of weakness was Cognitive Processing Speed, or the ability to quickly complete symbolic tasks of a clerical nature. On this cluster, her performance exceeded only 27% of her age peers. These results, as well as the findings from other tests that were integrated into the evaluation, support her need for extended time.

Conclusions Throughout her school career, Veronica has received accommodations because of her slow reading speed. She has been successful in both secondary and postsecondary settings when she has been provided with the necessary accommodations. Her SLD is dyslexia, or a specific learning disorder in basic reading skills and reading fluency. Even with three years of systematic reading intervention, she continues to have a functional limitation in the major life activity of reading when her performance is compared to most people of her age. In spite of her challenges with reading and spelling, Veronica is an intelligent and motivated student who excels in courses that are focused on math and science. Veronica's final GPA of 4.0 supports the fact that she is capable of high achievement when she is provided with the appropriate accommodations.

Recommendations

Accommodations

1. Based upon her slow reading rate as compared to most people her age, Veronica will require 50% more time (time and one-half) on time-limited tests. Veronica's slow reading rate, when compared to most people her age, requires the accommodation of extra time so that she can demonstrate her knowledge and not be penalized by her slow reading speed.
2. On high-stakes tests, because of a tendency to get distracted when in a room with others, Veronica requires testing to be conducted in a quiet room so that she can direct her full attention to taking the test.

For Veronica Prior to starting graduate school, it would be beneficial to work on improving your reading rate. If possible, spend 30 minutes 5 days a week doing the Mindplay program (MindPlay Individual Subscription link: https://bit.ly/42WRBTd). Another option would be: Great Leaps Tutoring Program online (15 minutes a day), using the version for high school students (https://tutoring.greatleaps.com/). You may also wish to explore the use of assistive technologies that can support reading, such as the C-Pen-2 or OrCam Learn.

TEST YOURSELF

1. **Why might Noah's evaluator have chosen to score the WJ V with grade norms rather than age norms?**
2. **Write a statement to describe Noah's RPI of 14/90 on the Basic Reading Skills cluster.**
3. **On the GIA/Achievement comparison procedure, explain the meaning of William's discrepancy percentile rank score of 6 in Math Problem-Solving.**
4. **Sophia has a significant difference between her score on the Semantic Word Retrieval test (100) and her scores on the Phonemic Word Retrieval (67) and Rapid Phoneme Naming (75) tests. This suggests her difficulty is primarily with tasks requiring the retrieval of phonemes, rather than the oral retrieval of words. True or False?**
5. **Victoria's low score in Listening Comprehension suggests that she might also have a low score in:**
   (A) Reading Fluency
   (B) Basic Reading Skills
   (C) Reading Comprehension
   (D) Math Problem Solving
6. **Which of the following would be most useful to test the hypothesis that an examinee has lower-than-expected performance in reading fluency specifically, using scores from only the WJ V ACH battery?**
   (A) Intra-Achievement Comparisons
   (B) Oral Language/Achievement Comparisons
   (C) GIA/Achievement Comparisons
   (D) Academic Skills/Fluency/Applications Comparisons
7. **An RPI below what level would suggest that a similar grade-level task would be extremely difficult for a student?**
   (A) 90/90
   (B) 70/90
   (C) 50/90
   (D) 25/90
8. **What does Evan's RPI of 100/90 mean on the Written Language Samples Test?**
9. **Veronica's low scores on RAN–Reading suggest that she will also have a weakness in:**
   (A) Basic Reading Skills
   (B) Reading Comprehension
   (C) Reading Fluency
   (D) Written Expression
10. **What does Veronica's percentile rank of <1 on the RAN–Reading cluster mean?**

ANSWERS

1. Since Noah is repeating first grade, it is reasonable to evaluate his performance against the children with whom he is being educated rather than his age mates, who are one grade ahead of him.
2. Compared to average first-grade students who would have 90% proficiency on word recognition tasks, Noah would have only 14%, or very limited, proficiency.
3. William scored significantly lower than predicted on the Math Problem Solving cluster, given his GIA, or overall cognitive ability. Only 6 out of 100 grademates with the same predicted Math Problem Solving score would have an actual score as low or lower than William's.
4. **True.**
5. **C.**
6. **B.**
7. **D.**
8. When average agemates have 90% success in expressing ideas in writing, Evan is expected to have 100% success, or very advanced proficiency. These types of tasks will be extremely easy for Evan.
9. **C.**
10. Veronica's score fell below the bottom 1% of her age peers.

Appendix

FREQUENTLY ASKED QUESTIONS

This appendix contains answers to the most frequently asked questions about the WJ V. It focuses primarily on questions about the battery structure, uses, administration, and score interpretation. The *Riverside Score®* digital platform will necessarily change when new features are introduced in the future, so this appendix does not provide detailed feature-specific information about the platform. Refer to the *Riverside Score®* website (www.riversidescore.com) for release notes and descriptions of new features.

QUESTIONS ABOUT THE WJ V BATTERY

What training do I need to administer the WJ V?

Before purchasing the WJ V, you will need to furnish evidence of your user qualifications to Riverside Insights. User qualifications vary for the COG and ACH batteries; generally, the COG battery requires a higher level of training and/or experience than the ACH battery to administer and interpret. Because the WJ V is administered from a new digital platform, even experienced WJ IV users may need some additional training to become familiar with the WJ V. Before administering the WJ V as part of an evaluation, administer several practice tests to become comfortable with using the digital platform. If you desire additional training beyond what is provided in the published test materials and this book, contact the publisher (www.riversideinsights.com) for more information about remote and in-person training options.

Essentials of WJ V™ Assessment, First Edition. Erica M. LaForte, Nancy Mather, and W. Joel Schneider.

What is the Virtual Test Library (VTL)?

The WJ V Virtual Test Library (VTL) is a collection of 15 tests that can be administered alone or in combination with tests from the WJ V COG and/or WJ V ACH batteries. It includes diagnostically useful tests measuring the phonological processing aspects of auditory processing (Ga), several tests measuring rapid automatized naming (RAN) aspects of retrieval fluency (Gr), and aspects of auditory working memory (Gwm). The VTL is available to both WJ V COG and ACH users on the *Riverside Score*® platform.

What is the age range for the WJ V?

With the exception of the Letter Writing Fluency test, norm-referenced scores are available for all WJ V tests and clusters for ages 4 years, 0 months through 100 years, 0 months. For Letter Writing Fluency, norm-referenced scores are available from 4 years, 0 months through 9 years, 11 months. The existence of norm tables at a particular age does not necessarily imply that the test is *appropriate* for all individuals of that age. For instance, administering the Passage Comprehension test, which requires the examinee to read short passages, to a 4-year-old child who is unable to read would be inappropriate; likely, the norm-referenced score would be uninterpretable.

To help guide you in selecting appropriate tests, the WJ V provides recommended age ranges for all tests and clusters (see Rapid References 1.7 and 1.8). Many tests are recommended for *all* examinees ages 4 and older. Some tests are recommended for ages 5 and older (e.g., Numbers Reversed, Spelling), ages 6 and older (e.g., Story Comprehension, Paragraph Reading Comprehension), or ages 7 and older (e.g., Symbol Inhibition, Sentence Writing Fluency). Two tests—Sound Deletion and Sound Substitution—have upper age recommendations (11 and 12 years, respectively) because they assess skills that tend to fully develop by early adolescence. In other words, median group scores from examinees older than age 11 or 12 in the WJ V norming sample were perfect or near perfect. Administering those tests to an adult examinee would not yield useful information unless the examinee was suspected of having weaknesses in phonological processing skills.

Generally, use your professional judgment when determining whether to administer a specific test or cluster to an examinee who is outside of the recommended age range. In most cases, only administer a test to an examinee who is younger or older than the recommended minimum age if you have reason to believe that the score will provide useful information (e.g., a 4-year-old examinee who is being evaluated for a gifted program or a college student who may have phonological processing difficulties).

What is the grade range for the WJ V?

With the exception of the Letter Writing Fluency test, norm-referenced scores are available for all WJ V tests and clusters for grades K.0 (the first month of Kindergarten) through 12.9 (the last month of 12th grade); the WJ V does not have college norms. For Letter

Writing Fluency, norm-referenced scores are available for grades K.0 through 4.9 (the last month of 4th grade). If you are testing a child who has not yet started Kindergarten or an adult who is no longer enrolled in K-12 schooling, score the WJ V using age norms.

How big was the WJ V norming sample?

The WJ V norming study included 5,837 individuals ages 3 through 90+. Although the WJ V does not provide norm-referenced scores for children younger than 4 years, some 3-year-old examinees were included in the norm sample to help estimate more precise reference score values for the youngest 4-year-old children. The norm sample was matched to the 2020 U.S. population proportions for geographic region, race/ethnicity, sex, and education level (LaForte et al., 2025).

What materials and equipment are required to administer the WJ V?

You will need the following materials to administer and score the WJ V: (a) a Mac or Windows laptop with 8 GB RAM or more (for optimal performance), screen resolution of 1,920 × 1,080 or higher, and a high-speed internet connection (consult the publisher's website at www.riversideinsights.com for current hardware and browser requirements); (b) a silent mouse; (c) an iPad 8th Generation or newer with a minimum screen size of 10.2 in and iOS 16 or higher; (d) a Response Booklet and at least two sharpened pencils, if you will be administering any ACH tests that require written responses (see Rapid Reference 3.1); and (e) a scoring guide, if you will be administering any of the tests that require you to score the examinee's written responses (see Rapid Reference 3.2).

If the WJ V is digital, why do I still need a Response Booklet?

The WJ V requires a paper Response Booklet for tests that require the examinee to write letters, words, and sentences, such as Spelling, Spelling of Sounds, and Written Language Samples, and for tests that require the examinee to work math problems, such as Calculation and Math Facts Fluency. Although the author team and publisher explored possibilities for capturing examinees' written responses digitally, studies have shown that writing with a stylus on a tablet screen is inherently different from writing on paper with a pencil (Alamargot & Morin, 2015; Guilbert et al., 2015). Therefore, the WJ V retains paper-and-pencil responding for tests that require writing, to avoid introducing construct-irrelevant variance into the WJ V test scores (LaForte et al., 2025).

Can I use a tablet that is not an iPad to administer the WJ V?

Wide variability exists among commercially available tablets in terms of size, price, and technical specifications. Of particular importance for WJ V administration are the differences among tablet devices in *touch latency*, or the amount of time that a device takes to register a user's tap on the screen. Consistency in touch latency is an important consideration for the

WJ V because many tests are administered under timed conditions. There is less variation in touch latency among iPad tablet devices than between and among other tablet devices. Because of this, and because the WJ V was normed on iPads only, it is not recommended that you use a non-iPad device to administer the tests (LaForte et al., 2025). While future comparability research may provide support for other devices, at the time of this book's publication, the iPad is the examinee device recommended by the publisher.

Is the WJ V accessible to individuals with disabilities?

The *Riverside Score®* platform was designed to be compliant with Web Content Accessibility Guidelines (WCAG; W3C World Wide Web Consortium, 2023). The WJ V Examiner's Manual and Chapter 3 of this book contain guidance for testing examinees with diverse needs. At the time of this book's publication, the *Riverside Score®* platform contains some, but not all, features that would be useful for testing an individual with visual or hearing impairments or other needs. For example, for tests with audio-recorded instructions, the examiner is able to view the instructional script onscreen and read it to the examinee if necessary. This may be useful for testing an examinee who has auditory processing difficulties. Future platform enhancements may contain new features that would be useful for testing individuals with disabilities; however, you should always exercise professional judgment and caution when making accommodations, as some accommodations may invalidate the interpretation of the test scores.

QUESTIONS ABOUT ADMINISTRATION

How long does it take to administer the WJ V?

WJ V administration times can vary significantly depending on the age and ability of the examinee you are testing and your level of proficiency with administration. When you create a Test Set on *Riverside Score®*, the platform calculates an estimated total administration time, in minutes, based on the average administration times gathered during the WJ V norming study. Keep in mind, though, that the norming study included individuals as young as 3 years and as old as 90+ years, of all different ability levels. If you are testing a younger child or a lower-ability examinee who is likely to reach a ceiling after just a few items, the actual administration time may be lower than the platform's estimate. If you are testing an adult or a higher-ability child, the administration time may be longer. Individual personality characteristics of the examinee also come into play; some examinees respond quickly, while others take their time and respond more slowly. Regardless of the examinee's age or ability level, there are several ways that you can keep the administration time to a minimum. These include (a) preparing for your testing session ahead of time so that it is ready to launch on *Riverside Score®* when the examinee arrives; (b) keeping the examinee on task by avoiding unnecessary conversation during testing; and (c) maintaining a brisk pace when advancing from one item to the next and from one test to the next.

What should I do if an examinee changes their response?

Sometimes, an examinee may think of an answer or change their response to an item after you have moved on to another item. If this happens, return to the item and score it according to the examinee's *last* response. For example, imagine that you are administering the Picture Vocabulary test and the examinee responds *I don't know* to Item 16. You select I Don't Know from the scoring interface and then click Next to advance to Item 17. Before responding to Item 17, the examinee tells you that they remember what the other picture (Item 16) was and provides the correct response. In this scenario, you should use your Test Navigation panel to return to Item 16, click the I Don't Know button to deselect it, and then click the correct response. When you click Next, the platform will advance to Item 17.

If you need to navigate to a previously administered item, do *not* use the Back button on your browser. Instead, always use the Test Navigation panel on the left-hand side of your examiner interface (see Chapter 3 of this book for more information). The platform will not allow you to navigate to an item that has not yet been encountered.

What should I do if I am not sure how to score an item?

Sometimes you may be unsure how to score an examinee's response "in the moment." If this happens on a *non-timed* test, do the following:

1. Click the Flag icon on the Bottom Ribbon.
2. Type the examinee's response in the Notes field for later evaluation.
3. Assign a tentative item score using the following rules:
   a. On tests with basal and ceiling rules, if a basal has not yet been established, score the item incorrect. If a basal has been established, score the item correct.
   b. On all other tests, score the item correct.
4. After testing is complete, review the flagged item and decide whether the score you assigned is appropriate. You may change the item score at this point if necessary.

You should not attempt to flag items during the rapid naming (RAN) tests because you are scoring examinee responses under time limits.

What if the *Riverside Score*® platform selects a starting point that is too high or too low for my examinee?

Suggested Starting Points (SSPs) help to reduce testing time by identifying an appropriate starting item for each examinee based on their age or grade. Depending on the selections you make when you assign a Test Set to an examinee, the platform will use either the examinee's age or current grade as the basis for the default SSPs. If you suspect that the examinee is performing above or below their age or grade level, you may override the platform-assigned default age- or grade-level SSP and select a higher or lower age or grade level. For example, an individual who is low functioning may need to begin with an easier item than indicated by their present age or grade placement to avoid frustration; in contrast, an individual who is higher-functioning or gifted can start testing with a more difficult item to avoid spending time on items that are too easy.

If you launch a test and determine immediately that the starting point selected by the platform is too high (i.e., the first item is too difficult for the examinee), do not worry. For most tests, the test logic will present easier items if the examinee is not successful on the first item or item set they encounter. The platform offers the option to edit the starting point each time you launch a new test; this way, you can use information about the examinee's performance from earlier tests to adjust the starting point on later tests.

Can I "test the limits" after an examinee reaches a ceiling or stopping point on a test?

Sometimes, evaluators will "test the limits" of an examinee's ability during a testing session by modifying standardized procedures to learn more about an examinee's particular abilities and potential. For instance, after an examinee reaches a ceiling on a test under the standardized administration procedures, the examiner may provide "coaching" on more difficult items to determine whether the examinee is able to generate correct responses with some assistance. Testing the limits can provide additional, qualitative insight into the examinee's cognitive processes, strategies, and instructional needs.

At the time of this book's publication, the *Riverside Score*® platform does not allow an examiner to administer items beyond a test's ceiling or stopping point. Future updates to the platform, however, may include this feature. Consult www.riversidescore.com for information about the current platform release and its features.

What should I do if a timed test gets interrupted?

The *Riverside Score*® platform contains a safeguard to ensure that if the initial administration of a timed test is spoiled (such as if an interruption occurs due to a fire drill), the test can be replaced with a parallel second form of the test in the Test Set. To replace a spoiled timed test in your Test Set, click Invalidate Test next to Score Check in the end-of-session review. The platform will offer an option to add the second form of the test to the Test Set.

How soon can I retest the same examinee with the WJ V?

There are no hard-and-fast rules about how soon you can re-administer a test such as the WJ V to an examinee; you must use your professional judgment to determine whether re-administration is warranted and what impacts, if any, the prior administration might have on the validity and interpretability of the scores from the second administration.

The *Riverside Score*® platform contains parallel second forms of many of the WJ V achievement tests. This is a useful feature if, for example, you need to conduct a follow-up evaluation with an examinee who was originally administered the WJ V ACH. The second forms were constructed to be parallel in both item content and difficulty to the first forms of the tests. See the WJ V Technical Manual (LaForte et al., 2025) for information about the equivalence of the parallel alternate forms of the WJ V ACH tests.

What should I do if an examinee provides a response that is not in English?

Sometimes, examinees who use more than one language may provide a response to a test item in a language other than English. Use your professional judgment to determine whether to accept a response in a different language. Generally, when English-language knowledge or ability is relevant to the construct measured by the test, do *not* accept responses in other languages. For example, Picture Vocabulary and Oral Comprehension are measures of English oral language. If an examinee provides a response in Spanish or any other language, say: ***Tell me in English***. If the examinee cannot provide a correct English response, you should make a note of it (because it may be clinically useful) but you should score the item incorrect. In contrast, on tests for which English-specific knowledge is not important (i.e., fluid-reasoning tests such as Concept Formation or Analysis-Synthesis, or math tests such as Applied Problems), accept non-English responses. For example, on Analysis-Synthesis, if the examinee says *circulo rojo* instead of *red circle*, provide the English words when you give feedback (i.e., *That is correct. Red circle.*) but do not require the examinee to use the English words. If you are not sure whether a non-English response is correct and the examinee does not know the English word, assign a tentative score and flag the item for review later.

If an examinee consistently responds to test items in a language other than English, consider whether it would be more appropriate to administer an assessment in their native language.

QUESTIONS ABOUT SCORES

What are Relative Proficiency Index (RPI) scores?

The Relative Proficiency Index, or RPI, is a score that predicts how successful an examinee will be on tasks similar to those on the test that the examinee's age or grade peers would find manageable. The RPI is expressed as a fraction where the denominator is always 90, representing the location on the *W* scale where the examinee's typical (i.e., *median*) peer will be 90% successful with tasks similar to the ones on the WJ V tests. The numerator ranges from 0 to 100 and reflects the examinee's *proficiency*, or likelihood of success, on those same tasks. For example, an RPI of 40/90 indicates that an examinee will be only 40% successful with test tasks that their median age or grade peer will be 90% successful with, while an RPI of 96/90 indicates that the examinee will be 96% successful on tasks with which a typical peer would be 90% successful. When you select the RPI score in the report generation options, the report includes verbal descriptors in addition to the RPI scores (see Rapid Reference 7.1).

How do I interpret age equivalent (AE) and grade equivalent (GE) scores?

An age-equivalent score, or AE, reflects an examinee's test or cluster performance in terms of the age (in months) in the norming sample at which the median *W* score is the same as the examinee's obtained *W* score. A grade equivalent score, or GE, reflects an examinee's test or cluster performance in terms of the grade level in the norming sample at which the median *W* score is the same as the examinee's obtained *W* score. Use caution when interpreting AEs and GEs. For example, it is not appropriate to say that a student who obtained a GE of 5.3 is "performing at a fifth-grade level" because the GE only describes how the student performed on the WJ V test items compared to norming examinees and does not take into account the local curriculum.

What is the Instructional Zone/Developmental Zone?

The instructional zone identifies an individual's present level of functioning from difficult (the frustration level) to easy (the independent level) on the WJ V achievement tests. The concept of the instructional zone is similar to that found in informal reading inventories, in which instructional reading levels are identified that range from the independent (easy) level to the frustration (difficult) level. Vygotsky's (1978) zone of proximal development is another similar concept, representing the distance between an individual's actual developmental level and the level of potential development when assisted by a more knowledgeable other. In the WJ V COG, the EASY to DIFF range is expressed in the same manner but is labeled as "developmental zone" in the score report.

For example, Ella, a fourth-grade student, obtained a GE of G2.3 on the WJ V Math Calculation Skills cluster. Her Instructional zone ranges from G1.4 to G3.3, suggesting that she will find math calculation tasks at grade level 1.4 easy but will find math calculation tasks at grade level 3.3 difficult. The concept of instructional ranges is helpful in planning interventions to support growth.

What are comparison scores and how do I interpret them?

The WJ V comparison score procedures use information from the WJ V norming study to make *predictions* about how an examinee will perform. These predictions are then compared to the examinee's *actual* scores, and the differences are expressed as *base rates*. A base rate is similar to a percentile rank and is used to describe how likely a phenomenon is to occur in a population. The WJ V has two types of comparison score procedures: Intra-Ability Comparisons and Ability/Achievement Comparisons. Intra-Ability Comparisons are useful for identifying strengths and weaknesses among an individual's cognitive abilities or academic achievement, whereas Ability/Achievement Comparisons are useful for determining if a discrepancy exists between an examinee's overall ability and their academic achievement. See Chapter 7 for more information about the derivation and interpretation of comparison scores.

Why are scores missing from my report?

Occasionally, you may notice that your score report is missing proficiency and relative standing scores for one or more tests or clusters. The *Riverside Score*® platform has built-in features to guard against the misinterpretation of zero raw test and cluster scores for children. In cases where an examinee obtains a very low *W* score on a test or cluster (usually, the *W* score associated with a raw score of 0), the platform may omit the test or cluster's proficiency, relative standing, and comparison scores from the report. This is because in some cases, very low or 0 raw test or cluster scores can yield derived scores that are spuriously high due to a lack of score variance at very young ages in the norming sample. For example, if a 4-year, 2-month-old child was administered the Sentence Writing Accuracy test and received a raw score of 0, then the child's standard score would be 108 (70th percentile). Clearly, this child is not performing in the "average" range on this test, because he was unable to write any correct sentences. The average-looking standard score simply indicates that *most* 4-year-old children in the norming sample also obtained raw scores of 0 on this test. When scores for a test or cluster are omitted from the WJ V Score Report for this reason, the report contains a footnote to explain the omission.

Why do I have to complete an examinee's testing within a specific number of days?

For tests and clusters to appear together in a report, *Riverside Score*® requires all testing for an individual examinee to be completed within 90 days from the date that the *first test* in the Test Set was administered. The platform will calculate all normative scores based on the *earliest* administration date among the tests in the Test Set. This requirement ensures that the validity of the cluster score and comparison score interpretations will not be significantly impacted by any developmental changes that may have occurred between the earliest and latest administration dates.

Can I interpret scores from individual tests?

Generally, it is recommended that you interpret WJ V results at the *cluster* level. Clusters are combinations of two or more tests that provide more reliable score interpretations. However, there are some instances where the interpretation of scores from individual tests may be appropriate. First, there are 13 tests on the WJ V that do not contribute to any clusters. While it would not be appropriate to make a clinical diagnosis based on any one of these tests, they may be useful for assessing very narrow or specific abilities as part of a more comprehensive evaluation. Second, examining qualitative patterns of score differences *within* a cluster (i.e., score scatter) can be useful for understanding the nature and underlying causes of an examinee's particular strengths and weaknesses. For example, comparing an examinee's scores from the WJ V Oral Comprehension and Passage Comprehension tests can help determine whether an examinee's weaknesses in comprehension are related to oral language, reading, or both (Mather et al., 2025). See Chapter 7 for more information about SS/PR profile analysis.

My examinee has the same standard score (SS) on two different tests or clusters, but different percentile rank (PR) scores. Is this OK?

It is not unusual for standard scores on the same test or cluster to yield a slightly different PR, or for different PRs to yield the same SS. For example, an examinee may have a percentile rank of 24 on two different tests but have different standard scores (89 and 90) on those two tests. Likewise, it is possible that an examinee could obtain a standard score of 90 on two different tests but have two different PR scores (24 and 25). Because the WJ V computes PRs directly from 2-decimal *z* scores (see Chapter 7), SS and PR category overlaps are possible due to integer-level rounding.

How do I evaluate an examinee's progress over time using the WJ V?

If you want to assess an examinee's absolute growth or change over time (for example, before and after receiving a targeted intervention), you should rely on Proficiency metrics in the WJ V (i.e., *W* Difference score and Relative Proficiency Index, or RPI). The proficiency metrics are based on the *W* score, which is an equal-interval metric. This means that a change in ability at any location on the underlying scale has the same meaning. In contrast, relative standing metrics such as standard scores and percentile ranks are dependent (for interpretation) upon the individual's relative position in a group of peers.

If you use the WJ V for research or program evaluation, you may want to assess change at the group level. For example, you may want to evaluate the effectiveness of an intervention by comparing WJ V scores for two different groups of students (i.e., those who received the intervention and those who did not) at two different time points (before and after intervention). For this type of analysis, the *W* score is the most useful metric. See Chapter 7 for more information about score interpretation.

Why does a cluster score seem too low (or too high) compared to the test scores that contribute to the cluster?

Sometimes, you may note that a cluster score seems "too low" when compared to the average of the standard scores from the tests that contribute to the cluster. For example, a 10-year-old examinee obtains standard scores of 86, 88, and 90, respectively, on the three tests that contribute to the Academic Applications cluster: Passage Comprehension, Applied Problems, and Written Language Samples. The examinee's Academic Applications cluster score is 77. Your intuition may tell you that something is wrong, because you expect the cluster standard score to be approximately the average of the test scores. However, your intuition in this case is not correct; a cluster, or composite, standard score is not necessarily always the average of the test-level standard scores, for two reasons. First, recall from Chapter 7 that WJ V cluster standard scores are not derived by averaging the contributing test-level standard scores. Instead, the test-level *W scores* are averaged, and then the cluster-level norm tables are used to derive cluster standard scores. Therefore, although we should expect the cluster-level *W* scores to be the arithmetic mean of the contributing test-level *W* scores, we should not have the same expectation for standard scores.

Second, one or more relatively low contributing test-level standard scores will often result in a cluster-level standard score that is even *lower*. (The reverse is also true: one or more relatively high contributing test-level standard scores will often result in a cluster-level standard score that is even *higher*.) This phenomenon is referred to by Schneider (2016) as the *composite score extremity effect*, and is not unexpected. The explanation is relatively simple: extremely low test scores are relatively rare. Having multiple low test scores is even more rare, and therefore, when multiple low test scores contribute to a cluster, the examinee's relative standing on the cluster will be even lower than for the individual test-level scores. The same is true in the reverse. An examinee with one or more relatively high test scores will likely have a cluster score that is even higher. While it is rare to be extremely good at one skill, it is even rarer to be extremely good at multiple skills.

REFERENCES

Alamargot, D., & Morin, M.-F. (2015). Does handwriting on a tablet screen affect students' graphomotor execution? A comparison between Grades Two and Nine. *Human Movement Science*, *44*, 32–41.

Guilbert, J., Alamargot, D., & Morin, M.-F. (2015). Handwriting on a tablet screen: Role of visual and proprioceptive feedback in the control of movement by children and adults. *Human Movement Science*, *65*, 30–41.

LaForte, E. M., Dailey, D., & McGrew, K. S. (2025). *Technical manual*. Woodcock-Johnson V. Riverside Assessments, LLC.

Mather, N., Wendling, B. J., Snader, E. H. (Contributor), & Jeantete, G. T. (Contributor) (2025). *Examiner's manual*. Woodcock-Johnson V. Riverside Assessments, LLC.

Schneider, W. J. (2016). *Why are WJ IV cluster scores more extreme than the average of their parts? A gentle explanation of the composite score extremity effect* (Woodcock-Johnson IV Assessment Service Bulletin No. 7). Riverside Assessments, LLC.

Vygotsky, L. S. (1978). *Mind in society: The development of higher psychological processes*. Harvard University Press.

W3C World Wide Web Consortium. (2023). *Web content accessibility guidelines (WCAG) 2.2*. https://www.w3.org/TR/WCAG22/.

Index

Essentials of WJ V™ Assessment, First Edition. Erica M. LaForte, Nancy Mather, and W. Joel Schneider.

Printed and bound by CPI Group (UK) Ltd, Croydon, CR0 4YY
17/09/2026
14964240-0001